W9-CMG-050

The Philadelphia Inquirer
Restaurant Guide

The Philadelphia Inquirer
Restaurant Guide

Craig LaBan

Camino Books, Inc.
Philadelphia

Copyright © 2007 by The Philadelphia Inquirer
All Rights Reserved

No part of this book may be reproduced in any form or by any electronic or
mechanical means including information storage and retrieval systems without permission in writing from the publisher, except by a reviewer who may
quote brief passages in a review.

Manufactured in the United States of America

1 2 3 4 5 10 09 08 07

Library of Congress Cataloging-in-Publication Data

LaBan, Craig, 1968-
The Philadelphia Inquirer restaurant guide / Craig LaBan.
    p. cm.
Includes index.
ISBN-13: 978-0-940159-98-3 (alk. paper)
ISBN-10: 0-940159-98-8 (alk. paper)
1. Restaurants—Pennsylvania—Philadelphia Region—Guidebooks. I.
Philadelphia Inquirer and Daily News (Firm) II. Title.

TX907.3.P42P455 2006
647.9509748'11—dc22

198   2006018

Cover and interior design: Jan Greenberg

Photo credits: frontispiece, Fork; p. 1, Fountain Restaurant; p. 6, Amada; p. 57,
John's Roast Pork; p. 75, Yue Kee; p. 89, Marsha Brown; p. 130, Lunch time in the
Reading Terminal Market; p. 166, Szechuan turnip patties at Szechuan Tasty
House; p. 183, Positano Coast by Aldo Lamberti. All photos courtesy of *The
Philadelphia Inquirer.*

This book is available at a special discount on bulk purchases for
promotional, business, and educational use.

Publisher
Camino Books, Inc.
P.O. Box 59026
Philadelphia, PA 19102

www.caminobooks.com

Contents

ESSAYS

CAPSULE REVIEWS

INDEX BY CATEGORY

Introduction

If you're counting in restaurant time, four years is an eternity. In a city as charged with culinary energy as Philadelphia, four years can represent an entirely new era.

And that is exactly what has happened since the last time I put together a guide to my 76 favorite restaurants in 2002. More than half of the names in this edition are different — 41 to be exact. A handful of those old favorites left the list because they closed or slid into natural decline. But for the most part, the members of this current class simply represent an exciting new energy pulsing through the city's kitchens, from the growth in value-oriented BYOBs and gastro-pubs, to small-plate wine and beer bars, and several emerging new ethnic flavors.

Few of these movements have done more to change the local dining landscape as much as the BYOB phenomenon, which began simmering several years ago, but erupted into an all-out regional obsession from Rittenhouse to Kennett Square. With the economy putting the brakes on all but a few big new expense account destinations (most of them now owned by Stephen Starr), the uniquely Philadelphian BYO boom has created an exciting outlet for young talents to craft their dining dreams on a budget — from cozy Italian trattorias to cutting-edge urban kitchens. It has also allowed burgeoning neighborhoods to jumpstart their nightlife with a hip piece of the gastronomic action. The result has been a wealth of intimate and personal new spaces that put the focus on good food at reasonable prices. And restaurants like Matyson, Marigold Kitchen, Alison at Blue Bell, and Melograno have been so successful that traditional wine list restaurants have felt the pinch of competition.

The entire city can now get a literal breath of fresh air as a result of the new smoking ban (effective January 2007) at virtually all restaurants and bars, bringing Philadelphia up to speed with New Jersey and Delaware. This should be an especially nice change for otherwise smoky gastro-pubs like the Standard Tap, N. 3rd, and Southwark, which have added a casual yet high-quality layer to the eating scene, bridging the bar and dining room with everything from gourmet burgers to roasted pheasant and an increasingly serious focus on good local and Belgian beers.

And with wine-by-the-bottle now becoming an endangered practice, by-the-glass wine bars and small plates have suddenly become the medium of choice through which our hottest young chefs express their talents, from the inspired Spanish tapas at Jose Garces's Amada to David Ansill's daring "snacks" of venison tartare and bone marrow crostini at Ansill.

The last few years have seen an amazing growth in new authentic ethnic flavors — especially Mexican taquerias like La Lupe and Vietnamese restaurants like Nam Phuong, which have added new depth and vitality to the Italian Market and Washington Avenue. Emerging neighborhoods like Northern Liberties and Graduate Hospital began to mature with serious new destinations like Sovalo and Pumpkin. Funky Queen Village has had a resurgent upgrade in serious dining, and Rittenhouse Square has acquired a youthful nightlife zone to its north to counter the staid luxury palaces of Walnut Street's Restaurant Row. East Passyunk Avenue has returned to life in Deep South Philadelphia with the likes of Paradiso. And Chester County has finally come into its own as a gastronomic center of suburban dining, from sophisticated Gilmore's in downtown West Chester, to Sovana Bistro in Kennett Square, Majolica in Phoenixville, Ristorante Alba in Malvern, and Berwyn's ultra-stylish Nectar.

All of these entries were easy choices as new favorites. But as I spent the last 10 months considering the dining scene as a whole — and nibbling my way through more than 120 reconnaissance meals spanning a broad range of price, styles, and neighborhoods — many stalwarts from the last round-up were not to be denied. Superstar chefs like Marc Vetri, Susanna Foo, Georges Perrier, and Martin Hamann at the Fountain are still cooking as well as ever. Veterans like Margaret Kuo, John Mims at Carmine's, and Rich Landau at Horizons successfully transferred their talents to new venues. Striped Bass survived the bankruptcy of its founder, to emerge even better than before under new ownership.

A couple restaurants I'd initially counted as favorites were caught in mid-transition as this book went into final production — Lacroix at the Rittenhouse (whose namesake chef retired), and Fuji Japanese Restaurant (which was planning a new Center City address after its Cinnaminson location was slated to be razed).

But then ... there were a couple classics — the Famous 4th Street Delicatessen and Villa di Roma, the unpretentious bastion of Italian Market red gravy — that happily found their way onto my favorites list for the first time, alongside other enduring touchstones like John's Roast Pork and the Sansom Street Oyster House. In a dynamic region where several hopeful places open each week, it can be startling to savor dishes that still resonate with the satisfying taste of Philadelphia history. When you live by the ever-evolving, quick-paced clock of restaurant time, it's reassuring to know that at least a few of our best flavors refuse to change.

How This Book Was Done

I created this guide in the same format as my previous collection, *Savoring Philadelphia*, with an in-depth look at 76 current favorites, plus tips and information on hundreds of other restaurants you should know. The favorites were chosen to reflect the true diversity and breadth of Philadelphia's restaurant scene — not just the obvious and expensive standbys of Old City or Restaurant Row, but also the authentic ethnic finds, vibrant street foods, neighborhood bistros, and traditional classics I often crave. All of them are, in the real sense, personal favorites. And that's no small recognition, considering I eat 500 restaurant meals a year.

Readers of my column in the Sunday *Inquirer* will find many of these familiar, especially the most recent favorites. But every single one has been carefully re-edited, re-fact-checked and, in most cases, revisited to be brought up to date. This is particularly true of holdovers from the earlier book, which each received a completely new review. All of the favorites have been revisited within the past year — often more than once.

This edition offers much more than reviews of the 76 favorites (whose names are printed in all capital letters throughout most of the book). It also offers smaller features that reflect my journey through hundreds of new restaurants since 2002, and it is considerably more comprehensive than the first edition, with information on nearly 700 establishments across the region, including special new sections dedicated to dining at the Jersey Shore, a listing of the coolest local cafes, and where to find the best ingredients, wines, and beers when you decide to cook at home. After this 10-month restaurant marathon, more of that would be nice.

About the Ratings

I've never had a scientific formula for rating a restaurant. But over the years, I've done my best to keep *The Inquirer's* scale of Liberty Bells consistent and fairly tough, from the rarified four-bell pinnacle, where currently only five restaurants reside, to the occasionally well-deserved spanking known as The No-Bell Prize. There will be no such "prize-winners" in this book, since it is a guide, after all, dedicated to good food.

But there are plenty of levels in between, from one bell to three, that bear a little understanding. To begin with, I give restaurants a bell rating based on a complete review process, including making multiple visits paid for by *The Inquirer* and (to the best of my ability) eating meals without being recognized. The rating categories are meant to have broad reach, since they must apply to restaurants of all ambitions, but they have come, necessarily, to mean a few specifics that are, I hope, true to their definitions.

A two-bell rating ("very good") tends to be my baseline for a solid recommendation and is generally given to a restaurant of interest — but still far from perfect. A three-bell restaurant ("excellent") isn't perfect either, but such an establishment is usually something special. In some rare cases, as with John's Roast Pork, it's not necessarily upscale. But that lofty rating is a proper acknowledgment for those classics that are the best in certain important genres.

A one-bell restaurant ("hit-or-miss"), contrary to popular opinion, is not necessarily a complete dud. I often find a lot to like about some of these places, but something — consistency of the food, value, service, or concept — is not yet clicking. But if they're in this book, they have some redeeming value.

In addition, there are hundreds of totally worthy restaurants without any ratings at all included in these listings. They are not "No-Bell Prize Winners." I simply haven't yet gotten around to putting them through the Liberty Bell wringer of a lengthy, formal review. At least, not yet.

The 76 Favorites by Bell Rating

🔔🔔🔔🔔 SUPERIOR
Fountain Restaurant
Le Bec-Fin
Susanna Foo
Striped Bass
Vetri

🔔🔔🔔 EXCELLENT
Alison at Blue Bell
Amada
Ansill
Barclay Prime
Birchrunville Store Cafe
Brasserie Perrier
Buddakan
The Capital Grille
Dilworthtown Inn
Gayle
Gilmore's
Horizons
Jake's
John's Roast Pork
Margaret Kuo's
Majolica
Marigold Kitchen
Matyson
Melograno
Meritage Philadelphia
Morimoto

Moro
Moshulu
Nan
Nectar
¡Pasion!
Pif
Radicchio
Savona
Southwark
Sovalo
Sovana Bistro
Standard Tap
Tangerine
XIX Nineteen

🔔🔔 VERY GOOD
Carmine's Creole Cafe
Cherry Street Chinese
  Kosher Vegetarian
  Restaurant
Devi
Django
Dmitri's
El Vez
Famous 4th Street
  Delicatessen
Fork (and Fork:ETC.)
Friday Saturday Sunday
Karma
Kristian's Ristorante

La Lupe
Lakeside Chinese Deli
L'Angolo
Lolita
Los Catrines Restaurant &
  Tequila's Bar
Marsha Brown
Monk's Cafe
N. 3rd
Nam Phuong
Paradiso
Penang
Positano Coast by Aldo
  Lamberti
Pumpkin
Rembrandt's
Restaurant Alba
Ritz Seafood
Rouge
Sabrina's Cafe
Sang Kee Asian Bistro
Sansom Street Oyster
  House
Siam Lotus
Sweet Lucy's Smokehouse
Szechuan Tasty House
Tierra Colombiana
Vietnam
Villa Di Roma

Key to Ratings and Icons

BELL RATINGS
🔔🔔🔔🔔 Superior
🔔🔔🔔 Excellent
🔔🔔 Very Good
🔔 Hit-or-Miss

AVERAGE ENTREE PRICES
I Inexpensive—$15 or less
M Moderate—$16-$20
E Expensive—$20-$27
VE Very Expensive—$28-$35
U-E Ultra-Expensive—Over $35

NOISE, IN DECIBELS
Quiet   below 75
Lively   75-79
Raucous   80-85
Deafening   over 85

The 76
Favorites

Alison at Blue Bell

♟♟♟ EXCELLENT

MENU HIGHLIGHTS Ginger squid; truffled salmon tartare; escargots with mushrooms "Stroganoff"; scallops with gnocchi; leg of lamb with lamb monti; chile-dusted skate; duck confit with couscous; swordfish with grits and salsa verde; chocolate-chile pot de crème; sticky bun ice cream sandwich.

BYOB

WEEKEND NOISE Deafening

IF YOU GO Lunch Tu-F 11:30 a.m-2:30 p.m. Dinner Tu-F 5:30-9:30 p.m.; Sa 5-10 p.m.
• **E** Dinner entrees, $18-$27.50
• Reservations highly recommended one month in advance of date
• Cash, checks only
• No smoking
• Wheelchair-accessible
• Free parking lot

It is hard to make a comeback when you never really left. But that is exactly what Alison at Blue Bell is: a happy resurgence for Alison Barshak's highly publicized roller-coaster career. Not to mention a boon for suburban dining.

Few can forget when Barshak shot to national prominence more than a decade ago as the sassy, cover-girl chef of Striped Bass. But after bolting the Bass, then flaming-out at her own Venus and the Cowboy, followed by a brief stint in New York (where she still lives part-time, but no longer works), few expected Barshak to rise again.

No wonder Alison at Blue Bell became one of the biggest culinary comebacks in recent years. Compared to the flash of her previous venues, the mood is refreshingly understated at this crisp blue-and-yellow BYOB, which is slipped into the patio-trimmed ground floor of an obscure suburban office park. When you walk in, you encounter Barshak orchestrating the open kitchen, that trademark braid of ginger hair swinging away from the crowds as she inspects every dish on its way to the tables.

With her attention now firmly focused on the food, Barshak's appealing culinary vision has finally come into view. The menu retraces themes that have outlined her career, with an emphasis on seafood and notes of Asian, Mediterranean, and Latin fusion. But there is none of the convolution that earned her earlier endeavor the nickname "Venus and the Corn Nut." The dishes are more stripped-down, the flavors more vivid, and good ingredients are on best display.

A cool timbale of smoked salmon tartare scented with truffle is served with warm coins of mini-potato pancakes. Tender escargots bask in a rich gravy of wild hedgehog mushroom "Stroganoff." A dusting of chili powder lets skate sparkle through its rich brown butter sauce and harmonize with Southwestern jicama and

NEW AMERICAN BYOB • NORTHERN SUBURBS

721 Skippack Pike, Blue Bell, Pa. 19422

215-641-2660 • www.alisonatbluebell.com

guacamole. And beautifully seared big scallops are served in a surprisingly subtle textural play, scattered over creamily tender gnocchi (cut to the shape of smaller bay scallops), soft morsels of sweet squash, chewy nuggets of prosciutto, and a light broth enriched with foie gras mousse.

Barshak has a knack for elevating more familiar dishes to something more personal. Her fried squid is among the best I've had, amazingly tender and scented with ginger beneath squiggles of wasabi sauce. Tacos appear with a stuffing of Asian duck. Seasonal soft-shell crabs come crisped beneath shards of smoky bacon with wilted greens and pan-fried ripe tomato.

The cooking here always beams with good produce and a decidedly light touch, which may partly explain why the dining room is so often dominated by a predominantly female clientele ("lots of cashmere, jeans, and $200-highlights," observed my fashion-savvy guest). Barshak even manages to present lamb with a surprising delicacy, fanning a beautiful slice of grilled leg over tangy yogurt sauce streaked with chile oil and pinenuts alongside a plump Turkish manti ravioli stuffed with ground lamb and mint.

With dishes like these, Barshak dispels any notions that her notoriety as a chef was built solely on hype. Her servers are also some of the best in the suburbs, an attentive but personable staff that dispenses helpful advice without pretense.

The restaurant also has a fine pastry chef in Amelia Dietrich, whose desserts capture a perfect sense of upscale comfort. From her awesome sticky bun ice cream sandwich to her mango upside-down cake to a silky chocolate pot de creme that tingles with an afterburn of pasilla chiles — these are the kind of finales that make a comeback like Alison at Blue Bell worth coming back for.

— OR TRY THESE —

Here are three other suggested Blue Bell restaurants:

Sushikazu 🗡 🗡
920 Dekalb Pike, Blue Bell, Pa. 19422, (610) 272-7767
The smart bungalow is home to a creative sushi counter, where premium ingredients, from toro to live scallops, are sliced with skill. Try off-the-menu specials such as spicy tuna over crunchy rice or Area 51 roll. There has been an ownership change since the review.

The Blue Bell Inn
601 Skippack Pike, Blue Bell, Pa. 19422, (215) 646-2010
Some contemporary flavors have appeared here of late, but this classic remains one of the region's best old-time establishments, with staples such as fried oysters, creamed spinach, great wines, and butter-fried prime steaks.

Coleman Restaurant
1401 Morris Rd., Blue Bell, Pa. 19422, (215) 616-8300
Celebrity chef Jim Coleman's suburban digs. The concept of an all-organic modern twist on Pennsylvania Dutch cooking is fabulous, but results have been inconsistent.

Amada

♟♟♟ EXCELLENT

MENU HIGHLIGHTS Cured meats (serrano; chorizo pampalona); cheeses (La Cerena; Monte Enebro); tortilla Española; salt cod croquettes; octopus; garlic shrimp; caldo gallego; duck flatbread; razor clams a la plancha; roast pork; tenderloin with cabrales; paella Valenciana; leche frita; crema Catalana.

WINE LIST Nicely focused selection from Spain and South America. Most less than $50 per bottle and around $10 per glass. Sangria and sherry make excellent starters. Full bar and wine list.

WEEKEND NOISE Deafening

IF YOU GO Lunch M-F 11:30 a.m.-2:30 p.m. Dinner M-Th 5-11 p.m.; F and Sa 5 p.m.-1 a.m.; Su 5-10 p.m.
• **E** Dinner tapas, $4-$19; paellas (for two), $38-$75
• Reservations required
• Wheelchair-accessible — from Strawberry St. entrance
• Valet parking W-Sa $16

When the sultry perfume of shrimp sizzling in terracotta crocks of garlic oil is not enough to keep them going, Jose Garces and his red-hot tapas kitchen will always have flamenco.

"The passion of flamenco inspires me," says Garces. "When you hear that guitar go *da-da-dam!* it can get kind of feverish in here."

Live flamenco would come off as a gimmick alongside most of the weak efforts I've seen at Spanish tapas. But the twice-weekly performances at Amada are a natural because Garces has done his part, crafting a genuine identity for this seductive Old City space.

Those are real Spanish serrano hams dangling over the bar, where a wall of sangria barrels nestled into dark wood cubbies lends the feel of a genuine bodega. A glass case harbors some perfect Spanish cheeses, like oozy sheep's milk La Cerena and ash-covered Monte Enebro. And the bar is stocked with an excellent list of Spanish wines, quenching sangrias, and bone-dry sherries that are ideal with olives and boquerone anchovies.

Garces's cooking, meanwhile, rarely disappoints. The Chicago-raised son of Ecuadoran parents spent nearly a year cooking on the Andalusian coast after culinary school. And he treats the Spanish palette with the same sophisticated modern touch that he brought to Mexican and Cuban cuisines at El Vez and Alma de Cuba.

The tortilla Española, traditionally cold, arrives here hot, to order — a crisp potato-filled round of egg served with a mini-pestle filled with saffron-dusted aioli. Deep-fried croquettes of salt cod melt in the mouth like fish-scented potato creams, chased by the salty fresh pop of caviar and the cool tomato puree. Dime-shaped rounds of tender octopus, dusted with smoked paprika beneath a sheen of arbequina olive oil, are irresistible. And when the lid is lifted from the terra-cotta dish with those sizzling shrimp, a puff of steam rises above us like a garlic cloud.

SPANISH TAPAS • OLD CITY
217 Chestnut St., 19106
215-625-2450 • www.amadarestaurant.com

The pacing of all those little plates is amazingly smooth, thanks to an impressive staff that was informative but not smarmy. The broad menu, meanwhile, offers more than 60 choices, from charcuterie nibbles and classic tapas to larger (albeit less successful) dishes to be shared by an entire table.

The "lobster" paella tinted black with squid ink was delicious, but for $75 didn't have nearly enough lobster. The enormous paella Valenciana, though, was a stupendous centerpiece, a broad pan of saffron rice studded with chorizo and sublimely tender chicken. And I can't wait to round up a group to special-order one of Garces's suckling pigs, especially if the smaller pernil asado was any preview. That pork shank — stewed in lard, then crisped over white beans beneath Seville oranges — was one of the best slices of pig I've ever eaten.

It was but one of many spectacular flavors. There was soulful caldo gallego stew of white beans, ham, and kale with potato foam. Harmonica-shaped razor clams were sauteed simply on the plancha with garlic butter, parsley, and lemon. The filet mignon over Cabrales demiglace topped with a torch-crisped slice of foie gras left an impression, too.

If there's still room — and those little dishes add up in every way — Amada also makes great desserts. They range from the traditional (orange-scented crema Catalan; fried leche frita custard with butterscotch) to modern fantasies like caramel bananas with chocolate cake and saffron custard.

But this still tastes like just a beginning. Garces's debut feels like the chef equivalent of that flamenco guitarist setting the tone for something special with that first heart-pumping, string-rattling strum. I can't wait to see how his tune at Amada plays out.

— OR TRY THESE —

Here are three other suggested upscale Latin restaurants:

¡PASION!
211 S. 15th St., 19102, (215) 875-9895
The brilliant ceviches and chile-kissed flavors of Nuevo Latino cooking blossom here. Chef Guillermo Pernot still creates most inventive cuisine; however, both kitchen and service have slipped a notch.

EL VEZ
121 S. 13th St., 19107, (215) 928-9800
Still the city's most sophisticated Mexican food, courtesy of Mexican-born chef Adrian Leon. A slip in service and over-iced margaritas, though, have dropped El Vez a notch from its three-bell rating.

LOS CATRINES RESTAURANT & TEQUILA'S BAR
1602 Locust St., 19103, (215) 546-0181
The elegant room is graced with beautiful Mexican art, charming servers, and a collection of fine tequilas. The menu aims for polished authenticity rather than creativity, but has real highlights, from the tortilla soup to langostinos in tequila sauce.

Date Restaurants

ROMANCE AND RESTAURANTS HAVE BEEN INTERTWINED since the very beginning. And aside from sustenance, I can think of no cause more noble for a restaurant than to become the featured backdrop for budding love. But how to define the romantic restaurant? Is it decked in linens and candelabras? Is it the latest Old City nightspot lounge? Or is the air scented with ethnic spice and the thrill of a food adventure? And what about that first date? Le Bec-Fin might be coming on a little strong.

The answers, I suspect, are different for all kinds of people. But there is clearly a great difference between the ideal place to meet someone for the first time and the setting for a proposal. "Date restaurants" are often "romantic," such as Amada in Old City, but they don't have to be.

They should be fun, with an ambience that applies minimal pressure, but allows you and your date enough culinary options to express your personalities through food. But it's been more than a decade since I had the chance to go courting in local restaurants. So I've asked a broad spectrum of my single (or recently single) friends to chime in on their favorite places for the entire date cycle, from that first meeting place to a setting for the big event. In their own words:

JEN: single white reporter, 31, "laid-back and probably way too picky"

FIRST DATE: You can't go wrong with **N. 3rd** on a first date. It's got dim lighting (makes everyone look better), a fun atmosphere (plenty of diversion if your date's a dud). Perhaps most importantly, it's got good, cheap drinks. If you want to go a little more swanky, another great first date place (or second or third, as far as I'm concerned) is **Southwark.**

SECOND DATE: **Lolita** has dependable upscale Mexican fare and a menu with veggie versions in case your date doesn't eat meat. Plus, it's got a fun little "shtick" — you bring the tequila, they'll do up the margaritas for you.

THIRD DATE: **La Locanda del Ghiottone.** You'll get lots of points for this little gem of an Italian joint. It has one of the more romantic atmospheres around, great down-home and Italian-speaking (or at least -sounding) waiters.

ROBERT: single African-American reporter, 37, "and Craig thinks I am some kind of Philly super-lover"

FIRST DATE: Since you can't go wrong with Chinese, I have been taking the ladies to **Shiao Lan Kung**. It is popular with Asians — which makes the date think you have some kind of inside scoop. The salt-baked dishes are to die for and there are excellent vegetarian dishes, so you won't play yourself if she doesn't eat meat.

SECOND DATE: The next level needs more romance. **Alma de Cuba** fits the bill. Not only is it classy; it won't kill your wallet. I can personally testify for the Fire and Ice Ceviche.

THIRD DATE: We are approaching the touchy-feely stages. Under such circumstances I am offering a curveball. The Moroccan restaurant, **Marrakesh,** offers a seven-course meal for around $30 per person. You'll both feel like royalty as your cushion-bound behinds feast on salads, lamb, chicken, couscous, fruits, and more. And you get to eat with your hands.

THE NEXT STEP: As you approach that rarefied air, this is what I call "romancing the stone," as proposal night is about the rock. Put on your very best, go see whatever she wants at the Academy, then head on over to **Lacroix at the Rittenhouse** (someone cue the angels' singing please!) Nothing is quite as romantic as looking out over Rittenhouse Square with a glass of wine in one hand and your partner's hand in the other while you wait for some of the best French cuisine this town has to offer. Yes, it is pricey, but so is marriage I'm told.

ROBIN: single African-American woman, personal trainer, in "my late thirties"

FIRST DATE: I would meet someone at **El Fuego** for a lunchtime burrito. Going on an initial date earlier in the day takes off some of the pressure. The burritos are freshly made, and the atmosphere is very casual and relaxed. Anyone that can consume one of El Fuego's giant burritos and maintain an intelligent conversation definitely deserves a second outing.

SECOND DATE: The **Continental Mid-Town** is great for a nighttime outing, with the triple-decker of tasty tapas, hip drinks, and even hipper people. Hopefully you will see at least 10 people that you know, making you seem attractively popular.

THIRD DATE: I actually went to **Friday Saturday Sunday** for a first date. It is too romantic for a first date, but is perfect for special occasions, i.e., you have given your date a special ring tone on your cell phone. Just kidding. This place has third date written all over it.

THE NEXT STEP: Eventually you may want to introduce the lucky guy or gal to your friends, and **Copabanana** on South Street is wonderful for group outings. Margaritas. Burgers. Tattooed waitresses. Enough said.

LINDA: single white divorced writer, "middle-aged, lives in South Philly and prefers to dine in the city — no treks to the suburbs, please!"

FIRST DATE: **El Vez:** claro que sí! It's fun, light-hearted, and just noisy enough to cover conversation gaps. Great food, and did I mention the blood-orange margaritas?

SECOND DATE: **Pif** is a charming and quiet BYO with a sophisticated, superb menu. OK, now we can really have a conversation, but first, could we peek at the wine? (You brought a Zind-Humbrecht gerwurtztraminer? How did you know, darling!)

THIRD DATE: Where else but **N. 3rd!** Let's keep it caz and head to Northern Liberties for the best pub food, great beer, and cheap bottles of wine. Maybe we'll eat outside? You gotta have a sporty side, baby.

FOURTH DATE: Time to invite you to the neighborhood for some nouvelle Italian delights! We're headed to **Tre Scalini** (langostinos all around!), and, no, that's not the Trevi Fountain, but imagination is a treasured attribute!

FIRST ANNIVERSARY: **Striped Bass** is absolutely perfect for sipping champagne and slowly devouring the finest sensual delights. And maybe later, **Chris'** for some jazz?

PAUL: a retired journalist and writer, 65, divorced

FIRST DATE: I definitely place a premium on ambience and quiet and one of my favorite places is **Khajuraho** in Ardmore. It's BYO, always the way to go if you like good wine and aren't loaded. **Lourdes Greek Taverna**, a BYO near the Bryn Mawr train station, serves great food in a really nice, brightly lit room.

SECOND DATE (and beyond): If I'm ready to spend a bit more I'd go for **Taquet** in the Wayne Hotel. If I'm really flush maybe **Savona** in Gulph Mills. For Chinese, **Yangming** in Bryn Mawr remains the class of the Main Line — gotta love those fortune cookies half coated in dark chocolate.

PATRICK AND KAITLIN: newlywed reporters, 27 and 30, the extreme foodie couple

FIRST DATE: **Tria** is a low-commitment, after-work meeting spot. Stay 20 minutes for a beer and make a quick getaway or linger over a bottle of wine and plates of cheese if the evening looks promising. Sushi is the perfect date food, and at **Morimoto** the Iron Chef never fails to impress. If conversation should lag, turn your attention to admiring the sushi chef's technique.

SECOND DATE: **Matyson** is a BYOB that's as romantic as it is tasty. The warmth between this husband-and-wife chef-and-pastry-chef team seems to spill over to your dinner table. All of South Philly's Italian charm can be found in a not-so-frenetic atmosphere at **Cucina Forte**.

THE MORNING AFTER: Go to **Cafe Sud** for an exotic and sumptuous breakfast in a cozy setting. Or **Beau Monde**, for oh-so-sultry crepes.

THE BIG DINNER: **Vetri** is special-occasion dining where the focus is the food. Marc Vetri's six-course tasting menu is a gift in and of itself.

Ansill

♟♟♟ EXCELLENT

MENU HIGHLIGHTS Venison tartare; scrambled duck egg with smoked trout; bone marrow crostini; charcuterie (speck, duck prosciutto); cheeses (Idiazabal, Taleggio); sweetbreads; grilled quail; langostinos; baby octopus; hanger steak; open-faced osso bucco; roasted porcini; panna cotta; saffron cheesecake.

WINE LIST Excellent mid-sized list focused on well-priced quality Europeans (most under $60) with nearly 20 by the glass. Try Southern French viognier from Domaine la Bastide ($8), or Spanish rioja crianza from Cune ($8). Great Belgian-centric beer list, with other unusual finds, like German black lager from Kostritzer.

WEEKEND NOISE Raucous

IF YOU GO Dinner Su-Th 5:30-11 p.m.; F and Sa until midnight. Brunch Sa and Su 11:30 a.m.-3:30 p.m.
• **M to E** Small plates, $4-$14
• No reservations
• Not wheelchair-accessible
• Street parking only

I can't blame diners for refusing to eat foods they consider scary. And there have been more than a few fearful gulps from less adventurous eaters who settled into the former meatloaf comfort corner that used to be Judy's and perused some of the new highlights from Ansill's little plates. Treats like lamb's tongue and bone marrow crostini surely sent a shiver down their squeamish spines.

But for anyone capable of setting aside inhibitions for a night, Ansill should be required eating.

The brainchild of Pif chef David Ansill and his chef de cuisine, Kibett Mengech, this casual bistro may just be the best destination I've found to discover the wonderful world of weird meat gastronomy. The exquisitely cooked plates are small and affordable — so the risk is minimal. But there's hardly a bum dish among the 40-plus items.

There's even a fabulous wine list and beer bar to loosen you up for the journey. So grab a glass of roasty black German lager or a goblet of Languedoc viognier, and buckle-up for a flavor adventure. Because you haven't lived until you've tasted the sensuously soft venison tartare shined with raw quail egg and mustard.

OK, maybe we shouldn't start there.

But there are a number of plates that even timid diners could love. There is a small but marvelous cheese board to choose from, ranging from nutty Idiazabal with homemade quince paste to a gouda-like slice of orange Mimolette paired with the spicy-sweet pear mostarda preserves. There is some fine charcuterie, including smoky speck ham with balsamic-soaked figs, and velvety slices of house-cured duck prosciutto.

A cool pea soup ringing with mint and yogurt, and a sublime plate of porcini mushrooms sauteed with morsels of taleggio cheese, are among the spectacular vegetarian options. There are also reasonably mainstream plates of beef (hanger steak with whole shallots)

EUROPEAN SMALL-PLATE WINE BAR • QUEEN VILLAGE
627 S. 3rd St., 19147
215-627-2485 • www.ansillfoodandwine.com

and shellfish (scallops with bitter endive; sweet langostinos striped with dark truffle vinaigrette.)

Beyond that, however, the familiar food beacons become more scarce. But anyone who has dined at Pif, the French BYOB where Ansill made his reputation, knows the chef has an affinity for turning offal into gold.

The daring discipline reaches new refinement here, though the space still has the casual warmth of a neighborhood haunt, its walls painted cozy pumpkin and goblin green. The service is an impressively unpretentious match — with the astute advice and polished pacing of a tricky multi-course meal.

It helps to have such a talented hand behind the stove as Mengech, whose crisp technique and smart ideas gain vivid focus inside the limited small-plate frame.

Perfectly crisped sweetbreads tumble with fava beans and fresh morels over a puree of tarragon-scented peas. Sublimely tender quail, darkened from its balsamic marinade, arrives over arugula pesto. Scrambled duck eggs are a billowing cloud around morsels of moist smoked trout. Tiny crostini rounds bear coins of creamy bone marrow, griddle-crisped and speckled with pink sea salt.

There were rare disappointments, like the surprisingly bland braised pork belly. But Ansill is usually a trove of bold flavors — even in miniature. A parcel of braised osso buco meat served over toasted brioche is dainty, but could be the centerpiece of a meal.

The desserts by Ansill's wife, Catherine Gilbert-Ansill, had their own intrigue. Panna cotta was scattered with bee pollen. A grilled panini sandwiched warm gianduja chocolate with fresh raspberries.

But the saffron cheesecake with spiced red wine syrup was the stunner — as gold as Spanish treasure and radiating the glow of saffron's sunny perfume. I wasn't going anywhere until it was done. On the city's most exotic menu, I'd found my comfort zone.

— OR TRY THESE —

Here are three other suggested small-plate restaurants:

AMADA ♟♟♟
217 Chestnut St., 19106, (215) 625-2450
Discover your inner flamenco at this tapas haven, where Jose Garces presents updates to classic Spanish flavors in an evocative space in Old City. Impressive service and well-tuned menu, but those small plates add up quickly.

POSITANO COAST BY ALDO LAMBERTI ♟♟
212 Walnut St., 19106, (215) 238-0499
The old pasta depot (Lamberti's Cucina) has gotten an upgrade in concept and look. A good wine bar and an appealing small-plate Italian menu (try the mahi crudo) make for a smart pre-movie meal.

Tria ♟♟
123 S. 18th St., 19103, (215) 972-8742
A great beer venue without the usual bar grunge, this chic Rittenhouse cafe has made strides. A recent visit brought more relaxed, less pretentious service and a much-improved cheese board.

Barclay Prime

★★★ EXCELLENT

MENU HIGHLIGHTS Kobe sliders; beef tartare; onion tart; Black Pearl caviar; shaved vegetable salad; kobe cheesesteak; all steaks (especially rib-eye); short ribs; butter-poached lobster; sides (truffled potatoes, creamed spinach, mushrooms); peanut butter s'mores; sundae; pineapple upside-down cake.

WINE LIST Extensive list of quality bottles emphasizes New World reds. Triple-plus markups excessive, making values under $70 hard to find, but Lucky Country shiraz-cabernet from Australia is worthy at $42. Beware steep bar prices.

WEEKEND NOISE Noisy

IF YOU GO Lunch M-F 11:30 a.m.-2:30 p.m. Dinner Su-Th 5-10 p.m.; F and Sa 5-11 p.m.
• **U-E** Dinner entrees, $25-$100
• Reservations recommended
• Most major cards
• Wheelchair-accessible
• Valet parking $15 ($20 SUV), Sheraton Rittenhouse Hotel, 18th and Locust Sts.

Barclay Prime is more than just another $100 cheesesteak. It's the decadent splurge we've been missing in our dalliances with BYOs, a sexy revamp of the staid chop house genre, and a second chance for glamour dining in one of the city's historic rooms.

Restaurateur Stephen Starr and Parisian designer India Mahdavi have captured here an ideal balance of old and new. The sprawling foyer bar is a netherworld of dark wood Ivy League accents, where diners sip on pomegranate martinis and nibble on a menu of tiny sliders stuffed with everything from kobe beef burgers to deep-fried blue goat cheese. The main dining room beyond is sleekly modern, a library of walnut wood cubes floating on ivory walls. With a gentle push from the server, green and white leather chairs glide beneath you. Settle in for extravagance.

The cheesesteak, by the way, is for showing off only, but as good as overpriced gimmicks come, a mouthful of fireworks — kobe beef, truffles, lobster, and molten Taleggio cheese — that arrives with a complimentary split of champagne.

The rest of the nouveau steak house menu, which recasts standards with better ingredients and refined trimmings, has been uniformly stellar down to the homemade tater tots.

All of the chops are superb. None are as extraordinary as the rib-eye, a 20-ounce slab of 21-day aged beef worth every cent of its $44. Each forkful stoked such a primal, savory glow, this was steak with a swagger.

Too bad our wine was meek. The overzealous markups make it hard to find a great wine with enough umph to stand up to those chops for $80 or less. (Drink gouging is one of the few reservations I had in bestowing a fourth bell.) The service could also tune down its chirpy enthusiasm a notch. The food is good enough that it requires no hard sell.

The $14 kobe "slider" mini-burgers were even better

STEAK HOUSE • RITTENHOUSE SQUARE
237 S. 18th St., 19103
215-732-7560 • www.barclayprime.com

than the cheesesteak — two White Castle-sized discs of meat on truffle-crisped buns with Gruyere cheese that deliver more beefy punch in a few bites than any super-sized pretender.

I've also been dreaming of the Barclay's butter-poached lobster, a three-pound beauty that looked like a fiery plume of crustacean on the plate. It was like eating butter with texture.

The kitchen pays a nice homage to all the luxury classics. Italian caviar came with coin-sized homemade blini. Beef tartare was cleverly presented two ways, minced with tarragon and toasted basmati rice, and shaved into a carpaccio fan sparkling with pepper.

The dry crabcakes were a mild disappointment. But the oysters Rockefeller were perfect, cooked just enough and draped with the nutmeg-scented silk of creamed spinach.

The spinach was only one of the great a la carte sides. The sauteed mushrooms were wild. The mashed potatoes come truffled. And there is a variety of marvelous a la carte sauces. But with meats like this, I hardly thought to use them.

That's how I usually feel about the pedestrian desserts at most steak houses. But Frank Urso's confections are a highlight. His all-American sundae was a standard at its most refined, with homemade ice creams and fruit compotes steeped from scratch. I loved the ginger-spiced pineapple upside-down cake, as well as the banana cream that unleashes a flood of caramel-soaked fruit when you crack the phyllo crust.

My favorite, though, was the toasted peanut butter s'mores, which slipped peanut butter ice cream into finger sandwiches between morsels of chocolate torte and disks of roasted house-made marshmallows that were sticky and warm to the touch. Now that's an updated decadence worth the splurge.

— OR TRY THESE —

Here are three other suggested steak houses:

THE CAPITAL GRILLE 🔪🔪🔪
1338 Chestnut St., 19107, (215) 545-9588
This clubby steak house is the best of the corporate steak chains, with consistently cooked chops, a first-class bar, and a power-lunch scene to rival the Palm's. Recent changes in management and kitchen have been seamless.

The Prime Rib 🔪🔪🔪
1701 Locust St. (in the Radisson Plaza Warwick Hotel), 19103, (215) 772-1701
Step back into the era of the steak house supper club, the ideal retro setting for a prime rib that is one of the region's best slices of beef.

The Saloon 🔪🔪
750 S. 7th St., 19147, (215) 627-1811
This South Philadelphia power-dining spot serves expensive (and often unspectacular) Italian cuisine, but it is rightly known for its garlic-infused chops that make it one of the area's most distinctive steak houses.

Birchrunville Store Cafe

♟♟♟ EXCELLENT

MENU HIGHLIGHTS Goat cheese souffle salad; Caesar salad with prosciutto and truffle dressing; foie gras pate; butternut squash bisque; mussel bisque; rack of lamb; venison chop; garlic-stuffed boar; stuffed rabbit; pomegranate-glazed pheasant; chocolate-hazelnut crunch tort; butterscotch cake.

BYOB French wines are a sure match.

WEEKEND NOISE Noisy

IF YOU GO Dinner W-Sa 6-9 p.m.
• **E** Dinner entrees, $23 to $30
• Reservations required
• Cash, check only
• Entire dining room nonsmoking, except sometimes, late evening, if no one objects
• Not wheelchair-accessible
• Free parking lot behind restaurant

The harvest moon hung like a big orange pumpkin over the Chester Country cornfields as we wound our way down into the hollow that hides the Birchrunville Store Cafe. As we pulled into the starlit gravel lot behind the cafe, with the sound of crickets and the dusky smell of herbs from the restaurant garden filling the air, it occurred to me that there are few — if any — dining destinations more picturesque than this old country store and post office-turned-gastronomic paradise.

But after you pass the rocking chair porch into the candlelit dining room, with its rustic country wood tables and Oriental rug-covered wood plank floor, it doesn't take long to realize that a trip to Birchrunville is more than a scenic drive. Chef Francis Trecziak's cooking, a sunny expression of his French and Italian roots, is absolutely the best part of the journey. And with only Trecziak and one sous-chef manning the tiny kitchen every night from Wednesday through Saturday, it has remained one of the area's most consistent (and popular) destinations for years.

With simple but perfectly executed dishes that highlight natural flavors and quality seasonal ingredients, it's easy to see the appeal. Trecziak's powers often seem at their height when his garden is in full summer bloom. But fall is also a particularly sweet time to experience his soulful cooking, inspired by Trecziak's youth in Aix-en-Provence and northern Italy.

A medley of real wild mushrooms — chewy black trumpets, snappy chanterelles, and meaty Italian porcini — are quickly sauteed in wine and cream, then ladled over a buttery puff pastry vol au vent. A quivering puff of goat cheese souffle plays against the gentle crunch of salad greens picked from the garden just moments before dinner.

The autumn menu also indulges heartily in the rich flavors of game. A crisply roasted breast of pheasant is

CONTEMPORARY FRENCH BYOB • WESTERN SUBURBS

Hollow and Flowing Spring Rds., Birchrunville, Pa. 19421
610-827-9002 • www.birchrunvillestorecafe.com

glazed with the sweet tang of pomegranate and fig molasses. A leg of rabbit comes stuffed with an herby mousse of pistachios and wild mushrooms. Seared leg of venison is sliced thin over silky mashed potatoes over a rich gravy of Burgundy wine sweetened with whole blackberries. Tender, ruby-colored slices of buffalo carpaccio are painted with piquant streaks of green peppercorn emulsion.

Some of his best dishes, though, transcend any season. The airy spinach gnocchi take on a bewitching twist in a light cream tinted by the woody smoke of cured salmon. A thick fillet of Chilean seabass in a green cream tingling with Champagne and wasabi show a rare but understated nod to fusion cooking, with the added surprise of tiny bay scallops hiding inside the sauce like exquisitely tender dumplings.

Birchrunville is a cash-only BYOB. But as suggested by the spent bottles scattered like trophies across the old store's cork-filled front windows — starring empty cadavers of '45 LaTour, '75 Petrus, and '67 d'Yquem — the regulars break out their big bottles for a proper meal here. And Birchrunville's charming young staff does the perfect job of delivering with effortless grace, yet casually, like the restaurant itself. How else does an unrequested birthday candle suddenly appear at our table in the warm croissant bread pudding unless the server was paying extra-close attention?

Pay close attention, indeed. Because that pudding didn't last long. And neither did the smooth ricotta torta with berries, or the silky Grand Marnier souffle, or the chocolate cake that oozed cocoa like hot lava, or the butterscotch soaked mini-bundt cake. I didn't drive all this way to leave even a crumb left on the plate. And it hasn't happened yet.

— OR TRY THESE —

Here are three other bucolic Chester County restaurants:

MAJOLICA 🔔🔔🔔
258 Bridge St., Phoenixville, Pa. 19460, (610) 917-0962, Phoenixville has a gem in this bistro, one of the area's best BYOBs. Chef Andrew Deery's New American menu showcases vivid combinations of good ingredients; wife Sarah Johnson guides the pleasant staff with grace.

RESTAURANT ALBA 🔔🔔
7 West King St., Malvern, Pa. 19355, (610) 644-4009 Former Rose Tattoo chef Sean Weinberg and wife, Kelly, have put Malvern on the culinary map with their ambitious BYO, warmed by the open wood grill and seasonal menu inspired by Italy, Mexico, and local ingredients.

Catherine's
1701 W. Doe Run Rd. (Rt. 82), Unionville Village, Kennett Square, Pa. 19348, (610) 347-2227 A popular showcase for chef Kevin McMunn's southwestern-tinged fare. Intense seasonings and sauces would benefit from more finesse, but the mushroom-crab soup is tremendous.

The BYOB Phenomenon

THE BYOB BOOM IS, DEPENDING UPON whom you ask, either the savior or death sentence for our restaurant scene. But the truth is hardly so red-and-white.

What we have here is a truly organic phenomenon, and it's far from its final state.

A survey last year by OpenTable.com, an online reservation service, found that Philadelphians are more than twice as likely to take their own wine to dinner than in most other American cities, including New York. And the phenomenon in this region has taken root here for many reasons. In New Jersey, the BYOs reflect growing restaurant scenes (like Collingswood) with too few liquor licenses. In Philadelphia, however, it is in many ways a response to a crisis in the city's official wine culture, exacerbated by a tenuous economy for expense account dining and Pennsylvania wine laws that have fostered wine lists that are 20- to 30-percent overpriced compared with those in free-market states.

The trend has been great for consumers eager to drink better wines in restaurants at retail prices. What's more, it has begun to reshape the identity of what dining in Philadelphia is all about. It has inspired a grassroots vitality that recalls the Restaurant Renaissance of the 1970s, which first put this city on the culinary map.

Since then, of course, Philadelphia has created a fair share of sophisti-cated full-service restaurants, from glitzy Walnut Street to Stephen Starr's empire of trendy eateries. But few reflect Center City's true spirit quite as much as these cozy storefront bistros — urban yet accessible, with the personal scale that still distinguishes Philadelphia from its East Coast rivals.

What began as a collection of affordable neighborhood spots and bare-bones starter restaurants has matured into a scene with consider-able ambition and variety, including a handful of bistros that now easi-ly rank among the city's most special dining experiences. Many of them also do a fine job serving wine, storing customers' bottles and special glassware, decanting wines, and tailoring dinners for wine events.

It remains to be seen whether the movement has staying power, as restaurateurs eventually confront the limited earning potential these mostly small venues produce. The original owners of Django eventual-ly sold their coltishly popular BYOB. David Ansill recently added a wine and tapas bar called Ansill to compliment his own seminal BYOB, Pif.

But the backlash effects of BYOs on the full-service restaurant scene may have the most lasting effects — and not all of them will be negative. There will always be plenty of greedy restaurants that regard their wine lists and bars as cash cows to be milked. But many of the best restaurants in town have learned to adapt to the competition by presenting an occasional BYO night, or simply building smart wine lists with fairer markups and the real added value of old-vintage bottles and other wines that are impossible to find in stores.

Value-oriented dining concepts like gastro-pubs and small-plate wine bars have also recently become the rage, proving that public interest in wine is clearly growing, not going dry. If the BYO camp can no longer be wooed to buy a good bottle, perhaps a good glass would do.

Here is a list of 50 great BYOBs followed by a roster of full-service restaurants and wine bars that still offer worthwhile wine lists:

NEW AMERICAN
Alison at Blue Bell
Bistro 7
Carambola
Carmine's Creole Cafe
Chloe
Django
Elements Cafe
Funky Lil' Kitchen
Mandoline
Matyson
Majolica
Marigold Kitchen
Maya Bella
Next
Pumpkin
Restaurant Alba
Rx
Sovana Bistro
The Orchard
Word of Mouth

FRENCH
Birchrunville Store Cafe
Gilmore's
La Boheme
Overtures
Pif
Spring Mill Cafe
Taste

MEXICAN
Lolita
La Cava
Las Cazuelas

ASIAN
Nan
Vientiane Cafe
Sagami
Sushikazu

GREEK
Dmitri's

SEAFOOD
Emerald Fish
Little Fish
Ritz Seafood

ITALIAN
Branzino
Caffe Casta Diva
L'Angolo
Melograno
Mercato
Porcini
Radicchio
Ristorante Pesto
Trattoria Lucca
Tre Scalini

RESTAURANTS WITH WORTHWHILE WINE LISTS

At the higher end, here are some restaurants with deep, prestigious cellars that are not outrageously priced (a la Fountain and Le Bec-Fin): Savona, Dilworthtown Inn, Vetri, La Famiglia, Moro, the Capital Grille, Meritage Philadelphia, Strawberry Hill (Lancaster), and Rat's (Hamilton, N.J.).

On a slightly lower price point, these restaurants work hard to present a smart selection of interesting wines that are not available at retail in Pennsylvania: Jake's, Fork, Friday Saturday Sunday, Bistro St. Tropez, and Sovalo.

I also appreciate restaurants such as Morimoto, ¡Pasion!, Estia, and Amada that look at their cellars as an extension of their kitchens and create thoughtful lists that are best suited to the identity of their cuisines.

Perhaps most telling, though, is the recent growth of wine bars and the availability of wines by the glass. The best of these wine bars are Ristorante Panorama, Ansill, XIX Nineteen, Amada, Tria, Vintage, Positano Coast, Penne, Paradiso, and Domaine Hudson.

Many BYO fanatics have begun insisting on bringing their own wine even to restaurants that serve wine. Here's a sampling of some full-service restaurants and their policies regarding bring-your-own wine (for a more complete listing on corkage policies, go to the informative Web site, www.byophilly.com):

- **Ansill:** $15 corkage fee
- **Barclay Prime :** $25 corkage fee
- **Bliss:** $10 corkage fee
- **Brasserie Perrier:** No corkage fee on Sundays; not permitted other days
- **Buddakan:** $12 corkage fee for wines not on wine list; must have Pa. sales receipt
- **The Capital Grille:** $25 corkage fee for wines not on wine list; otherwise, not permitted
- **The Chophouse:** Not permitted
- **Cork:** Not permitted
- **Dilworthtown Inn:** $15 corkage fee
- **Ernesto's 1521 Cafe:** No corkage fee
- **Farmacia:** No corkage fee
- **Friday Saturday Sunday:** $10 corkage fee
- **Fork:** $15 corkage fee
- **Gayle:** $35 corkage fee first bottle, $20 subsequent bottles
- **George's:** $5 corkage fee on Sundays; not permitted other days
- **Giumarello's:** Not permitted
- **Lacroix at the Rittenhouse:** $40 corkage fee for wines not on wine list
- **Le Bec-Fin:** Not permitted
- **Morimoto:** $25 corkage fee; Pa. sales receipt required
- **Moro:** Prohibited by Delaware law
- **Nectar:** Not permitted
- **Ristorante Panorama:** Not permitted, with rare exceptions
- **Savona:** $25 corkage fee
- **Sovalo:** No corkage fee on Mondays; not permitted other days
- **Susanna Foo:** Not permitted
- **Striped Bass:** $35 corkage fee for wines not on wine list; otherwise, not permitted
- **Trattoria Prima Donna:** No corkage fee

LIQUID PHILLY

When it comes to alcohol, Philly is much more than a wine town. This is also considered one of the greatest beer-bar cities in America. Here is a list of some of the best venues for beer and other drinks:

BEER

Belgian or local craft brews
Monk's, Eulogy, Bridgid's, The Standard Tap, The Grey Lodge Pub, The Bishop's Collar, N. 3rd, Johnny Brenda's, Drafting Room, The Farmhouse, Tria, Ansill, McMennamin's, The South Philadelphia Tap Room, Chaucer's Tabard Inn, Ten Stone, Nodding Head, The Abbaye

A great pint of Guinness
The Dark Horse, The Black Sheep, The Plough and the Stars, Fado, Tir Na Nog

German beer
Ludwig's Garten, Otto's Brauhaus

WHISKEY
The Dark Horse, Drafting Room, The Vault at the Ritz-Carlton, Mahogany, XIX Nineteen, Twenty21, the Royal Tavern, The Black Sheep (Irish whiskey), Jack's Firehouse (small-batch bourbon)

TEQUILA
Los Catrines Restaurant & Tequila's Bar, Zocalo, El Vez, El Sarape, Horizons, Cantina Los Caballitos

RUM
Cuba Libre, Alma de Cuba, Horizons, ¡Pasion!, Cafe Habana

GRAPPAS
La Famiglia, Vetri, Le Castagne

SAKE
Raw Sushi and Sake Lounge, Morimoto, Genji, Margaret Kuo's, Teikoku

GREAT PLACES TO MEET FOR A DRINK
Southwark, Brasserie Perrier, XIX Nineteen, the Happy Rooster, SoleFood, the Swann Lounge, the Capital Grille, Taquet, Twenty21, Jake's, Washington Square, Mahogany (with cigars), Bar Saigon (Vietnam), Continental Mid-town (roof), The Tank Bar (over Friday Saturday Sunday), l'Etage (over Beau Monde)

Brasserie Perrier

♟♟♟ EXCELLENT

MENU HIGHLIGHTS Lounge: salmon carpaccio; cheese ravioli; cheese or mushroom fondues; steak-frites; salmon with lentils; burger. Restaurant: Potato and goat cheese terrine; lobster risotto; choucroute (Monday); bouillabaisse (Friday); black bass a la nicoise; veal tenderloin; lacquered duck; stuffed chicken; homemade ice cream; rice pudding with brandied cherries.

WINE LIST Substantial list from both the New and Old Worlds, but maddeningly overpriced, with three- to five-times markups, decent wines beginning around $60. Excellent selection of quality wines by the glass.

WEEKEND NOISE Quiet to Noisy

IF YOU GO Lunch M-Sa 11:30 a.m.-3:30 p.m. Dinner M-Th 5:30-10 p.m. (until 11 p.m. in the lounge); F and Sa 5:30-11 p.m. (until midnight in the lounge); Su 5:30-9:30 p.m.
- **M to VE** Dinner entrees, dining room, $29-$43; lounge, $12-$19
- Reservations strongly recommended
- Wheelchair-accessible
- Valet parking $15

On the most prestigious restaurant street in a city of marquee chefs, Chris Scarduzio may be among the least known stars. But one gets the sense he likes it that way, thriving happily in the long shadow of his mentor, Georges Perrier.

Perrier's name, of course, lends cachet to this brasserie. But it is Scarduzio's steady, low-key excellence that has kept Brasserie Perrier (of which he is co-owner) near the pinnacle of local restaurants for nearly 10 years. And with Perrier's luxurious Le Bec-Fin nearby constantly working to redefine French haute cuisine for the 21st century and his Georges' in Wayne perpetually grappling to find its suburban groove, Brasserie has been the steadiest ship in Perrier's fleet.

It, too, struggled with its own identity early on, juggling Perrier's desire for an affordable neighborhood boite (which is, after all, the "brasserie" spirit) with the financial need for an upscale room to pay the bills on Restaurant Row. But this was resolved long ago by presenting both concepts under one roof.

The true brasserie can be found at the sidewalk cafe and in the boisterous front lounge, where the well-heeled crowds are often three deep at the bar, trading in restaurant dish and Rittenhouse gossip and splendid happy hour hors d'oeuvres. The lounge's dedicated menu, meanwhile, offers affordable bistro fare at its highest gloss.

There are plateaus of pristine oysters and house-smoked salmon carpaccio with preserved lemon creme fraiche. You can savor a luxury burger, a croque monsieur, or the definitive steak-frites, dry-aged in-house for an amazingly reasonable $17. Roasted salmon poses classically over lentils with red wine lobster sauce. There are also fun fondues for sharing, traditional with Kirsch and Savoie cheeses, or infused with cepes and served with risotto beignets.

Stride past the host stand at the rear of the bar, however, and you will enter into the sleek poshness of the

CONTEMPORARY FRENCH BISTRO • RITTENHOUSE SQUARE

1619 Walnut St., 19103
215-568-3000 • www.brasserieperrier.com

main dining room. With its deco colors, crackle-glass mural walls, and supple leather banquettes, it's like visiting an entirely different restaurant. The veteran servers pad around with suave and professional grace, ably helping diners navigate the well-stocked (but maddeningly overpriced) wine list. And the menu is every bit a showplace for high-end contemporary cuisine.

To begin, there is the signature goat cheese and potato terrine, a roulade of shaved potato sheets wrapped around tangy curds. There are also impressive risottos, homemade pastas, and raviolis.

I especially loved the ravioli stuffed with pureed celery root and artichokes that lent Provencale flair to the black bass "a la Nicoise." A honey-lacquered duck with gingered anise sauce was beautiful, one of the last relics of the initial Asian-fusion theme that Brasserie has been slowly shedding. A luscious veal tenderloin, meanwhile, served over puff pastry with crispy sweetbreads, chanterelles, and sweet roasted garlic, could have been at home at Le Bec-Fin.

But Scarduzio has also maintained a measure of brasserie flavors in the dining room's weekly "plats du jours" and they are among his best dishes. I love Monday's Alsatian choucroute, stewed with malty Meteor beer, duck confit, and boudin blanc; Friday's lobster-rich bouillabaisse; and the Thursday prime rib that cooks 13 hours before it arrives alongside creamy macaroni studded with peas and ham.

For dessert, Brasserie offers simple but sophisticated twists on familiar flavors, slipping creme brulee inside a pyramid of chocolate mousse, churning superb house ice creams, and serving warm steel cocottes of rice pudding topped with liquor-soaked cherries.

They could be more showy, perhaps. But the Brasserie and its chef have proven over time that quiet elegance is the essence of their success.

— OR TRY THESE —

Here are three other restaurants that serve authentic French bistro fare:

Bistro St. Tropez 🍴 🍴
Marketplace Design Center, 2400 Market St., 19103, (215) 569-9269
An upbeat bistro with a fantastic Schuylkill view, St. Tropez has a creative take on French cuisine at reasonable prices.

Caribou Cafe
1126 Walnut St., 19107, (215) 625-9535
This handsome cafe is historically inconsistent, but the current owner, chef Olivier de St. Martin, has redirected the menu toward its classic French bistro roots. Service, though, can be painfully slow.

Slate Bleu 🍴 🍴
100 South Main St., Doylestown, Pa. 18901, (215) 348-0222
A classic French bistro in downtown Doylestown's historic Agriculture Works building. The menu features well-crafted retro standards drawn from Mark Matyas's years as chef at Manhattan's La Grenouille. The low-energy service staff and weak wine list, though, need serious attention.

Buddakan

♟♟♟ EXCELLENT

MENU HIGHLIGHTS Ginger-cured salmon; hot eel dice; edamame ravioli; wasabi tuna pizza; king crab tempura; tea-smoked spareribs; pad Thai; char-grilled aged beef; duck breast; Asian barbecue pork; chocolate bento box; dip-sum donuts.

WINE LIST Decent list with focus on crisp New World whites, spicy-ready reds (zin-fandel and syrah), and an excel-lent (albeit pricey) selection of sake.

WEEKEND NOISE Deafening

IF YOU GO Lunch M-F 11:30 a.m.-2:30 p.m. Dinner Su-Th 5-11 p.m.; F and Sa 5 p.m.-mid-night
• **V E** Dinner entrees, $20-35
• Reservations required, avail-able two months to the date in advance
• Wheelchair-accessible
• Valet parking $16

It's hard to feel sorry for Buddakan, which has been for much of the last decade the most popular and finan-cially successful dining destination in the city. Since it opened eight years ago, this Old City palace of Asian-fusion chic has served up to 500 diners a night in the shadow of its giant golden Buddha.

With a soaring room draped in gauzy white curtains, a steady flow of celebrities, and a solid menu of contem-porary Asian flavors, this was the mega-hit that marked Stephen Starr's ascendancy to dining dominance, gave Old City its glamour, and defined a generation of concept eater-tainment halls that melded splashy ambience with first-rate food.

But if any great restaurant risks being stifled by its own success, Buddakan might be the one. The restau-rant has become such an icon that it has hardly changed from the day it opened — a boon to its devo-tees, perhaps, but also a danger for a restaurant created to set trends. Much of the rest of the food scene has evolved from simple Asian fusion to updating more authentic flavors — even Starr's new Chinese-centric Buddakan in Manhattan bears little resemblance to the original. But to step into this dining room is like walking backwards to 1998.

There is the same crush of stylish patrons hovering near the water wall beside the hostess stand, a mix of middle-aged Main Liners, wannabe boy-band posses, leggy models, and athletes, who are among the VIPs that can show up with a call to the kitchen and be fed with-out reserving weeks in advance.

The menu has also remained virtually identical to when the restaurant opened. It is in some ways a waste of chef Scott Swiderski's talents (he receives anguished letters any time he tries to remove an item from the menu). Then again, his creations are a big reason Buddakan struck a magic chord from the start — one that still resonates each time I return.

ASIAN FUSION • OLD CITY
325 Chestnut St., 19106
215-574-9440 • www.buddakan.com

The room vibrates with noise, but also a serenity radiating from the giant Buddha. Swiderski's kitchen, meanwhile, operates with Zen-like consistency, turning-out stunning plates that are, if not cutting-edge, the epitome of accessible exotic. Dumplings filled with gingered-chicken get dipped in sesame soy. Tea-smoked ribs shine beneath a hoisin barbecue glaze. Crisp flabread is draped with sheets of sushi tuna and streaks of wasabi mayonnaise. Batons of sweet king crab legs are tempura fried and crossed over spicy ponzu. A pork spring roll brings fried pastry cigars stuffed with meat infused with the anise aromatics of a slow braise. Skewered kobe shortribs are skimpy for $16, but undeniably tasty.

Of Buddakan's entrees, I find the popular miso-glazed black cod overly sweet. But the char-grilled sirloin, crusted in togarashi spices beside a haystack of shoestring potatoes, is irresistible. The tender duck is my favorite entree, with its garlicky five-spice jus and corn pudding of scallion-flecked spoonbread. The "angry lobster," however, can be missed. This $65 stir-fry showpiece of de-shelled crustacean comes menacingly draped over an edible basket. But it's weighed down by retro gobs of lobster mashed potatoes with a dull sauce that's more of a bland bore than angry with spice.

Buddakan delivers the promised drama with desserts. They range from the chocolate pagoda ice cream sandwich to the multi-chocolate bento box spectacular to the clever "dip-sum," which brings an overturned Chinese take-out box with freshly fried, sugar-dusted donuts. The dip-sum hasn't changed in years, down to its chocolate, blackberry, and gingered cream dips. But they're still so good, like much of the Buddakan experience, I'm reminded that the status quo can sometimes be worth holding on to.

— *OR TRY THESE* —

Here are three other Asian fusion restaurants:

SUSANNA FOO ✕ ✕ ✕ ✕
1512 Walnut St., 19102, (215) 545-2666
Susanna Foo's French-Chinese cuisine sets the city's benchmark for creative but natural fusion cooking. Foo's kitchen does a nice job melding new ideas with her classic repertoire, and the service is polished.

NECTAR ✕ ✕ ✕
1091 Lancaster Ave., Berwyn, Pa. 19312, 610-725-9000
This pan-Asian palace has become the Buddakan of the 'burbs, with its big Buddha and talented chef. The menu from former Susanna Foo chef Patrick Feury is a French-Asian blend that ranks among the most ambitious dining experiences in the suburbs.

Roy's ✕
124-34 S. 15th St., 19102, (215) 988-1814
An old bank has been transformed into a branch of this Hawaiian-fusion chain, but the creative fare, from wasabi spaetzle to pork chops with plum sauce is too inconsistent for these prices, and service has been iffy.

The Capital Grille

♟♟♟ EXCELLENT

MENU HIGHIGHTS Fried calamari with hot peppers; crab and lobster cakes; wedge salad; ribeye steak sandwich; kona-crusted sirloin; porcini-rubbed Delmonico; lamb chops; grilled tuna; baked potato; creamed spinach; cottage fries and onion strings; coconut cream pie.

WINE LIST Microscopically printed wine list, over 450 choices. Relatively reasonable mark-ups focus on usual California cabs and cult wines (like Diamond Creek, Shafer, and Peter Michael); fewer good choices below $50 than in the past. Nice selection of wines by the glass.

WEEKEND NOISE Lively

IF YOU GO Lunch M-F 11:30 a.m.-3 p.m. Dinner M-Th 5-10 p.m.; F 5-11 p.m.; Sa 4:30-11 p.m.; Su 4-10 p.m.
 • **V E** Dinner entrees, $22-$38
 • Reservations highly suggested
 • Wheelchair-accessible
 • Valet parking $18

I've never been a big fan of chain steak houses because so many seem to be cut from the same proverbial side of corporate beef. They're essentially high-end clubhouses built to pamper the expense-account crowd with red meat and wood-paneled pomp. Ordinary diners, though, often feel overlooked. The a la carte menus are predictable. As for local character, very few manage to capture that elusive trait.

The Capital Grille is a notable exception, although not because it reinvents the chophouse formula. It simply works to refine it.

The Capital Grille appears, in many ways, to be cast from the familiar chain mold, a posh, woody restaurant filled with mounted animal heads and private wine lockers, and a Broad Street clientele to rival that of the Palm's across the avenue. But its consistently high-quality menu, its fairly priced deep cellar, and its outgoing service, have made it the most reliable standout in a city flush with competition.

I worried when the manager and chef who opened the local branch five years ago departed. But a recent meal under the new team, managing partner Miguel Miranda and chef Norman Reola (formerly at Pappas Bros. in Dallas), was as smooth as it could be.

The service was a picture of professionalism, formal but not stuffy, and with plenty of helpful advice on the menu and enormous list of microscopically printed wines. Tables of families with children were treated just as royally as big-spending conventioneers.

The food, meanwhile, was an impressive display of classic indulgences, from the rich lobster bisque and silky asparagus soup filled with nuggets of crab, to an ice-cold wedge glazed with creamy blue cheese and freshly crumbled bacon. There are a number of great appetizers that are hard to pass up, like fried calamari sauteed with

STEAK HOUSE • AVENUE OF THE ARTS

1338 Chestnut St., 19107

215-545-9588 • www.thecapitalgrille.com

hot peppers in garlic butter and a generous crab cake starter studded with bonus morsels of lobster.

But you'll want to save room for the main event. At lunch, the ribeye sandwich may be one of the best cheesesteaks in town, with 10 oz. of sliced ribeye on a sourdough roll with caramelized onions and havarti cheese. At $15.95, it's also a great value. The super-sized dinner chops are priced in the mid-$30s, but this is fair given their consistent quality.

I'm particularly fond of the cuts the Capital Grille dry-ages in house — the sirloin, the porterhouse, and Delmonico rib steak. I tried a couple dressed-up variations on my last visit — a sirloin rubbed in kona coffee and a Delmonico dredged in porcini dust — and both were excellent, each seasoning adding an extra layer of depth without obscuring the complex flavors of the meats. A gorgeous rack of American lamb was virtually unadorned, but its tender, rose-colored meat was simple perfection.

There's plenty to choose from for non-carnivores, too, from broiled lobsters to sesame-seared tuna. They're fine, but not a reason to come.

The a la carte sides, however, are the stuff of cravings. The rich nutmeg-scented creamed spinach, the football-sized fresh-baked potatoes, and the mountain of crisp cottage fries and crunchy onion strings are all worth the splurge.

And so is dessert, though the choices are fairly traditional. Among the best were the cheesecake, the white chocolate mousse, and a coconut cream pie with whipped cream billowing over its macaroon crust. It also arrived, quite surprisingly, with a candle ablaze — thanks to the cheery reservationist who noted a phantom anniversary by mistake. We were buoyed, nonetheless, by this typical Capital Grille hospitality. Even if it wasn't our anniversary, a corporate steak house meal this good was worth the celebration.

— OR TRY THESE —

Here are three other upscale restaurants on the Avenue of the Arts:

The Grill 🔪🔪🔪
Ritz-Carlton Philadelphia, 10 Avenue of the Arts, 19102, (215) 523-8000. The departure of star-chef Terrence Feury has taken some inventiveness from Ritz-Carlton's premier dining room, but you'll still find high-quality updates of American grill cooking and classy service.

Estia 🔪🔪
1405-07 Locust St., 19102, (215) 735-7700. An elegant Greek seafood palace with a display of imported Greek fish, the kitchen's signature. The whole fish are exquisite, but high prices and a limited menu have kept the vast dining room feeling empty.

Bliss 🔪🔪
220-224 S. Broad St., 19102, (215) 731-1100. One of the few local restaurants on the Avenue of the Arts, serving fusion fare with a minimalist look. After a disappointing debut, the kitchen has shown some imagination, from venison with chestnut ravioli and cheesesteak empanadas. But service remains inconsistent.

Carmine's Creole Cafe

🎭🎭 VERY GOOD

MENU HIGHLIGHTS Gumbo of the day; crab and smoked gouda tart; crawfish spring rolls; blackened maple-glazed duck special; Cajun seafood pasta; braised short ribs with crawfish mac 'n' cheese; chicken-andouille fricassee; pecan pie.

BYOB Hearty red (shiraz or zinfandel) or quenching white (sauvignon blanc) pairs well with the assertive spice. Crisp beer works, too.

WEEKEND NOISE Deafening

IF YOU GO Dinner Su 5-9 p.m.; Tu-Th 5-9:30 p.m.; F and Sa 5-10 p.m.
• **M to E** Entrees, $15-$28
• No reservations, except for chef's tasting
• Visa, MasterCard only
• No smoking
• Not wheelchair-accessible
• Street parking only

My frequent longings for a good gumbo or Monday bowl of red beans took a kick in the gut when Hurricane Katrina nearly destroyed my former city, washing so many New Orleans chefs into exile across the country that it will be years before the Crescent City recovers.

Selfishly, I can only hope a good "Yat" lands at a stove somewhere near Philadelphia. Because as I surveyed our realm for a few Creole gems, the pickings were lean, and not exactly authentic.

There is at least one local chef who best understands the Big Easy palate — most likely because he's from there — and that is John Mims, who last year moved his wildly popular BYOB, Carmine's Creole Cafe, from Havertown to Narberth.

The move from his former deli space to a refurbished house in the middle of a residential neighborhood has afforded Mims a more upscale look, if not necessarily more seats (at 40, it's still tiny). The room's tile floor, brick walls, wrought-iron work, and bustled burgundy drapery lend the space an appropriately New Orleans feel.

It is the full-flavored Louisiana cooking emerging from Mims's open kitchen, though, that has folks lined up on the sidewalk porch, sipping wine for up to an hour on weekends as they wait for a table. Luckily, it was worth the delay.

The daily gumbo was a highlight, a hearty bowl thickened with mahogany-colored roux, but also a delicate undertow of sweet lump crab. Beautifully blackened shrimp streaked with remoulade sauce had a surprise scattering of tart pickle chunks that really lit the dish up.

Carmine's crispy seared scallops were succulent next to a syrupy black currant-balsamic glaze. The fried crawfish spring rolls, meanwhile, were better than ever with their gingery soy Asian dip. For pure indulgence, it

CAJUN/CREOLE • MAIN LINE
232 Woodbine Ave., Narberth, Pa. 19027
610-660-0160 • www.carminescreole.com

would be hard to top Mims's crab tart, a creamy cheesecake that adds some zippy Acadian edges with a green scallion mayo and smoky gouda cheese. The buttery crab claws and wine over toast pushed the legal limit on garlic.

Such rewards, however, are not always certain as Mims is prone to inconsistency — an oversalted duck gumbo, a dry pork loin, or the occasional kitchen-sink special.

How else to describe a platter with bacon-wrapped scallops, blackened shrimp, ribs, and filet mignon? Down South, that'd be called "redneck surf 'n' turf." And it would have been great had the filet been even remotely well cooked. On the third try, Mims himself brought it to the table with this oath: "If that isn't perfect, why don't I just slit my throat right here!"

No need. It was really, really good. And so were many of the other entrees (especially since Mims vowed to do more of the cooking himself). Our daily duck special was blackened and maple-glazed, a combination that was both lusty and sweet. The amazing short-rib special came topped with wonderfully crisp, cornmeal fried oysters, and also a creamy side of broiled mac 'n' cheese scattered with fried crawfish.

For something less dressy, we enjoyed the Cajun seafood pasta with fistfuls of shrimp, crab, and crawfish in a cream sauce that tingled with spice. I was also especially fond of the chicken and andouille fricassee over mashed potatoes. Sadly, Mims declared self-consciously that he planned to remove it from the menu because it's a homely brown dish that doesn't look nice.

Neither did Carmine's usually ice-cold pecan pie when they (begrudgingly) heated it up on special request. But really, when a taste of true New Orleans home-cooking finally warms my fork, I'm simply grateful that it exists anymore at all.

— OR TRY THESE —
Here are three other worthy New Orleans–themed restaurants:

Melange Cafe 🔔🔔
1601 Chapel Ave., Cherry Hill, N.J. 08002, (856) 663-7339
Chef Joe Brown's upscale restaurant is South Jersey's best bet for a Mardi gras fete, with a menu inspired by Louisianan and Italian ideas, from creamy smoked tomato crab bisque to tasty mixed-grill jambalaya.

MARSHA BROWN 🔔🔔🔔
15 S. Main St., New Hope, Pa. 18938, (215) 862-7044
Marsha Brown has transformed a former church into a Southern-inflected grill where the best dishes reflect her New Orleans roots. It's an impressive destination for a New Hope splurge, but some of the Louisiana flavors still need fine-tuning.

High Street Caffe
322 S. High St., West Chester, Pa. 19382, (610) 696-7435
This funky BYOB has a gutsy kitchen that indulges in high-octane Cajun flavors. Ignore the gratuitous flame-throwing voodoo crawfish; the andouille gumbo and fine blackened catfish are authentic.

Cherry Street Chinese Kosher Vegetarian Restaurant

🏛🏛 **VERY GOOD**

MENU HIGHLIGHTS Emerald 3 Mix soup; winter-melon soup with golden-needle mushrooms; house-special wonton; rose dumpling; mushroom rice noodles; stuffed fried bean curd with black-bean sauce; dynasty mock shrimp; mushroom winter-melon roll; mock fish with ginger and scallion.

BYOB Try the whole flower tea.

WEEKEND NOISE Quiet

IF YOU GO Entire menu Su-Th 11 a.m.-10 p.m.; F and Sa 11 a.m.-11 p.m.
• I Entrees, $7.25-$12.95
• Reservations recommended
• Most major cards
• Wheelchair-accessible
• Free parking, 10th and Filbert St. lot, with validation

Chinatown has a number of vegetarian Buddhist restaurants where the "beef" is made from seitan (wheat gluten), and textured soy stands in for everything from pork to shrimp. But most of them make a gloppy mockery of mock duck, and vegetables, which should play a prime role, too often seem like an afterthought.

The Cherry Street Chinese Kosher Vegetarian Restaurant is a major exception. Take one spoonful of their amazing soup called Emerald 3 Mix, and you'll taste a vegetarian masterpiece — a broth filled with shiitake caps and golden needle mushrooms and a color that radiates the vibrant green of freshly juiced asparagus and spinach.

Cherry Street dabbles in mock meats, too, and for a change, the results are convincing. The steamed mock fish — thin slices of textured white soy edged with a dark seaweed "skin" and slicked with gingered soy sauce — had a firmness and a mild flavor that could be mistaken for monkfish. The imported Japanese jumbo mock shrimp were also shockingly authentic, especially good in a tangy dark glaze of Dynasty sauce.

I must admit to a curiosity about faux foods, but such culinary trickery, even at its most clever, delivers limited satisfaction. What sets apart this kitchen, run by chef/co-owner Bao Xin Shen, is attention to sharp flavors and creative presentations that highlight, rather than mask, the ingredients.

Shen's restorative soups and sauces begin with a giant pot of fresh, full-flavored vegetable stock enriched with caramelized bok choy. This versatile building block is then spiked with soy sauce and rice vinegar for a delicate hot-and-sour soup, or sweetened with milky yellow kernels of corn for tofu soup, or shined with sesame oil and filled with plump vegetarian wontons.

One of my favorites is a soup with finely diced savory winter melon and strands of golden needle mushrooms. In a non-soup entree, that winter melon is shaved into

CHINESE VEGETARIAN • CHINATOWN
1010 Cherry St., 19107
215-923-3663

crisp sheets and wrapped, like pasta, around chewy mushroom caps, springy mock ham, and crunchy asparagus.

The vegetables here are stars. Carrot not only gives the steamed rose dumplings their orange tint; a little carrot puree sweetens and binds their mung-bean noodle, mushroom, and cabbage filling. Jade dumplings get their verdant color and flavor from spinach juice.

Mushrooms are also given a prime role. I loved the mushroom rice noodles, a dish that brings five varieties of mushrooms atop a nest of tangled noodles. The fried oyster mushrooms coated with spicy salt were a clever twist on salt-encrusted fried seafood that crackled with high-voltage flavor.

There were a couple dull dishes. A curious creation called Golden Feather Knishes, a potato-stuffed pastry aimed at the restaurant's large kosher clientele, was unappealingly bland. The non-dairy dessert "blintzes" also disappointed.

But the crowd at my table didn't need dessert. We were savoring the orange-flavored mock beef, made of crisped house-made seitan with a dark, citrus-peel-infused sauce, and heat-blistered string beans tossed in a spicy-sweet Szechuan sauce.

I even loved the subtler tofu dishes, which are favored by old-school Buddhists over the trendier gluten-based mock meats. Both the crispy bean curd and the fried tofu blossoms were stuffed with a comforting soft tofu mash scented with mock ham and sweet bell peppers.

Our teapots were filled, not with standard Chinatown oolong, but ethereal brews steeped from whole heads of flowers — tiny marigolds and roses — that, like the rest of the meal, were light but satisfying from start to finish.

My fortune cookie proclaimed that my wishes would be granted if my "desires are not extravagant." But it was too late. My meals here had been extravagant feasts indeed.

— *OR TRY THESE* —

Here are three other Chinatown restaurants specializing in vegetarian cooking:

Charles Plaza
234-236 N. 10th St., 19107, (215) 829-4383
This haven for seitan-seekers offers both mock and real versions of fish and meat. The "paradise goose" — bean-curd-wrapped veggies glazed with tangy peanut sauce — is truly inspired. But the crispy mock fish tastes a bit too much like turkey stuffing.

Harmony Vegetarian Restaurant
135 N. 9th St., 19107, (215) 627-4520
Delicate veggie dumplings, wafer-thin scallion pancakes, and zippy Hunan-sauced mock beef made from wheat gluten are the highlights at this serene cafe. The service could be warmer.

Singapore
1006 Race St., 19107, (215) 922-3288
The mock-meat Chinese specialties have the added flair of Southeast Asian curry. Unfortunately, the kitchen hides many of its fresh flavors inside big puffs of deep-fried dough.

Devi

♟♟ VERY GOOD

MENU HIGHLIGHTS Idly; gunpowder idly; medhu vada; samosas; mulligatawny; dosas — butter masala dosa, spinach dosa, spicy Mysore dosa, giant "family" dosa; channa bhatura; malai kufta; dal makhani; coconut rice; lemon rice; gulab jamum; semiya payasam.

BYOB Crisp (or off-dry) white wine or brisk lager works well for the spicy cuisine. Try mango lassi or exotic lime and garam Nimbu soda.

WEEKEND NOISE Lively

IF YOU GO Lunch M-F 11:30 a.m.-2:30 p.m.; Sa 11:30 a.m.-3 p.m.; Su 11:30 a.m.-3 p.m. Dinner M-F 5:30-9:30 p.m.; Sa 5:30-10 p.m.; Su 5:30-9 p.m.
• I Buffets $7.95-$11.95; menu entrees, $9.95
• Reservations for 6 or more only — and highly suggested
• Most major cards
• No smoking
• Wheelchair-accessible
• Free parking

At the edge of exurbia in Exton, not far from where the Lancaster County farmland meets the Chester County sprawl, the crowds are coming to Devi. But not for mainstream American-chain fluff.

Devi is a destination extraordinaire for ultra-authentic South Indian vegetarian cuisine — a distinct, rice-based tradition that is finally emerging here from the shadows of more familiar North Indian cuisine. And the featured attraction is the dosa, the giant, crispy crepe made of ground rice and lentils that is the signature home-food of South Indian cooking.

Dosas issue from Devi's kitchen with a dizzying variety of shapes and fillings alongside dips of tangy sambar lentil stew and cooling white coconut chutney. Buttery cone-shaped dosas arrive, like dunce caps on a plate, before wide-eyed children. Masala dosas are curled into tubes around mounds of curried potatoes. And then there was the amazing family dosa, a five-foot roll of crepe spanning the length of two platters. It drew so many envious stares on its way to our table, I looked up to see a nearby table of 12 grinning at us with a unanimous thumbs-up.

It was a proud moment. And it was well rewarded by chef Xavier George, whose vivid cooking draws on a broad repertoire of Hindu-inspired vegetarian cuisine far beyond the dosas.

A visit to Devi's lunch buffet is a primer on many dishes from the subcontinent that Philadelphians rarely see. There are crisp rounds of deep-fried donuts called medhu vada made from ground lentils and ginger. Like the fluffy steamed idly cakes made from ground rice, these are wonderful dunked into sambar or hot mulligatawny soup, a chickpea lentil brew racing with cumin and curry.

Coconut is one of the primary ingredients in the South Indian palette — like turmeric, it aids the digestion of

SOUTH INDIAN/VEGETARIAN • WESTERN SUBURBS
151 Whiteland Town Center, Exton, Pa. 19341
610-594-9250

spice. It appears at Devi in the ever-present chutneys, but also in the marvelous "coconut rice," which blends sweet coconut meat into fragrant rice with crunchy bits of fried lentils, snappy cashews, and onions.

Other unusual items on the buffet: deep-fried pakora cabbage; creamy tomato curry filled with chickpeas and cubes of homemade paneer cheese; and a saute of snake gourd, a ring-shaped zucchini-like vegetable sauteed with turmeric and onions.

While the buffet is a bargain, it's worth venturing onto the large menu for variations like the gunpowder idly, which earns its name from an incendiary spice crust. The puli kozhambu is a rare example of cooking from the state of Tamil Nadu, a deeply tangy gravy steeped from tamarind pulp and ginger filled with whole cloves of roasted garlic.

George also produces superb renditions of some more familiar vegetarian curries. His dal makhani is a simultaneously buttery and earthy ragout of black gram lentils, split yellow peas, and red beans. The channa masala is a rich, cuminy stew of tender chickpeas, but it's the airy bhatura bread that wows the table, an immense balloon of deep-fried dough that breathes buttery steam when we pierce it.

For dessert, there are crisp balls of syrup-soaked gulab jamun, tart mango mousse, and vermicelli floating in milky semiya payasam pudding. Frothy cups of Madras coffee are a wake-up from the food stupor.

For the rest of the well-spiced meal, consider bringing a crisp white or hoppy IPA, because Devi is BYOB. Otherwise, try the house-made "Nimbu" soda, which is essentially seltzer blended with lime juice and a pinch of garam masala. The aromatic powder swirls through the glass like a fizzy, spicebox brew, but magically harmonizes with virtually every curry. A sip of true exotica at exurbia's edge.

— OR TRY THESE —

Here are two other restaurants that serve South Indian cuisine:

Uduppi Dosa House
2163 Galloway Rd., Bensalem, Pa. 19020, (215) 638-4008
Destination for South Indian specialties, such as dosa crepes with coconut chutney, steamed idly rice cakes, hot pickles, Madras coffee, and extensive vegetarian offerings; the giant dosa is a real treat.

Jewel of India
53 W. Lancaster Ave., Ardmore, Pa. 19003, (610) 645-5502
Wide-ranging menu spans varieties of Indian cooking (including non-vegetarian), but also has decent South Indian specialties like dosa and pizza-like uthappam. Closer to Center City, but the cooking's not as sharp as the others.

Cafe Spice 🔨 🔨
35 S. 2nd St., 19106, (215) 627-6273
This hip Indian bistro has contemporary decor, but classic dishes prepared with quality ingredients and sharp flavors.

Dilworthtown Inn

♟♟♟ EXCELLENT

MENU HIGHLIGHTS Caesar salad for two; foie gras; ginger crisp lobster; braised buffalo ribs; wagyu cheesesteak spring roll; crab and corn chowder; rack of lamb; wagyu oxtail cannelloni; duck breast with duck confit "knish"; scallops with beef cheeks; chateaubriand for two.

WINE LIST One of the best cellars in the region with over 800 selections, the 29-page list is strong in French prestige labels, but has lately deepened its reach into California cult labels, Italy, and Australia. The cellar master is well informed and helpful. A planned upgrade in wine glasses will be welcome.

WEEKEND NOISE Lively to Raucous

IF YOU GO Dinner M-Sa 5:30-10 p.m.; Su 3-9 p.m.
- **V E** Entrees, $22-$37; tasting menus, $30 (3 courses), $65 (5 courses)
- Reservations strongly requested
- Smoking, bar only
- Wheelchair-accessible
- Free parking lot

The Pennsylvania countryside is dotted with dozens of charming old inns, but few have remained as relevant as the one named for the tiny historic Village of Dilworthtown.

The Dilworthtown Inn, which survived the damage wrought by redcoats after the Battle of Brandywine in 1777, is now in its 30th year as a fine-dining destination. And it certainly has colonial ambience to spare. The inviting glow of candlelight flickers through its paned windows, and many of its 15 intimate dining rooms are filled with brick hearths and Colonial-style tables hand-crafted on the premises, which lend it a cozy romance. During warm weather, diners can gaze at the starry West Chester sky from the open-air ruins of 18th-century stables that are now the restaurant's al fresco terrace.

But no institution survives three decades at this level on quaint ambiance alone. And for the Dilworthtown Inn, remarkable longevity can also be attributed to one of the region's best veteran service teams, a spectacular wine cellar (over 800 selections), and a constant, yet measured, pursuit of progress.

In some regards, progress has meant expanding the property, with the opening of a large banquet and cooking-event facility across the street (The Inn Keeper's Kitchen) and the new addition of a casual cafe with prepared foods take-out, The Blue Pear Bistro.

But progress has also meant keeping the kitchen up to date. That isn't easy for a standby revered by West Chester's blue blazer crowd as a bastion of Continental classics, from one of the last great Caesar salads made tableside by tuxedoed servers, to Kennett Square mushroom soup, stuffed lobster tails, and Cheateaubriand for two.

But owners Jim Barnes and Bob Rafetto have always insisted on hiring talented young chefs to keep the menu fresh. And the current chef, David Intonato, is no exception. The veteran of Ritz-Carlton kitchens in Atlanta and New York has been presenting a contemporary

NEW AMERICAN/CONTINENTAL • WEST CHESTER
1390 Old Wilmington Pike, West Chester, Pa. 19382
215-671-4088 • www.dilworthtown.com

approach and some exotic high-end ingredients that few might expect at this old-line address. So along with the usual crab cake and rack of lamb, there is also a trendy "cheesesteak" springroll made from wagyu (a.k.a. kobe) beef, ginger-fried lobster, game, and other daring meats.

To begin with, there were braised shortribs of buffalo rubbed with exotic garam masala that were glazed with pomegranate-scented jus. House-cured pork belly is mashed into creamy rillettes alongside poached foie gras blended with truffles streaked with persimmon syrup. Braised oxtail of wagyu beef is blended with pumpkin and folded into cannelloni packages over creamy bechamel and wild mushroom ragout.

There were rare disappointments. An upscaled macaroni and cheese with lobster sounded irresistible, but the pasta was flabby and the fontina cream was surprisingly bland. A grilled boar sausage, served with the massive braised boar shank, was disappointingly dry.

But we loved seared duck breast with bacon-braised cabbage and a clever "knish" of puff pastry stuffed with duck confit, goat cheese, and smoked paprika. Luscious seared scallops were paired with a strikingly earthy stew of beef cheeks and porcini, with creamed salsify.

As intriguing as the savory menu has become, Dilworthtown's desserts remain yawningly dull (mousses, tarts, and vanilla ice cream). Another nit is the clunky glassware, which has always been surprisingly low-end considering the restaurant has one of the greatest cellars in Pennsylvania, where one can sample verticals of Chateau Cheval Blanc, obscure Hungarian dessert wines, or the latest California Rhone Ranger.

Jim Barnes, though, promised me that serious stemware was at last next on his list of big improvements. When you're running the region's best country inn, real progress sometimes is found in the smallest details.

— OR TRY THESE —

Here are three other destinations near West Chester:

GILMORE'S 🔔🔔🔔
133 E. Gay St., West Chester, Pa. 19380, (610) 431-2800
Peter Gilmore's dining room has earned the ex–Le Bec-Fin chef a third bell, with innovative French cuisine (try the "corndog" shrimp and "candied apple" chocolate mousse) and poised service.

Roux 3 🔔🔔
4755 West Chester Pike, Newtown Square, Pa. 19073, (610) 356-9500
This ambitious restaurant has survived well despite a series of chef changes. The New American menu highlights natural flavors, with occasional Asian and Mediterranean accents. The eclectic wine list is also strong.

Simon Pearce on the Brandywine 🔔🔔
1333 Lenape Rd., West Chester, Pa. 19382, (610) 793-0948
Watch artisan glass blowing, then enjoy creative regional American cooking with some Irish accents that has improved over time.

Django

🎖🎖 VERY GOOD

MENU HIGHLIGHTS Bay scallops with blood orange and crab salad; octopus with socca crisp; cassoulet; oysters with horseradish-Champagne gelee; skate with avocado-beet salad; duck breast with salsify and mulled jus; venison with chestnut spaetzle; veal steak with veal cheeks; chocolate-almond terrine; goat cheese cake; cheese plate.

BYOB

WEEKEND NOISE Noisy

IF YOU GO Dinner Tu-Sa 5:30-10 p.m.; Su 5:30-9 p.m.
• **E** Entrees, $21-$28
• Reservations required, accepted up to one month to numeric date
• Not wheelchair-accessible — small step at entrance; restroom accessible
• Street parking only

One of the greatest joys of our BYOs — their ability to so clearly reflect the efforts of a few talented individuals — is also one of their biggest perils.

What happens when that talent hits the road?

Ironically, it is Django, the celebrated little bistro off South Street that inspired the BYO boom, that has been the most visible test of such growing pains. Considering the sentimental pull of this cultishly popular destination, it will be worth watching this transition play out.

Founding chef Bryan Sikora and his wife, Aimee Olexy, cheeseplate goddess and dining room manager, transformed a homey yellow room dressed in burlap linens into one of the hardest reservations around. So they shocked the food scene last fall when, after five years, they sold their business and left town.

New owners Greg Salisbury and chef Ross Essner, who a few years ago teamed-up for West Philly's Rx, have made some upgrades, but wisely attempted few obvious changes — aside from replacing Django's clunky old wine glasses with finer crystal. Adorning the exposed brick walls here is some nice local art (occasionally by one of the servers). And dinners here still begin with that signature loaf of warm flower-pot bread. The servers orchestrate the meal with a casual yet graceful skill uncommon in a neighborhood bistro. (Manager Christina McKeough even sounds like Olexy when she sidles up to describe the famous cheese plate).

But the old Django didn't earn four bells because of its cozy setting, or because it was the iconic BYO. Sikora's cooking was simply that good — intensely seasonal, uniquely inventive, and flawlessly done. The difference, so far, has been most obvious in the kitchen.

Essner is no slouch, and shares Sikora's love of good local ingredients. And many of his dishes show legitimate three-bell potential. Succulent caramelized bay scallops line the plate alongside a lively salad of fennel and blood

NEW AMERICAN BYOB • SOCIETY HILL (South Street East)
526 S. 4th St., 19147
215-922-7151

orange tossed with peekytoe crab. Crisped skate wing pairs with avocado and beet salad with spiced pumpkin seeds. Tender duck breast evokes fall flavors with a mulled jus and caramelized salsify. Salty Cape May oysters sparkle beneath a minted apple relish and champagne gelee spiced with horseradish.

However, both the concepts and execution of Essner's early menus have been considerably less elegant than the Django norm. There are some holdovers, like the goat cheese gnocchi, but they were chewy and incidental beneath a barrage of too many ingredients, from mushrooms to squash to greens and more cheese.

That cluttered feeling weighed down many of Essner's best ideas. The soups, which were served in tiny cups, were crammed with so many things — creamed chestnuts, duck confit, brandied apples in one — there was no room for interplay.

But basic technical goofs also held some promising ideas back from their true potential. Venison loin would have been great with chestnut spaetzle if it hadn't been totally overcooked (they graciously recooked it). The veal sirloin was also overcooked, not to mention lukewarm. Two other intriguing dishes — a Mediterranean octopus with chickpea "socca crisp" and butter poached escargots with Pernod and celery root puree — also arrived already less than hot.

McKeough has done a decent job maintaining Django's 12-cheese cheeseplate, though it could use more diversity and ripeness. But several desserts — a crunchy praline variation on the original chocolate almond terrine, and the goat cheese cake with lemon curd — were among the true winners. And they hint at the rosy horizons the new Django can hope for.

In the minimalist setting of the BYO, the chef behind the menu has to lead it there every night.

— OR TRY THESE —

Here are three other BYOBs near South Street:

Next 🍴 🍴
223 South St., 19147, (215) 629-8688
New American food that offers reasons to reconsider South Street as a dining destination. The emergence of young talents — in both dining room and kitchen — makes this more than just the next BYO.

Overtures 🍴 🍴
609 E. Passyunk Ave., 19147, 215-627-3455
This stalwart BYO features chef-owner Peter Lamlein's classic French menu. Despite inconsistencies, it satisfies with the timeless appeal of good ingredients cooked with simple care.

Ava
518 S. 3rd St., 19147, (215) 922-3282
This Society Hill BYOB from Le Castagne veteran, Michael Campagna, offers contemporary twists on Northern Italian cooking, from homemade pappardelle with rabbit ragu to shrimp sauteed with limoncello, and ravioli stuffed with eggplant and Taleggio cheese.

Dmitri's

🗡🗡 VERY GOOD

MENU HIGHLIGHTS
Mediterranean plate; beets;
grilled octopus; shrimp pil-pil;
spinach pie; grilled whole fish;
sauteed shrimp; grilled bluefish; panfried breaded flounder;
grilled scallops; grilled lamb;
creme caramel; rice pudding.

WINE LIST Queen Village is
BYOB, but Fitler Square has a
decent list of affordable wines.

WEEKEND NOISE Noisy

IF YOU GO Fitler Square: Su-Th
5:30-10 p.m.; F-Sa 5:30-11 p.m.
Queen Village: Tu-Sa 5:30-11
p.m.; Su 5-10 p.m.; M 5:30-10
p.m.
• **M** Entrees, $14-$21
• No reservations
• Fitler Square: most major
  cards; Queen Village: cash
  only
• Not wheelchair-accessible —
  steps, both locations; Fitler
  Square, restroom accessible
• Street parking only

The Dmitri loyalists will forever tout the original BYOB, of course, that eternally crammed 35-seat Greek corner nook at 3rd and Catherine where a former rock guitarist named Dmitri Chimes built a cult following on simply grilled octopus and fish.

But I long ago lost my desire to wait an hour for a seat at that tiny spot — though not because Queen Village doesn't have its charms. Quite simply, Dmitri's newer second location on the west side's Fitler Square is more spacious and accessible, not to mention equipped with an affordable little bar. And with original Dmitri's first chef, Chong "Hua" Xiong cheerfully navigating the open kitchen, the menu differences between the two are negligible, if any.

Stripped of the Queen Village aura of exclusivity, the West Side Dmitri's has proven itself to be a very good affordable neighborhood seafood restaurant, which is what the concept was intended to be all along. The service is pleasant and casual. And the room has a family-friendly comfort the other Dmitri's doesn't have, its clay-pot-colored walls whimsically scrawled with Greek motifs, and bright windows that look out from the narrow room onto quaint Fitler Square. The major appeal, though, is the clarity of its menu — Greek seafood done as simply as possible, splashed with garlicky oil and lemon, and rarely more than $20 a plate. And judging from my recent visit, the concept is still as satisfying as ever.

The octopus, now much imitated across the city, arrives blushing pink and touched by char, splashed with just the right amount of olive oil and herbs, with a mild chew that recalls grilled chicken salad with a Mediterranean flair. Shrimp pil-pil, perfectly fried beneath a micro-crust and splashed with a perfect twinge of red spice, are impossible to stop eating. Greaseless tubes of fried calamari were fresh and nicely

GREEK SEAFOOD • FITLER SQUARE • QUEEN VILLAGE
Fitler Square: 2227 Pine St., 19103 • 215-985-3680
Queen Village: 3rd and Catharine Sts., 19147 • 215-625-0556

tender. The triangles of feta-tangy spinach pie wrapped in a crisp phyllo sandwich were pure taverna comfort.

A plate of creamy feta cheese cubes and salty Greek olives is also a nice way to begin. Or you can go for the Mediterranean platter, which brings grill-charred pita wedges to dip into musky chickpea hummus, smoke-tinged baba ghanoush, garlic-and-walnut-thickened skordalia, cucumber and yogurt tzatziki, and salty orange tarama salada. A salad of avocado, slivered almonds, citrus wedges, and romaine is another great starter.

The main event here, though, is always the whole grilled fish. Like the octopus, these are far more widely available now than when Chimes first opened, and Dmitri's fish are on the small side compared to some of the competition. But for consistency and value, with sides of yellow rice pilaf and a garlicky mound of the signature escarole, they are still hard to beat. My favorite is the grilled pompano, the snub-nosed silver-skinned fish with a luxuriously moist flesh. But I was just as pleased recently with a one-pound striped bass — though, unless you're proficient in boning fish, it can be a pretty light meal. For those who don't like the dirty work, the pan-fried flounder, dusted in a perfectly browned crust, is also a satisfyingly straightforward plate of fish.

I've had mixed luck here with meat, but the kitchen was on target at my last visit. Thin slices of lamb were perfectly pink and tender with marinated flavor. A big terra-cotta crock filled with soulfully good ground lamb and eggplant moussaka, meanwhile, would have been hearty enough for two.

The baklava remains one weakpoint. But other comfort classics, like the creme caramel or cinnamon-dusted rice pudding, more than compensate. Like Dmitri's itself, their appeal is simple, but irresistible simplicity.

— OR TRY THESE —

Here are three other suggested Greek restaurants:

Estia 🗡 🗡
1405-07 Locust St., 19102, (215) 735-7700
An elegant Greek seafood palace with a display of imported Greek fish, the kitchen's signature. The whole fish are exquisite, but high prices and a limited menu have kept the vast dining room feeling empty.

Effie's 🗡 🗡
1127 Pine St., 19107, (215) 592-8333
Classic Greek home foods, from moussaka to baklava, can be savored in the lovely brick patio or the cozy cottage behind Effie's townhouse-turned-taverna. A recent meal, though, was a bit sloppy.

Lourdes Greek Taverna
50 N. Bryn Mawr Ave., Bryn Mawr, Pa. 19010, (610) 520-0288
The menu offers a list of Hellenic classics, from moussaka to souvlaki and spinach pie, but the flavors lack the zip of a little opa! to energize the fare.

El Vez

🔔🔔 VERY GOOD

MENU HIGHLIGHTS
Guacamole; melted manchego salsa; sopes mixtos; tortilla soup; mahi-mahi taco; carnitas taco; tamale; carne asada; sea scallops with horchata sauce; shrimp with pasilla cream; sopapillas; Mexican coffee.

WINE LIST Small list of decent $40-and-under bottles, many Latin American, but focus clearly is on great tequilas and sour margaritas.

WEEKEND NOISE Deafening

IF YOU GO Lunch M-Sa 11:30 a.m.-3 p.m. Dinner Su 3-10 p.m.; M-Th 5-11 p.m.; F 5 p.m.-midnight; Sa noon-midnight
• **E** Entrees, $8-$25
• Reservations suggested
• Discover card not accepted
• Wheelchair-accessible
• Parking discounted ($9) with validation, Park-A-Way lot, 12th and Sansom Sts.

Being crowned Philadelphia's best Mexican restaurant would have been no big deal a few years back, when the genre was one of our weakest ethnic specialties. But we've received a host of down-home taquerías since 9/11, when a diaspora of displaced Mexican workers from New York came our way. And the best highlight gutsy, homespun flavors that made our more established, upscale places pale.

But Stephen Starr manages to capture the best of both worlds at El Vez (which is named for the Mexican Elvis impersonator). His chefs build upon the labor-intensive traditions of authentic Mexican cooking, but elevate the quality of ingredients and present them with contemporary vision and polish, not to mention Starr's patented pink-and-chrome low-rider flash.

I get a serious craving for fresh guacamole whenever I settle into the oversize plush of the tufted red velvet booths at El Vez. Made to order from a cart near our table, it's a green goddess of cream that swirls with the snap of fresh citrus and a crack of chile spice. Wash it down with a salty-sour splash of blood orange margarita, grab a fistful of chipotle-spiced nuts, and you're ready to fiesta.

A crisp baton of mahi-mahi wrapped in a soft tortilla with pepper remoulade and pickled red cabbage redefines the classic fish taco. The tortilla soup draws a bottomless depth from a broth of guajillo and ancho chiles thickened with tortilla. Crunchy flauta tubes come stuffed with chipotle-tinged duck confit over avocado cream. Succulent shrimp marinated in pasilla peppers are seared with a chile-spiked lobster cream.

I worried when El Vez's opening chef, Jose Garces, left to open his own restaurant, Amada. But he has a capable successor in Adrian Leon, a Mexican-born chef, who, like Garces, worked under Nuevo Latino innovator, Douglas Rodriguez.

CONTEMPORARY MEXICAN • AVENUE OF THE ARTS
121 S. 13th St., 19107
215-928-9800 • www.elvezrestaurant.com

Very little of the winning original menu has been changed. The carne asada remains beautiful, a shingled stack of adobo-rubbed tenderloin ringed by dabs of green and brown sauce. It's electric over the crunch of a sour tomatillo-pepper salad. A classic rendition of piquant Veracruzana sauce, filled with capers, tomatoes, and green olives, takes an upscale polish with a thick slice of Chilean sea bass.

Seared sea scallops are the centerpiece of a contemporary study in subtle Mexican flavors. Posed over a thick pillow of sope tortillas layered with sweet corn and crab, they are ringed by a milky pool of horchata rice cream streaked with nutty green pipian. Half-moon pillows of authentic Mexico City quesadillas, more like empanadas, are puffed with hearts of creamy crab. The slow-cooked carnitas were among my few disappointments, nicely flavored with all-spice and orange juice, but chewy.

Even the sides here are usually a treat — creamed corn and rice flecked with spicy poblanos, frijoles charros stewed with Negro Modelo beer, and grilled ears of corn glazed with an orange blush of chipotle mayonnaise.

I had fretted about changes in the kitchen, but it is the usually perky and confident service that has slacked off the most of late, acting more than a little lost — if they remember to stop by at all. The bar also has a maddening habit of padding their margaritas with too much ice.

But with some exceptional desserts, complaints are quickly sated. The "El Vez" combines rich chocolate with caramelized bananas and peanut butter mousse. The sopapillas, though, are the best. Served with a honeyed cream flavored with Jamaica tea, these beignets are crisply fried pillows of air dusted with cinnamon sugar, and ooze goat's milk caramel when you take a bite. It couldn't have been a sweeter adios.

— *OR TRY THESE* —

Here are three other suggested upscale Mexican restaurants:

LOS CATRINES RESTAURANT & TEQUILA'S BAR 🔨🔨
1602 Locust St., 19103, (215) 546-0181
The room is graced with beautiful Mexican art, charming servers, and a collection of fine tequilas. The menu has real highlights, from tortilla soup to langostinos in tequila sauce.

LOLITA 🔨🔨
106 S. 13th St., 19107, (215) 546-7100
The BYO boom takes a Mexican turn here, with affordable fare that feels more New American bistro than authentic Mexican. But warm service and killer margarita punch make this spot worth trying.

Paloma 🔨🔨
6516 Castor Ave., 19149, (215) 533-0356
Chef Adan Saavedra's French-influenced "haute Mexican" is one of the more intriguing menus in the city — let alone Northeast Philly. Inattentive service has held the restaurant back from the next level.

Famous 4th Street Delicatessen

🔔🔔 VERY GOOD

MENU HIGHLIGHTS All corned beef and pastrami sandwiches; hard salami; mushroom barley soup; split pea; cheese blintzes; all smoked fish (especially sturgeon); whitefish salad; special chopped liver; brisket platter; chicken-in-a-pot; stuffed cabbage; "black-out" cake; carrot cake.

BYOB A hoppy beer or a tannic Rhone red would work, but I opt for the Cel-Ray soda.

WEEKEND NOISE Noisy

IF YOU GO Entire menu served every day 8 a.m.-9 p.m.
- **I to M** Sandwiches, $9-$16; entrees, $16-$24
- No reservations
- Most major cards
- Wheelchair-accessible — request portable ramp for entrance step
- Street parking only

The new Famous 4th Street Delicatessen is a vast improvement over the old one, a power-brunch destination that was known more for its cookies and crumbs than good corned beef. It's been completely rehabbed by Russ Cowan, who has brought along the fragrant towers of hot corned beef and giant bowls of chicken-in-the-pot that made him the region's undisputed king of deli at three former locations called Kibitz (in Center City, Cherry Hill, and down the Shore); Pastrami & Things; and the Bread & Bagel.

Whether Cowan will stay for a while at 4th and Bainbridge remains uncertain, but the Famous is a classic that merits his attention, with all the ingredients to become the great sit-down Jewish deli Philadelphia has long been lacking. He's taken great care to respect the historic feel, refurbishing the paned window atrium, replacing the vintage 1930s tile, and installing deco lights and a wall of memorabilia from his family's own four-generation legacy of Radin's delis in Brooklyn.

But the longtime Famous waitstaff occasionally struggles with the weighty new gravity of Cowan-style deli, groaning "Oh my God!" under their heaping trays as they teeter toward a table. The portions are that big. My friend Dave claims he sprained his jaw biting into his corned beef reuben. And that was a "regular." However, it is the pure quality and consistency of the food — more than sheer girth — that sets Cowan's places apart. And Famous is no exception.

The little pre-dinner touches let you know a true deli man is behind the counter: the carafes of seltzer water, the sour pickle plates and house-baked onion-poppy rolls, and those cute freebee ramekins of tiny matzo balls in broth.

But the hot corned beef here is king. Glistening pink with melted fat and stacked six inches high on a crisply grilled rye, it calls to me with the mystery of clove and

JEWISH DELI • QUEEN VILLAGE
700 S. 4th St., 19147
215-922-3274

garlic. The lean pastrami is made especially for Famous with an extra whiff of smoke and mustardy pepper spice. And the hard salamis that hang in the window like shriveling torpedoes of mahoganied beef are a rare indulgence that I savor plain.

The smoked fish case here is also superb, from meltingly soft nova to the luxuriously meaty white sturgeon. The smoked whitefish salad was memorable, with a chunky consistency I prefer to the usual fine puree.

Other standouts were Famous's delicate homemade cheese blintzes. And Cowan's "special chopped liver" (modeled after the Sammy's Roumanian version) is an instant classic, infused with extra fried onions, and the spark of fresh horseradish.

Famous makes great soups (hearty mushroom barley and split pea with sausage) with one exception — an elephantine matzo ball of such an unwieldy heft that it suffocates the wholesome chicken broth.

But I devoured the beef brisket with garlic gravy over challah stuffing. The sweet and sour stuffed cabbage had the perfect balance of meat and rice. The chicken paprikash and beef goulash were among Famous's weakest efforts. Meanwhile, the Roumanian tenderloin (flank steak) buried in onions and mushrooms was undeniably delicious.

After such a filling meal, it's unlikely there's enough appetite left to attempt, say, a chocolate eclair as big as a clown shoe. But the sweet case has other treats worth sharing — the buttery rugelach, the intensely chocolatey "black-out" cake, or the checkerboard, whose moist squares of chocolate and vanilla cake are joined with mocha cream. And then, of course, there are still those big cookies, which were about the only things that Cowan didn't change. But thankfully, this new and improved classic now has plenty of real deli to be famous for.

— OR TRY THESE —

Here are three other worthy destinations for a corned beef sandwich:

Pastrami and Things
24 S. 19th St., 19103, (215) 405-0544
This cafeteria deli still slices one of the best hot corned beef sandwiches in town (though the pastrami's just OK). It has held up better than most of founder Russ Cowan's other former delis.

Murray's Deli
285 Montgomery Ave., Bala Cynwyd, Pa. 19004, (610) 664-6995
In the battle for Bala's deli soul, I tend to side with the old-fashioned mood in Murray's dining room, where one can taste one of the best examples of a Philly-style corned beef special.

Koch's Deli
4309 Locust St., 19104, (215) 222-8662
Devotees swear by the garlic-infused corned beef special at this cramped take-out deli as the definitive Philly-style corned beef. But the colorful counter-side banter and complimentary cold-cut noshes are also a draw.

Fork (and Fork: Etc.)

♟♟ VERY GOOD

MENU HIGHLIGHTS Grilled flatbread; clams in black bean sauce; chimichurri hanger steak; beef-tongue tacos; mustard seed encrusted fish (skate, trout, or scallops), cheeses; ricotta gelato.

WINE LIST Small, notable selection of quality smaller label wines, with focus on Europe; several quality choices by the glass. Good selection of local microbrews and Belgian beers.

WEEKEND NOISE Lively

IF YOU GO Fork: Lunch M-F, 11:30 a.m-2:30 p.m. Mid-day menu M-F, 2:30-5 p.m. Sunday brunch 11 a.m.-3 p.m. Dinner M-Th 5:30-10:30 p.m.; F until 11:30 p.m.; Sa 5-11:30 p.m.; Su 5-10:30 p.m. Late night menu Th 10:30 p.m.-midnight; F and Sa until 1 a.m. Fork:Etc.: Breakfast M-F 7-11:30 a.m.; Sa 8 a.m.-1:30 p.m.; Su 8 a.m.-2:30 p.m. Lunch and prepared foods daily, 7 a.m. (8 a.m. weekends)–8 p.m.; until 9 p.m. (June-Sept.). Chef's bistro dinner, W 8 p.m.
  • **M to E** Dinner entrees, $17-$32; chef's bistro dinner, $40 (4 courses, including wine)
  • Reservations recommended in restaurant; chef's bistro, walk-in only
  • Wheelchair-accessible
  • Street parking only

Fork was one of the first restaurants to bring the taste of a contemporary bistro to Old City when it opened in 1997. Nearly a decade later, it remains one of the most reliable destinations for a grown-up meal in a neighborhood that now caters increasingly to twentysomethings looking for a lounge.

Fork has smartly deepened its ties to Old City's rapidly growing residential population with the addition of Fork:Etc., a handsome cafe and prepared foods take-out emporium directly next door to Fork's main room.

That original space, transformed from an old sock shop into a sophisticated room decked out with tall-back quilted banquettes, velvet curtains, and hand-painted lamps, has always been a prime spot for a business meal. I love eating at the square front bar — especially at lunch — with its bird's-eye perch over the bustling back dining room and open kitchen.

With a menu that pairs seasonal ingredients with wide-ranging international flavors, Fork has always delivered thoughtful, modern cooking at fair prices. A lack of attention to some finer details has always held it back from being a truly elite kitchen, and it may never attain that level. But Fork is still one of the classiest, most comfortable restaurants around, and the addition of the Etc. space has added some impressive depth, from excellent house-baked breads to one of the best artisan cheese selections in town to a handsome private room for events.

Some recent meals in the restaurant were a little more polished than in the past, with sharper flavors that showed real attitude.

A lunch brought crisp pesto-smeared flatbread topped with arugula and grilled baby octopus. Frisee salad took on the hearty Greek flair of flaky strudel stuffed with ground lamb and eggplant and a side of yogurt tzaziki.

NEW AMERICAN/PREPARED FOODS · OLD CITY
306-308 Market St., 19106
215-625-9425 · www.forkrestaurant.com

Fork served up a fabulous grilled hanger steak, marinated in gingery chimichurri and served with irresistible hand-cut frites (at dinner, yucca fries). By contrast, the seafood curry had plenty of shellfish for $12, but was bland considering the exotic promise, with a garnish of mushy coconut rice — exactly the kind of details that have nagged this kitchen for years.

Fork's chef, Thien Ngo, is Vietnamese-born and trained in France, so the menu has evolved over the years from updated American comfort to a more pronounced French-Asian bent. Judging from the fixed-price bistro meals Ngo prepares each Wednesday night for the big community table in Etc., his true interests are even more adventurous than the regular menu shows.

The four-course menu with wine for $40 is an incredible bargain, and the first-come no-reservation meal is currently Fork's most intriguing feature. Co-owner Ellen Yin hosts it like a casual dinner party, while Ngo's changing blackboard menu is for food adventurers only.

Ours began with little clams and tofu stir-fried in an electric black bean sauce (fabulous, except for the broken shells). Next came spectacular skate wings, crisped beneath a tangy mustard seed batter and draped over a warm roasted tomato. Ngo showed some Latin moves with a tender beef tongue taco, poblano salsa, and diced mangos — though half the big table's guests were too timid to eat it. There were no such problems with the sublimely creamy ricotta gelato.

We were served refills on both a crisp Scherer pinot blanc and a fresh red Arva Vitas tempranillo from Spain — each typical of the value-oriented small labels that co-owner Roberto Sella has collected for Fork's smart wine list. That alone would distinguish Fork in a scene awash with overpriced wine lists and BYOs. But this is one restaurant that admirably never stops trying to become the full package.

— OR TRY THESE —

Here are three other suggested Old City restaurants:

Mandoline ♟ ♟
213 Chestnut St., 19106, (215) 238-9402
Restaurants don't get much smaller than this, but Old City locals will be pleased with a spot that takes its food seriously. It's a nice debut for chef Todd Lean's contemporary fare, but awkward service and the tight room limit the restaurant's potential.

The Continental
138 Market St., 19106, (215) 923-6069
This Old City diner-turned-martini-bar serves global tapas and high-style salads to an endless supply of buff swingers in black.

Bistro 7 ♟ ♟
7 N. 3rd St., 19106, (215) 931-1560
This dining room brings the respite of a food-focused BYO to the heart of Old City. The room and service are pleasant, and the New American menu from chef Michael O'Halloran is appealing, though nagging details keep the food from achieving full potential.

Fountain Restaurant

🗡🗡🗡🗡 SUPERIOR

MENU HIGHLIGHTS Foie gras and squab terrine; sweetbreads in pepperpot sauce; cheesesteak spring roll; Dover sole brandade in potato surprise; venison over salsify; black bass with corn and mushroom ragout; lobster trio; chocolate soufflé, baba au rum; cheese cart.

WINE LIST Enormous international cellar with focus on premier French and California labels, most with healthy markups. Some worthy sub-$75 wines from Southern France, Italy, Spain, and Austria. Extensive selection of quality wines by the glass, but also a bit overpriced, from $11-$36.

WEEKEND NOISE Quiet to Lively

IF YOU GO Breakfast M-F 6:30-10:30 a.m.; Sa 7-11 a.m.; Su and holidays, 7-10:30 a.m. Sunday brunch 11 a.m.-2:15 p.m. Lunch M-Sa 11:30 a.m.-2:15 p.m. Dinner every day 5:45-10 p.m.
- **U-E** Dinner entrees, $44.50-$58; dinner tasting menus, from $85 (4 courses) to $110 (6 courses); brunch entrees, $45-$65
- Reservations preferred
- Most major cards
- Wheelchair-accessible
- Valet parking $20, 2-4 hours; self-park, 2 Logan Sq., $19 for longer than 100 minutes

If you spend much time in some of the city's hotter new restaurants, where the quality of cooking has advanced so impressively in bargain venues like BYOBs, gastropubs, and neighborhood bistros, it might come as a shock when you crack the menu to see the price of dining at the Four Seasons hotel these days.

Entrees in the Fountain Restaurant start at $29 — and that's just lunch. You can count on $45 to $50 for the main course at dinner. But you can also count on something else. The Fountain still delivers one of the most impressive all-out dining experiences the city has to offer. The grand hotel and its staff swaddle guests in regal luxury from the moment they step through the Fountain's hushed vestibule into the warm wood dining room resplendent with gold and green linens, sparkling crystal, and a grand view onto the bubbling Swann Fountain. You're also likely to see famous faces like Governor Rendell or Sam Katz doing deals amidst the poshly spaced tables. But the best service staff in town knows how to make any plain Philadelphian feel like a regular big-shot, with a perfect balance of outgoing warmth and professional grace.

I wish the Fountain's enormous international wine cellar were more democratically priced (especially by the glass). But there are intriguing sub-$70 bottles if you look beyond the prestige French labels and verticals of California cult wines.

It is the powerhouse kitchen overseen by executive chef Martin Hamann, though, that assures the Fountain its place in our culinary pantheon, with an ever-evolving display of international haute cuisine built on premier ingredients, meticulously labor-intensive cooking, and a clever modern touch.

Classic Philly pepperpot stew undergoes a stunning contemporary deconstruction as its richly steeped broth of bell peppers and tripe is reduced to sauce around

NEW AMERICAN / HAUTE HOTEL • LOGAN SQUARE

Four Seasons Hotel, 1 Logan Sq., 19103
215-963-1500 • www.fourseasons.com/philadelphia

sweetbreads and croutons smeared with shredded ossobucco. A reinvention of brandade brings a hollow tower of carved potato filled with creamed Dover sole and a dollop of caviar. An Asian-scented shrimp arrives suspended inside a crispy "nebulous" of shredded kataifi phyllo. And foie gras terrine is a marvel of technical prowess, a luscious slice of Tokaj-marinated liver marbleized with slivers of wild mushrooms and a ruby circle of tender squab breast.

Over years of eating here, I've only had a handful of disappointing bites — all of them at lunch. Then again, something as incidental as a doughy pumpkin gnocchi, or a pedestrian French fry with their famous cheesesteak spring roll (yum!) tends to stand out when perfection is the standard.

Mostly, this kitchen has refined and focused ideas that, a few years ago, seemed bent on overpowering the diner. Butter-poached black bass was divine over a ragout of late-harvest corn and chanterelles mushrooms. Burgundy-colored medallions of venison offered startling contrast to a sugar white pedestal of salsify logs. And a two-pound lobster was transformed into triple-take luxury — tucked into a raviolo with truffles and mushrooms, paired with celery root and capers, and sauteed with bok choy in exotic Asian lobster sauce.

Dessert here is predictably more conservative, but it's hard to complain about a perfect chocolate souffle, rum-soaked baba, or pineapple upside-down cake with pink peppercorn ice cream.

Or that amazing cheese cart. As it rolled beside our table, its elegant shelves ripe with 25 gorgeous cheeses, I actually tried to resist. Then I broke down and ate nearly a dozen, plus every last sweet grape on the side. There is something to be said for pleasures you can count on — even at this price. And the Fountain may just be the one we can count on most.

— OR TRY THESE —

Here are three other haute-hotel dining rooms:

XIX NINETEEN 🍴🍴🍴
Hyatt Bellevue, Broad and Walnut Sts., 19102, (215) 790-1919. Hyatt's stellar renovation of these dining rooms swaps a modern look for fusty old Founders. Raw bar and wines by the glass are a treat. Contemporary menu from new chef Marc Plessis is often spectacular.

Lacroix at the Rittenhouse 🍴🍴🍴
210 W. Rittenhouse Sq., 19103, (215) 790-2533. Chef Jean-Marie Lacroix has departed the Rittenhouse Hotel, succeeded by talented Matthew Levin, but it's too soon to know if he can maintain the city's best cutting-edge brunch, and a luxury dining room that has always flirted with elite four-bell status.

The Grill 🍴🍴🍴
Ritz-Carlton Philadelphia, 10 Avenue of the Arts, 19102, (215) 523-8000. The departure of star-chef Terrence Feury has taken some inventiveness from the Ritz-Carlton's premier dining room, but you'll still find high-quality American grill cooking and classy service in this classic room.

Friday Saturday Sunday

✠✠ VERY GOOD

MENU HIGHLIGHTS Cream of mushroom soup; chilled sesame tuna; chipotle barbecued shrimp; chicken Dijon; crab cake; crab and brie-stuffed flounder; rack of lamb; ancho strip steak; banana cream pie; chocolate mousse; carrot cake.

WINE LIST Home of the $10 mark-up, this amazingly well-priced wine list has grown and matured, and acquired special bottles (try Jaffurs viognier, $37) that make it feel like a real deal.

WEEKEND NOISE Lively

IF YOU GO Dinner M-Sa 5:30-10:30 p.m.; Su 5-10 p.m.
- **E** Entrees, $18-$27
- Reservations recommended during week, required weekends
- Most major cards
- Not wheelchair-accessible
- Street parking only

It's hard to believe that a restaurant started on $14,000 and a dare between seven friends could ever have lasted this long. That any neighborhood restaurant built on cream of mushroom soup and a fluorescent blackboard menu would ever have enough staying power to stick around 33 years — especially in today's intensely fickle dining scene — is an impressive feat, indeed.

But Friday Saturday Sunday has done more than simply survive. It has thrived in the cozy corner townhouse with the striped awnings near Rittenhouse Square as one of the most enduring institutions from the city's first Restaurant Renaissance.

Of course, its wide-ranging menu and low-lit decor no longer seem quite as revolutionary as they did back in 1973, when quality dining was defined by fish houses and stuffy private clubs. But there is still real romance to the main dining room, ringed by mirrored walls and a handsome new 60-foot mural by local artist, Tom Judd, which wraps the room in a dreamlike collage of flowers, kangaroos, and a reclining nude. The Tank Bar upstairs, where a tented ceiling and fish tank lend a feeling of mellow seclusion, remains one of the city's secret corners for seduction. There is a nice selection of spirits to soften the mood. Then again, Friday Saturday Sunday has been a drinker's haven ever since owner, Weaver Lilley, who long ago bought out his other partners, began the revolutionary practice of adding only $10 to the cost of his wines compared to the triple mark-ups more commonly seen.

The cellar has grown nicely to about 60 bottles over the last few years, including an exotic California viognier we enjoyed from Jaffurs ($37) and a lush Jordan cabernet for only $66 (usually $100).

The kitchen, meanwhile, has remained a picture of reliability under chef Reese Skulteti, who has done a

NEW AMERICAN • RITTENHOUSE SQUARE
261 S. 21st St., 19103
215-546-4232 • www.frisatsun.com

fine job maintaining the restaurant's repertoire of popular standards, a blend of basic French and American stalwarts from the '70s, with an occasional Asian flair, and daily specials ranging from Creole to Southwestern. The result is an easy hodgepodge of gently updated comfort food that proved at a recent visit to be as satisfying as ever.

Cream of mushroom soup is intensely rich and earthy, its creamy mushroom broth enlivened with a whiff of brandy. The silky smooth house pate of pureed chicken livers, still pink from their cognac flambe, is impossible to resist. Other retro classics were also expertly done. The breaded chicken breasts napped in a yellow streak of Dijon-spiced cream were amazingly tender and crisp. The garlic- and herb-crusted rack of lamb was memorably juicy and perfectly pink. The crabcakes aren't unusual, but the lump crab was so sweet and so delicately bound over a sweet white wine butter sauce, that they easily rank among the best in town.

While this menu can seem somewhat dated at times, it still has some exotic moves, a little Asian accent remaining from previous chefs (sesame-crusted sashimi tuna), as well as an occasional Southwestern flair. The chipotle barbecued shrimp weren't exactly fiery, but the chile rub and cool green avocado dip lent the tender crustaceans a lively tang. Likewise for the ancho-rubbed strip steak, which bolstered the excellent beef's savory gusto.

The homey dessert list is as much a blast from the past as anything else — a thick wedge of creamy banana pie, rich chocolate mousse over a delicate cookie crust, bread pudding moist with bananas. But they're so satisfyingly well made, Friday Saturday Sunday's longevity isn't so surprising after all.

— OR TRY THESE —

Here are three other survivors from the Restaurant Renaissance:

Rose Tattoo Cafe ☓ ☓
1847 Callowhill St., 19130, (215) 569-8939
The gallery remains a pleasant perch for a lunchtime rendezvous spiced with jambalaya and Texas chili. The cooking has lost a little finesse since the departure of ex-chef Sean Weinberger for his own place in Malvern.

Roller's
8142 Germantown Ave., 19118, (215) 242-1771
Paul Roller last year moved his longstanding Chestnut Hill favorite, a reliable destination for updated comfort food, from the top of the hill down to his former Flying Fish.

Astral Plane ☓
1708 Lombard St., 19146, (215) 546-6230
The time-capsule decor and charismatic owner, Reed Apaghian, have drawn loyalists to the tented dining rooms for more than three decades. The kitchen strives for updated flavors, but is too inconsistent to carry these off. Service also lags.

Gayle

♟♟♟ EXCELLENT

MENU HIGHLIGHTS Risotto fingers; winter wings; smoked salmon with apples and potato; #9 combination; lobster roll with lavender; skate; beef tenderloin shepherd's pie; veal stew; endive parfait; breakfast.

WINE LIST One-page list showcases high-quality, versatile wines from the Northwest, with fair range in prices; several wines by the glass.

WEEKEND NOISE Lively

IF YOU GO A la carte dinner M-W 5:30 to 10 p.m.; Tasting menu only Th-Sa 5:30 to 10 p.m.; after-hours a la carte menu Th-Sa 10 p.m. to midnight
• **E to V E** A la carte entrees, $20 to $25; tasting menus, $45 (3 courses), $62 (5 courses)
• Reservations strongly recommended
• Not wheelchair-accessible
• Street parking only

Daniel Stern seems to revel in turning expectation on its ear at Gayle, his new Queen Village restaurant in the terra-cotta-tiled bistro bones of the old Azafran on 3rd Street.

Potato soup becomes a sauce, and clams casino become a soup. Stews and casseroles are deconstructed, then put back together again. You'll encounter basmati rice churned into ice cream for your entree. Bitter Belgian endive is transformed into dessert.

But the most amazing thing about these dishes is not simply that they are strange — shock value is an easy trick. The catch is that the food works. Even a seemingly random creation like the "#9 Combination," which poses cylinders of braised lamb shoulder opposite tuna sashimi glazed in yogurt tzatziki, suddenly harmonizes around a silky dollop of avocado-cucumber puree. In a few bites, it evolves from dubious to memorable.

Of course, this modernistic culinary juggling is not obvious from the sparsely worded menu, which teases with cryptic descriptions like "Chicken, Purple and Green." But Stern, a Cherry Hill native who worked in Manhattan landmarks like Jean-Georges and Daniel before coming home to run the kitchen at Le Bec-Fin, turns them into unexpected delights.

One called "Beef Tenderloin, Shepherd's Pie" is unlike any pub casserole I've seen. Potatoes are wrapped inside a crisp parcel of bacon filled with Gruyere and shredded short rib. Meanwhile, three morsels of tenderloin that line the plate exude a double-layered gusto — from their two-hour hickory smoking and the rendered bacon fat used to sear the meat. Another treat transforms chicken wings into exotic "winter wings" glazed with juiced butternut squash and Moroccan spice. The "summer wings" are infused with watermelon.

Despite its haute ambitions, Gayle has a comfortable 35-seat room that feels like a neighborhood bistro, with sage green walls and a back patio for pleasant warm-

NEW AMERICAN • QUEEN VILLAGE
617 S. 3rd St., 19147
215-922-3850 • www.gaylephiladelphia.com

weather dining. The portions are rather small, but the weekday a la carte entrees and weekend tasting menus are reasonably priced considering the level of cooking.

The one-page wine list has an intriguing selection that should grow, but focuses on the versatile pinots of the Northwest and some eclectic whites. And the restaurant's service staff is gracefully attentive, at ease answering the inevitable questions about the food.

Some of these precious dishes still need tweaking, like the fishy crab dumplings wrapped in dough made of pureed scallops. Or the seared tuna entree that should have been renamed "Things You Can Do With Basmati," for its feverish five-part riff on the rice.

Mostly, though, Stern's vision was clear. Lavender added elegance to a luscious lobster salad cradled in a house-baked potato roll. Deep-fried risotto balls came with a sabayon tinted by soy and truffles. Creamy foie gras played against the crunch of water chestnuts cooked in red-wine syrup. Textures are also key to skate accented with the gentle pop of lotus seeds and peanuts and chile-spiced orange segments.

The veal stew, meanwhile, was a fascinating assembly of separately cooked parts — slow-stewed shank; crispy veal mini-spring roll; deep-fried trotters; tender morsels of poached tongue — that were satisfyingly reunited in a rich dark gravy.

Gayle's desserts sustain its topsy-turvy tune, with thyme ice cream atop classic apple pie and an ever-changing item called "Breakfast" that plays games with French toast soaked in white chocolate custard and amazing banana sticky buns with mocha pot de creme.

The unorthodox chef even steeps the famous Belgian salad green with beer and cream and candied orange zest for a custard of stunning complexity. It may be Stern's greatest trick of all, bringing unexpected sweetness right down to the bitter endive.

— OR TRY THESE —

Here are three other restaurants turning Queen Village and nearby Bella Vista into a gastronomic destination:

SOUTHWARK 🍴🍴🍴
701 S. 4th St., 19147, 215-238-1888
A Queen Village gem, with a lively eat-at-the-bar scene and a dining room that opens onto a large patio. An impressive debut for Sheri Waide, whose New American fare blends seasonality and a light touch.

ANSILL 🍴🍴🍴
627 S. 3rd St., 19147, 215-627-2485
The small-plate phenomenon meets strange meats at David Ansill's daring Queen Village wine and "snack" bar. While the offerings may be exotic, chef Kibett Mengech spins them into exquisite bites served with style and a smart wine-and-beer list.

HORIZONS 🍴🍴🍴
611 S.7th St., 19147, (215) 923-6117
You don't have to be a vegan to appreciate the city's only serious vegetarian restaurant. Rich Landau's exotic and inventive preparations of seitan and tofu are spectacular.

Gilmore's

♖♖♖ EXCELLENT

MENU HIGHLIGHTS Scallop-short rib "surf-n-turf"; pheasant consomme; "corndog" shrimp; butter poached lobster; crab-cake; lamb loin with leek puree; duck with celery root; pheasant with red wine risotto; venison strip steak au poivre; babas au rhum; "candied apple" choco-late mousse.

BYOB

WEEKEND NOISE Lively

IF YOU GO Dinner seatings Tu-Sa 6 p.m. and 8:30 p.m.
- **E** Entrees, $20 - $35
- Reservations suggested
- Most major cards
- No smoking
- Not wheelchair-accessible
- Street parking (free after 5 p.m.); free lot parking off Walnut St. behind post office

It isn't hard to book an 11-table dining room solid for two months in advance when you have a reputation like Peter Gilmore's, earned in his 22 years as one of the esteemed chefs at Le Bec-Fin. Yet in many ways, his great-est achievement has been to overcome the baggage of those expectations, to create a restaurant that exists in diners' minds as something quite separate from Georges Perrier's gastronomic palace on Walnut Street.

His tiny self-named BYOB has been a smash hit for downtown West Chester's burgeoning dining scene since the day it opened six years ago — even if it showed some growing pains early on. Judging from my most recent spectacular meal, however, Gilmore's has at last found its own true voice as one of the region's finest con-temporary French restaurants.

Rich pheasant consomme comes with fresh porcini mushroom ravioli bobbing in its tea-colored broth. Perfectly seared scallops become the "surf" to Gilmore's clever "turf" of slowly braised shortribs, anchored by a silky puree of celery root. Poached lobster over spinach-flecked orzo and orange sauce is so sweet, its tender meat tastes as if it has been injected with butter. Seared strip steak of venison captures the essence of luxury game, its ruby, berry-flavored meat sparked by a pepper-corn crust and the bitter richness of a creamy Brussels sprout gratin.

If Gilmore's were be compared to Le Bec-Fin, it should be to that institution's first venue, at 1312 Spruce St. (the storied 35-seat townhouse now occupied by Vetri), where young Gilmore arrived in 1980 fresh from the Culinary Institute of America, and reveled in the magical ambience of such an intimate yet ambitious culinary enterprise. The physical similarity between Perrier's orig-inal dining room and Gilmore's is almost uncanny: Both are snug, homey spaces aspiring to a formality beyond

CONTEMPORARY FRENCH • WEST CHESTER
(Western Suburbs; Chester County)

133 E. Gay St., West Chester, Pa. 19380

610-431-2800 • *www.gilmoresrestaurant.com*

the atmosphere of the typical bistro. Gilmore's packs in the tables a bit tight for complete comfort, but it still spins a convincing fine-dining feel with the old-fashioned parlor decor of chintz curtains, salmon walls, and mirrored centerpiece mantel.

Veteran servers like Stephanie Hoster and Richard Rooney have mastered the close quarters, presenting the food with both drama and sincerity, while maintaining the tables with clockwork grace.

It isn't hard to see where the staff's enthusiasm comes from. This menu is easy to love, a blend of technically perfect classics relying on fine seasonal ingredients and the occasional twist of creativity. Dishes like the wonderfully roasted pheasant over red wine risotto, or the rose-colored breast of duckling with celery root puree ringed by a dark Bordelaise, or the succulent veal chop with fresh morel mushrooms, have a simple elegance that reveals Gilmore's decades long immersion in the French tradition.

Every so often, though, Gilmore displayed sparks of a more personal vision trying to emerge. His "corndog" shrimp, for example, were inspired by a family trip to the Shore. But the giant crustaceans (sometimes lobster) that arrived on skewers inside the crunch of a sweet polenta batter were more than just a whim — they were a surprisingly playful stroke of personality.

The desserts also delight with their own blend of classics (boozy babas au Rhum) and clever twists, like the surprise core of banana cream at the heart of the molten chocolate cake. Most stunning was the "candied apple," which is not an apple at all, as we discovered with one swift crack of the spoon. Inside this gorgeous scarlet "fruit" made of spun sugar was a cloud of silken chocolate mousse. Like Gilmore's itself, it isn't just the treat you expect it to be — it's even better.

— OR TRY THESE —

Here are three recommended ventures from other Le Bec-Fin alumni:

GAYLE ✗ ✗ ✗
617 S .3rd St., 19147, (215) 922-3850. Former Le Bec-Fin chef Daniel Stern gives modern twists to familiar foods: soups become sauces, stews are deconstructed, and endive will never be the same. The gambles almost always pay off, and service is superb.

The Restaurant at Doneckers ✗ ✗ ✗
333 N. State St., Ephrata, Pa. 17522, (717) 738-9501. Former Le Bec-Fin chef Greg Gable blends French haute cuisine with regional flavors at this upscale shopping complex. Dinners are more interesting than the shopper-friendly lunches.

Moore Brothers Wine Co.
7200 N. Park Dr., Pennsauken, N.J. 08109, (856) 317-1177. 1416 N. DuPont St., Wilmington, Del. 19806, (877) 316-6673. Founded by Gregory Moore, former Le Bec-Fin sommelier, who specializes in importing lesser-known high-quality European wines at fair prices. Quality has been most reliable in wines priced at $12 and up.

Horizons

EXCELLENT

MENU HIGHLIGHTS Chilled cucumber-avocado soup; olive tasting; Portobello carpaccio; edamame hummus; Jamaican BBQ seitan; Yucatan chopped spinach salad; rum-glazed tempeh; grilled seitan; Pacific Rim tofu; paella; sopa de tortilla; seared tofu with fregola and leeks; vegan cheesecake.

WINE LIST Mid-sized but smart selection of fairly priced craft beers and international wines (all "vegan") with focus on hearty reds and exotic whites to match menu's spice. We loved the plush Aussie shiraz from Carlei ($54), and crisp Quivira sauvignon by the glass. Excellent rums, cocktails, and tequila.

WEEKEND NOISE Deafening

IF YOU GO Dinner Tu-Th 6-10 p.m.; F and Sa until 11 p.m. Lounge closes one hour later than dining room.

- **M** Entrees, $16-$19
- Reservations recommended
- Visa, MasterCard only
- Not wheelchair-accessible
- Street and lot parking only

When Rich Landau first announced plans to move his groundbreaking vegan restaurant, Horizons Cafe, from Willow Grove to Center City, he hoped the move would bring it "the credibility" of a downtown location.

But I'm thinking it's quite the opposite. No sophisticated restaurant scene is complete anymore without some serious vegetarian cooking (let alone non-dairy, animal-free vegan.) And until February, when Landau and his wife, Kate Jacoby, opened their extraordinary new venture in Bella Vista, Philly's veggie landscape was borderline pitiful.

But the new Horizons is more than a kind oasis for the long wandering Tofu Tribe. The food is so carefully wrought, so vividly infused with satisfying flavors, that any meat-eater with a half-open mind is in danger of being impressed.

That could be the rum talking (since Horizons has a primo list.) But as a longtime fan of Horizons' efforts, I was astounded to see how far this restaurant had evolved from its funky BYOB beginnings attached to a strip-mall health food store.

Landau and Jacoby have left the old co-op look far behind. The two-story space still has a bohemian feel with pulsing bright colors, but its peach-colored upstairs dining room is surprisingly pretty. Gauzy curtains, synthetic leather chairs, and turning fans in the rafters lend the feel of a Caribbean getaway.

And not only does the new Horizons have a smart little wine list and bar — all of it vegan-vetted — the staff knows how to serve it, and the meal too. Our waitress lucidly explained the fine points of seitan (textured wheat gluten), tempeh (soy bean cakes), and tofu (soy curd) without apology or pretense.

More important, that's now how Landau cooks. Gone are the cutesy mock labels of "tofu scallops" and "seitan wings." These dishes can stand on their meatless own. Cast in vibrant Latin and Caribbean flavors and beautiful-

VEGAN · BELLA VISTA

611 S. 7th St., 19147

(215) 923-6117 · www.horizonsphiladelphia.com

ly presented, this is some of the most interesting cooking in town — vegan or otherwise.

Landau coaxes real flavor from tofu through a three-day brine in tamari and Old Bay, then crisps it with an aromatic seed crust over Sardinian couscous, sweet leeks, and wild mushrooms. Tempeh is moistened by a gingered curry stock then served over coconut-calabaza stew beneath a tangy tamarind-rum glaze. Korean gochu jang chile paste warms the Pacific Rim tofu.

There are several worthy Horizons classics — the Jamaican grilled seitan strips shined with a beguiling barbecue sauce; crispy seitan sopes tacos over chayote and avocado stew; and salsa-striped enchiladas stuffed with smoked tofu and wild mushrooms.

But Landau's pure vegetable dishes were also memorable. His chilled cucumber soup is brilliant, buttery with avocado, vibrant with lime, and earthy with cumin oil and snappy smoked pumpkin seeds. Deconstructed paella brings a crisped cake of La Bomba rice ringed by saffron sauce and gorgeous grilled vegetables. A spectacular Yucatan spinach salad, festooned with tortillas, smoke-dried olives, and creamy cilantro dressing, was the most festive plate of roughage I've ever eaten.

Jacoby runs the dining room, but is also an impressive pastry chef who brings Caribbean inspirations to her desserts. Rum stands in for one of the milks in coconut tres leches cake, which gets layered with tart lime sorbet into the Mojito Perfecto parfait. And a liberal use of coconut milk, blended with soy milk and tofu, goes a long way towards the convincing texture of her cheesecakes. They're so startlingly creamy, they've finally defined the seemingly contradictory notion of vegan indulgence.

Then again, Horizons is bursting with many such taste revelations. So many, in fact, it's hard to believe it took so long for them to make it downtown.

— OR TRY THESE —

Here are three other suggested vegetarian-friendly restaurants:

Blue Sage 🍴🍴
772 2nd St. Pike, Southampton, Pa. 18966, (215) 942-8888
One of the region's few worthy mainstream veggie alternatives. Chef Michael Jackson's menu is not vegan, opting for a vegetable-centric cuisine that offers international takes on every thing from blue corn–asparagus tacos to goat cheese gnocchi.

CHERRY STREET CHINESE KOSHER VEGETARIAN RESTAURANT 🍴🍴
1010 Cherry St., 19107, (215) 923-3663
The kitchen is right on the mark. It defies the stereotypes of deep-fried mock-meat Chinese cooking with creative, well-seasoned dishes that emphasize good ingredients, whether in pure veggie cookery or convincing mock shrimp.

Citrus 🍴🍴
8136 Germantown Ave., 19118, (215) 247-8188
A tiny bistro-bakery that offers modern seafood and vegetarian dishes with a light Asian touch and a heavy dose of animal-rights activism.

Jake's

♦♦♦ EXCELLENT

MENU HIGHLIGHTS Soft-shell crabs with melon; duck spring rolls; veal dumplings; tuna tartare with watermelon; short rib-lobster surf-n-turf; venison with kimchee; barbecued salmon; veal with lobster-mashed potatoes; cookie taco; profiteroles; homemade ice cream.

WINE LIST One of the finer wine lists in town, with focus on New World wines. Bar also stocked with top spirits.

WEEKEND NOISE Lively

IF YOU GO Lunch M-Sa 11:30 a.m.-2:30 p.m. Dinner M-Th 5:30-9 p.m.; F 5:30-10:30 p.m.; Sa 5-10:30 p.m.; Su 5-9 p.m. Sunday brunch, 10:30 a.m.-2:30 p.m.
• **V E** Dinner entrees, $24.50-$32.50
• Reservations recommended
• Discover card not accepted
• Not wheelchair-accessible — small step, entrance and main dining room
• Valet parking available after 5 p.m., $10

The rise and fall of Manayunk dining is one of Philly's more puzzling tales. It still has the happening Main Street that made it such a trendy draw in the '80s and early '90s, not to mention the well-heeled Main Line crowds. But its eating scene has never quite recovered from the five-year moratorium that put the kabosh on new restaurants — just as Center City was hitting its stride.

With the ban now lifted and many of the neighborhood's big players losing their grip to nightclubs and bars, the continued success of Jake's is an especially impressive feat. Not only is chef Bruce Cooper's standby easily the best fine-dining spot in Manayunk, it has remained for nearly two decades one of the best restaurants in the entire region.

The sunrise-colored dining room, with banquettes along its walls and dramatic stage lights running down its barrel-shaped acoustical ceiling, is a superbly comfortable and handsome modern space. The long-time service staff is the picture of a clockwork veteran team. And the wine program remains one of the best around, with a smart selection of high-end New World wines and a number of quality selections by the glass.

But it is Bruce Cooper's kitchen that has really managed to keep this address relevant, blending many of the stylish classics that have long anchored Jake's menu with a continuous quest for fresh seasonal and contemporary flavors.

The old favorites remain popular for a reason. The barbecued salmon glazed in tangy apple cider and soy sauce is impossible to resist. The veal medallions in bright green chive sauce with lobster mashed potatoes may be so 1980s, but they are nouveau luxury at its best. The crispy duck confit spring rolls — standing on end tied with a string of chive and ringed by a colorful necklace of

NEW AMERICAN • MANAYUNK

4365 Main St., 19127

215-483-0444 • www.jakesrestaurant.com

dotted blackberry, orange, and mustard sauces — are an ideal example of Asian fusion done right. And Cooper has singlehandedly kept calves' liver on the map by grilling it with red wine jus, apple hash, and port-soaked onions.

Most impressive, though, are newer dishes that show this kitchen is still drawing nimbly from a deep creative well. An ingenious tartare plays trompe l'oeil tricks, mixing diced red tuna with look-alike cubes of crunchy, sweet watermelon. A braised beef short rib over earthy parsnip puree anchors a stylish twist on surf-n-turf with a lobster tail stained pink with beet juice. Succulent scallops give a nod to the Mediterranean with a dark olive tapenade and lemony artichokes. Ruby rare medallions of venison crusted with pink peppercorns depart from the usual mellow wine sauce in favor of an electric jolt from kimchee, whose sour and spicy cabbage contrasts the natural richness of the meat.

Jake's desserts are nearly as satisfying as the rest of the meal, though the best efforts are refined classics rather than notably creative. The timbale of cheesecake is memorably light and creamy with plum and lemon sauces. A trio of crisp choux pastry puffs filled with homemade vanilla ice cream and glazed with patent black fudge sauce were a convincing reminder of why profiteroles were a favorite to begin with.

And then there is that Jake's classic, the cookie taco. Cradled inside a tortilla shell dusted with cinnamon sugar, this mountain of vanilla ice cream is baubled with jumbo berries and curls of white chocolate that is the ultimate sundae indulgence, re-envisioned for the go-go nights of Manayunk's halcyon days. Yes, that era may be waning. But Jake's and its sweet taco are definitely still thriving on Main Street in style.

— OR TRY THESE —

Here are three other suggested Manayunk restaurants:

Derek's
4411 Main St., 19127, (215) 483-9400
At chef Derek Davis's remake of his former Sonoma, the vodka bar has been revamped to a casual neighborhood feel, with space for eating and an American grill menu that ranges from wood-fired pizzas to big salads and burgers.

Il Tartufo
4341 Main St., 19129, (215) 482-1999
Alberto Delbello's "Roman-Jewish" trattoria is tight inside, but has a lovely sidewalk cafe from which to watch Main Street pass by while you nibble fried artichokes, homemade mozzarella, and truffle-sauced veal scallopini.

Fish Tank on Main
4247 Main St., 19127, (215) 508-0202
This sleek corner room brings a stylish new spot with an Italian bent (and yes, a fish tank) to Manayunk's Main Street. Still too new for a verdict.

Cheesesteaks, and Other Essentials for Paradise on a Roll

A FEW YEARS AGO, I TRAVELED ACROSS THE REGION accompanied by four high school eating machines on a quest (for their senior class project) to answer the age-old question of Philadelphia street food: Who makes the best cheesesteak?

The result was The Cheesesteak Project, a gustatory marathon that would take us more than 110 miles, through two states, 23 steakeries, 65-plus sandwiches, and countless hours of challenging digestion. In four days.

Well, I'll never do that again. I love a great cheesesteak as much as the next guy — probably more. But I'm a hedonist, not a masochist. And that was a lifetime achievement. Not to say we didn't try to recapture the road food magic. The guys and I piled into a car on one of their college holiday breaks the following year and mopped up some of the places we missed. But really, not much had changed. We added a few good new addresses to the roster of worthy steaks — Pudge's in Blue Bell, Frusco's in the Northeast — but our thoughts on the matter hadn't changed. So I've reprinted our essential rankings from the first go-round, plus some notable additions below.

But first, for those who missed The Cheesesteak Project to begin with, here is an essential primer in the science of cheesesteak scrutiny:

There is the meat itself. It can range from rib-eye to top round to, yes, even beef knuckle (gulp!?). But most important, how it is cooked? Look at the color of the meat before it hits the griddle. Is it as faded as an unripe tomato, drained of its flavorful juices? Or does it have a fresh crimson blush, marbled with the lacy white lines of fat that will baste it?

Is the griddle a glorified factory, lined with a tall berm of pre-cooked steaming meat? Or is each sandwich cooked to order, seared to a caramelized brown around the edges and placed on a roll, still dripping its natural essence? Is it shredded to a hamburger fineness (a method I always find dry), or is the thinly sliced meat left largely intact? Is the meat seasoned?

These essentials, we decided, was key. But there was so much more. The crusty rolls versus the soft ones. Whether the onions were fried to a sweet golden brown. The girth of the sandwich (for which we were armed with a ruler) mattered. So did the quality of the cheese (was it real Cheez Whiz, or imitation?). The fire of the chiles and sauces on the condiment bar counted for extra points. As did an authentic level of atty-tude at the cashier's window. Ultimately, we judged each restaurant on three sandwiches: a traditional steak with Whiz or American cheese, a specialty steak, and a chicken cheesesteak.

The truth, however, is that a transcendent steak must exist in perfect harmony, an ethereal melding of cheese and onion and juicy meat, swirling at the height of its flavors through your roll at that very moment you take a bite. Call it the perfect storm of steaks. One of my student companions had his own name for this elusive trait: Good Drip.

Here is the straight list of our top destinations for a good cheesesteak, more or less in order, including some recent additions:

- The Pantheon: **John's Roast Pork**
- Pretty Darn Great: **Tony Luke's, Chink's, Pudge's, Frusco's, Cosmi's Deli, Grey Lodge Tavern, Donkey's Place,** and **McNally's H&J Tavern** (which also sells their famous Schmitter salami cheesesteak at Citizens Bank Park)

- Still Good Enough to Stand in Line: **Steve's Prince of Steaks, Sonny's Steaks, Chick's Deli of Cherry Hill, White House Sub Shop, Pagano's Market** (in Market Place East)
- Fading Notables: **Pat's King of Steaks, Dalessandro's, Rick's Steaks, Mama's Pizzeria, Geno's Steaks**

There has been some curiously creative cheesesteak-fusion of late, from haute faux-steaks like the "cheese skate" at **Striped Bass** (great) or the $100 kobe steak at **Barclay Prime** (go for the sliders instead) to the sudden popularity of cheesesteak "springrolls." Here are a few places that have actually made it palatable: the **Swann Lounge, Deuce,** the **Dilworthtown Inn, Moro, TSOP, Bliss** (the cheesesteak empanada).

The cheesesteak is only part of the city's love affair with sandwiches. Here are some of my other, non-steak favorites:

- The roast pork with spinach and provolone sandwich at John's Roast Pork, followed by pork sandwiches at **DiNic's,** the **Standard Tap,** and **Porky's Point**
- The sloppy roast beef on kaiser at the original **Nick's Roast Beef**
- The chicken cutlet with spicy roasted peppers at **Shank's & Evelyn's Roast Beef**
- Traditional Italian hoagies at **Ricci** (1165 S. 11th St., 19147, 215-334-6910); **Lombardi"s Specialty Hoagies; Cosmi's Market** (1501 S. 8th St., 19147, 215-468-6093); and the small sandwich (the big ones have too much meat) at **Primo Hoagies** (2043 Chestnut St., 19103, 215-496-0540)
- The awesomely satisfying vegetarian hoagie at **Chickie's Italian Deli**
- The hot, thick-sliced New York–style corned beef from **Pastrami and Things** and the **Famous 4th Street Delicatessen**
- The cold, thin-sliced Philadelphia-style corned beef from **Koch's Deli**
- The grilled panini with mozzarella, basil, tomato, and prosciutto at **Paninoteca**
- The toasted "House of Cheese" foccacia in the upstairs cafe at **Di Bruno Bros. House of Cheese**
- Baguette with pate and brie and toasty croque monsieur at **Cafe Lutecia**
- The Countryside, a hot muffuletta taste-alike at **The Countryside Market & Deli.**
- The Vietnamese chicken hoagie at **Ba Le Bakery**
- The authentic Israeli falafel sandwich at **Mama's Vegetarian**

Great burgers also abound. Here are some of the best:

- The giant **Rouge** burger
- The burger stuffed with bleu cheese at **Good Dog**
- The caramelized-leek and bleu cheese burger at **Monk's Cafe**
- The kobe burger sliders at **Barclay Prime**
- The toasty bun, buttery burger at **Loie Brasserie**
- The English muffin burger at **London Grill**
- The triple sampler of three miniature burgers at **Copa Too**
- The big, beefy steakhouse burgers at the downstairs grill of **Smith & Wollensky,** at the Rittenhouse Hotel, and at **Jolly's Sporting Saloon**

- The Old Bay-laced Chesapeake burger at **Chaucer's Tabard Inn**
- The lunchtime burger with brioche and farmhouse cheddar cheese at **Matyson**
- It's hard to find a great burger for $5 or less, but you can still find a reliable one at **Tangier Restaurant**

Another major food group not to be overlooked is this shortlist of prime pizzas:

- The Margherita pizza and creative alternative pizzas (clam chowder pie?!) at **Sovana Bistro** in Kennett Square currently gets my top vote.
- The **Couch Tomato Cafe** in Manayunk serves up some of the best gourmet pies-by-the-slice.
- Reserve your dough for the garlicky white pies and meat-lover pizzas laden with prosciutto and sausage, pulled from the immense brick oven at **Tacconelli's Pizzeria** in Port Richmond, but they're best when requested without the powdered garlic.
- Some of the best thin-crusted pizzas and strombolis come from **By George** in the Reading Terminal Market.
- For pizza simplicity, try the thin-crusted Margherita pizzas at **Rembrandt's** and **Illuminare**.
- Classic Philly-style pizza can be found in the heart of the Italian Market at **Lorenzo's Pizza.**
- And few pizzerias are more classic than **Marra's**, where the Margheritas are superb as long as you request fresh mozzarella.
- **Georges'** in Wayne creates some amazingly good creations, including an ususual but tasty French-centric pizza topped with Dijon and Gruyere cheese.
- The no-cheese tomato pies of Trenton are famous, but **People's Pizza** in South Jersey makes a fine one (as well as hefty stuffed pizzas) just across the Ben Franklin Bridge.
- Some of the most unusual pizzas are the gourmet wood-grilled pies at **Carambola**, in Dresher.
- When it comes to the category of cheap-but-decent pizza, the massive, slightly sweet pizzas at **Lazaro's Pizza House** have become a bargain staple near Graduate Hospital.

John's Roast Pork

♣♣♣ EXCELLENT

MENU HIGHLIGHTS Roast pork (with greens and sharp provolone on a seeded roll); cheesesteak wid'; chicken cheesesteak wid' (and tomato gravy); chicken cutlet; roast beef sandwich; French fries.

WINE LIST Alcoholic beverages not allowed.

IF YOU GO Entire menu M-F 6:45 a.m.-3 p.m.
- I Cheesesteaks and pork sandwiches, $5.50-6.25
- Can place big orders by phone in advance
- Cash only
- Wheelchair-accessible lunch line, but not restroom
- Ample free street parking

John Bucci Jr. could have gotten a head as big as his pork sandwich. But it's unlikely that any overly grand ambitions would make it too far down the luncheonette counter before his mother, Vonda, perched like a hawk beside the cash register, would stop them in their tracks.

After all, Vonda's idea of a major expansion after John's Roast Pork won an *Inquirer* cheesesteak competition four years ago and the stand, a well-kept secret for 70 years, was suddenly swamped by ravenous masses, was to add a few new picnic benches to the concrete patio outside the old shack's door.

But after a taste of John Jr.'s two-fisted cooking, a repertoire of classic South Philly Italian sandwiches that are still near the top of their respective genres — zesty roast pork and beef, roll-busting cheesesteaks, and tender chicken cutlets — the crowds have never stopped coming. The James Beard Foundation recently named it an American Classic.

And John's fortune did not stop there. Until two years ago, its humble wedge of South Philadelphia was an out-of-the-way industrial zone, trimmed on one side by a chemical plant and on the other by train tracks that made the counter vibrate every time some freight went by. Now it's suddenly smack in the heart of Big Box heaven. There was always a great urban view of the Center City skyline from its picnic tables — a favorite perch during pleasant weather. Now you also see Ikea, Target, Lowe's, and Famous Dave's.

All that development brought a major infrastructure project in 2006 that inconveniently fenced John's off from Snyder Avenue. But the lunch shack's faithful have always been determined, especially with a schedule that is limited from early morning to 3 p.m. ("You gotta come

ROAST PORK AND CHEESESTEAKS • SOUTH PHILADELPHIA
14 E. Snyder Ave. (at Weccacoe), 19148
(215) 463-1951

early, kid," Vonda once told me. "We're dedicated here to the working man.")

If the Buccis had even a slivered onion's worth of the marketing chutzpah that turned far lesser cheesesteak stands into national icons, there's no telling the amount of neon signage that would be blinking from the corner of Snyder Avenue and Weccacoe Street. But I never get the sense, when I slide into the long line that snakes up to the fragrant grill, that quick riches are the main goal here. Short-cuts are never taken. Everything is cooked to order (best by John himself). And the result is a taste of Philadelphia soul food that is as true as it ever gets, passed down through three generations of Bucci men.

When I first wrapped my hands around a crusty, sesame-seeded roll stuffed with John's pork and garlicky greens, I knew immediately how a pork sandwich could become a legacy. Flavor filled my mouth like a cascade nuanced with rosemary and bay. A hovering shade of clove was flowing through this river on a bun.

The pork was so good that it took me years to order anything else. But there is also excellent roast beef sauced with dark gravy, perfectly crisp chicken cutlets, fabulous fries, and hearty Italian wedding soup. Somehow, I wasn't surprised to learn that John Jr. also makes some of the best cheesesteaks in town, whether it's beef or chicken (never pre-cooked) streaked with sausagey tomato gravy. Bucci caramelizes onions to order on his hot griddle, seasoning his meat and searing it brown and tasty around the edges. Then he blends in a hefty amount of real cheese. Ask for whiz on your steak and you will get a cold stare and a "No" as sharp as the provolone. The atty-tude isn't conceit. It's an authentic taste of cheesesteak tough love

— OR TRY THESE —

Here are three other venues for great pork sandwiches:

Tony Luke's
39 E. Oregon Ave., 19148, (215) 551-5725. The homemade rolls elevate the broccoli rabe-topped steak Italian and pork sandwich at this take-out (which also has an open-air seating shelter), making this branch the best of the famous big-crowd steak emporiums.

Tommy DiNic's
Reading Terminal Market, 12th and Arch Sts., 19107, (215) 923-6175. This lunch counter is a longtime destination for a proper pork sandwich and zesty banter. Juicy brisket and super slow-roasted pork shoulder dressed in spicy long hots, greens, and sharp provolone have taken DiNic's to a new level.

Porky's Point
3824 N. 5th St., 19140, (215) 221-6243. The Latino equivalent of Tony Luke's, where cars triple-park and the line grows long with people hungry for homemade blood sausage, red beans with chopped pig ears, and one of the city's tenderest pork sandwiches.

Karma

♟ ♟ VERY GOOD

MENU HIGHLIGHTS Salmon raita; chana Peshawari; rogan-josh; chicken hara bara kabob; butter chicken; chicken vindaloo; baingan bharta; prawns moilee; malai kofta.

WINE LIST Usual assortment of Indian beers; unique mango-tini; good, modest list of international wines. For something special, try spicy, fruit-forward shiraz from d'Arenberg or Groom.

WEEKEND NOISE Noisy

IF YOU GO Lunch M-F 11:30 a.m.-2:30 p.m.; Sa and Su noon-4 p.m. Dinner M-Th 4:30-10 p.m.; F 4:30-11 p.m.; Sa 4-11 p.m.; Su 3-10 p.m.
• **M** Dinner entrees, $9.95-$18.95; lunch buffet, $9.95 (weekends, $11.95)
• Reservations recommended
• Wheelchair-accessible
• Street parking only

Stylish but unstuffy, Karma occupies a comfortable niche between the inexpensive buffets in University City that have ill defined Indian food for so many diners as lowbrow cheap eats and the chic polish of nearby Cafe Spice, the high-quality New York chain that caters to Old City's martini-swilling yuppies.

Karma has a lunch buffet, but it is classy, with creamy lentil dal, silky spinach curry, and hot-pink drumsticks of moist chicken mounded inside shiny copper chafing dishes. The room isn't nearly as sleek as Cafe Spice, but it has a homespun style nonetheless, its tandoori-red and curry-yellow walls covered with abstract murals by local artists. And this being Old City, Karma makes a nice mango-tini — though its fairly priced wine list is also worth a look.

Most important, Karma's food is authentic enough to attract large tables of Indians of all generations, but also accessible enough for the mainstream Center City crowd. It should also appeal to hungry travelers who pause for a meal just off the turnpike in Mount Holly, N.J., where expansion-minded owner, Munish Narula, a former regional manager for Denny's, opened a second Karma in an old Howard Johnson.

The addictively tangy crunch of cold aloo papri chaat salad or marinated cauliflower phool are a popular way to start. For something spicy, the Goan chicken vindaloo topped with crimson chile peppers will make you weep. But most of Karma's cooking is judiciously spiced, focusing on good ingredients and sauces that offer a variety of vivid flavors.

The butter chicken is one of the better chicken curries I've eaten, its tender morsels of dark meat sauced in a buttery tomato bisque that unfurled with spice and the underlying sweetness of jaggery palm sugar. The South Indian–style prawns moilee brought tender, butterflied crustaceans in an earthy yellow coconut curry that popped with mustard seeds.

INDIAN • OLD CITY
114 Chestnut St., 19106 • 215-925-1444
2015 Burlington Mt. Holly Rd., Mt. Holly, N.J., 08060
609-914-0800 • www.thekarmarestaurant.com

I also loved the salmon raita, a thick piece of fish submerged in a bowl of cool yogurt tinged with mint and spice. The hara bara kabob was another winner, morsels of chicken sizzling on a platter tinted an unearthly shade of green by a marinade of cilantro and mint. Set alongside vibrant red butter curry, it looked like Christmas in Calcutta.

There were a few disappointments — such as Karma's odd take on Scotch eggs, and breads that could also have been more supple and fresh (though the mint-dusted whole-wheat paratha was a delight). The desserts were also weak, an assortment of standards (cakey gulab jamun; thin rice pudding) and not-so-standards (cinnamon-scented flan) that had me opting instead for another cup of chai.

But Karma easily compensates for its slips with accommodating service and a command of the Northern Indian basics. The chana Peshawari rises on sweet onions and tender chickpeas that pop between the teeth, releasing an herby trail of cilantro and spice. The black lentil dal called Maharaja Punjab turns creamy from eight hours cooked over a slow fire. The roasted eggplant curry (baingan bharta) is exceptionally light and fluffy, punctuated by the snap of fresh green peas.

And then there is the lovely lamb roganjosh, a classic stew that brings tender chunks of yogurt-tenderized meat in a deeply steeped gravy perfumed with ginger and cardamom.

The Indian crowd, Narula says, prefers this dish with the more flavorful goat, and I wouldn't mind that extra baaa boost, either. But I can see why Narula might want to play his menu mellow. As he pursues his expansion plans into unexotic territory more accustomed to the white-bread blandness of Howard Johnson, he'll need all the good karma he can get.

— OR TRY THESE —

Here are three other Indian restaurants:

Cafe Spice 🍴🍴
35 S. 2nd St., 19106, (215) 627-6273
This hip Indian bistro has contemporary decor, but classic dishes prepared with quality ingredients and sharp flavors.

Khajuraho 🍴🍴
Ardmore Plaza, 12 Greenfield Ave., Ardmore, Pa. 19003, (610) 896-7200
Exotic food and sensuality are tastefully linked at this Main Line ethnic, where some of the region's finest Indian cuisine is served under the gaze of erotic sculptures from ancient Khajuraho.

DEVI 🍴🍴
151 Whiteland Town Center, Exton, Pa. 19341, (610) 594-9250
Dosa lovers should make the trek to this obscure suburban Indian find — a rare example of South Indian vegetarian cuisine (think gunpowder idlys, sambar, and coconut chutneys) that is so finely prepared, it transcends the modest steam table buffet format.

Kristian's Ristorante

🖈🖈 VERY GOOD

MENU HIGHLIGHTS Crabcakes; stuffed pepper; risottos (sausage, goat cheese and raisins; grape tomatoes and crab; seared tuna with risotto puttanesca; osso buco; trout with pancetta; rack of lamb; galletto; beef marsala; spinach-stuffed chicken; braised red snapper; pasta Bolognese.

WINE LIST Small selection of good Italian table wines (Zenato valpolicella, $42), but few special bottles. Corkage fee $15.

WEEKEND NOISE Lively

IF YOU GO Dinner M, W-Th, 5-10 p.m.; F and Sa 5-11 p.m.; Su 3:30-8 p.m.
• **E** Entrees, $20-$30
• Reservations for 5-8 p.m. seatings only
• Most major cards
• Wheelchair-accessible
• Free valet parking

It has been eight years since chef Kristian Leuzzi's contractor father, Dominick, transformed an old butcher shop next to their home into one of South Philadelphia's most elegant restaurants.

The 50-seat gem at the corner of 11th and Federal Streets called Kristian's Ristorante is trimmed with white corral tile and crisply striped canopies on the outside, and a local power crowd inside that remains fiercely devoted to Leuzzi's osso buco and risottos.

The neighborhood's dining scene has evolved considerably since Kristian's opened, with vibrant new Mexican and Asian options to the north, and a host of intriguing new Italian BYOBs appearing on all sides. The much larger Paradiso, which anchors East Passyunk's resurging restaurant district to the south, is the only newcomer that rivals the elegance of Kristian's. But Leuzzi is still one of my favorite young cooks in South Philadelphia, capable of bringing a sophisticated uptown touch to traditional downtown flavors.

That Leuzzi makes the best osso buco in town is worthy in itself of a spot on my list. It's not one of those big, flopping-all-over-the-place osso bucos, but a carefully trimmed and neatly presented one that rides atop a golden mound of saffron risotto. Despite its refined look, the thick mahogany colored meat is bursting with flavors steeped from hours in a richly fortified stock, so tender that it unfolds at the tap of a fork. It's a Milanese classic done to perfection.

Leuzzi's mastery of risotto, though, is perhaps even more noteworthy than his osso buco. So few chefs capture the tricky texture of risotto in a restaurant setting (par-cooked ahead of time, it's usually too sticky, too mushy, too crunchy, or too creamy). But Leuzzi has made arborio rice his creative canvas. There is risotto filled with bursts of grape tomatoes and sweet lump crab. There is risotto

CONTEMPORARY ITALIAN • SOUTH PHILADELPHIA
1100 Federal St., 19147
215-468-0104 • www.kristiansrestaurant.com

enriched with goat cheese and studded with the zesty contrast of sausage and sweet dots of golden raisins. Risotto brushed with the tart tomato-caper piquance of a puttanesca sauce is the ideal pedestal for a lusty slice of grilled tuna. Ratatouille risotto rings true beneath a fillet of seared black bass and littleneck clams in saffron sauce.

Kristian's could achieve a third bell if only it could iron out some persistent issues. The service is always friendly, from the firm-gripped welcome handshake to one of the city's only free valets. But the waiters rarely maintain their focus, drifting off to the front bar to chat with their buddies (or slip out for a smoke) just when tables need them most.

With increasing competition from nearby BYO's, Kristian's might also upgrade its modest little wine list. We enjoyed a simple valpolicella from Zenato, which was recommendable for the price ($42). But Leuzzi's food is worthy of some finer bottles. And there are highlights beyond risotto.

His crabcake is always exceptional, its sweet lump meat bound by creamy bechamel. The pastas offer familiar combinations, but cooked with an artful touch. A pappardelle with creamed mushrooms and peas was intensely flavored, but admirably light. A special pasta Bolognese sauce of pancetta stewed with ground veal and pork in milk and tomatoes was hauntingly good. Pan-fried whole trout sandwiching a ribbon of crisped pancetta was both delicate and rustic. And Leuzzi's roasted galletto was simply one of the best Cornish hens I've ever eaten, the tender little butterflied bird rife with the vibrance of its herb and garlic marinade.

The desserts are homemade, but less inspired than the rest of Kristian's cooking. Then again, South Philadelphia is stocked with great pastry shops. Talented young cooks like Kristian Leuzzi are a rarer find.

— OR TRY THESE —

Here are three other suggested Italian restaurants in South Philadelphia:

Mezza Luna   🍴 🍴
763 S. 8th St., 19147, (215) 627-4705
This crisp, contemporary space has one of South Philly's more upscale dining rooms, and an affordable Italian wine list, to go with airy ricotta gnocchi in gorgonzola sauce, rabbit stew, and fine seafood; worth the trip.

Tre Scalini   🍴 🍴
1533 S. 11th St., 19147, (215) 551-3870
Central Italian home cooking, from fresh pasta al la chitarra to grilled polenta with broccoli rabe and veal with mushrooms, is served with warmth in this BYOB.

Cucina Forte   🍴 🍴
768 S. 8th St., 19147, (215) 238-0778
Ebullient chef-owner Maria Forte's simple but pleasant South Philly BYOB emphasizes warm hospitality and elevated Italian home cooking, from cloudlike ricotta gnocchi to sublime leg of lamb.

La Lupe

🎖🎖 VERY GOOD

MENU HIGHLIGHTS Tacos: queso, al pastor, barbacoa; huaraches with meat (try carnitas); quesadillas with huitlacoche; posole stew; enchiladas suizas; enchiladas de mole Poblano; pierna adobada; chicken al pipian special; chile relleno special with chipotle sauce; bistec with nopales special; flan asada.

BYOB Beer always works, but nice selection of Mexican sodas and homemade agua fresca juices — try watermelon (sandia).

WEEKEND NOISE Lively

IF YOU GO Entire menu M-Th 10 a.m.-midnight; F-Su until 1 a.m.
  • **I** Tacos, $2; platters, $9.50-$14.95
  • Reservations suggested for large parties
  • Not wheelchair-accessible
  • Street parking only

There is no comfort quite like a fresh tortilla. Steaming hot from the griddle and rolled into a perfect taco cone, the velvety-soft white wrapper warms the fingers as a prelude to the fireworks tucked inside.

At La Lupe in South Philadelphia, where the tacos come with a cool green dollop of guacamole, the payoff could be any number of stellar fillings. There's a fire-orange mince of chile-rubbed pork al pastor studded with bursts of pineapple. Or white clouds of queso fresco fried to a golden cheese crisp. Or sublimely tender barbacoa goat, slow-cooked to gamy sweetness with avocado leaves.

But it's the hand-pressed and cooked-to-order tortillas that make the tacos sing. It's amazing that more local Mexican restaurants don't make their own. That attention to detail, though, is a factor that distinguishes La Lupe as the best of our recent wave of authentic taquerias. And with its perch just north of the Italian Market crossroads where Pat's and Geno's duke it out, La Lupe has a chance to show that there's much more to South Philly street food now than the cheesesteak.

It's about time someone on 9th Street offered a steak "wid" cactus. La Lupe's garlicky bistec smothered in strips of green nopales would look mighty tempting on a roll.

Inside the glass garage-door facade of its dining room, a former cheesesteakery now festooned with the colors of the Mexican flag, there are few concessions to gringo palates. For one, this is anything but fast food, as evidenced by the painfully long waits and spacey service. But the delays were always rewarded with satisfying plates.

There are the thicker "sopes" tortillas, whose sides are crimped into ridges that hold a smear of creamy refried beans and shredded lettuce. I'm especially partial to the huaraches, sandal-shaped sopes that come topped with your choice of meats. The pork carnitas were a great

MEXICAN TAQUERIA • ITALIAN MARKET
1201 S. 9th St., 19147
215-551-9920

choice, a mound of pulled pork roasted with orange juice and beer that had tender, fatty flesh and edges that crackled with caramelized garlic.

The quesadillas are essentially a hearty platter of three tacos that offer some extra-intriguing fillings like huitlacoche, the black corn mushrooms that have a trufflelike intensity and come threaded with jalapeños and stringy Oaxaca cheese. Few bites anywhere in the city deliver an earthy gusto as profound.

There are some less inspired options, like the carelessly wrapped burritos, and less than stellar seafood.

But La Lupe is impressive, nonetheless, for the breadth of its menu. The pungently spiced soups, filled with seafood or honeycomb tripe could be a meal unto themselves. The milder-flavored posole stew was my favorite, the puffs of hominy corn bobbing alongside nuggets of tender pork.

There are also the delicate, cheese-stuffed chile rellenos ringed with smoky chipotle gravy. The enchilada suizas tingle with a tart green salsa of tomatillos. The special chicken pipian is napped with vibrant salsa verde enriched with cream and pureed pumpkin seeds. The pierna adobada brought tender pork in a cuminy red mole made from guajillo chiles.

Guadalupe Bravo, who owns La Lupe with her husband, Gabriel, also makes a marvelous chocolate-based mole learned from her mother in Puebla. The nearly black puree tingles the minute it crosses your lips. It swirls through deep notes of bitter cocoa, cinnamon, dried chile peppers, almonds, ground tortillas, and a tangy backbone of plantains. And like the best moles, it's sweet but not candy. It's toasty but not burnt. It's rustic but amazingly suave. It's hot but doesn't burn.

It changes every time I take a bite, and calls me back for more. Much like La Lupe itself.

— OR TRY THESE —

Here are three other suggested taquerias:

Mexico Lindo 🍴🍴
3521 Federal St., Camden, N.J. 08105, (856) 365-9004
Some of the area's most genuine Mexican cooking, from quesadillas made with hand-pressed tortillas to my favorite mole poblano. The homey cooking is worth a trip across the border (to New Jersey, that is).

Taco Riendo
1301 N. 5th St., 19122, (215) 235-2294 . This colorful little taqueria from Armando Castro, father of Las Cazuelas chef, Alfredo Aguilar, brings authentic, affordable Pueblan street food — tamales; tacos dorados; stuffed poblanos; posole stew — to a cheery corner room. Can be very slow.

Restaurant Acapulco
1144 S. 9th St., 19147, (215) 465-1616. Another authentic newcomer to Baja Filadelfia, this simple Mexican cafe specializes in seafood cocktails from the Acapulco coast, as well tender barbacoa tacos and Thursday special posole stews that come flavored with red or green chiles.

Lakeside Chinese Deli

🪧🪧 VERY GOOD

MENU HIGHLIGHTS Dim sum: chiu chow shrimp rolls; meat-and-peanut dumplings; crispy vegetable rolls; steamed barbecued pork buns. Spicy satay beef appetizer; cold sesame noodles; Hong Kong shrimp wonton soup; stir-fried clams with peppers and pork; sauteed baby bok choy; General Tso's chicken; crispy fried squid; crispy fried soft-shell crabs.

BYOB

WEEKEND NOISE Reasonable

IF YOU GO Entire menu F-W 11 a.m. to 8 p.m. Closed Th.
• **I** Entrees, $5.50-$15
• Reservations suggested
• Cash only
• Not wheelchair-accessible — step at entrance; restrooms accessible
• Street parking only

Contrary to logical first impressions, the hole smashed in the sign that has long hung above the Lakeside Chinese Deli at 207 N. 9th St. is not evidence of the restaurant's demise. Things have gone so well at Lakeside over the past 15 years, in fact, that owner Brenda Leung refuses to fix the sign because she believes it has brought good luck.

Good fortune, indeed, comes to anyone who ventures beyond the broken facade and into the utilitarian dining room of this, the definitive Chinatown joint. And it arrives in the form of the city's best dim sum, made to order by Leung's brother, partner and chef, Eric Ng.

There are, of course, plenty of typical dim sum carts rolling around bigger banquet-hall restaurants in Chinatown such as Ocean City, H.K. Golden Phoenix, and Imperial Garden. But none of these would I call great.

Ng eschews the roving steam carts for bite-size dumplings, buns, and appetizers that are prepared fresh in the kitchen, a practice I grew fond of as the dishes arrived, delicately steamed or crisply fried, hot from the wok to our table. And, unlike the dim sum at most other places, where the same gristly pork-and-shrimp stuffing is simply repackaged into different shapes, each had clean flavors and distinct textures.

There were square little chiu chow shrimp rolls, with crisp sheets of fried bean curd wrapped around tender shrimp and crunchy water chestnut stuffings. Deep fried teardrops of mashed taro root were stuffed with crumbles of fresh pork. And steamed vegetable dumplings stuffed with Chinese chives so fresh that they shone vibrant green beneath the rice-dough skins. Meat and peanut dumplings are redolent of the roasty snap of sweet nuts. Steamed buns as puffy and white as clouds conceal a sweet dark heart of tangy barbecued pork. No gristle anywhere.

CHINESE DIM SUM • CHINATOWN
207 N. 9th St., 19107
215-925-3288

Most of the large round tables and 60 metal chairs in this yellow tiled box of a room are filled with a predominantly Asian crowd, who slurp down shiny dark cubes of duck's blood with scallions ("Chinese chocolate!" says Leung) and other delicacies listed among the specials hand-scribbled on construction paper taped to a room-length mirror. Of course, those specials haven't been touched for more than a decade.

"Good luck," Leung shrugs again.

They aren't all fabulous. The conch with snow peas was a bit crunchy for my taste. The duck feet are an acquired taste. But usually these specials led me to wonderful discoveries, like the steamed salted chicken with minced raw ginger sauce that is among the moistest birds I've had. Or the baby clams stir-fried with hot peppers and ground pork, an awesome dish that tastes like Chinese clams casino.

The printed menu, meanwhile, has its own gems. The thick slices of tender slow-stewed brisket were fragrant with five spice. The Hong Kong–style wonton soup was brimming with thin-skinned dumplings stuffed with chopped shrimp. Lakeside's wok-fried greens are also special, especially the micro–baby bok choy that arrived heaped on a plate with whole cloves of roasted garlic and homemade oyster sauce.

The house chow fun brought wide rice noodles tossed with a brown sauce that magnified the flavor of every ingredient it covered — strips of chicken, big shrimps, and Chinese broccoli. A stir-fried pork lo mein found a perfect foil in ribbons of spicy pickled cabbage.

One caveat: Lakeside's unglamorous look may make it a logical candidate for take-out. But the food just doesn't taste the same, especially the deep-fried squid and salt-baked soft-shell crabs that are among its best dishes. So much for logic. Just go, and consider it good luck to eat-in.

— OR TRY THESE —

Here are three other great Chinatown joints:

SZECHUAN TASTY HOUSE 🟥🟥
902 Arch St., 19107, 215-925-2839. Get a rare taste of authentic Szechuan cooking at this Chinatown newcomer. Vibrant dishes make the meal, with careful preparations and a peppercorn-flared chile heat that is both stinging and seductive.

Shiao Lan Kung 🟥🟥
930 Race St., 19107, (215) 928-0282. The busy, no-frills room has grown worn around the edges since my last visit, but the kitchen still turns out some of the brightest Cantonese cooking: awesome salt-baked seafood, made-to-order wontons, and memorable orange beef that draws crowds into the early morning hours. Not open for lunch.

Lee How Fook 🟥🟥
219 N. 11th St., 19107, (215) 925-7266. The family-owned Chinatown veteran is still one of the neighborhood's most dependable standbys for great hot pots, restorative soups, crispy Buddha rolls, and delicious whole fish at affordable prices.

L'Angolo

🎐🎐 VERY GOOD

MENU HIGHLIGHTS Antipasto misto; spicy calamari and shrimp; grilled calamari; penne melanzane; chicken with balsamic sauce; veal chop with mushrooms; veal medallions with porcini; paillard di vitello; mixed seafood grill special; monkfish special with clams; espresso chocolate torte; cheesecake with almond praline crust; Italian risotto pudding.

BYOB Bring a rustic Italian red.

WEEKEND NOISE Noisy (82 decibels)

IF YOU GO Dinner Tu-Th 5-9:30 p.m.; F and Sa 5-10:30 p.m.; Su 4-8:30 p.m.
- **M** Dinner entrees, $13-$19
- Reservations strongly suggested
- Most major cards
- Not wheelchair-accessible
- Street parking

For the uninitiated, the food world of South Philadelphia becomes a foggy landscape below Washington Avenue and that well-trod cheesesteak crossroads at 9th and Passyunk. Yet the area is rich with treasures, from the bakeries and hoagie shops of Ritner Street and Oregon Avenue, to East Passyunk Avenue's recent revival.

How ironic that Kathryn and Davide Faenza once counted themselves among the clueless when it came to Deep South Philly. Now, after six years at the corner of Porter and Rosewood, a half-block west of Broad, their 35-seat trattoria, L'Angolo, ranks among its best hidden gems.

Hidden, of course, doesn't necessarily mean undiscovered. And judging from the crowds that pack its cheery brick-arched rooms, L'Angolo (which means "the corner") is already inscribed on the agendas of most of the BYOB hounds who scour our region for great food at fair prices. And it has only improved since my first visits a few years ago, with a splendid crew of charming young Italian servers and one of the most authentic menus in town.

Among the unique items are Davide's antipasto, which draws from the many plates of salads and nibbles that line the counter of the open kitchen near the door. Inspired by Faenza's native Puglia, there are wedges of frittata flecked with vegetables and mint, florettes of deep-fried cauliflower, and chickpeas baked with mushrooms. A typical antipasto might also include marsala-splashed carrots, creamy Pugliese rice salad, irresistible eggplant Parmesan, and a tangy potato-tomato cake layered with olives and capers. Called pitta di patate, it's an homage to Faenza's hometown of Gallipoli.

The rest of the menu is pure trattoria, with entrees priced at $19 or less — a bargain for the quality. Faenza has cooked at a number of local spots, from Mediterraneo

ITALIAN TRATTORIA · SOUTH PHILADELPHIA
1415 Porter St., 19145
215-389-4252

in Horsham (where he met Kathryn, who was a waitress just back from a year in Rome) to Il Portico and La Baia. But this is, by far, his best performance.

The grilled calamari were not only tender from a day-long bath in olive oil and garlic, but also beautiful, sliced into pompons that looked like ivory orchids hot off the grill. A gorgeous swordfish steak special was topped with caramelized onions and golden raisins splashed with tangy white balsamic. Perfectly sauteed monkfish arrived under a mountain of tiny cockles and shrimp. The flavors were more elegant than the presentation, elevated by a zesty white-wine broth.

The balsamic-sauced chicken (a better bet than my overcooked chicken saltimbocca) luxuriated in a dark balsamic reduction. Nuggets of filet mignon came gratineed with smoked mozzarella. And virtually every veal dish was ideal, including a veal chop propped up over a ragout of oyster mushrooms and crimini, and a mushroom-stuffed braciole glazed in amaretto-kissed demiglace. The pounded paillard, a pounded sheet of herb-infused veal flashed on the grill and paired with creamy polenta, was the essence of simple but satisfying trattoria cooking — especially at $17.50.

Most of the pastas are made in-house, and the effort pays off. Among the best were special broccoli rabe ravioli shined with garlicky olive oil and crowned with sweet roasted cloves. The tiny ricotta gnocchi were so incredibly light, despite a glaze of gorgonzola cream, they simply evaporated when I took a bite.

Kathryn Faenza, meanwhile, makes some wonderful desserts, from a sublimely rich mascarpone cheesecake over a praline crust, to an intensely dark espresso chocolate torte. It's so silky that it triggers an exquisite calm as each fudgy forkful melts in slow, slow motion. And suddenly, the uncharted reaches of South Philadelphia do not seem so foggy anymore.

— OR TRY THESE —

Here are three other finds in Deep South Philly:

South Philadelphia Tap Room
1509 Mifflin St., 19145, (215) 271-7787
A gastro-pub for Deep South Philly, with a stellar selection of local craft brews and an ambitiously eclectic menu that ranges from deep-fried asparagus to wild boar burritos.

Ristorante Pesto   🔔 🔔
1915 S. Broad St., 19148, (215) 336-8380
One of the more polished entries in a crop of new South Philadelphia BYO trattorias. The kitchen isn't perfect, but Neapolitan-style pizzas are a highlight, as are several homemade pastas and veal dishes.

Dad's All Natural Stuffings
1615 W. Ritner St., 19145, (215) 334-1934
312 S. Black Horse Pike, Blackwood, N.J. 08012, (856) 228-7744
This prepared foods market has some of the best crab cakes in town (perhaps better than Bobby Chez), excellent meat loaf, and a surprisingly good cheesesteak

Le Bec-Fin

🍴🍴🍴🍴 SUPERIOR

MENU HIGHLIGHTS Galette de crabe; pesto risotto with garlic emulsion; wild mushroom ravioli; sauteed scallop with red cabbage; escargots; tuna tartare; black bass with squash three ways; black bass with chorizo emulsion and squid ink; veal and sweetbreads; rack of lamb; roasted whole birds (wild partridge); cheese cart; dessert cart.

WINE LIST Prestige French crus are the meat of this big cellar, though there is also a selective international collection of premium labels. Great values are few. But excellent wines by the glass work well for modest budgets and tasting menus. Wine flights: lunch $45; dinner $80.

WEEKEND NOISE Lively

IF YOU GO Lunch seatings M-F 11:30 a.m., 1:30 p.m. Dinner seatings M-Th 6, 9 p.m.; F and Sa 6, 9:30 p.m. Closed Su.
• **U-E** Lunch tastings, $54 (3 courses), $70 (6 courses); dinner tastings, $138 (6 courses), $165 (10 courses); garden room menu, $39 (3 courses)
• **M to E** Le Bar Lyonnais, dinner entrees, $15-$42
• Reservations required
• Wheelchair-accessible
• Valet parking $15, across Walnut at Sharper Image.

There are days when Georges Perrier blusters that he plans eventually to walk away from Le Bec-Fin, the gastronomic jewel of Walnut Street that is the closest thing we have to a palace of French dining.

"This kind of restaurant, unfortunately, is on the way out," says Perrier.

Then there are other days when the capricious chef, now in his early sixties, declares he will keep it open "until I die."

Personally, I'm betting on the second option. But he's right to predict the decline of multicourse blowouts like Le Bec-Fin, a truffle-'til-you-drop culinary orgy in which no luxury is spared, and more than a few expense accounts have met their maker in a blinding flash of polished silver and premier cru Bordeaux. People no longer need to gorge themselves on six courses (and spend about $200 a person doing it) to approach culinary nirvana. Le Bec's Old World formality, though conscientiously un-snooty, isn't for everyone.

And yet, a meal at Le Bec-Fin remains an experience unlike any other, a rarefied pursuit of dining perfection in its most symphonic expression, from the lavishly gilded room (think King Louis) to the legions of genuflecting tuxedoed servers and a cellar stocked with some of the world's most prestigious wines.

Most impressive, though, is how Perrier's kitchen has remained up-to-date, all the while honoring the many signature dishes that made it legendary to begin with. First-timers, for example, might not want to miss the escargots, which arrive inside a snail-crowned silver pot in champagne butter with hazelnuts and garlic. Or the galette of lump crab suspended in a disc of creamy seafood mousse. Or the superb wild mushroom–chicken ravioli. Or succulent game birds like the wild Scottish partridge or poussin that are carved tableside and glazed with the essence of their natural juices.

CLASSIC AND CONTEMPORARY FRENCH • RESTAURANT ROW
1523 Walnut St., 19102
215-567-1000 • www.lebecfin.com

Anyone seeking a taste of refined contemporary cooking, meanwhile, will quickly discover that is the rule at Le Bec-Fin, not the exception. This is especially true at lunch, where day chef, Jerome Bacle, presents the restaurant's most daring palette. The old familiar tuna tartare becomes electric with pickled raspberries that tingle with gingered spice. Black bass sits atop a stunning evocation of Spain, a vivid orange emulsion of cuminy chorizo butter swirled with black squid ink. Rack of lamb strikes a Mediterranean pose over creamy white beans greened with vibrant pesto.

Dinner chef Pierre Calmels is no less modern, with dishes like pesto risotto topped with a mousse of garlic foam, or tomato water shots with olive oil and candied pumpkin. But his menus rely more on soulful seasonality than startling combinations. Luscious scallops pair with a honeyed red cabbage tarted up with currants, port, and dried apricots. Black bass luxuriates over a fall study of squash: shaved kabocha marinated in beer, caramelized butternut, and spicy segments of Cinderella pumpkin pickled with honey and peppercorns.

Few of these plates are petite. And by the time you make it even halfway through one of the exquisite meat dishes — veal medallions tiered with sweetbreads over chestnuts and celery root, or lamb chops with sausage-studded flageolet beans — the mere notion of three more courses sounds absurd.

Oh well, you're here. Your bank balance already will never be the same. So why even pretend to resist the chariot of ripe cheeses, the silver chalices of sublime sorbets, and the multi-tiered pastry cart that glides to your table laden with frozen souffles, pistachio-creamed tartes, and chocolate-ribboned temptations?

They will be history someday, no doubt. So enjoy them for however long they last.

— OR TRY THESE —

Here are three other suggested upscale French restaurants:

Deux Cheminees 🍴🍴🍴
1221 Locust St., 19107, (215) 790-0200
Turn back the clock to an era of classic French dining in an elegant 19th-century townhouse, beautifully maintained by the jovial and scholarly chef Fritz Blank, whose massive cookbook library upstairs is as famous as the stunningly rich soups served from antique terrines.

GILMORE'S 🍴🍴🍴
133 E. Gay St., West Chester, Pa. 19380, (610) 431-2800
Peter Gilmore's dining room has earned the ex-Le Bec-Fin chef a third bell, with polished French cuisine that shows innovation (try the "corndog" shrimp and "candied apple" chocolate mousse) and poised service.

Pond/Bistro Cassis 🍴🍴🍴
175 King of Prussia Rd., Radnor, Pa. 19087, (610) 293-9411
New owner and chef, Abde Dahrouch, formerly at nearby Taquet, has added a French tone (with Moroccan accents) to a dual-venue concept that is a welcome, sophisticated addition to the Main Line scene.

Truck Fare

FOOD TRUCKS ARE A PHILADELPHIA-WIDE PHENOMENON.

But in University City, trucks are a way of life, feeding the campus culture's insatiable hunger for good, cheap eats. Nowhere in the city is there such an intense concentration of food trucks, and the result is a healthy competition, both for rock bottom values and menu diversity. Whether you want kung pao chicken, vegetarian meatballs, incendiary vindaloo curry, or a plantain burrito, there is a truck that can feed you for $5 or less.

But are these mobile kitchens any good? I've eaten at dozens of trucks and carts, in University City and elsewhere across the metropolis, and the verdict is mixed at best.

Filling your belly will never be a problem. But most trucks served up ordinary fare, and some were downright awful. I found a few worth noting, but one in particular stood out as special: Yue Kee.

It is common knowledge among habitues of the Yue Kee mobile kitchen that one should never, ever, simply walk up to the truck's open window and expect an order to be speedily noted and prepared.

It might help if you speak Cantonese. But a simple call to Bi Pang's cell phone is really all that's needed.

"Twenty minutes!" she'll bark. Then she'll return to her brusque flurry of packing and organizing the mountain of orders for a lunchtime rush that gathers impatiently on the shaded sidewalk of South 38th Street, across from the Wharton School.

But some people learn the hard way, like the fellow who waited 15 minutes in line behind me before finally giving up in exasperation. He whipped out a cell phone and called Pang, just five feet away, who promptly took his order for ginger chicken and string beans with beef before hanging up: "Twenty minutes!"

I suspect there are two reasons Yue Kee has flourished here since 1983 despite an inefficiency bordering on rudeness that makes it the "Soup Nazi" of Chinese trucks. The first is that Pang's husband, Tsz Pong, expertly wok-cooks each order fresh in the back of the truck, and his food is worth every minute of the wait.

The second reason is that Yue Kee's ancient Grumman truck is so dilapidated — a beat-up metal hulk that croaks like a lawn mower and looks as if it just returned from a tour of duty on the front lines — that it attracts few newcomers, allowing the couple to focus on loyal customers who know better than to judge them by their cover.

w/ 1 egg roll & (1 soup or 1 can of soda)

ONLY $4.50

eet & Sour Chicken
echuan Bean Curd (Spicy)
xed Vegetables
icken with Peanuts (Spicy)

pper Steak
occoli with Chicken, Beef,
Pork
xed Vegetables with
icken, Beef, or Pork
chuan Chicken or Beef
icy)
k with Mushrooms

ow Peas with Chicken,
ef, or Pork
an Sprouts with Chicken
Shrimp
w Mein with Chicken,
ef, Pork, or Shrimp

After several memorable lunches there, however, I've come to believe that Yue Kee is not the grungy, grouchy, excruciatingly slow food truck it first appears to be. It is one of the better Chinese kitchens in the city.

I find myself with regular cravings for the Beijing "hot noodles," which are essentially a Chinese dan-dan spaghetti bolognese with a fiery, complex spice. But there are so many other dishes I also love.

The ma pao tofu delivers a sharp and punchy spice tweaked with the rich saltiness of dark soy, and is also a study in textures — crumbles of ground pork playing against the silken tofu and the crunchy snap of shredded bamboo. The ginger chicken might aptly be renamed scallion chicken, because it appears to be little more than a mound of tender white meat tossed with a fistful of crunchy onion greens. But a swelling heat in the clear sauce rings brightly with ginger spice. The chicken with string beans is a look-alike, but tastes completely different, with a nutty shade of garlic sweetness.

Beef with eggplant in black bean chile sauce is another simple winner, setting the tender meat against meltingly soft half-moons of violet-skinned Asian eggplants. Even better were the Singapore noodles, which may be the best in the city. The fabulous "pork billy," made from a recipe handed down from Tsz's father, is essentially thick slices of Chinese bacon, steamed with leaves of medicinal herbs to a tender sweetness perfumed with Asian spice.

For connoisseurs of old-time chop suey–house cuisine, meanwhile, Yue Kee also makes a standout egg foo young. But one of the richest treats of dining at Yue Kee is the sheer value of its food, which tops out at $4.50 a dish. It is, after all, a truck.

Yue Kee 🍴🍴
238 S. 38th St. (between Walnut and Spruce Sts.), 19104, (610) 812-7189

Here is a short list of some of other highlights in truck dining; phone numbers generally are not available:

IN NORTH PHILADELPHIA

The Creperie
13th and Norris Sts.
Owner Vasilios "Bill" Zacharatos ladles out the crispy crepe cones for the Temple crowd at his lunch truck, then heaps them with a pound of fillings ranging from grilled meats with homemade feta spread to "savory pizza" crepes and more traditionally French ones for dessert with Nutella.

IN WEST PHILADELPHIA

Aladdin
33rd and Spruce Sts.
This tiny Middle Eastern food cart in front of the University of Pennsylvania Hospital is a favorite for its platters of couscous (or lentil rice) with grilled kofta and chicken kabobs.

Denise's Soul Food
30th and Market Sts. (S.E. corner)
The jerk chicken platter with rice and beans is a mouthful of Caribbean flavor, best washed down with a big gulp of sweetened iced tea.

Koja
38th and Walnut Sts. (N.W. corner)
Along with notably friendly service, this truck serves extremely tasty Korean fare, including a hearty mound of sesame-tinged beef bulgogi, refreshing cubes of kimchee radish, and an addictive stir-fried tofu tossed with a chile sauce that glows like fire.

IN CENTER CITY

Christis's Unnamed Lunch Cart
20th and Market Sts. (N.E. corner)
There's a reason a long line can always be found leading up to this unusual cart bedecked in potted plants, flowers, and copper pots. Gregarioius owner Konstandinos Christis cooks excellent marinated chicken sandwiches over a charcoal-fired grill, and his crisp falafel — fluffy and herbaceous inside and vibrant with green herbs — is one of the best in town. It's slow, but worth it.

King of Falafel
16th St. and JFK Blvd. (S.E. corner)
This little food cart parked across from Love Park at 16th and JFK fires up one of the most reliable falafels in town, as well as a delicious weekly special of oniony lentil rice called mjadra.

Spice Mexican Food

400 block of North Broad St. (west side, in front of The Inquirer *building)*

You know it's a tight deadline day when I'm standing in line at this cheery Mexican cart, but the hearty, black-bean–laden platters are honestly cooked and deliver satisfying flavors, from the open-faced belly-busting enchiladas (chicken and spinach is a fave) to the occasional special of excellent mole tamales. Beware the "hot" salsa — it'll make you breathe fire.

IN WEST CHESTER

Wally's Wiener World

High and Market Sts. (N.W. corner)

Scott Vassil has been serving tasty wieners for nearly two decades from his cart outside the Chester County Courthouse, in the shadow of the statue "Old Glory." He closes on the early side and takes the winter months off, but his dog topped with excellent homemade chili is one of the best ways I can think of to spend $1.50. Vassil, by the way, made a splash on David Letterman's "stupid human tricks" by stopping a fan with his tongue.

Lolita

🗡🗡 VERY GOOD

MENU HIGHLIGHTS
Guacamole; tostaditas de salmon; queso fundido; puya chile braised veal cheeks; beef tenderloin (carne asada); pistachio-crusted duck; lamb barbacoa; enchiladas verdes; halibut with chorizo and clams; cheesecake with ancho crust.

WINE LIST Bring your own tequila to mix with addictive margarita setups. Try good but affordable brands like Herradura, Cuervo Tradicional, or Sauza Hornitos. For beer, go with lager; for wine, spicy red zinfandel or earthy syrah.

WEEKEND NOISE Raucous

IF YOU GO Su-Tu 5-10 p.m.; W and Th until 10:30 p.m.; F and Sa until 11 p.m.
- **E** Entrees, $18-$23
- Reservations suggested
- Cash only
- Wheelchair-accessible
- Street parking

There comes a moment in the life cycle of ethnic foods when a signature dish — be it curry, spring rolls, or pesto — ceases being ethnic at all.

It simply melts into the proverbial sauce pot of a progressive restaurant scene and re-emerges beneath a tuft of microgreens (and no doubt ringed by huitlacoche vinaigrette) as yet another bright color in the palette of the New American menu.

That cycle has come nearly full circle at Lolita, the charming 13th Street bistro where Mexican flavors are an inspiration rather than an exercise in authenticity.

Not to say the sauces and ingredients here aren't faithful to tradition. Chef and co-owner Marcie Turney, known for her neo-Mediterranean flavors at Audrey Claire and Valanni, has worked hard to use the labor-intensive techniques of proper Mexican cooking. The velvety soft, steaming-hot tortillas she makes for the carnitas and queso fundido, for example, are superb.

But when you tuck into a plate of tequila-cured smoked salmon draped over malanga chips with jalapeño crema and crunchy heirloom radish salad, it's clear Lolita is more contemporary BYO than barrio taqueria.

There's nothing wrong with that, especially when it's BYOT (as in tequila), and the margarita punch is as lip-smackingly fresh as Lolita's virgin mix. The servers are welcoming and attentive, and impressively attuned to customers' special needs.

The space is just right, too, an angular glass storefront that opens onto a slender, urbane room with exposed brick walls and steel air ducts, and a fire-red glass tile mosaic fronting the open kitchen. Lolita generates a lively buzz, but it's more mellow than the fiesta-like frenzy at flashy El Vez across the street. The food is also lower-key, but always interesting enough to merit a visit.

Dishes like the meltingly tender (and trendy) veal cheeks braised in puya chile spice, or the beef tender-

CONTEMPORARY MEXICAN • AVENUE OF THE ARTS

106 S. 13th St., 19107

215-546-7100 • www.lolitabyob.com

loins glazed in smoky cream that fly to the table beneath wings of plantain chips, are among Turney's best proto-BYO-Mexi-fusion.

The classic guacamole, meanwhile, is simply a fresh green cream topped with jicama slaw for crunch. The queso fundido is also impossible to resist, a bubbling crock of Oaxaca cheese laced with cuminy chorizo that was weirdly topped with delicate tufts of microgreens. If Turney has a weakness, it's that penchant for piling boutique produce on every plate, a steady shower of tiny leaves, shaved organic roots and a surfeit of other ingredients that detract from the earthy flavors her kitchen so painstakingly creates.

I loved the depth of the red mole chicken-and-corn stew in the tamal. But freshly ground masa was unsatisfyingly thin, as was the coveted huitlacoche. The carnitas stewed with orange and cinnamon was on the sweet side, but at least it was in the right hemisphere.

The halibut was also excellent, posed over a hash of chayote squash, tender clams, and spicy chorizo. Satisfying enchiladas verdes filled with shiitakes and Lancaster jack cheese came topped with bright tomatillo salsa and succulent grilled shrimp. The barbacoa roasted lamb flavored with Mexican aromatics was another classic Turney nailed, with a clever contemporary bonus of grilled pasilla lamb loin with hazelnut-huitlacoche stuffing.

There were other smart tweaks for dessert, like the milk-soaked tres leches cake alongside creamy chocolate pot de creme, or the hot spiced nuts and coconut that topped the moist flourless chocolate cake. It was the cheesecake, though, that I remember best. The creamy wedge was scattered with pecans, streaked with goat's milk caramel, and set in a chocolate cookie crust that left a warming surprise. When I licked my lips, they tingled with Lolita's kiss of ancho chile spice.

— OR TRY THESE —

Here are three other suggested hotspots at the corner of 13th and Sansom:

EL VEZ 🔔 🔔
121 S. 13th St., 19107, (215) 928-9800
Still the city's most sophisticated Mexican food, courtesy of Mexican-born chef Adrian Leon. A slip in service and over-iced margaritas have dropped El Vez a notch from its three-bell rating.

Capogiro
117 S. 20th St., 19103, (215) 636-9250
119 S. 13th St., 19107, (215) 351-0900
If there is better gelato in America, I haven't tasted it yet. The midnight dark chocolate is an addiction. Both locations are also stylish lunch cafes, with great panini, coffee, and sweets.

Vintage
129 S. 13th St. (at Sansom), 19107, (215) 922-3095
This appealing new wine bar with simple French bistro eats is yet another addition to developer Tony Goldman's growing entertainment crossroads just a block off Broad. Still too new for a verdict.

Los Catrines Restaurant & Tequila's Bar

♟♟ VERY GOOD

MENU HIGHLIGHTS Nachos; taquitos de pollo; empanadas; sopa de tortilla; posole; seviche; crab tostada special; pollo entortillado; langostinos con salsa Tequila's; filete grito; carne aguacate; caramel crepes; churros.

WINE LIST Small list of affordable Latin wines, but 50-plus tequila list is stellar, from Porfidio to El Tesoro de Don Felipe to outstanding house-produced label, Siembra Azul. The margaritas are also dangerous.

WEEKEND NOISE Noisy

IF YOU GO Lunch M-F 11:30 a.m.-2 p.m. Dinner Su-Th 5-10 p.m.; F and Sa 5-11 p.m. Bar open M-F 11:30 a.m. until close; Sa and Su 5 p.m. until close.
- **M to E** Dinner entrees, $15.95 to $23.50
- Reservations accepted Su-Th for parties of 8 or more
- Wheelchair-accessible (motorized lift at entrance)
- Valet parking, dinner only, Th-Sa, $15

Mexican cooking has come a long way in Philadelphia since David Suro-Piñera opened his suave cantina on Locust Street almost 20 years ago, introducing the area to the universe of authentic flavors beyond Tex-Mex chimichangas.

But Los Catrines Restaurant & Tequila's Bar has assured itself a steady place in the hearts of local diners by moving into one of the city's most beautiful and storied dining rooms, where its outgoing staff is the epitome of professional charm, and the kitchen reliably delivers high-quality Mexican cuisine. These classic plates might lack the look and creativity of some of the nuevo competition. But creations like the profoundly earthy tortilla soup, or those grilled langostinos splashed with tequila butter and garlic, really don't need much embellishment.

The restaurant, confusingly, will probably always be known to locals as Tequila's, which was the restaurant's name at its original location a block away. It's also a nod to Suro-Piñera's passion for the national drink. Not only does he have one of the finest lists of artisan tequilas in the country (from Chinaco to Porfidio), he recently began producing his own excellent brand of the agave elixir called Siembra Azul.

Still, I'm fond of the new name, Los Catrines, which refers to the whimsical mural of skeletons dressed like dandies in the foyer, whose image is a symbol of the 1910 Mexican Revolution's victory over the country's aristocratic dictatorship. They are a prelude to the impressive collection of Mexican art that brings new life to the grand chandeliered space once occupied by La Panetiere and Magnolia Cafe.

Dozens of other beautiful artworks fill the moody, votive-lit dining rooms with romantic intrigue, including a mural by Jose Clemente Orozco-Farias (grandson of the famed Jalisco artist) depicting Suro-Piñera's children in the agave fields, along with Zapatista Sub-Comandante

MEXICAN (UPSCALE TRADITIONAL) • RITTENHOUSE SQUARE
1602 Locust St., 19103
215-546-0181 • www.tequilasphilly.com

Marcos. But it is los catrines that best symbolize the restaurant's spirit — at once serious and irreverent and fiercely rooted in authentic Mexico.

There is classic mole Poblano sauce rich with chocolate and spice and an aftertaste of sesame. There are soft tacos topped with shredded pork "enchilada," and pillowy empanadas stuffed with ground meat moistened with tart tomatillos. The huachinango red snapper comes traditionally done with a wonderful Veracruz salsa of tomatoes, capers, and olives. Los Catrines also indulges diners with huitlacoche, the earthy corn mushroom that gets pureed into an inky sauce beneath crab-stuffed zucchini blossoms.

The tortilla soup was a soulful gem, its rust-colored chile broth ribboned with noodles of sliced tortilla. But the occasional special of posole soup is also worth seeking.

Los Catrines is a bit more expensive than a typical Mexican restaurant, and while the kitchen could be a bit more inventive, I still consider it fairly priced considering the ambiance, fine service, and ingredients used by chef Carlos Molina. The huge langostinos are nearly as big as lobsters and as tender as butter. And the numerous variations on filet mignon are among the restaurant's most interesting offerings, from the mushroom-stuffed "carne aguacate" ringed by green avocado and cilantro cream to the "filete grito," whose dark tamarind sauce and bed of cactus leaves give it gusto. The grito's meat has also been shot through with whole serrano chiles that riddle the filet with little explosions of heat.

There are some satisfying sweets to soothe the heat, including crepes with warm goat's milk cajeta caramel. My recent favorite, though, were the traditional churros, the grooved beignet sticks dusted in cinnamon sugar. Crisp and warm, with dips of chocolate and caramel, I found them to be much like Los Catrines itself. An irresistable classic.

— OR TRY THESE —

Here are three other suggested upscale Mexican restaurants:

Las Cazuelas   ☓ ☓
426-28 W. Girard Ave., 19123, (215) 351-9144. This BYO on Northern Liberties' northern border is a step up from most bare-bones taquerias, but the food is classic Puebla home cooking, ranging from mole-sauced enchiladas to fresh sopes and Veracruz-style whole snapper.

Zocalo ☓ ☓
3600 Lancaster Ave., 19104, (215) 895-0139. In Powelton Village, contemporary updates on authentic Mexican flavors, with house-made tortillas, Puebla mole, fresh guacamole, and one of the best tequila bars in town. A recent lunch was excellent.

Coyote Crossing
Market and Walnut Sts., 19382, West Chester, Pa, (610) 429-8900. 800 Spring Mill Ave., Conshohocken, Pa. 19428, (610) 825-3000. I never loved the Conshohocken original, but this newer West Chester branch brought careful renditions of tequila-soused shrimp, a hearty stuffed pepper, and decent mole.

Majolica

♟♟♟ EXCELLENT

MENU HIGHLIGHTS Mussels with Pernod butter; veal sweetbreads; corn soup with fried clams; duck with apricot marmalade; steak frites; porcini-dusted halibut; lamb loin; salmon with truffle nage; Hendricks Farm cheese plate; profiteroles; figs with honey ice cream.

BYOB Superb selection of Spiegelau glassware.

WEEKEND NOISE Noisy

IF YOU GO Dinner seatings on half-hour Tu-Th 6-9 p.m.; F and Sa seatings only at 6, 6:30, 8, 8:30 p.m.
  • **E** Dinner entrees, $20-$24
  • Reservations highly recommended
  • Most major cards
  • Wheelchair-accessible
  • Small free lot behind restaurant accessible from Gay St.; street parking free after 6 p.m.

Chef Andrew Deery and his wife, Sarah Johnson, no doubt, had something elegant in mind when they resurrected the bones of the derelict Phoenix Tavern into a charming 40-seat eatery called Majolica. The name alludes to a type of glazed earthenware that was the late–19th-century glory of Phoenixville, where Griffin-Smith-Hill Pottery produced sardine boxes and strawberry platters that are still collectible.

A key to the pottery's continued value is colorful glazes that remain vivid over the course of time. If my impressive meals here are any indication, Majolica the restaurant has a bright future, too, with the kind of sophisticated dining that can jump-start any aspiring downtown revival.

Majolica delivers that sophistication with an unpretentious ease. The decor is simple yet elegant, a polished glass storefront giving way to a plush waiting couch, exposed brick, copper-top tables, and an antique breakfront filled with Spiegelau glassware — one of the many elegant touches that are a step above what you'll find in most neighborhood BYOBs.

The service team led by Johnson, who worked at the Birchrunville Store Cafe, is also a delight. But it is Deery's kitchen that makes the biggest impression, putting fine ingredients in striking combinations so focused, that little touches — a dusting of thyme petals or a few dabs of aged vinegar — are able to transform a dish.

Beautifully crisped sweetbreads, for example, took on surprising shades of flavor with a glaze of hazelnut oil, and a finely diced salad of apples, currants, and celery. A tiny cube of malt vinegar gelee sparks a complimentary amuse-bouche of fried halibut brandade.

Deery revels in the bounty of local, seasonal ingredients, from the ripe blueberries he turned into an intermezzo sorbet glossed with extra-virgin olive oil and ribbons of basil to the sweet peaches that bolstered seared

NEW AMERICAN • WESTERN SUBURBS (Chester County)

258 Bridge St., Phoenixville, Pa. 19460

610-917-0962 • www.majolicarestaurant.com

foie gras scattered with sea salt. Even the wonderful coffee is blended for Majolica and roasted nearby at Kimberton Coffee Roasters.

No dish spoke more clearly of its season than the milky white summer corn soup, poured from a carafe tableside around a mound of crisply fried cherrystone clams. Steamed mussels — a dish I've grown tired of — were among the best I've had, completely perfumed by the Pernod flambe.

The deconstructed frisee salad and classic hanger steak frites (complete with amazingly crisp hand-cut french fries) show Deery's affinity for bistro cuisine. A meaty breast of duck was sparked by the yin-yang flavors of finely shaved bitter Belgian endive and sweet apricots spiced with peppercorns.

A thick piece of porcini-dusted halibut was also splendid, posed over a vibrant green parsley butter with chanterelle mushrooms. And an amazingly good Scottish salmon was set over the double crunch of a brioche crouton and braised celery ringed by truffle butter.

Majolica's cheese plate gives some much deserved attention to the cheeses of Hendricks Farm in Telford, Montgomery County, siding its tomme-style and soft-rind cheeses with honeycomb, roasted hazelnuts, and sweet berries.

The heart of its dessert offerings, however, centers on homemade ice creams and sorbets. Coconut sorbet, cradled in a macadamia nut tuile, has an exotic flair with ginger-poached pineapple. Profiteroles with vanilla ice cream are classic, but elicit aahs when a server pours a carafe of warm dark chocolate sauce over top. The best, though, was a hazelnut cake ringed by a sunburst of roasted figs, then crowned with honey ice cream and a fragrant purple shower of lavender flowers.

It was an elegant finish to a memorable meal. I can only hope it is as enduring as Phoenixville majolica.

— OR TRY THESE —

Here are three other suggested BYOBs along the 422 corridor:

Funky Lil' Kitchen 🍴 🍴
232 King St., Pottstown, Pa. 19464, (610) 326-7400. This Center City–style bistro adds a spark to Pottstown's revival. It has a spunky personality and an adventurous New American menu from chef-owner Michael Falcone that should draw fans from beyond the nearby 'burbs.

Mosaic Cafe
50 Glocker Way, Suburbia Shopping Ctr., Rt. 100, North Coventry, Pa. 19465, (610) 323-9120. A splash of color from this BYO, where an upscale menu ventures from kobe burgers to lavender-glazed salmon. My meal brought an excellent crabcake but awkward service.

Sly Fox Breweries
312 N. Lewis Rd., Royersford, Pa. 19468, (610) 948-8088. 519 Kimberton Rd., Pikeland Village Sq., Phoenixville, Pa. 19460, (610) 935-4540. This mini-chain of the brewpubs turns out some of the best local craft beers, especially the impressively Guinness-like O'Reilly's stout.

Margaret Kuo's

♜♜♜ EXCELLENT

MENU HIGHLIGHTS Chinese menu: Shandong wonton soup; Shanghai steamed buns; Peking duck square appetizer; Peking duck; Mandarin braised duck; lamb stew; Shanghai provincial pork; tofu with bamboo heart; ginger steamed whole fish. Japanese menu: iso maki roll; otoro sashimi; usuzukuri.

WINE LIST Superb international selection; several fine choices by the glass. Try an excellent cold sake (Iyo Densetsu or Itten). Premium teas — Dragonwell, Pouchong — also a delight.

WEEKEND NOISE Quiet

IF YOU GO Lunch daily, 11:30 a.m.-3 p.m. Dinner M-Th 3-10 p.m.; F and Sa 3-11 p.m.
• **E** Dinner entrees, $9.95-$32.95
• Most major cards
• No smoking
• Wheelchair-accessible
• Street parking only

The carved stone dragons and warrior horses that grace the walls of the Dragon's Lair at Margaret Kuo's pay homage to the great Tang Dynasty. But it is the dynasty of Margaret Kuo herself that finally gets its due at her Asia-plex in downtown Wayne, a handsome pink facade with burgundy trim that houses the region's most elegant, authentic Chinese restaurant downstairs, and the stylish Japanese Akari Room on the second floor.

Kuo's three-decade career is notable for the quixotic nature of her restaurants — two called Peking, and a Tokyo, all in Media, and a Mandarin in Frazer. Though she serves a mainstream crowd that would do just fine with General Tso's chicken, Kuo has always also presented authentic regional rarities such as braised Shanghai pork shoulder, spicy Mandarin stews, and exquisite steamed Shanghai buns that gush streams of broth when you take a bite.

It's thrilling to stumble upon an elegant gem like Peking hiding in the Granite Run Mall. But there is no element of surprise at this newer outpost on the Main Line. It has all the markings of a centerpiece destination, from the plush banquettes, tall ornate vases, and carved stone reliefs in the Dragon's Lair to the contemporary black Akari Room, with its illuminated rice paper wall booths and sleek tatami rooms.

Service here has evolved into a finely tuned machine, and there is also a first-class wine list (a great selection of premium sakes), and special loose teas served in artful wrought-iron pots.

The Japanese menu is particularly strong with sushi, including buttery otoro tuna belly, a ponzu sauce-splashed fan of sliced fluke called usuzukuri, and the marvelous iso maki special, which rolls tuna, yellowtail, and crunchy apple with tempura flakes in tender white seaweed.

UPSCALE CHINESE/JAPANESE • MAIN LINE
175 E. Lancaster Ave., Wayne, Pa. 19087
610-688-7200 • www.margaretkuos.com

But Kuo's Chinese specialties are what really set the restaurant apart. It's obvious from the moment a gong rings and you have the duck chef tableside, masterfully cleaving an entire Peking duck down to a sweet pile of satiny moist meat and crisply honeyed skin that a veteran waiter rolls up in delicate housemade pancakes. I doubt there is a better Peking duck in town. For the quick version, try the "duck square" appetizer, in which shredded meat and skin are pressed and crisped — like Peking Power Bars.

Most Chinese kitchens never get beyond quick stir-fries. But Kuo's best dishes come from hours of preparation. The Shanghai pork shoulder is like an exotic pork osso buco, a massive ring of meat in a deep, mildly sweet anise-flavored gravy. Chile spice sings more assertively through the Mandarin lamb stew, which brings lean, tender meat and chunks of daikon radish.

There were a few disappointments, such as the overcooked orchid shrimp and the oddly mundane list of brought-in Italian desserts.

But there is far more here to love. There are delicate wonton soups laced with chicken and pork in the house-special version, or spiked with scallions and spicy Szechuan pickles in the Shandong style. There are kobe beef steaks with maitake mushrooms, whole dover soles pan-seared with a garlicky-scallion crust, and fresh Maine lobsters stir-fried with zesty ginger and scallion sauce to the perfect tender sweetness.

Kuo says Main Liners have been more adventurous than her Media crowd. One unlikely item, though, has been popular: tofu with bamboo, essentially cloudlike fritters of mashed tofu and scallops topped with a velvety crab sauce and gauzy ribbons of bamboo heart.

They're savory and crunchy and fluffy, and I couldn't stop eating them — even if they were tofu. That shows what a great dynasty can do.

— OR TRY THESE —

Here are three other suggested restaurants in or near Wayne:

Georges'
Spread Eagle Village, 503 W. Lancaster Ave., Wayne, Pa. 19087, (610) 964-2588
Georges Perrier's gorgeous French farmhouse has struggled to find the perfect identity. A recent lunch with Dijon mustard-Gruyere pizza, spectacular Iberian clams, and refined-but-unstuffy service felt just right.

Restaurant Taquet 🔔 🔔
Wayne Hotel, 139 E. Lancaster Ave., Wayne, Pa. 19087, (610) 687-5005
Clark Gilbert is the new chef at this posh perch in the Wayne Hotel, an elegant, palm-fringed room and outdoor terrace. Gilbert has updated the French cuisine, but the place still exudes Main Line stuffiness.

Teresa's Cafe Italiano
124 N. Wayne Ave., Wayne, Pa. 19087, (610) 293-9909
Decent brick-oven pizzas and affordable pastas make this an appealing destination for a casual, family-friendly meal on the avenue. Has plans to open a bar next door, but won't change its BYO-friendly policy.

Marigold Kitchen

♟♟♟ EXCELLENT

MENU HIGHLIGHTS Pink lentil soup with lamb-stuffed cabbage; escargots with honey mushrooms and Israeli couscous; beef carpaccio and tartare; filet mignon with cardoon gratin; scallops with oxtail tagine; striped bass in grape leaf papillote; kataifi with truffle honey semifreddo; chocolate hazelnut rows.

BYOB

WEEKEND NOISE Lively

IF YOU GO Dinner Tu-Sa 5:30 to 10 p.m.
- **E** Entrees, $22 to $30
- Reservations recommended
- Not wheelchair-accessible
- Street parking only

It isn't often that a restaurant gets struck by culinary lightning twice, but that is exactly what happened to Marigold Kitchen.

The first came when chef Steven Cook gave the homey old Victorian townhouse a contemporary makeover in late 2004, and Cook's startling modern cuisine transformed a Spruce Hill dining room long known as a cozy parlor for blue-plate comfort into one of the city's most cutting-edge BYOBs.

The next bolt came with Cook's sudden departure from the kitchen less than a year later, and the subsequent lucky arrival of Michael Solomonov, a talented Vetri sous whose head chef debut here has been stunning. His food has retained the wit that made Cook's food so appealing — a knack to recast familiar flavors in surprising and artful ways. But if Cook, the son of a rabbi, had a distinctly "haute deli" Ashkenazi flair, with specialties like chicken liver croquettes, deconstructed borscht risotto, and pumpernickel bread pudding, the Israeli-born Solomonov has lent a decidedly Sephardic touch.

For an avant-garde aesthetic that always risks being too cool (a legacy of Cook's work at the old Salt), the new Mediterranean flavors have brought an extra dose of warmth, even in an amuse-bouche of three marble-sized savory truffles: foie gras dusted in pistachio; goat cheese showered with Jerusalem z'atar herbs; and pureed chicken rolled in smoked paprika.

Solomonov expands on these Middle Eastern flavors throughout the meal. A puree of cuminy pink lentil soup is poured from a carafe around a plump stuffed cabbage that has been sliced into medallions to reveal the exotic warmth of lamb kofte sausage. Pearls of Israeli couscous are the perfect textural foil for the tender chew of snails, pine nuts, and the slender-stemmed snap of intensely foresty honey mushrooms. The seared sea-sweetness of huge scallops is heightened by the earthy contrast of a

NEW AMERICAN BYOB/
CONTEMPORARY MEDITERRANEAN • WEST PHILADELPHIA
501 S. 45th St. (at Larchwood), 19104
215-222-3699 • www.marigoldkitchenbyob.com

Moroccan oxtail tagine, slow-stewed with sweet root vegetables into silken threads tinged with North African spice. A thick piece of wild striped bass is wrapped tightly into a package by grape leaves, whose briny tang and parchment-like snap is softened by pureed chickpeas topped with chanterelles.

Marigold's entrees have climbed about $8 during its starry first year, the liver croquettes now replaced by foie gras. But an essential homeyness remains in the old residential building, whose tenants occasionally still schlep home through the dining rooms to the six rental units upstairs — a curious quirk that is the legacy of Marigold's antiquated boardinghouse license. The bay windows with stained glass preserve the feel of a converted home in the dining rooms, but a banquette, modern art, and a fireplace wrapped in blue steel lend it a chic modern touch.

The staff is low-key but usually smooth — though I've had reports of the occasional weekend meltdown. Ultimately it will be Solomonov's menu that keeps Marigold among the city's hottest tables.

With delights such as a brioche-crusted cardoon gratin for the filet mignon, or a spicy paprika emulsion to spark the barramundi, or house-cured lemons and fennel to ignite the beef tartare, Marigold is clearly delivering quality for its prices.

And that continues with dessert, whether one opts for the excellent little cheese plate, or the elegant cardamom-scented creme brulee, or the dense chocolate-hazelnut bars with orange-glazed chestnuts. The black walnut kataifi with truffled honey semifreddo, though, best sums up all the excitement in Marigold's new kitchen. With local nuts wrapped in a Middle Eastern fantasy of shredded phyllo, each crunchy, earthy, divinely honeyed bite is the taste of lightning striking twice.

— OR TRY THESE —

Here are three other recommended restaurants west of 40th Street:

Rx 🔔 🔔
4443 Spruce St., 19104, (215) 222-9590
This pioneer has matured nicely over the last three years. The creative menu doesn't always taste as good as it sounds, but a commitment to local ingredients and fair prices keeps it on the go-list.

Vientiane Cafe
4728 Baltimore Ave., 19143, (215) 726-1095
This cheery Asian cafe provides a welcome oasis for striving Baltimore Avenue, a simple but pleasant destination for crisp Thai and Laotian cuisine. The ground chicken laab salad dressed in spicy-tangy vinaigrette was a hit.

Kabobeesh
4201 Chestnut St., 19104, (215) 386-8081
A Pakistani kabob house where especially vibrant flavors from the subcontinent arrive in the form of spicy skewered meats and fragrant curries come with puffy, homemade naan.

Worthy Stops Far Afield

SOME RESTAURANTS ARE WORTH A ROAD TRIP. Others can be a godsend when you're already far afield. Here's a short list of some favorites I've enjoyed when traveling more than an hour from Center City:

TOWARDS LANCASTER

General Sutter Inn
14 East Main St., Lititz, Pa. 17543, (717) 626-2115, www.generalsutterinn.com
When in Lititz for a visit to the Wilbur chocolate factory and Sturgis pretzelry, try this rambling old hotel (circa 1764), a reliable stop for a quality meal. The upscale dinner menu has a surprisingly adventurous focus on game with a French twist. Our lunch, meanwhile, brought a very impressive broiled crab cake and a tasty weinerschnitzel.

Good 'n' Plenty
150 Eastbrook Rd., Smoketown, Pa., 17576, (717) 394-7111, www.goodnplenty.com
You'll get your fill of Amish kitsch (and then some more) at this sprawling Lancaster County feed hall. But for a place where tourists arrive by the busload, the country cooking is surprisingly good (from fried chicken and ham loaf to excellent shoo-fly pie). The family-style service is preferable to the competition's free-for-all buffets.

The Restaurant at Doneckers   ✗ ✗ ✗
333 N. State St., Ephrata, Pa. 17522, (717) 738-9501, www.doneckers.com
Former Le Bec-Fin-chef Greg Gable blends French haute cuisine with regional flavors at this upscale Lancaster County shopping complex. The dinners are considerably more interesting than the shopper-friendly lunches.

Silk City Diner
1640 N. Reading Rd., Stevens, Pa. 17578, (717) 335-3833
Not to be confused with the recently closed Northern Liberties diner, this Lancaster County standby is a favorite lunch stop on our westbound turnpike roadtrips. It's a family-friendly venue that is one of the last bastions of old-time Dutch country and diner cooking, from noodle-topped chicken pot pies and smoked pork chops with kraut to meatloaf and good house-baked pastries.

Strawberry Hill   ✗ ✗ ✗
128 W. Strawberry St., Lancaster, Pa. 17603, (717) 393-5544, www.strawberryhillrestaurant.com
This warm tavern offers a surprising slice of California wine country in historic Lancaster, with an extraordinary cellar of 1,400 wines and a creative contemporary menu that uses excellent local ingredients.

FAR CHESTER COUNTY

BIRCHRUNVILLE STORE CAFE   ✗ ✗ ✗
Hollow and Flowing Spring Rds., Birchrunville, Pa. 19421, (610) 827-9002 www.birchrunvillestorecafe.com
Few destinations combine relaxed country charm with refined cooking

as seamlessly as this bucolic general-store-turned-BYO. The seasonal French menu was at its game-inspired height recently, ranging from buffalo carpaccio and wild mushroom pastries to fabulous pistachio-stuffed rabbit.

FAR NORTHERN MONTGOMERY COUNTY

Funky Lil' Kitchen   🏮🏮
232 King St., Pottstown, Pa. 19464, (610) 326-7400, www.funkylilkitchen.com
This surprising Center City-style bistro adds a real spark to Pottstown's downtown revival. With its groovy lava-lamp decor, it has a spunky personality and an adventurous New American menu from chef-owner Michael Falcone that should draw fans from beyond the nearby burbs. Great half-way meeting place between Philly and Berks County.

NEAR ALLENTOWN

The Farmhouse   🏮🏮🏮
1449 Chestnut St., Emmaus, Pa. 18049, (610) 967-6225, www.thefarmhouse.com
This charmingly restored farmhouse has a world-class beer collection to accompany a New American menu bursting with local ingredients and vivid flavor combinations. It's a malt drinker's haven that takes food and ambience seriously. Well worth the hour-plus drive from Center City.

IN DOYLESTOWN

Domani Star
57 W. State St., Doylestown, Pa. 18901, (215) 230-9100, www.domanistar.com
Look out through the window-paned storefront onto charming downtown Doylestown from this always-packed BYOB, where the Italian menu has an authentic touch, from the generous

antipasto platter to the hearty, lightly creamed bolognese sauce and the excellent tomato-basil soup.

Slate Bleu　🔔🔔
100 South Main St., Doylestown, Pa. 18901, (215) 348-0222; www.slatebleu.com
Mark and Susan Matyas have brought a classic French bistro to downtown Doylestown's historic Agriculture Works building. The menu is upscale and features well-crafted retro standards drawn from Mark's years as chef at Manhattan's La Grenouille. The low-energy service staff and weak wine list, though, need serious attention.

NEAR LAMBERTVILLE AND NEW HOPE

Frenchtown Inn　🔔🔔
7 Bridge St., Frenchtown, N.J. 08825, (908) 996-3300; www.frenchtowninn.com
This historic inn beside the Delaware River has a long tradition of sophisticated dining, with an ambitious menu rooted in seasonal French cooking, fine wines, and cozy fireplace dining rooms.

The Harvest Moon Inn　🔔🔔🔔
1039 Old York Rd., Ringoes, N.J. 08531, (908) 806-6020, www.harvestmooninn.com
This old stone inn, set in picturesque Hunterdon County, has a talented chef-owner whose complicated but inspired modern cuisine is fueled by heirloom and local ingredients.

Inn at Phillip's Mill　🔔🔔
2590 River Rd., New Hope, Pa. 18938, (215) 862-9919
The French country fare is better than average, but the inn's real draw is candlelit ambience that breathes

romance, from the fireplace lounge to the lush patio.

MARSHA BROWN　🔔🔔
15 S. Main St., New Hope, Pa. 18938, (215) 862-7044, www.marshabrown-restaurant.com
Marsha Brown, who also owns the local Ruth's Chris franchise, has transformed a former Methodist church into a dramatic Southern-inflected grill where the best dishes reflect her New Orleans roots. It's an impressive and reliable destination for a New Hope splurge, but some of the Louisiana flavors still need fine-tuning.

Sergeantsville Inn　🔔🔔
601 Rosemont-Ringoes Rd., Sergeantsville, N.J. 08557, (609) 397-3700; www.sergeantsvilleinn.com
This cozy 18th-century stone inn has ambitious young owners and an adventurous fine-dining menu that ranges from game to great tomato soup. The wine list is also excellent.

TRENTON AND SOUTH

Rat's　🔔🔔
16 Fairgrounds Rd., Hamilton, N.J. 08619, (609) 584-7800, www.ratsrestaurant.org
J. Seward Johnson Jr.'s Giverny-like sculpture park outside Trenton offers one of the region's most fantastical settings for ambitious French cuisine and a tremendous wine cellar. Only steep prices and pretentious service hold it back. A new chef has taken over since my last visit.

ALONG THE NEW JERSEY TURNPIKE

KARMA　🔔🔔
2015 Burlington Mt. Holly Rd., Mt. Holly, N.J. 08060, (609) 914-0800; www.thekarmarestaurant.com

This South Jersey branch of my favorite Old City Indian sits just at the bottom of Exit 5 off the Jersey Turnpike, and is a convenient early dinner stop on the way home from weekends in New York City.

WILMINGTON

The Chef's Table   ♟♟
222 Delaware St., New Castle, Del. 19720, (302) 322-6367, www.chefs-tablerestaurant.com
Former Deep Blue chef Robert Lhulier has revived the colonial-era David Finney Inn in charming old New Castle. With a contemporary menu that stresses seasonal ingredients and reasonable prices (including wine), the inn's warm tavern-style rooms feel as much like a neighborhood spot as a destination. Green service, though, still needs polish.

Domaine Hudson Wine Bar & Eatery   ♟♟
1314 N. Washington St., Wilmington, Del. 19801, (302) 655-9463, www.domainehudson.com
Wilmington gets into the small-plate wine-bar craze at this clubby little eatery, where a huge selection of intriguing wines by the glass is paired with ex-Dilworthtown chef Jason Barrowcliff's New American fare. The wines are worthwhile, the service is fine-tuned, and though the menu sometimes lacks focus, it's good enough to help the affordable wines shine.

Eclipse Bistro
1020 N. Union St., Wilmington, Del. 19805, (302) 658-1588; www.eclipse-bistro.com
This contemporary bistro has a colorful dining room and an open kitchen, with a fun fusion menu to match, from pulled pork–sweet potato spring rolls

to excellent wild boar tacos and a dangerous Cosmo sorbet. Entrees could be more carefully cooked.

821
821 N. Market St., Wilmington, Del. 19801, (302) 652-8821, www.restaurant821.com
Across from Wilmington's Grand Opera House, this sophisticated restaurant has been a mainstay of foie gras decadence and wood-roasted gusto for the credit-card city. There has been a change in ownership and in the kitchen since its former three-bell rating, but the overall buzz has been positive.

Hotel DuPont   ♟♟
11th and Market Sts., Wilmington, Del. 19801, (302) 594-3100, www.hoteldupont.com
The soaring, oak-clad Green Room offers unmatched classical grandeur. The service and the wine cellar are first-class, but the kitchens, while better than average, are rarely magical.

Krazy Kats   ♟♟
Rt. 100 and Rockland Rd., Montchanin, Del. 19710, (302) 888-2133, www.montchanin.com
A wacky animal motif somehow fits in at this beautifully refurbished inn with adventurous New American cooking and a fine wine list.

MORO   ♟♟♟
1307 N. Scott St., Wilmington, Del. 19806, (302) 777-1800, www.mororestaurant.net
This seductive spot in Trolley Square offers a stunning stage for talented young chef-owner Michael DiBianca. From his freewheeling New American cuisine to the awesome wine list and intimate atmosphere, this restaurant has only gotten better with time.

Marsha Brown

🛇🛇 **VERY GOOD**

MENU HIGHLIGHTS Gumbo; shrimp maison; crabcakes; blackened shad roe; cowboy rib-eye; catfish; eggplant Ophelia; Granmere's comfort custard.

WINE LIST 150-bottle list focuses on known wineries, most in California. Lower-tier wines not exciting; not much to choose from in $50-$75 mid-range.

WEEKEND NOISE Noisy

IF YOU GO Dinner M-Th 5-10 p.m.; F 5-11 p.m.; Sa 2-11 p.m.; Su 2-9 p.m.
• **V E** Entrees, $18.95-$35.95
• Smoking, bar only
• Wheelchair-accessible
• Valet parking $10

Marsha Brown is an avowed "steak house girl," which you might expect from the woman who owns the Philadelphia area's Ruth's Chris franchise.

But Brown is also a New Orleans girl. So when she embarked on a project in New Hope that would bear her own name, the old steak house formula needed a new twist: a homage to gumbo and "Granmere's comfort custard."

She isn't the first restaurateur to canonize her family's down-home flavors. But one taste of eggplant Ophelia, a classic Creole home dish renamed for her mother that mixes mashed eggplant with nuggets of shrimp and crab, and it's clear she plans to do this right.

For someone who has played the corporate sure-bet for so long, Marsha Brown's self-named restaurant is a considerably ambitious and personal gamble. But her $2.7 million investment to convert a 125-year-old stone Methodist church into her vision of a Southern grill has resulted in one of the most satisfyingly consistent restaurants New Hope has seen in a while.

The space itself is spectacular, with a great raw bar and bordello-like private room downstairs. The dining room awaits upstairs in the massive, cathedral-ceilinged former sanctuary, complete with stained-glass windows, church pew banquettes, and a towering mural of lions mauling their attackers.

Despite the theatrical ambience, the menu here is rooted in accessible comfort. Brown hasn't abandoned her steak house pedigree altogether. There is the usual assortment of a la carte chops and classic sides, and for their part, they are superior to those I've tasted at various Ruth's Chris locations over the years.

The dry-aged steaks are sublimely tender, full of the complex flavors that are the hallmark of great beef. The big cowboy rib-eye is a freewheeling, zesty wallop of meat. The New York strip is more refined, with a peppery crust that gives way to a juicy interior.

SOUTHERN STEAK HOUSE • NEW HOPE

15 S. Main St., New Hope, Pa. 18938

215-862-7044 • www.marshabrownrestaurant.com

But what really sets Marsha Brown apart is its deft New Orleans flair. The gumbo is thickened with rich, chestnut-brown roux and filled with chunks of chicken and earthy smoked Cajun andouille sausage. The seasonal blackened shad roe with alligator sausage is a true bit of Mid-Atlantic-Cajun fusion.

I didn't love the crawfish spring rolls, which were too mushy inside. The jambalaya was also disappointing, since it was really a soupy bowl of duck gumbo instead of a more rice-based dish. The shrimp maison was far more satisfying, its mustard- and anchovy-laced dressing highlighting the delicacy of the shrimp.

The blackened lollipop lamb chops were perfectly cooked, with an exotic mango chutney to quench the spice. The juicy pork chop was topped with whiskey-soaked raisins that brought boozy bursts of sweetness.

Add a number of winning sides — divine creamed spinach; giant onion rings; wonderful whipped cauliflower — and Marsha Brown is a total splurge.

The restaurant's early staff jitters have calmed over the past couple years. Much of the staff is young, but they were courteous and outgoing, and their basic advice on the big wine list was generally on target.

If I did have quibbles, they were completely forgotten by dessert, a parade of homespun New Orleans sweets from rice pudding to fruit cobbler to chocolate mousse laced with Oreos. None, though, were better than Granmere's comfort custard. This parfait glass of vanilla-tinged pudding silk was crowned with an unexpected fluff of meringue. But there was also something intriguing inside with a subtle crunch and a faintly salty tinge....

"Saltine crackers!" our waiter chimed in on cue.

Saltine crackers, indeed. The secret ingredient to Marsha Brown's success was the gamble to finally sell herself.

— OR TRY THESE —

Here are three more restaurants in or near New Hope:

The Harvest Moon Inn
🔪 🔪 🔪
1039 Old York Rd., Ringoes, N.J. 08531, (908) 806-6020
This old stone inn, set in picturesque Hunterdon County, has a talented chef-owner whose complicated but inspired modern cuisine is fueled by heirloom and local ingredients.

Inn at Phillip's Mill 🔪 🔪
2590 River Rd., New Hope, Pa. 18938, (215) 862-9919
The French country fare is better than average, but the inn's real draw is candlelit ambience that breathes romance, from the fireplace lounge to the lush patio.

Sergeantsville Inn 🔪 🔪
601 Rosemont-Ringoes Rd., Sergeantsville, N.J. 08557, (609) 397-3700
This cozy 18th-century stone inn has ambitious young owners and an adventurous fine-dining menu that ranges from game to great tomato soup. The wine list is also excellent.

Matyson

♟♟♟ EXCELLENT

MENU HIGHLIGHTS Lobster salad; duck confit with fig sticky bun; rock shrimp tempura with hamachi tartare; braised shortribs; scallops with fregola sarda; lamb loin with cannellini beans and wild mushrooms; pork chop with spaetzle; seared hamachi with chipotle sauce; cheddar burger (lunch); coconut cream pie; apple strudel; creme caramel.

BYOB

WEEKEND NOISE Noisy

IF YOU GO Lunch M-F 11:30 a.m-2:30 p.m. Dinner M-Th 5-10 p.m.; F and Sa until 11 p.m.
• **M to E** Dinner entrees, $18-$27
• Reservations highly recommended
• Most major cards
• Wheelchair-accessible — notify when reserving preferential table
• Parking discount $7 (M-Th), $9 (F-Sa) with validation, William Penn garage directly across 19th St.

The story behind Matyson has, in one respect, happily repeated itself many times. A talented young married couple does time in big-name restaurants, then strikes out on their own in a modest neighborhood space. It's a scenario that has infused fresh and accessible dining life into every corner of the region.

Matyson's story, though, also represents something a bit more rare. After a promising but somewhat uneven start, owners Matt and Sonjia Spector have made impressively steady improvements. And over the last two years, Matyson has actually blossomed from just-another-aspiring-bistro into one of the area's most exciting restaurants.

At 56 seats, this converted butcher shop north of Rittenhouse Square is slightly larger than your average BYO, but the concept is the same. The decor is low-budget but cleanly styled in a Pottery Barn kind of way, with throw pillows in a window banquette, bright food paintings, and bouquets of flowers splashing color across the earth-toned room. Some welcome sound-proofing to mute the roar that plagued the space early on was one of the couple's more important recent investments, making Matyson as fine a choice for a civilized business lunch as it is for a romantic dinner. The opening service jitters have also disappeared.

But for the Spectors, who met at Novelty (he was the chef, she was the pastry queen who seduced him with brownies), the most impressive strides have been made in the kitchen.

Matt, a veteran of Jake's and Brasserie Perrier, is a creative and sophisticated cook who eagerly crosses borders for weekday tasting menus with themes that range from Basque cuisine (scallops with chickpeas and chorizo) to Chinese New Year (red mullet in black bean sauce). And he's capable of finding just the right flavor to give an uncommon spark to an old dish, like a burst of grapefruit

NEW AMERICAN • RITTENHOUSE SQUARE
37 S. 19th St., 19103
215-564-2925 • www.matyson.com

and a brush of vanilla to warm the saffron sauce for butter-poached lobster salad.

There were moments in the beginning when Matt's kitchen only sporadically connected those creative dots. A recent visit, though, revealed a chef who has matured and focused his ideas for maximum effect. Salty shreds of duck confit arrive over a warm "sticky bun" with sweet fig and onion jam rolled inside buttery brioche. A hot cigar-shaped beignet of tempura-fried rock shrimp made a startling contrast to its cool garnish of soy-splashed hamachi tartare.

The entrees were equally exciting. A side of mustard-laced mashed potatoes had the perfect tang to enliven the hearty richness of braised beef short rib. Grilled lamb loin came with delicately crisped cannellini beans and snappy hedgehog mushrooms. The luscious sea-sweetness of big scallops played against the tangy pearls of fregola sarda couscous sauteed with chewy nuggets of pancetta. Australian hamachi showed a lighter Pacific Rim touch with colorful purees of mango and raspberry that also swirled with dusky chipotle spice.

Of course, Sonjia's meticulous updates of homey desserts may, in fact, be the best part of the meal.

I still dream of her apple strudel, an orchard of cinnamon-scented fruit wrapped in a band of sour cream pastry. But her ice creams are also superb, and her creme caramels melt on the tongue like silk. Her double-chocolate bundt cake is both airy and intense, and topped with caramelized bananas in bay-scented marsala wine.

But nothing beats her coconut cream pie. From its chocolate-lined macadamia crust to the cool custard steeped with natural coconut, everything about this pie is as good as it can be. Even the cloud of Lancaster cream on top is whipped to order for every slice. It's one happy ending I'll never get tired of.

— OR TRY THESE —

Here are three other husband-and-wife-run BYOBs:

Chloe 🔔 🔔
232 Arch St., 19106, (215) 629-2337
Chefs Dan Grimes and Mary Ann Ferrie run this homey neighborhood BYO warmed by a deftly rendered, affordable menu of international comfort food, ranging from Indonesian prawns with corn cakes to pork chops and spaetzle.

L'ANGOLO 🔔 🔔
1415 W. Porter St., 19145, (215) 389-4252
This cozy corner grotto is always jammed with diners seeking simple, deftly prepared trattoria fare, from the unusual antipasti to the wonderful desserts. Service can be a little brusque but not when the charming owners are around.

PIF 🔔 🔔 🔔
1009 S. 8th St., 19147, (215) 625-2923
David Ansill's BYO, now earning its third bell, with a market menu that elevates French bistro cooking, from crispy pig's feet to ice cream scattered with bergamot candy. Bring your best bottle.

Melograno

♟♟♟ EXCELLENT

MENU HIGHLIGHTS Grilled scallops; spinach crepe; pappardelle tartufate; potato ravioli; penne with pancetta and pomodoro; bistecca alla fiorentina; pork chops special; chicken senese; ginger creme brulee; pistachio ice cream.

BYOB

WEEKEND NOISE Deafening

IF YOU GO Dinner Tu-Sa 5-9:45 p.m.; Su 5-8:45 p.m.
• **M to E** Entrees, $14-$28
• No reservations (but accepted Tu-Th during winter months)
• Most major cards
• Wheelchair-accessible
• Street parking only

Melograno is the Italian trattoria I've been waiting for, an affordable, unpretentious corner pocket where the food actually tastes like Rome and the air is perfumed with crisped pancetta and sage.

And wait you will, sometimes more than an hour, for a seat at this 30-seat cafe, which remains after four years one of the city's hottest and most consistent little BYOBs. A passing glance at this bright nook at the corner of 22nd and Spruce — its window walls revealing a minimalist white room with an open stainless-steel kitchen and dangling strings of garden lights — evokes instant comparisons to Audrey Claire, two blocks away.

Co-owner Rosemarie Tran could well be the Vietnamese-born incarnation of Audrey Taichman, taming the eager sidewalk hordes with a coquettish smile, a reliable list of cell phone numbers to summon waiting diners, and a plate of free bruschetta.

But it is the cooking from her Italian husband, chef Gianluca Demontis, that really wins hearts. (He won over Tran when she was a student in Rome and happened to stop him on the street for directions.)

His menu isn't complicated or exotic. But Demontis can make food sing, adding personal touches to specialties from Tuscany, Umbria, and his native Rome.

Wide ribbons of homemade pappardelle arrive tangled among truffled mushrooms and toasted walnuts. Another pappardelle has a tomato sauce studded with salty olives, sweet scallops, and shrimp.

The ravioli stuffed with airy mashed potatoes and leeks are like divine Italian pierogi, shined with brown butter and sage. He finishes cooking his penne in its pancetta-tomato sauce so the pasta absorbs that smoke and spice. And his fresh fettuccine has such a perfect al dente snap that the ingredients that grace it — sweet peas, roasted cherry tomatoes, and garlicky white wine sauce — taste all the more alive.

ITALIAN TRATTORIA • FITLER SQUARE

2201 Spruce St., 19103

215-875-8116

Demontis isn't perfect, but he pulls off memorable dishes with a consistency that sets Melograno apart from most other Italian BYOBs. And the service is remarkably efficient and poised considering the lively pace and noisy tenor of this bustling room.

Of course, when you serve food this tasty, a waiter's job can be downright pleasant.

A pork chop special was a succulent, herby cut. The bistecca alla fiorentina was ridiculously delicious, the porterhouse soaking in the garlicky herb marinade of the white bean salad served with it. And the cute little quails were stuffed with figs and walnuts, then glazed with the sweet and sour darkness of marsala and pomegranate molasses. (Melograno is Italian for pomegranate.)

Some of Demontis's best dishes reveal how effective familiar ideas can be with the addition of a simple tweak: linguine with tiny whole clams in wine sauce threaded with arugula and chopped tomatoes; a simple appetizer of grilled scallops paired with an elegant, long-stemmed artichoke.

I find myself craving the chicken senese, a deconstructed chicken parmigiana that brings a delicately breaded breast wrapped in a veil of soft prosciutto and topped with milky chunks of fresh mozzarella and slices of tomato.

Demontis puts effort into the desserts, too, in the particularly oozy chocolate souffle, the rich creme brulee piqued with ginger, the crepes wrapped around wine-poached pears and sweetened goat cheese, and housemade gelato filled with salty pistachios.

But I was seduced long before the dessert. How else to explain the odd sensation of feeling lucky to snag a table in only one hour and 10 minutes? Yes, reservations would be nice. (Or try arriving early on a mid-week night.) But Melograno is one little gem worth waiting for.

— OR TRY THESE —

Here are three other Italian BYOBs near Rittenhouse Square:

Branzino 🔔 🔔
261 S. 17th St., 19103, (215) 790-0103
A touch of Old World elegance to this Italian BYO. The menu is stocked with standard dishes, but they are carefully done, from the airy gnocchi to delicate stuffed veal and the signature whole fish.

Porcini 🔔 🔔
2048 Sansom St., 19428, (215) 751-1175
A no-frills trattoria, this closet-sized BYOB remains consistent, with a well-prepared menu of homemade pastas, grilled chicken with balsamic sauce, and hospitality from the brothers Sansone.

Caffe Casta Diva 🔔 🔔
227 S. 20th St., 19103, (215) 496-9677
This storefront Italian BYO near Rittenhouse Square serves carefully wrought homemade pastas (try the spinach fettuccine with walnut pesto), interesting salads, and nice veal dishes in a tranquil room with an opera theme.

Monk's Cafe

🍺🍺 VERY GOOD

MENU HIGHLIGHTS Mussels; veal cheeks; duck spring rolls; rabbit terrine; boudin blanc; octopus; lapin a la Gueuze; burgers; key lime tart; chocolate-hazelnut tart.

BEER LIST Amazing international list of more than 200 beers, with focus on Belgian greats such as Duvel, Chimay, and Cantillon. Special treats include Achel Extra Trappist ale, Dupont Avec Les Bon Voeux saison ale, Rochefort 10, and creamy Westmalle Triple.

WEEKEND NOISE Deafening

IF YOU GO Entire menu Su-Sa 11:30 a.m.- 1 a.m. Sunday brunch 11 a.m.-5 p.m.
• **M** Entrees, $6.95-$25.95
• Reservations not accepted
• Not wheelchair-accessible
• Street parking only

Jolly Tom Peters became Sir Thomas of Monk's not long ago, a Knight of the Brewers' Mashstaff, the 400-year-old brewers guild of Belgium. But I doubt Peters's knighthood carries much sway with your typical barhoppers, who wedge their way through the vortex of sound and smoke that pulses inside Monk's Cafe only to find that, no, there is no Coors Light on tap.

Still, the more than 200 artisanal beers that Monk's has amassed since it opened in 1997 have transformed this cafe into not just a bar, but an institution.

It's a place where brewers from around the world come to debut their newest beers, and a destination where star chefs linger after their own kitchens have closed, wolfing down boudin sausage and meltingly tender veal cheeks stewed in Leffe brown ale.

The cafe's frequent special beer dinners also give guest chefs such as Daniel Stern a chance to expand the preconceived boundaries of beer cuisine with creations like bacon-wrapped rabbit with coppery Westmalle Tripel, rare medallions of venison marinated in Grottenbier herbed brown ale, or Belgian endive custard parfait with sweet brown Rochefort 10.

The Monk's that patrons usually find is a considerably more raucous place, with a beer-hall dynamic that can overwhelm the laid-back Belgian bistro. But for those who don't mind the ridiculously long wait for tables, the throbbing din, and the occasionally sticky floors, there are plenty of rewards on the menu.

Monk's is rightly renowned for its burgers, which are juicy and substantial, dressed in sweet Ardennes ham, blue cheese, and caramelized leeks, or in truffled cheese and shiitake mushrooms.

The obligatory mussels are also good, whether the simple house-style made with beer, or the "red light"

BELGIAN PUB • RITTENHOUSE SQUARE

264 S. 16th St., 19102

215-545-7005 • www.monkscafe.com

mussels flavored with fragrant Hoegaarden and spicy chile de arbol oil. Whichever you get, the crisp and lacy frites are the main attraction. They're inconsistent, but on good days, they are undeniably irresistible with their spicy mayo dip.

The menu also offers more unusual examples of beer cuisine. There is marvelous grilled octopus tenderized by hours of braising in Flemish sour ale. Spring rolls filled with duck confit that has been stewed in Hoegaarden come with a tangy sauce made of pureed cherries moistened with cherry-flavored lambic ale. The rabbit terrine, also tarted-up by cherry ale, is excellent. Gueuze, an intensely funky, sour lambic, has a natural acidity that braised the lapin a la Gueuze into one of the most marvelous rabbit stews I've ever eaten.

Cooking with other famous beers can be tricky, since their distinctive traits can disappear when the carbonation is cooked out. They sometimes add depth to a dish the way your typical wine might, such as the Madeira-like Gale's Prize Old Ale that glazed the tender rack of lamb. But if I was looking to taste the fruity tang of Dupont saison ale, I didn't find it in the trout saison, an overcooked piece of ordinary fish. Delaware's Dogfish Head Raison d'Etre ale was also wasted on the chewy pheasant.

Monk's typically has a respectable dessert tray of brought-in pastries. But really, the best dessert at Monk's is the kind you drink — an apricot lambic or a toffee-dark Westvleteren or a bottle of Christmas-spiced Stille Nacht. Or a vintage English strong ale. Or a high-octane World Wide Stout from Dogfish Head.

Whatever your brew, chances are that Monk's will pour it — if it's any good, that is. One isn't invited to join the Knights of the Brewers' Mashstaff for serving anything less.

— OR TRY THESE —

Here are three more Belgian beer destinations:

Tria 🍴🍴
123 S. 18th St., 19103, 215-972-8742
A great beer venue, this chic cafe with Italianesque nibbles has made strides since opening. Some recent visits brought more relaxed, less pretentious service and a much-improved cheese board with riper, powerful cheeses.

The Farmhouse 🍴🍴🍴
1449 Chestnut St., Emmaus, Pa. 18049, (610) 967-6225
This charming farmhouse has a world-class beer collection to accompany a menu bursting with local ingredients and vivid flavor combinations. It's a malt drinker's haven, well worth the hour-plus drive from Center City.

Eulogy
136 Chestnut St., 19106, (215) 413-1918
The Flemish pub fare has been inconsistent here. You can lay your Corsendonk on a pine box in the Coffin Room lounge, but stick with moules and frites, and any number of the 300-plus ales.

Morimoto

🗡🗡🗡 EXCELLENT

MENU HIGHLIGHTS Omakase tasting — toro tartare; yellowtail carpaccio; broiled jackfish salad; lobster sashimi; hot rock-seared abalone, kobe tartare. Sushi — needlefish; Japanese shad; otoro; uni; Morimoto sashimi; spicy tuna roll. Cooked menu — rock shrimp tempura; 10-hour pork belly; zaru soba; lobster epice; ishi yaki buri bop; yuzu panna cotta; oolong-poached pears.

WINE LIST Medium-size cellar, excellent international selection; many bottles under $50, including strong group of crisp, aromatic whites, like Spanish Albariño from Morgadio ($47), that are good match for cuisine. Very good house sakes served in neat bamboo carafes.

WEEKEND NOISE Deafening

IF YOU GO Lunch M-F 11:30 a.m.-2 p.m. Dinner M-Th 5-11 p.m.; F and Sa 5 p.m.-midnight; Su 4-10 p.m.
- **V E to U-E** Entrees, $17-$34; dinner omakase menus, $80-$120; lunch omakases, $40-$60
- Reservations strongly recommended
- Most major cards
- Wheelchair-accessible
- Valet parking $13

It was virtually inevitable from the moment he arrived that we'd eventually watch our Iron Chef return to New York City. But while the plans for a second Morimoto in Manhattan dragged on through years of delays (finally opening this winter), Masaharu Morimoto and his impresario, Stephen Starr, have honed one of the most consistently exhilirating dining experiences in the city.

The pony-tailed celebrity chef himself may be seen less frequently bounding around the color-shifting glass-topped booths posing for pictures with his Philadelphia fans. But this sleek and undulating bamboo hall remains a true paradise of sushi wonders. And it is no doubt one of the finest Japanese restaurants this side of Tokyo, as refined as the rice that gets polished from brown to white in the basement, as vivid as the house-fermented soy sauce, as pristine as the buttery pink slices of toro tuna belly that get minced into spectacular tartare.

That tartare, formed into a timbale of sweet fish sparked with garlic, caviar, and crunchy shallots, is one of the signature flourishes that can be expected on Morimoto's omakase tasting menus. Ranging from $80 to $120 for dinner, an omakase with a sushi bar view (far more intriguing than the noisy dining room) is easily among the city's ultimate eating thrills. The lunchtime version, at half the price, is a gastronomic bargain.

At a recent $60 lunch tasting, we sailed from the tartare to yellowtail carpaccio, half-raw and half-seared with a splash of hot sesame oil. A pristine salad of microgreens and yuzu vinaigrette tangled with strips of char-broiled jackfish skin and fragrant shavings of smoke-cured bonito. Crisply fried rock shrimp tossed in spicy gochu jang aioli initiated the cooked portion of the tasting, followed by a buttery hunk of Chilean steam bass steamed in sake beneath a salty smear of fermented black beans.

JAPANESE • WASHINGTON SQUARE WEST

723 Chestnut St., 19106

215-413-9070 • www.morimotorestaurant.com

A board laden with pristine sushi — supremely good otoro; brilliant orange salmon; a crunchy fan of fluke flipper wrapped around minty shiso — were the final savory highlight before a flourless chocolate cake topped with green tea ice cream.

As good as the omakase is, it offers only a glimpse of Morimoto's deep repertoire. There are also refined takes on traditional dishes, such as the restorative dobin mushi soup of shrimp and chicken that comes in a teapot, the tender 10-hour braised pork belly over rice porridge, and zaru soba noodles that arrive over ice in a bamboo basket with a gingery side of dashi broth for dipping. The meticulously crafted sushi is the region's gold standard, bolstered by the perfect texture of Morimoto's rice and the extraordinary quality of his fish, from the chantilly-sweet sea urchin to rare varieties of mackerel, needlefish, jack, and baby snapper.

The Iron Chef's reputation as an innovator, though, is also well displayed in off-beat fusion fantasies like the tempura veggies with gorgonzola sauce, the kobe beef tartare seared with hot sesame oil, and roasted wild salmon with foie gras and pineapple fried rice.

Morimoto's servers are impressively trained to deliver the meal with a blend of unpretentious knowledge and skill, whether describing the exquisite sakes or deftly searing slices of yellowtail tableside against the hot stone bowl for ishi yaki buribap.

The kitchen has particular East-West fun with dessert, giving tiramisu a tingle of wasabi, tarting panna cotta with yuzu citrus, poaching pears in oolong tea.

The evening is complete, of course, when the magnetic man himself makes the scene. But over time, Morimoto's greatness has become even more obvious when he's gone. Because even in his absence, few restaurants can match Morimoto's vibrant personality.

— OR TRY THESE —

Here are three more recommended Japanese restaurants:

Sagami
37 W. Crescent Blvd.,
Collingswood, N.J. 08108, (856) 854-9773
One of the area's finest sushi haunts, this restaurant keeps strictly to tradition, resisting overly trendy maki rolls in favor of pristine fish (and perfect tempura) served in classic, artful ways.

Teikoku 🍶🍶
5492 West Chester Pike, Newtown Square, Pa. 19073, 610-644-8270
This stylish restaurant combines Thai and Japanese flavors in a stunningly handsome space. The kitchen uses superb ingredients, from Kobe beef to fine sushi, but could be more consistent.

Hikaru
607 S. 2nd St., 19147, (215) 627-7110
Get your toro tuna fresh and your scallops alive at this Queen Village sushi standby, which recently underwent a handsome renovation, with beautiful tatami booths for an intimate group dinner.

Moro

♟♟♟ **EXCELLENT**

MENU HIGHLIGHTS Butter-braised lobster tart; littleneck clams with jalapeños, soppresatta and plums; duck confit salad; study of oysters; seared escolar; braised lamb shank with sage grits; filet mignon with Stilton-whipped potatoes; duck with gorgonzola spaetzles; venison with red wine risotto; buttermilk panna cotta with caramelized pineapple; pignoli tart.

WINE LIST Huge cellar for a new restaurant, with 700 different wines, many of them sought-after vintages at extremely fair prices. Try tropical chardonnay from California's Peter Michael or Mer Soleil, or tasty Oregon pinot noir from Adelsheim or Archery Summit.

WEEKEND NOISE Lively

IF YOU GO Dinner Tu-Sa 5-11 p.m.
 • **E** Entrees, $23-$30
 • Reservations strongly recommended
 • No smoking
 • Wheelchair-accessible
 • Street parking only

A sultry Mediterranean fruit like the Moro blood orange may not be the image most people associate with straitlaced Wilmington. But to a corporate-driven restaurant scene that can be described as snoozy, at best, the restaurant called Moro has delivered a much-needed burst of juicy excitement. Edgy, like that deep-purple citrus, but ultimately irresistible.

With its stunning decor, a talented young chef-owner in Michael DiBianca, and serious cellar, this gem has only gotten better over the last four years. Set on a tree-lined block in the Trolley Square neighborhood, Moro's jaunty copper and glass facade peeks out from between its unassuming rowhouse neighbors with a contemporary swagger. The two-story building is parceled into a series of intimate dining rooms rich with patterned fabrics in shades of burgundy, clay, and spice. Cozy circular wooden booths with textured-glass partitions are illuminated by Italian lights.

The ambience is matched by the vibrance of DiBianca's New American menu, which changes weekly, and presents a collage of powerful flavors and great ingredients together with an element of surprise. And yes, fruit is a recurring theme.

Cherries add their rich, round sweetness to the duck breast with piquant gorgonzola spaetzles, as well as a giblety venison special, which came with a luscious red wine risotto. Giant scallops with leek ravioli are sparked by a refreshing salsa of asian pear and cucumber. And the quenching burst of sweet plums added to spicy steamed littleneck clams with soppresatta sausage was an epiphany on the half shell.

Speaking of which, DiBianca also has his way with oysters. He presented them in a "study" of three preparations: topped with blood orange aspic and fried basil leaves; dolloped with tomato salsa; and deep-fried with a touch of lavender honey and nestled with a cool slice of grapefruit.

NEW AMERICAN • WILMINGTON

1307 N. Scott St., Wilmington, Del. 19806

302-777-1800 • www.mororestaurant.net

DiBianca is a Flemington native and Culinary Institute of America graduate who cooked at Wilmington's other trendsetter, 821, and, before that, at the Ajax Tavern in Aspen, Colo. And he has virtually every trendy culinary flourish in his quiver, be it fried herbs, three-way "studies," homemade mozzarella, or his unorthodox use of fruit and vanilla.

His penchant for offbeat embellishment can get the best of him, overwhelming an onion-crusted, vanilla-sauced red snapper with so much sweetness that it tasted more like a bonbon than a fish. But usually, the 29-year-old DiBianca cooks far beyond his years.

He has also assembled a massive wine cellar with 700 labels that is befitting of a much more established restaurant, with numerous California cult wines, like Peter Michael chardonnay, that are not only sold at a fraction of what they'd be in Pennsylvania, but often served by the glass.

DiBianca's cooking deserves a great wine. A lush and tropical chardonnay from California's Mer Soleil, for example, was a perfect match for the exotic seared escolar with roasted fingerling potatoes and tarragon-amaretto butter. It also worked for the zesty, lemon-oil-splashed tuna with fresh avocado salad and roasted-onion risotto.

Though the menu roams wide — ranging from creative Mediterranean wood-fired pizzas to an oddly traditional list of steak house chops — it's clear from dishes such as the whole roasted lobe of foie gras with roasted fruit, inspired by his days at 821, that DiBianca's true mission is pure indulgence.

At Moro, it continues full-throttle through mega desserts like the eight-person "gluttonous" brownie sundae. I'm partial to the more elegant confections like mascarpone cheesecake with blackberry coulis, or the low-rise pignoli tart studded with dried cherries and topped with a scoop of refreshingly tart sour cream gelato. There will be no snoozing in Wilmington, for sure, until it's gone.

— OR TRY THESE —

Here are three other suggested Wilmington restaurants:

The Chef's Table 🔔🔔
222 Delaware St., New Castle, Del. 19720, (302) 322-6367
With a contemporary menu that stresses seasonal ingredients and reasonable prices (including wine), the inn's rooms feel as much like a neighborhood spot as a destination. Green service, though, still needs polish.

Domaine Hudson Wine Bar & Eatery 🔔🔔
1314 N. Washington St., Wilmington, Del. 19801, (302) 655-9463
Wilmington gets into the small-plate wine-bar craze. A huge selection of wines by the glass is paired with New American fare. Service is fine-tuned, and the menu good enough to help affordable wines shine.

821
821 N. Market St., Wilmington, Del. 19801, (302) 652-8821
This sophisticated restaurant has been a mainstay of foie gras decadence for the credit-card city. A change in ownership and in the kitchen since its former three-bell rating has generated a positive buzz.

Moshulu

♙♙♙ **EXCELLENT**

MENU HIGHLIGHTS Scallop "Benedict"; shrimp with short-rib appetizer; crabcake; quail; foie gras grilled cheese; chorizo-crusted mahimahi; duck; lamb loin; frozen chocolate parfait.

WINE LIST Decent-sized international list with great choices, both by glass and bottle, at reasonable prices.

WEEKEND NOISE Raucous

IF YOU GO Main dining room: Lunch M-Sa 11:30 a.m.-3 p.m. Dinner M-F 5:30-10:30 p.m.; Sa 5-10:30 p.m.; Su 5-9 p.m. Sunday brunch, 11 a.m.-3 p.m. Bongo Bar: M-F 5-10:30 p.m.; Sa 11 a.m.-10:30 p.m.; Su 11 a.m.-9 p.m.
- **V E** Dinner entrees, dining room, $22-$36
- **M to E** Bongo Bar, $8-$26
- Wheelchair-accessible
- Parking lot (with complimentary valet) $10

In the three decades it has been docked in Philadelphia, the Moshulu has been a star-crossed ship. A floating fern bar when it opened in 1975, it has since been plagued by fire, then by the tragic collapse of Pier 34, where it was moored in 2000, and by a reputation as a tourist trap.

Over the past few years, though, lucky winds have blown the Moshulu's way, as the majestic tall ship was transformed under new ownership headed by Marty Grims and executive chef Ralph Fernandez into the classy riverside dining venue the city has always deserved. The result is a rare harmony of first-class food with stunning views and ambience.

Precious few restaurants feel unmistakably Philadelphian. But as I stood on the deck of the 400-foot-long vessel under a full moon, I scanned a horizon that could be no other, flanked by Center City's electric skyline on one side, and Camden's riverfront attractions on the other.

As we arrived to eat in the starboard-side dining room, all done up in South Seas rattan and palms, etched Victorian glass partitions, orchids, and rich mahogany, it was as if we'd been seated on cue: Fireworks exploded over Campbell's Field across the river and the food began to arrive.

Delicately grilled quail came tiered between goat cheese–smeared croutons and applewood-smoked bacon. Beautiful scallops posed over a tumble of buttery chanterelle mushrooms. And a sublime grilled cheese sandwich oozing pungent Swiss raclette was decadently topped with foie gras and ringed with pureed huckleberries and a scattering of spicy candied pecans.

At a recent meal, executive sous-chef Adam DeLosso's kitchen turned out a sea scallop "Benedict" layered with ham and an English muffin toasted with truffle butter, then topped with lobster hollandaise. An enormous roasted shrimp came atop tender shreds of wine-braised

NEW AMERICAN • PENN'S LANDING

Penn's Landing, 401 S. Columbus Blvd., 19106
215-923-2500 • www.moshulu.com

shortribs and a ravioli filled with brie-creamed leeks. Homemade gnocchi basked in a ragout of fresh wild mushrooms. And a luxuriously thick piece of mahimahi was crusted with moist breadcrumbs infused with chorizo sausage and ringed by saffron beurre blanc.

Such carefully crafted and beautifully presented dishes are far better than one would normally expect from such an enormous restaurant that, despite its vast improvements, still caters largely to a tourist and suburban trade. The massive 400-seat ship offers menus and settings for every sort of diner, from the ambitious fine-dining room to the more casual fare in the front lounge, or a seafood platter and ceviche at the fun Bongo Bar on the deck. On busy weekend nights, it can serve 600 meals.

But while the kitchen can handle the crowds with aplomb, the service team has been less reliable. Our most recent waitress was friendly but less than sharp, unable to make useful suggestions on the extensive wine list, and so taxed with bigger parties — the boat is a party factory — that she brought my wife the entirely wrong entree.

The correct dish was prepared relatively quickly, and the cost of the entree was properly removed from our bill — though not without some extra complaining (a manager made the petty gesture of offering only one free dessert). I would have been more annoyed, but the duck entree that eventually arrived was delicious, a sublimely tender breast served with five-spice sweet potatoes and pomegranate glaze.

A subsequently smooth visit suggests that rocky night was a fluke. Plus, all was forgiven by the time we dove into pastry chef Ernie Rich's elegant desserts, including a puff pastry apple tart topped with cardamom ice cream, and a frozen chocolate parfait shaped like a boat and wrapped in sails of chocolate lace. Even in miniature, the new Moshulu promised sweet sailing ahead.

— OR TRY THESE —

Here are three more dining spots with river views:

Rock Lobster
221 N. Columbus Blvd., 19106, (215) 627-7625
The chef changes each year at this seasonal outdoor seafood grill, so quality always varies. But stick with the basics (steamed lobster's a good bet); few terraces have a more pleasant riverside view.

La Veranda 🔔 🔔
Pier 3, N. Columbus Blvd., 19106, (215) 351-1898
A large selection of whole fish and a wood-burning Tuscan grill (also good for meats) at this pricey Italian spot. The 2-pound salt-crusted fish of the day is a treat but reports have been mixed since the most recent ownership change.

Bistro St. Tropez 🔔 🔔
Marketplace Design Center, 2400 Market St., 19103, (215) 569-9269
An upbeat bistro with a fantastic Schuylkill view, St. Tropez has a stylish, retro decor and a creative take on French cuisine at reasonable prices.

N. 3rd

🎗🎗 VERY GOOD

MENU HIGHLIGHTS Soups of the day (cream of chicken, lentil and sausage, curried carrot); calamari; spring rolls; shrimp dumplings; hamburger; fish and chips; tuna burger; wild striped bass with eggplant; pork cutlets with apples and cabbage.

WINE LIST Super value list — 10 wines at $19.95 a bottle, $6 a glass — but also quite drinkable; highlights from California's Fess Parker, bargains from Argentina and Chile. Superb craft beers, big-bottle Belgians, and excellent selection of well-priced top-shelf liquor.

WEEKEND NOISE Deafening

IF YOU GO Dinner W-Sa 5 p.m.-1 a.m.; Su-Tu 5 p.m.-midnight. Brunch Sa and Su 11 a.m.-3:30 p.m.
• **M** Entrees, $8-$19
• No reservations
• Not wheelchair-accessible — one step, front door
• Street parking only

Ever since Mark Bee turned from plumbing to the restaurant business five years ago to open N. 3rd, this hip corner space has always seemed the ideal destination for diners seeking ambitious yet affordable food in the casual comfort of a neighborhood bar. The rooms have the unmistakable funkiness of a Northern Liberties taproom, from the handcrafted ironwork windows to the myriad masks, giant bird kites, Christmas lights, and illuminated blowfish hanging from the ceiling.

As for the food, well — it took Bee four chefs in a few years to find the one who hit the mark. But now he has a good one, if Peter Dunmire sticks around. Dunmire is working to refine a gastro-pub aesthetic here that he describes as "white trash meets white tablecloth," with a menu that takes its chicken wings as seriously as its seared tuna.

The task is a stretch for most kitchens, but N. 3rd has it down, with a solid repertoire of house favorites supplemented daily by an entire page of considerably more ambitious specials.

Fried calamari have a delicate cornmeal crunch. Steamed littlenecks soak in a punchy broth perfumed with chile and cilantro. The burgers are deliciously meaty. The fish and chips, served with malt vinegar atop a folded newspaper, present two beautifully battered fillets of flaky white cod.

All of it goes down delightfully with help from N. 3rd's bar, whether you indulge in the incredibly cheap but good wine list or, as I did, in one of the better beer selections in town, with local drafts as well as Belgian classics like La Rulles and Triple Karmeliet.

N. 3rd's waitstaff is also surprisingly polished for a neighborhood restaurant, let alone a bar. Then again, that is the beauty of this gastro-pub scene, as casual spaces such as N. 3rd expand our expectations of sophistication and value.

GASTRO-PUB • NORTHERN LIBERTIES
801 N. 3rd St., 19123
215-413-3666 • www.norththird.com

Even the restaurant's daily specials never rise above $20, though, judging from the day-boat scallops or the luxuriously thick slice of wild striped bass, many could easily sell for much more in Center City. That slice of seared wild striped bass, for example, comes over meltingly soft morsels of Asian eggplant ringed by Thai curry. Crispy-skinned salmon is paired with a rich risotto studded with tender shrimp.

N. 3rd also served me the first tuna burger I actually liked — the meat diced to just the right texture, blended with the hot sparks of ginger and wasabi mayo, then served on a perfectly soft challah bun. I also loved the restaurant's variations on pork and kraut, with braised napa cabbage and tender cutlets luxuriating in a mustard-tinged jus one night, with caramelized apples glazed in Yukon Jack another.

There were a few less-inspired dishes — a rubbery halibut, boiled ribs, and a heavy croque monsieur. N. 3rd's limited desserts also lacked the thoughtful spark found in the rest of the meal.

Dunmire does manage to capture that special flair, however, in nightly soup specials that are perhaps the restaurant's most distinctive course. A soulful Hungarian goulash was ribboned with cabbage and morsels of hanger steak. Curried carrot soup balanced the richness of coconut cream and swelling Thai spice. A portobello soup touched with truffle oil found an elegant contrast to its earthiness in a goat cheese–smeared crouton.

Best of all, though, was Dunmire's cream of chicken. Filled with tender shreds of simmered meat, the herb-flecked broth was ever so lightly thickened, then crowned with two cheddar-cheese biscuits that floated like fluffy rafts atop the soup. With bowls of $5 comfort like this, I just might join the chorus at N. 3rd howling for more.

— OR TRY THESE —
Here are three other suggested gastro-pubs:

Deuce Restaurant and Bar
🍴 🍴
1040 N. 2nd St., 19123, (215) 413-3822
A slice of Old City in Northern Liberties, with corny cocktails and homemade ketchup. The kitchen tries hard to deliver affordable, creative upgrades to pub comfort food. There's been a chef change since the review.

Johnny Brenda's   🍴 🍴
1201 N. Frankford Ave., 19125, (215) 739-9684
This vintage dive in Fishtown still looks like a '60s watering hole, but local beers and tasty Mediterranean-style tapas — from grilled octopus to fried mushroom "cigars" — reflect an exciting new neighborhood spirit.

Royal Tavern
937 E. Passyunk Ave., 19147, (215) 389-6694
This South Philly spot has a menu of updated comfort food — stuffed meat loaf, great burgers, tangy short ribs, mac-n'-cheese — to go with its smoked-duck club sandwich and other creations.

Nam Phuong

🖈🖈 VERY GOOD

MENU HIGHLIGHTS Ba vi sampler platter; roast quail; papaya salad; fresh beef with lime juice; duck and bamboo-shoot soup; country beef cubes; avocado shake.

WINE LIST Small list, but stick with the Vietnamese beer, '33' Export, and fruit and bubble-tea shakes (avocado is a favorite).

WEEKEND NOISE Lively

IF YOU GO Entire menu daily, 10 a.m.-10 p.m.
  • I Entrees, $4.95-$18
  • Most major cards
  • Wheelchair-accessible
  • Free parking lot

Just surviving the parking lot is an adventure, especially on weekends, when the Asian strip malls around the Italian Market are choked with shoppers. But Nam Phuong, which happens to be at the very rear of a perpetually busy lot at 11th Street and Washington Avenue, is worth navigating the throngs.

It's one of the better restaurants to emerge on the thriving multi-ethnic corridor that is Washington Avenue, and the first big Vietnamese restaurant to really compete with Chinatown stalwarts, Vietnam and Vietnam Palace.

Named for a beloved mid-20th-century South Vietnamese empress, Nam Phuong lacks the romantic Indochine ambience of those Chinatown spots. But its 200-seat dining room is pleasant enough, with chandeliers and the requisite red velvet-draped stage.

More notable, however, is the authentic menu overseen by chef Tieng Nguyen, who, with her husband, Kim, moved Nam Phuong here a few years ago from 8th and Christian Streets.

This is classic Vietnamese fare, from spring rolls to vermicelli bowls topped with charbroiled meats. But those spring rolls are perfectly crisped and filled with the ideal measure of noodles and flavorful ground meat. The summer rolls are carefully assembled, their translucent wrappers harboring fresh shrimp, pickled daikon, and soft slices of pork.

The appetizer combo platter (ba vi) is another great way to start, with an enticing assortment of grilled nibbles to wrap inside lettuce leaves along with pickled vegetables and herbs. The grilled grape leaves filled with sesame oil–seasoned beef are another treat. Even the sugarcane-skewered shrimp balls, which elsewhere tend to be spongy, have a perfect texture, their fresh flavor sweetened with sugarcane juice. Giant soups, such as the flavorful wonton or classic steak pho, were also superb.

While most restaurants offer just one type of nuoc

VIETNAMESE • WASHINGTON AVENUE
1100-1120 Washington Ave., 19147
215-468-0410 • www.namphuongphilly.com

mam, the clear fish sauce that gives Vietnamese cuisine its sour twang, Nguyen prepares seven different versions, modulating the balance of sweet and sour and saltiness to complement each dish.

A more assertively sour nuoc mam is served with a refreshing salad of shredded green papaya laced with carrots, tender curls of shrimp, toasted peanuts, and Thai basil. A squirt of lime juice enlivens a fish sauce–splashed appetizer of thinly sliced rare beef topped with fried garlic, raw onion, and basil. For the eggless Vietnamese crepe, a crisp yellow half-moon made with flour and curried coconut milk, the nuoc mam is sweet and salty.

My favorite nuoc mam was spiked with ginger that lent an almost electric zap to a giant bowl of musky duck and bamboo shoot soup. Your taste buds need to pause a moment while they register a different key and then happily proceed. Likewise when sampling the unusual avocado shake, a creamy green whip that coats the mouth with a subtle but lasting sweetness.

There are a few dishes to miss — the doughy soft-shell crabs, for example, and the sticky-sauced crispy shrimp appetizer.

The country beef cubes, meanwhile, are fantastic, especially when you swab those tender, buttery morsels of beef in the delightfully simple sauce of lime juice, salt, and pepper. A similar dip cut through the dark sweetness of the hoisin-lacquered quail.

Nam Phuong's big portions don't leave much room for dessert. But the trendy fruit shakes with tapioca bubbles are fun. There are sweet mango and jackfruit for beginners, but the more daring might try a shake made with durian, whose famously jarring aroma will take more than a few sips for your taste buds to get used to.

Still, if you've managed to survive the parking lot, the durian shake will seem like an exotic prize worth the adventure.

— OR TRY THESE —

Here are three more Southeast Asian restaurants on the Washington Avenue corridor:

Pho 75
1122 Washington Ave., 19147, (215) 271-5866
Dive into a satisfying meal-in-a-bowl at the city's best (and most utilitarian) Vietnamese pho hall, where the menu's focus (soup, soup, and soup) is a clue to its specialty.

Pho Ha
600 Washington Ave., 19147, (215) 599-0264
For soup alone, I'm partial to nearby Pho 75. But the menu at this bustling cafe is broader (with the added bonus of bun noodles and fried springrolls), so it's a frequent take-out stop for my family.

Cafe de Laos 🔔 🔔
1117 S. 11th St., 19147, (215) 467-1546
This tidy new spot has added Thai and Laotian flavors to the diverse Asian hub around Washington Avenue. The sharp flavors of its uncommon Laotian dishes (not the more standard Thai fare) are its best draw.

Nan

🂠🂠🂠 EXCELLENT

MENU HIGHLIGHTS
Lemongrass soup; escargots; chicken sate; satay chicken; Thai noodles; roasted tamarind duck; seared duck breast with black vinegar; pad Thai; sea bass with ginger-miso sauce; lemongrass crusted salmon; sweetbreads in puff pastry; steak au poivre; venison; creme brulee; apple tart; ginger ice cream.

BYOB

WEEKEND NOISE Quiet

IF YOU GO Lunch M-F 11:30 a.m.-2:30 p.m. Dinner M-Th 5-10 p.m.; F and Sa 5-11 p.m. Closed Su.
• **M to E** Dinner entrees, $15.95-$24.95
• Reservations recommended
• Most major cards
• Wheelchair-accessible
• Street parking only

Happily cloistered in the pastel serenity of the University City restaurant called Nan, Kamol Phutlek remains one of Philadelphia's most underappreciated chefs. His graceful fusion cooking, though, has also been one of the most widely copied influences on the local restaurant scene for the past three decades.

There are at least a half dozen other restaurants across the region offering menus rooted in the union of Thai and French cooking — a notion that first took root in the early 1970s when refugee chefs fleeing Southeast Asia helped shape the city's first Restaurant Renaissance. But none I've tasted can match the elegance and effortlessness of Phutlek's skill to float from Asia to Europe and back.

He'll serve you the most convincing pad Thai one moment, its lightly dressed rice noodles fragrant with crushed peanuts, succulent shrimp, and a balanced beam of sweetness, tamarind tang, and spice. Then the next moment will bring a parcel of gorgeous French puff pastry sandwiching creamed leeks and crispy sweetbreads over a classic reduction of port.

There is a certain dated feel to Phutlek's early style of Asian fusion, in which the two traditions happily co-exist rather than always forcibly meld. But a mastery of both cuisines comes naturally to the 62-year-old Thai-born Phutlek, who was a major figure of the Restaurant Renaissance in seminal kitchens such as the Frog, La Terrasse, La Panetiere, and his own Alouette. Few chefs of any pedigree can match the stunning consistency and elegant touch of Phutlek's cooking at Nan.

As with his pad Thai, the other Thai specialties display perfect balance. The satay chicken is sublimely tender (not dry as it commonly is elsewhere), and the curried meat shines beneath a peanut glaze that is both sweet and prickly with red Thai curry. A mound of cold Thai egg

THAI-FRENCH • UNIVERSITY CITY
4000 Chestnut St., 19104
215-382-0818 • www.nanrestaurant.com

noodles are fragrant with sesame oil and palm sugar. A salad of grilled squid is tossed over greens with an irresistible vinaigrette that blends spicy soy and lime with the fresh spark of mint.

Phutlek does create true fusion with a couple of excellent Nan standbys — seared duck breast dusted with five-spice over gravy that rings with the balsamic-like Chinese black vinegar; and black bass with a classic butter sauce turned exotic by miso and ginger.

But the heart of his menu also offers some of the most reliable French cooking in town. A special of sauteed bay scallops in chive-flecked cream was simultaneously rich and light. Beautiful medallions of venison basked in a Cumberland-style gravy blushing with red wine and currant jelly. For the filet mignon, a perfect peppercorn crust ignited just the right flicker of heat without overwhelming the steak. And crispy roast duck might have been a proper Gallic bird, but the tawny sauce was sparked with tamarind instead of citrus — a gentle reminder of Phutlek's Thai perspective.

With entrees no higher than the low-$20s, Nan remains one of the better values in town, not to mention one of the few dependable fine-dining options in University City. It wouldn't hurt to do a little more with the ficus tree non-decor, which has an almost Zen-like austerity. But if Nan has a true weakness, it remains a matter of service, which is pleasant and skilled enough, but prone to lethargic bouts of inattention.

Manager Flo Mayes, however, turns out to be a fine pastry chef, and she bakes satisfying renditions of bread pudding (soft pannetone glazed with apricot), pecan tart touched with frangelico, and rich homemade ice creams flavored with espresso and candied ginger. At Nan, that subtle twinkle of exotic spice is all a diner needs.

— OR TRY THESE —

Here are three other suggested Thai-French restaurants:

Trio
2624 Brown St. (at Taney), 19130, (215) 232-8746
This pleasant Asian venture offers affordable, fairly well-prepared Thai-fusion cuisine in a pretty multi-level space. Service is friendly but uneven, and the place feels more like a welcome neighborhood haunt than a destination.

Alisa Cafe
112 Barclay Farm Shopping Ctr., Rt. 70 E., Cherry Hill, N.J. 08034, (856) 354-8807
This French-Thai BYOB has outgoing service and good ingredients, but the cooking can feel too dated and inconsistent for the price. Some improvement since opening earned its second bell.

Siri's Thai French Cuisine
2117 Rt. 70, Cherry Hill, N.J. 08002, (856) 663-6781
One of South Jersey's favorite fusion spots. I've had mixed success here; my latest lunch showed it in fine form, from tangy coconut milk–shiitake soup to excellent shrimp-stuffed salmon with pungent green curry.

Nectar

♟♟♟ EXCELLENT

MENU HIGHLIGHTS Sushi: lobster roll; steak tartare roll; marinated tuna sashimi. Cooked menu: foie gras; pot stickers; beef teriyaki with blue cheese; celery-pear soup; monkfish with curried cauliflower; striped bass with mushrooms; grilled tuna; squab with chanterelles; venison with truffled potato-fennel tart; quince strudel with cheese.

WINE LIST Well-chosen, menu-friendly wines (rieslings, pinot noirs); excellent sakes (Kaori, Karatamba); surprising selection of local and Asian beers, including Hitachino Nest and Sapporo Reserve.

WEEKEND NOISE Deafening

IF YOU GO Lunch M-F 11:30 a.m.-4:30 p.m. Dinner M-Th 5-10 p.m.; F and Sa until 11 p.m.; Su until 9 p.m. Sushi bar M-Sa 2:30 p.m. until an hour after kitchen closes; Su 5-9 p.m.
- **V E** Dinner entrees, $9-$29
- Reservations highly recommended
- Most major credit cards
- No smoking
- Wheelchair-accessible
- Free valet parking Tu-Sa

Scott Morrison can expound at length on the Tibetan themes that are woven into Nectar, which rises from Berwyn's suburban landscape like a contemporary stone palace.

From the long gold and burgundy velvet curtains modeled after monks' robes to the $250,000 silk-print Buddha that hovers over the bar with ethereal serenity, it is a restaurant conceived to evoke both a spiritual glow and urban sophistication.

The obvious similarities to Stephen Starr's Buddakan may hint at a lack of originality, but the positive comparisons are also valid. Morrison and his partners, Yangming owner Michael Wei, chef Patrick Feury, wok chef Kenny Huang, and manager Henry Chu, have created a seminal restaurant for the suburbs just as Buddakan raised the style bar for Center City.

Not only is it a multi-million beauty, from the glass-enclosed balcony to the tubular red silk lamps dangling from the soaring 19-foot ceilings. It also acts like a serious restaurant in every way.

The service has settled over the past two years into an efficient and professional groove, helping smooth diners' decisions between the perfect riesling or cold sake or navigate the choice of wild striped bass versus tea-smoked duck.

I went for the bass and wasn't disappointed, swabbing every last bit of luscious, thick fish through its truffled stew of chanterelle mushrooms. But that's what I've come to expect from Feury, the former Susanna Foo and Avenue B chef who ultimately gives Nectar its stamp of class.

There are inevitable echoes of Susanna Foo. But the cooking here is decidedly more French with Asian accents than the other way around. The influences also go beyond Chinese, to the fresh chiles and curry of Thailand, the lemongrass and fish sauce of Vietnam, and a decent sushi bar.

It's not especially exotic sushi, and the construction of

ASIAN FUSION • MAIN LINE (Chester County)
1091 Lancaster Ave., Berwyn, Pa. 19312
610-725-9000 • www.tastenectar.com

some items — like the rice-heavy tuna tasting — can be unwieldy. But the quality of the fish is undeniably pristine. It is Feury's cooking, though, that is clearly Nectar's strongest draw. Traditional pork pot stickers became memorable with the clever garnish of bittersweet kumquat skins. Skewers of marinated beef offered a tender nibble of teriyaki alongside greens tossed with creamy Harmonyville blue cheese. Nectar's reinvented crab cake was also a surprise, a deep-fried cube of tofu stuffed with creamy, spicy crab, and posed over a vibrant green basil-edamame puree. Foie gras terrine came rolled in pomegranate molasses spiced with anise. Dark oxtail consomme was filled with duck and foie gras wontons.

The entrees have been equally elegant. A Barnegat tuna steak sparkled over spicy kimchee encircled by tomato butter. Poached lobster and gigantic seared scallops benefitted from a yellow lobster bisque infused with lemongrass.

The meat dishes were also sharp. I adored the tangy garlic-sauced beef tenderloin, wok-fried with giant shrimp. Medallions of tender tea-smoked venison were luxurious next to an elegant tart filled with fennel and potatoes laced with Burgundian truffles.

Even the sides were intriguing. Smoked wild boar jazzed-up lo mein with crunchy bits of broccoli and sweet rounds of cured Chinese sausage. Morsels of purple eggplant with cubes of fried tofu and fresh black bean sauce were a vegetarian hit.

Nectar's desserts were also impressive, including fine homemade ice creams and sorbets, and a warm chocolate "Black Forest" cake served with a malted chocolate milk shake. But Nectar should drop the mini doughnuts, which are too chewy to merit the splurge. Worse, it's reminiscent of one of Buddakan's signature desserts.

I'm not sure Morrison and company want — or need — any more such comparisons. Nectar is already a venture that stands just fine on its own.

— OR TRY THESE —

Here are three other upscale suburban Asian restaurants:

MARGARET KUO'S 🗡 🗡 🗡
175 E. Lancaster Ave., Wayne, Pa. 19087, (610) 688-7200
No one presents classic Chinese cuisine with more elegance than Margaret Kuo. Superb Chinese dining on the main floor and excellent sushi upstairs. Service has become professional and polished.

Teikoku 🗡 🗡
5492 West Chester Pike, Newtown Square, Pa. 19073, (610) 644-8270
This stylish restaurant combines Thai and Japanese flavors in a stunning space. The kitchen uses superb ingredients, from Kobe beef to fine sushi, but could be more consistent.

Yangming
1051 Conestoga Rd., Bryn Mawr, Pa. 19010, (610) 527-3200
One of the trailblazers in blending East with West. It's pretty, and reliable, but my meals here rarely have the bright flavors of CinCin, its sister restaurant in Chestnut Hill.

Paradiso

♟♟ VERY GOOD

MENU HIGHLIGHTS Cannellini with shrimp; beet salad; pappardelle with wild mushrooms; gnocchi; orecchiette with sausage; rabbit cacciatore; stuffed pork chop; braised shortribs; osso bucco; tuna with shaved fennel; rice pudding with grappa cherries.

WINE LIST Excellent cellar with fair mark-ups focused on Italian bottles, but good values from Australia and California; 15 quality wines by the glass (try Conundrum, Stump Jump, Gea, or Palazzo della Torre) and fine starter collection of grappas.

WEEKEND NOISE: Lively

IF YOU GO Lunch Tu-F 11:30 a.m.-3 p.m. Dinner Tu-Th 5-10 p.m.; F and Sa 5-11 p.m.; Su 4-9 p.m.
• **E** Dinner entrees, $13.50-$24
• Reservations suggested weekends
• Wheelchair-accessible
• Free municipal lot across street

So much attention has been lavished upon our little Italian BYOBs that it would be easy to forget the pleasures of a nice wine list in a grander, more upscale space. Just take a sip of cool Conundrum at the polished granite bar and let Paradiso be a nice reminder.

This contemporary Italian is not only the centerpiece of East Passyunk Avenue's dining revival; it is also the most elegant addition to the South Philly dining scene in years.

Folding glass cafe windows adorn the double-wide storefront, just waiting to fold open onto sidewalk tables during the warm weather. Inside the spacious ground-floor room, buttercup-colored walls lined with a cranberry-striped banquette stretch back to an open kitchen where owner and chef Lynn Marie Rinaldi toils away, dabbing garlicky bruschetta with silky white-bean puree.

Her Italian-centric menu has a number of other highlights, but Paradiso's wine program is also ambitious. The list of 60-plus labels targets both quality and value, with a smart selection from Italy, California, and Australia. There are also several excellent wines by the glass, from the full-bodied red Palazzo della Torre to the off-dry nectar of Caymus Conundrum.

The service here also has a professional tone that is rare in the neighborhood. All Paradiso really lacks in its bid to become South Philadelphia's first three-bell Italian restaurant is more consistency and finesse from its kitchen. Considering this is Rinaldi's first crack at fine dining (she previously owned a cafe in the Pennsylvania Academy of the Fine Arts), her debut efforts are impressive.

Her potato gnocchi are as light as diamond-shaped clouds that melt on the tongue. Beautiful shrimp come alongside white beans glazed with olive oil and a sparkle of lemon zest. Braised meats are also a Paradiso forte. I loved the wine-infused osso bucco and the massively

CONTEMPORARY ITALIAN • SOUTH PHILADELPHIA (East Passyunk)

1627-29 E. Passyunk Ave., 19148

215-271-2066 • www.paradisophilly.com

tender shortrib that arrived still attached to an arching long bone.

Pastas were also well done, from the orecchiette cradling bits of sweet sausage and bitter broccoli rabe, to the sheer pappardelle wrapped around earthy mushrooms.

But the kitchen still has work to do. A rabbit cacciatore that I loved during the initial review was dry on a revisit. A linguine with tiny clams had marvelous flavor, but also lacked juice. Previous visits stumbled over cooking times and careless prep work, but conquering such details will be key to unlocking Paradiso's considerable potential.

There are already promising signs of Rinaldi's inspiration. Her crespelle crepes came filled with an evocative stuffing of butternut squash and ricotta cheese. The beet salad captured the root's sweet essence, playing off salty gorgonzola and snappy pine nuts. The big stuffed pork chop brought a surprisingly tender pocket of meat wrapped around fontina cheese and mortadella.

Rinaldi also showed a delicate touch with fish. A black cod came over brothy Swiss chard and white beans. A whole branzino was sublimely moist and herby. And grilled tuna stoked a Sicilian mood with salty olives, sour blood orange, and a noodle-like nest of shaved fennel.

Paradiso's desserts are adequate, but hardly as intriguing as the rest of the meal. A sweet rice pudding topped with grappa-soaked cherries might be your best bet.

Then again, why not just go straight to the collection of grappas that perch behind the bar? Or consider a nice glass of port-like recioto, and savor it slowly with a plate of artisan cheese from Paradiso's cart — an oozy wedge of Humboldt Fog, a shaving of butterscotch gouda, or the creamy piquance of gorgonzola dolce.

If that's not my idea of pure paradiso, it's getting pretty close.

— OR TRY THESE —

Here are three other restaurants on or near East Passyunk Avenue:

Trattoria Lucca
1915 E. Passyunk Ave., 19148, (215) 336-1900
At this friendly trattoria, the affordable menu is classic South Philly — veal and chicken parm, fettuccine Bolognese, tiramisu — but updated with good ingredients and an authentic touch. It has continued to improve.

Tre Scalini ✗ ✗
1533 S. 11th St., 19147, (215) 551-3870
Authentic Central Italian home cooking, from fresh pasta al la chitarra to grilled polenta with broccoli rabe and veal with mushrooms, served with familial warmth in a bi-level BYOB. The menu almost never changes.

Roselena's Coffee Bar
1623 E. Passyunk Ave., 19148, (215) 755-9697
The quirky Victorian coffee parlor offers multicourse dinners upstairs, but the main attractions are the after-dinner desserts by lamplight in the charmingly old world downstairs rooms.

¡Pasion!

♟♟♟ EXCELLENT

MENU HIGHLIGHTS Ceviches (tuna in coconut; mackerel in mint sauce; scallops in tomatillo truffle salsa); calypso calamar; arepas; guacamole Cubano; vaca frita; suckling pig with feijoada sauce; baby goat; merluza; pescado; smoked ribeye; chocolate bunuelos; la torre.

WINE LIST Growing list has excellent focus on Latin and Spanish wines, plenty to choose from around $50 or less; small reserve list drawing on the best of Chile (Montes), Argentia (Catena), and California (Paul Hobbs; Diamond Creek). Tropical cocktails a delight.

WEEKEND NOISE Noisy

IF YOU GO Dinner M-Th 5-10 p.m.; F and Sa 5-11 p.m.; Su 5-9 p.m.
• **E** Dinner entrees, $21-$45
• Reservations suggested
• Wheelchair-accessible
• Parking discount with validation about $15, Parkway's valet garage directly across 15th St. Self-park discount $10, Avenue of the Arts Garage, 15th St. between Latimer and Spruce.

If ever there were a chef who transcended the fleeting nature of food trends, it would be Guillermo Pernot.

It remains to be seen whether the vibrant Nuevo Latino cuisine he helped introduce a decade ago will have the broad and lasting impact of Asian fusion. But when he opened ¡Pasion! seven years ago, he created a restaurant that had all the hallmarks of an enduring favorite. And it still does, despite a recent slip to three bells from its perch among the city's four-bell elite.

Few dining spaces are as beautiful as ¡Pasion!, whose tented, palm-fringed room evokes a sultry tropical courtyard. The intriguing wine list offers both quality and value and an appropriate Latin accent, from great Argentine malbecs and Spanish riojas suited to Pernot's full-flavored meats, to brisk albarinos ideal for his ceviches.

Pernot is also still a creative genius who, one former ¡Pasion! sous-chef told me, "would dream his menu at night, then have us figure out how to cook it the next day."

Who else could make a hit of lamb's tongue ceviche, dress humble arepas in foie gras luxury, or even attempt a frito ice cream?

The house-special ceviches, the cured seafood fantasies Pernot literally wrote the book on, are the best way to start a meal, and reveal the scope of his creative sorcery. A recent mackerel ceviche with pureed black mint and ruby grapefruit was positively electric. Pulled strips of seared and marinated skate, sparkling with tomatillos and cachucha chiles, brought the surprise of a fried goat cheese croquette. Past ceviche wonders include scallops with truffled tomatillos, habanero-cured sturgeon and the classic raw tuna in gingered coconut milk — though they change constantly to reflect the market and chef's whims.

But it's a difficult gambit to depend on such relentless innovation. And when the basics of such an intricate enterprise begin to waver, the novelties don't always hit their mark.

NUEVO LATINO · RESTAURANT ROW

211 S. 15th St., 19102

215-875-9895 · www.pasionrestaurant.com

The service staff has always been well trained to explain and serve the menu efficiently, but has noticeably lost a shade of its energy and polish. A waiter on one of my recent visits practically ignored us for his larger party.

Pernot's intricate dishes find their vividness through sound technique, and have paid off with multi-layered fantasies like camarones and pollo (shrimp and jerked chicken over coconut rice pudding), or garlicky braised ribeye "deckle" with spicy sour cherry chimichurri. Even desserts like those chocolate-filled bunuelo beignets, or the La Torre study in lime show an exteme attention to subtle contrasts in texture, temperature, and flavor.

The cooking of late, though, hasn't been as crisp as usual, either. A lobster chupe bisque was achingly over-salted. The octopus ceviche was chewy. The plantain-wrapped shrimp (just one per appetizer) lacked crunch.

But you need only one bite of Pernot's suckling pig over crunchy chicharrones and feijoada black bean sauce, or a forkful of his rabbit and salt-cod paella in chorizo broth, to be reminded of how spectacular ¡Pasion! can be. The big smoked ribeye with moro black beans is amazing. His tender lobster a la Cubana is an elegant spin on shrimp Creole. And he's taken a similar approach to other classic Latin flavors, elevating humble staples like arepas, empanadas, or braised goat to gastronomic heights.

While such wonders haven't been quite as certain as when I left the restaurant with four bells in 2002, few restaurants still can match Pernot's vision and originality. Perhaps a new menu and new sous-chef (both started weeks after my last visit) will energize ¡Pasion! to reclaim its place at the summit.

— OR TRY THESE —

Here are three other Nuevo Latino restaurants:

Alma de Cuba 🔔 🔔
1623 Walnut St., 19103, (215) 988-1799
Douglas Rodriguez, the nation's godfather of Nuevo Latino cuisine, has paired with Stephen Starr to bring culinary fireworks, from ceviches to flaming chocolate cigars, to light this chic and dark Walnut Street space.

Isla Verde 🔔 🔔
2725 N. American St., Plaza Americana (at Lehigh Ave.), 19133, (215) 426-3600
You'll find a surprising slice of South Beach in North Philly at this sleek restaurant and lounge, where the salsa crowd pulses across the weekend dance floor and the young chef, Juan Carlos Rodriguez, delivers an upscale Nuevo Latino menu.

Cuba Libre 🔔
10 S. 2nd St., 19106, (215) 627-0666
Tropicana, The Quarter, 2801 Pacific Ave., Atlantic City, N.J. 08401, (609) 348-6700
A fantasy dining room hosts an awesome rum list, though the Nuevo and Viejo Latino cooking have been inconsistent.

Penang

🎋🎋 VERY GOOD

MENU HIGHLIGHTS Roti canai Indian pancakes; satay chicken; baby oyster omelet; poh piah Malaysian spring roll; watercress with preserved bean curd; mee siam fried noodles; nasi lemak coconut rice; mango chicken; curried beef rendang; Malaysian Buddhist; house special prawns; whole steamed striped bass in hot bean sauce; cheng-lai stingray; peanut pancake.

WINE LIST Small selection of beer is available.

WEEKEND NOISE Raucous

IF YOU GO Whole menu served every day, 11:30 a.m.-1 a.m.
- **I to M** Dinner entrees, $5.50-$21
- Reservations accepted for 6 or more
- Cash only
- Wheelchair-accessible
- Street parking only

The Malaysian oasis that is Penang opens onto Chinatown's pagoda-topped arch with a strikingly modern iron smile. Welded at the seams in a post-industrial fantasy, copper coils dangle from its ceiling. And on hot summer days, young Asian women can often be seen at the tall wok-shaped tables in Penang's cafe windows spooning through mounds of shaved ice confections that look like rainbow-colored volcanos.

Behind them, a battery of chefs work away at flaming woks in the open kitchen. And it's what emerges through their window that really makes Penang so intriguing.

The cuisine of Malaysia, the part-peninsular, part-island nation that arcs into the South China Sea below Indochina, is a unique prism that binds the lights of Chinese, Indian, and Thai cooking into its own vibrant beam of fragrant coconut milk curries and chile-spiced sweet and sour sauces.

There is some of the best satay I've tasted, moist charcoal-grilled skewers of curried chicken or beef topped with an amazingly good tamarind peanut sauce. There are soft crepe spring rolls filled with crunchy shredded jicama. And there is a wide selection of live seafood along the wall, waiting to be steamed or fried and then sent through the dining room in an aromatic cloud of lemongrass and ginger.

Watch as a chef twirls a gossamer sheet of dough above his head. This is the roti canai, a bundled veil of pancake ready for dips in a dish of coconut chicken curry. There are also, in cautionary red ink, less familiar options — fish-head casseroles, treated duck web, and crispy pork intestines — that are almost too daring not to try. More than once, Penang's efficient and outgoing staff stopped at our table to ask if we liked our dish.

Their concern was rarely necessary. The crispy, lac-

MALAYSIAN · CHINATOWN
117 N. 10th St., 19107
215-413-2531 · www.penangusa.com

quered calamari was one item that challenged my taste buds, but I've come to regard them as delicious, fishy candy. The chewy duck web salad is not for me.

Still, authentic flavors and an admirable consistency are what draw me back to Penang. The menu's range might be a bit too wide for its own good. But our adventures usually ended with pleasant discovery.

There was a perfectly fluffy omelet full of tender little oysters bound with tapioca. Sweet and tender mango chicken, meanwhile, is an ideal dish for adjusting Western palates.

Penang makes frequent use of an unusual dark sauce based on shrimp paste. It's not for everyone, but it lent the giant "house special" prawns a complexity I can only liken to an Asian mole — fermented and spicy with lemongrass and chiles, rich with dark soy and subtly sweet.

To prevent palate fatigue, it's a good idea to order a few blander flavors as ballast. The Malaysian version of pad Thai, mee siam, was excellent for this purpose, a stir-fried vermicelli that is less assertive than its Thai cousin. Coconut rice dishes like nasi lemak are a delight, as was the gently coconut curried beef rendang. Even the wonton soup is exceptional. Also, the "Malaysian Buddhist" plate of steamed vegetables and gauzy bean curd skin was so pristinely plain that it was striking, especially with a salty brown miso dip served on the side.

Few things quench the meal's adventure quite like "ABC," a curious Malaysian dessert that transforms water ice into an exotic showpiece streaked with sweet colored syrups and mounded into a peak over jellied candies, red beans, and corn. Perhaps that does not sound appealing. But you'll have to trust me here. Like so much at Penang, this is discovery dining that delivers easy rewards.

— OR TRY THESE —

Here are three other Southeast Asian restaurants in Chinatown:

Banana Leaf
1009 Arch St., 19107, (215) 592-8288
Former Penang employees have opened Chinatown's second Malaysian restaurant to rival their former haunt. The big menu is virtually identical (plus sushi), and is also well prepared, from roti to the chicken satay.

Rangoon 🔪🔪
112 N. 9th St., 19107, (215) 829-8939
A worthy Chinatown standby, still the city's only destination for Burmese food, a unique hybrid of Indian, Thai, and Chinese cuisines that brings fabulous cold ginger salad, spicy lentil patties, and thousand-layer bread.

Indonesia
1029 Race St., 19107, (215) 829-1400
Spicy peanut curries and multi-course rice table feasts of Indonesia have found a home in this friendly Chinatown dining room. Prices are reasonable, but flavors a bit bland to qualify this as a truly special Indonesian kitchen.

Pif

⚜⚜⚜ EXCELLENT

MENU HIGHLIGHTS Escargots with roasted garlic; crispy pig's feet; gravlax; foie gras terrine; skate; lamb chops; cote du boeuf; crepinettes; garlic sausage with cabbage; chestnut-stuffed quail; chicken with chanterelle cream; panna cotta with bee pollen; Coupe Lorraine (ice cream with Bergamot candy).

BYOB Bring your best bottle. The chef may want a sip.

WEEKEND NOISE Lively

IF YOU GO Dinner Su 5-9 p.m.; Tu-Th 5:30-10 p.m.; F and Sa 5-11 p.m.
- **E** Entrees, $21-$30
- Reservations strongly recommended
- Cash, check only
- Not wheelchair-accessible
- Free street parking; free municipal lot next door, 8th and Kimball Sts.

When Pif first opened five years ago, it was a southern outpost of our budding BYO boom, a charming but modest little nook dedicated to French bistro cooking and the bounty of the nearby Italian Market, where chef David Ansill shops each day for his blackboard menu.

Named for a French comic book character, Pif is still all those things. But, as the service and cozy dining room were steadily polished (including the addition of a small private room), and as Ansill continued to refine his iconoclastic French cuisine, this 40-seat corner nook has grown into one of the city's unique gastronomic destinations. It's a favorite among wine aficionados looking to uncork their cellar treasures, as well as pilgrims of the Slow Food movement on the hunt for unique and forgotten European flavors.

They will find them just beyond the sculpted snail (Slow Food's international symbol) that hangs outside Pif's front door.

The escargots are more than decoration here. Simmered to sublime tenderness in red wine then flamed in Pernod, they tumble with herb butter and bits of pancetta over heads of sweet roasted garlic in Pif's signature dish — one of just a few specialties regularly found on a menu that changes with a vengeance. A thick slice of foie gras terrine is another standard, though the accoutrements vary depending on which preserves Ansill's French-born wife, Catherine Gilbert-Ansill, happens to be making that season. It was quince jam during our fall visit, adding the ideal tartness to the creamy pink liver.

Past favorites include chicken with creamed chanterelles and crepinettes veal patties with tarragon. House-cured gravlax with creme fraiche, pickled onions and salmon caviar is another regular treat, as is the best skate wing in town, perfectly seared beneath a dusting of flour, then ringed by a brown butter tinged with balsamic vinegar.

FRENCH BISTRO BYOB • ITALIAN MARKET (South Philadelphia)

1009 S. 8th St., 19147

215-625-2923

And so, with the winged fish, snails, and fattened duck liver, concludes the conventional portion of Pif's repertoire. Ansill's true calling, it seems, is to resurrect the daring days of French offal cooking, from pig tails to pot au feu with veal tongue and marrow. Along with chef de cuisine, David Kane, he does it with an uncommon sophistication, turning some unique ingredients into memorable and accessible meals.

Crispy pig's feet, for example, aren't as scary as they sound. They're stewed, deboned, chopped, and formed into pan-fried coins that have a bacony chew and sparkle with shallots, garlic, mustard, and herbs. A rare delicacy of monkfish livers with tangy brown butter sauce are seared crisp, but have a subtle brackishness to their creamy centers that taste like foie gras from the sea.

There are moments the kitchen could ease up. The marvelous one-pound rib steak with pureed parsnips, for example, would benefit from a lighter touch of anchovy butter. In entrees that showed more restraint, you could taste every nuance of great ingredients treated with care, from the bacon-scented potato cake alongside the gorgeous lamb chops to a delicately spiced, sherry cream that napped a casserole of lobster thermidor.

Dessert follows the same aesthetic of classics with a personal tweak. Mascarpone mousse comes with homemade biscotti. A doughy turnover is saved by a filling of wonderful quince compote. And two otherwise plain desserts are transformed by the garnish of rare flavors: a Coupe Lorraine of vanilla ice cream with mirabelle eau-de-vie made by Catherine's parents in France and the startling Earl Grey crunch of Bergamot candy; and rich panna cotta is dusted with the nutty sweetness of bee pollen gathered from the hives of her parents' neighbors. Now that's putting some authentic buzz into a bistro.

— OR TRY THESE —

Here are three other sophisticated French BYOBs:

GILMORE'S 🔔🔔🔔
133 E. Gay St., West Chester, Pa. 19380, (610) 431-2800. Peter Gilmore's dining room has earned the ex-Le Bec-Fin chef a third bell, with innovative French cuisine (try the "corndog" shrimp and "candied apple" chocolate mousse) and poised service.

Taste 🔔🔔
161 W. Girard Ave., 19123, (215) 634-1008. Jovial Billy Wong has teamed with talented Jimmy Ng to open this BYO on the urban frontier. The corner room is rarely busy, but the crowds should come once word of Ng's artful French bistro cooking spreads.

BIRCHRUNVILLE STORE CAFE 🔔🔔🔔
Hollow and Flowing Spring Rds., Birchrunville, Pa. 19421, (610) 827-9002. Relaxed country charm combines with refined cooking seamlessly at this bucolic BYO. The French menu was at its game-inspired height recently, ranging from buffalo carpaccio and wild mushroom pastries to pistachio-stuffed rabbit.

Positano Coast by Aldo Lamberti

♚♚ VERY GOOD

MENU HIGHLIGHTS Mahi crudo; Positano harvest; crabcake; N.Y. strip Bolognese; short rib; osso buco; veal parmesan; snapper and chips; swordfish; stuffed rigatoni.

WINE LIST Small list focuses on affordable regional Italian wines — whites from Campania, Nero d'Avola from Sicily — many available by quartino carafe. BYOB permitted Sunday and Monday.

WEEKEND NOISE Deafening

IF YOU GO Lunch M-Sa 11 a.m.-3 p.m. Dinner M-Th 3-10 p.m.; F and Sa 3-11 p.m.; Su 12:30-10 p.m.
- **M to E** Most dinner plates, $11-$17
- Reservations suggested
- All major cards
- Wheelchair-accessible
- Valet parking every day from 5 p.m., $10 weekdays, $15 F and Sa

Aldo Lamberti, the chain-maestro of South Jersey Italian dining, would take no fewer than two redos to be taken seriously at his location in Old City. But he has struck Amalfi gold with Positano Coast. The once awkward second-floor space known as Pasta Blitz, and then Lamberti's Cucina, now hovers like a crystal box that glows a deep Mediterranean blue.

Hand-painted Italian tiles cover the columns, bar, and walls. Tented linens billow from the ceiling. Lemon trees bear fruit near the open terrace porches. And the enormous illuminated photos that span the inside walls offer images of Positano so real — its terraced villas and whitewashed chapel domes framed by cerulean waters — you can almost smell Italian sea air wafting in off Walnut Street.

Lamberti spent more than a million dollars to reinvent this room, and it is one of the most evocative spaces in town.

The new menu, however, does not take its cues from Positano, which sits along the Amalfi Coast south of Naples. Lamberti turned instead to a menu of contemporary small plates (most under $16) that redefine some Italian classics with French techniques and modern presentations. A deconstructed osso buco Milanese removed the tender meat from its bone, and posed it atop a saffron risotto ringed by orange-saffron gravy. Crisp veal parmesan is turned into a clever roulade in which the traditional toppings ooze from the inside out. Creamy, cheese-stuffed rigatoni stand on end in a pedestal edged by a green halo of parsley puree.

The petite portions and trendy raw fish crudo (Italianized ceviche) may throw the old spaghetti-and-veal crowd for a loop. But along with a wine bar that serves interesting Italian vino by the quartino (a small carafe), I find this an appealing concept for a pre-movie nibble before heading to the Ritz. And Lamberti's son, Pippo, has done a nice job executing the menu with style and consistency.

CONTEMPORARY ITALIAN SMALL PLATES · OLD CITY
212 Walnut St., 19106
215-238-0499 · www.lambertis.com

The mahi crudo is sublime, a fine mince of olive-oiled fish pressed into a round on the plate topped with a cascade of smoked mozzarella, polenta croutons, bitter radicchio, fried garlic chips, and microgreens. The daily trio of crudos was less complex, but highlighted fresh seafood in refreshing preparations. Scallops tossed with radishes and lime. Rounds of razor clams mingled with celery and chile-spiced tomatoes. Tuna made a fine showing in the tonnato, which paired both raw and cooked fish beneath a creamy vinaigrette studded with fried capers.

There were some duds, such as the stuffed calamari and deep-fried "tuna fingers" that were a strange nod to bar food.

Most of the cooking was more ambitious. The lobster salad paired beautifully with creamy avocado and refreshing citrus salad. Pan-fried crabcakes had a zesty sauce of pureed squash and mustard. A seared swordfish steak came with tender littleneck clams and garlic-scented vermouth foam.

Meats are also well presented. The braised short rib is as tender as the osso buco. A simple trio of nicely grilled lamb chops plays against salty olives and rich creamed leeks. Even the strange meat-on-meat creation called N.Y. Strip Bolognese was undeniably satisfying, the chunky short rib ragu smothering the half-size slice of juicy steak.

The in-house desserts are mundane, with the usual tiramisu and cannoli, as well as a respectable chocolate mousse. More intriguing are the great gelati brought in from Capogiro.

Perhaps there was just too little energy left for dessert after the impressive effort devoted to transforming the room, wine bar, and menu at Positano Coast. But with a start like this, Aldo Lamberti won't need another do-over to get it all right at last.

— OR TRY THESE —

Here are three other suggestions for "dinner and a movie":

Pagoda Noodle Cafe
125 Sansom Walk, 19106, (215) 928-2320
This spacious sibling of the Sang Kee duck house is a reliable destination for affordable and tasty Chinese fare, with a focus on Hong Kong-style noodles, salt-baked seafood, greens, and Peking duck.

Marathon Grill
40th and Walnut Sts., 19104, 215-222-0100
In University City, a stylish step up for this chain of lunch-centric eateries, melding Marathon's updated take on affordable grill fare, which often seems like Caesar salad fusion, with the collegiate lounge scene of the Marbar upstairs.

RITZ SEAFOOD 🗡 🗡
Ritz Center, 910 Haddonfield-Berlin Rd., Voorhees, N.J. 08043, (856) 566-6650
This diminutive BYO is a homey setting for chef Daniel Hover's innovative pan-Asian seafood, ranging from fabulous Korean calamari pancakes and tuna tartare to Thai fried devil fish.

Pumpkin

📌📌 VERY GOOD

MENU HIGHLIGHTS Gratineed radicchio; salsify gratin; scallops with beets and lentils; potato-leek soup with finnan haddie; veal cheeks; swordfish with braised fennel; pork with lentils; chocolate pot de creme; blue-cheese cake.

BYOB

WEEKEND NOISE Deafening

IF YOU GO Dinner Tu-Th 6-10 p.m.; F-Su 5:30-10 p.m.; Closed M.
- **E** Entrees, $19-$25
- Reservations recommended
- Cash only
- Wheelchair-accessible
- Validated discount parking ($7) at garage, south side, 1700 block of South St.

Candlelight beams through the cheery orange logo in Pumpkin's storefront window like a jack o'lantern ablaze. And as wine-toting customers eagerly stream into the celery-colored shoebox of its tiny dining room, it is almost impossible to fathom why it took so long for this struggling commercial strip on South Street near Graduate Hospital to land a legitimate dining draw.

It helps when a place has Pumpkin's charms. Owner Hillary Bor has managed with relatively little to transform a long-defunct deli into a room of considerable charm. Votives flicker atop railroad ties turned into shelves. Salvaged antique window frames and shutters on the walls add the suggestion of a wider world peeking in. And gauzy orange curtains soften the square room, near a banquette snuggled into a nook, and beside the open kitchen, where Bor's fiance, chef Ian Moroney, toils away.

At only 28 seats, it's hard to believe Pumpkin is actually bigger than Moroney's last work address, Little Fish in Bella Vista, where he first wooed Bor with a taste of his clam chowder. They've been calling each other "Pumpkin" ever since.

Moroney is a talented self-taught chef still at the beginning of his own exploration, and his cooking reminds me of Pif in its early days — Mediterranean-inspired fare that changes daily, with simple dishes that stand on good ingredients and the whim of clever combinations.

A simple fall gratin at a recent visit brought chunks of sweet salsify root with bitter Belgian endive and Gruyere cheese. Beautifully grilled loin of pork was sparked by mustard cream over a mound of bacony French lentils. Irish blue cheese found its way into dessert.

These dishes showed some welcome improvement from the kitchen, whose technique occasionally fell short during earlier visits (undercooked quail; over-

NEW AMERICAN BYOB • GRADUATE HOPSITAL (South Street West)
1713 South St., 19146
215-545-4448

charred branzino). The pleasant but occasionally choppy service has also gained some composure since Pumpkin's early days.

Even then, however, Moroney's instinct for satisfying flavors made this affordable little nook impossible to resist. Given his Little Fish history, it's no surprise that seafood is ably done. Seared scallops over lentils get a surprise boost from finely diced beets. And a bistro classic such as potato-leek soup bounds from the mundane to the exciting when garnished with a thick smoky morsel of finnan haddie. A thick steak of grilled swordfish was given a Moroccan touch of preserved lemons, fennel, and olive tapenade.

There have been a number of memorable meat dishes, as well. Braised veal cheeks were one unlikely star, impossibly tender nuggets of meat posed around a cream-layered pillar of potato gratin. I also loved the simply prepared grilled hanger steak, with its rich red-wine gravy and homemade frites, as well as the medallions of tender veal loin that came showered with buttered chanterelles. Only a $22 chicken breast with polenta struck me as overpriced (entrees top out at $25).

There is clearly room at Pumpkin for growth, and Moroney has added help in the kitchen to elaborate on his good ideas. Most notable among them is pastry chef James Palazzo. In the past, I've adored Pumpkin's dark chocolate pot de creme, but it has been recently replaced by an equally rich, low-rise chocolate tart. Palazzo's most intriguing invention, though, has been the curiously good blue cheese cake, a creamy timbale tinted a robin's egg hue with Irish Cashel Blue, whose mild salty tang is perfectly balanced with the sweetness of candied walnuts and a frothy port sabayon. It's a dessert course, cheese course, and after-dinner drink all in one. But at tiny Pumpkin, efficiency is more than a way of life, it's an inspiration.

— OR TRY THESE —

Here are three other worthwhile additions around West South Street:

LaVa Cafe
2100 South St., 19146, (215) 545-1508
This handsome newcomer with an Israeli touch serves authentic "upside down" Nespresso cafe au lait, panini, and flaky bureka pastries filled with feta and spinach.

Grace Tavern
2229 Grays Ferry Ave., 19146, (215) 893-9580
The team behind Monk's Cafe has taken over a classic neighborhood bar. The beer is wonderful (try Nodding Head B.P.A.), and the menu is limited but tastily focused on gourmet sausages and burgers.

Balkan Express Restaurant
🍴 🍴
2237 Grays Ferry Ave. (at 23rd and Kater Sts.), 19146, (215) 545-1255
An American luncheonette by day and a trove of Serbian comfort foods by night. Still a bit awkward, but owner Radovan Jacovic's passion for the home-smoked flavors of his native land is satisfyingly evident.

Radicchio

♟♟ VERY GOOD

MENU HIGHLIGHTS Warm buffalo mozzarella special; scamorza al Radicchio; grilled shrimp appetizer with cannellini beans; steamed mussels and clams in white sauce; insalata di campo; rigatoni amatriciana; seafood fusilli special with spicy white wine sauce; grilled chicken paillard (lunch only); veal Milanese; whole fish.

BYOB

WEEKEND NOISE Deafening

IF YOU GO Lunch M-Sa 11:45 a.m.-2:30 p.m. Dinner daily, 4-10:30 p.m.; Su 4-10 p.m.
• **M** Dinner entrees, $10-$22
• No reservations
• Most major cards
• Not wheelchair-accessible
• Street parking only

Slipped into an isolated sliver of Old City, a charming urban valley of 19th-century rowhouses bordered by the Ben Franklin Bridge to the south and interstate on-ramps to the north, the trattoria called Radicchio remained a neighborhood secret for all of a week or two.

Grilled whole Dover sole de-boned tableside for $22? Warm slices of sweet buffalo mozzarella nestled alongside grilled zucchini? Pounded veal chops topped with lemony arugula salad? Just try to keep it quiet.

The crowds pouring into this small, ochre-colored room bounded by airy floor-to-ceiling cafe windows seem divided between two camps: beautiful, leather-clad Italians seeking out an authentic taste of home, and another group that owner Luigi Basile calls "the Moore Brothers crowd," the monied wine aficionados from Society Hill and Rittenhouse Square who flock to BYOBs with bottles that often cost more than their meals.

The hand-flailing Italians are no doubt better equipped than the silver-haired wine crowd to deal with the din — though much needed sound-proofing has recently been added to the ceiling, making conversation at least possible.

But don't speak. Just eat. Because Radicchio has continued to impress since it opened four years ago with a consistency that any restaurant would envy, and an elusive authenticity to its affordable fare that has made it the equivalent of "Melograno East."

Whole fish is clearly Radicchio's calling card. And it's worth ordering just to see the fast-moving servers suddenly stop for a moment to undress a whole sole with such grace that they seem to merely unzip the browned fillets from their bones, swish the pan, and drizzle the plate with spoonfuls of balsamic-infused oil. The fish itself is exquisite, but also a great bargain considering that most restaurants would charge anywhere from $28 to $42 for the same. A plump branzino was

ITALIAN TRATTORIA BYOB • OLD CITY
4th and Wood Sts., 19106
215-627-6850 • www.radicchio-cafe.com

equally delicious, its downy white moist flesh the essence of fish.

Virtually everything at Radicchio, though, is prepared with that effortless Italian touch (Basile, who also owns Laceno Italian Grill in Voorhees, was born near Naples.) Fusilli Positano brings corkscrews glazed in toasty garlic oil scattered with lumps of sweet fresh crab. The rigatoni amatriciana is so perfectly al dente that my teeth slow halfway through before they snap the pasta tubes. It's like a textural drum roll that makes way for the taste of the sweet onion and porky pancetta cradled inside.

Veal dishes are equally good, but prepared with tender pads of meat sauteed in a light brown sauce that rings with lemons, or flattened into a pan-fried Milanese chop mounded with a salad of arugula and tomatoes. A chicken paillard at lunch was also sublimely moist, the thinly pounded white meat flashed on the grill and topped with an arugula salad ribboned with artichokes and roasted sweet peppers.

Radicchio's other great mastery is mozzarella. Thick wedges of buffalo mozzarella, flashed in the oven and served with roasted vegetables, were so sweet that each warm mouthful was like an ambrosial milk pudding. The best cheese appetizer, though, was the scamorza al Radicchio, smoked mozzarella briefly grilled and then splashed with balsamic and white wine over a bitter bed of shredded radicchio. The purple leaf also makes a clever cup for succulent grilled shrimp over creamy white beans and asparagus.

There are a handful of standard but satisfying desserts, including one of the better tiramisus in town. It comes in a little glass bowl that, when your spoon pierces its cocoa-dusted crust, reveals creamy layers of rich mascarpone and a suprisingly dark little heart of espresso soaked cake. At Radicchio, secrets like this never last long.

— OR TRY THESE —

Here are three other Italian restaurants that specialize in cooking whole fish:

Ristorante La Buca 🐟 🐟
711 Locust St., 19106, (215) 928-0556
This downstairs grotto off Washington Square is an often-forgotten hideaway with black-tie service and classic Italian specialties, such as grilled langostinos, whole fish, and ribollita, executed with perfect understatement.

Gioia Mia 🐟 🐟
2025 Sansom St., 19103, (215) 231-9895
Yet another Italian restaurant at Rittenhouse Square, but worthwhile, with authentic flavors from chef Fabrizio Pace focusing on seafood, simple pastas, and quality meats. The space is roomier than much of the competition.

Marco Polo
8080 Old York Rd., Elkins Park, Pa. 19027, (215) 782-1950
Ignore the decor and strip-mall location; this Jenkintown mainstay serves a reliably decent Italian menu specializing in whole fish. A recent change in owner has brought few obvious changes.

The Reading Terminal Market

THE READING TERMINAL MARKET IS THE KIND OF MAGICAL PLACE that would be the envy of any city, a unique intersection of people, food, commerce, and history that presents an amazingly varied snapshot of Philadelphia.

During the work week, the Market, located at 12th and Arch streets (www.readingterminalmarket.org), has a bustling lunch scene that draws the single greatest slice of the city's diverse population — many of whom are well practiced in the tricky art of snagging an empty table. Convention Center tourists, school groups, and jurors from the nearby courthouse wander about its 76 merchants in hungry wonder. Colonial re-enactors pause for a coffee break next to Market Street suits out for a casual quick lunch. Construction crews kick back with a Bud in the beer garden. And music fills the air, from amateur jazz bands jamming near the statue of Philbert the pig in the central court to the eccentric performers that can often be found howling on the upright piano in back, where the heated banter at the shoeshine stand is already a show in itself.

On weekends, the aisles are crammed with shoppers stocking up on everything from Amish scrapple to organic local produce, turkey chops, imported cheese, and flowers. During the holidays it hits a frenzied buzz that is, for me, a rite of the season's excitement.

It is in the Reading Terminal's role as retail marketplace that Philadelphia's past and present intersect most vividly. There has been a market here since 1893, when the now-defunct Reading Railroad opened its headhouse and train shed as a gateway for farmers to bring their produce to the city from Lancaster and Berks counties. The well-preserved building, a National Historic Landmark, remains one of our most vital historic sites. But keeping-up with the modern challenges of city living (tough parking) and big supermarket competition hasn't been easy.

The Market's management has made some important improvements to remain relevant, with a recently built parking structure conveniently across the street that offers reasonable $2 parking with validation. It has also begun to cull some of its weaker vendors and make a stronger effort to actively reconnect the Terminal to its waning farm market roots by encouraging stands like Kauffman's, Livingood's, and the new Fair Food Project, which distributes some of the best artisan agricultural products from the region. That bump up in quality has reaffirmed the Reading Terminal as probably the city's premier one-stop shop for great ingredients. And it has a festive old-world energy that no 21st-century market could ever duplicate.

If you're lucky to work close enough to walk to it, the Market offers an endless selection of affordable possibilities, whether you're shopping for dinner or stopping in for lunch. I've been going once every two weeks now for over eight years, and I'm still always stumped by the selection — at least for a moment.

Here are some of my highlights:

RESTAURANTS

Bassetts Ice Cream
(215) 925-4315
An old-fashioned ice cream stand dedicated to America's oldest ice cream company, a Philadelphia classic founded in 1861.

By George
(215) 829-9391
This market standby serves up excellent brick-oven pizza slices, hearty strombolis (including one filled with a cheesesteak), veggie hoagies, and tasty homemade pastas.

Carmen's Famous Italian Hoagies
(215) 592-7799
The former Rocco's remains one of the purveyors of the best traditional Italian hoagie in the Reading Terminal Market, with good crusty bread, meats freshly sliced to order and a good balance of stuffings.

Delilah's Southern Cafe
(215) 574-0929
Also at 30th Street Station, 30th and Market Streets, 19104, (215) 243-2440

Before Delilah Winder attempted nouveau soul food at her stylish Bluezette in Old City, these casual food stands set decent local benchmarks of the Southern classics.

Dienner's Bar-B-Q Chicken
(215) 925-8755
One of the city's best stops for whole roasted chickens basted to a BBQ crisp in their own fat on large rotisseries.

DiNic's
(215) 923-6175
This lunch counter is a longtime destination for a proper pork sandwich and zesty Terminal banter. However, some recently added sandwiches — juicy brisket and super slow-roasted pork shoulder dressed in spicy long hots, greens, and sharp provolone — have taken DiNic's to an entirely new lofty level.

Down Home Diner
(215) 627-1955
Jack McDavid's Reading Terminal outlet for hog-jowl soup and pan-fried chicken could be so good if the food were more consistent.

Dutch Eating Place

(215) 922-0425

Squeeze in at this perpetually busy counter for a taste of simple but authentic Pennsylvania Dutch flavors, from the pork and kraut to tasty sloppy joes. Too bad those homey apple dumplings get nuked soggy.

Fisher's Soft Pretzels and Ice Cream

(215) 592-8510

For my money, this Pennsylvania Dutch pretzel stand makes the best soft twists in the city. The "smoky cheesers" — little cheese-stuffed pigs in soft pretzel blankets — are one of my guilty pleasures. The ice cream side of the stand also makes a nice shake — especially when its Lancaster County strawberries are fresh.

Little Thai Singha Market

(215) 873-0231

This stand has become one of the tastiest spots in the market, as evidenced by reliably long lines of lunchers waiting for grilled fresh salmon,

basil chicken, and the crab dumplings topped with crunchy garlic.

Mezze

(215) 922-2707

This stylish prepared food stand from the owners of By George is one of the more recent (and more upscale) additions to the market, serving great Mediterranean sandwiches, soups, and thin-crust pizzas with unusual toppings.

Nanee's Kitchen

(267) 918-0786

This friendly lunch counter serves mildly spiced but homey renditions of Indian and Pakistani cuisine to the Reading Terminal lunch crowd. It's improved over time. And there are also delicious house-labeled mango lassi shakes bottled to go.

Olympic Gyro

(215) 629-9775

I regularly crave a warm pita sandwich filled with shaved gyro meat and tzatziki yogurt at this simple Greek lunch counter. If I'm feeling indulgent, I'll add in a spinach pie and sweet baklava.

Rib Stand

(215) 925-3155
Who knew the Pennsylvania Dutch did good pork barbecue? The tasty boneless rib sandwiches at this steady little lunch stand are proof.

Rick's Philly Steaks

(215) 925-4320
The Reading Terminal steakerie descends from the Olivieri family that founded Pat's, but the water-steamed meat is served in small, unseasoned portions. It's better than the original, but far from the best. Word is Spataro's will be making steaks at its new location across from DiNic's — it's about time the Market had a good steak.

Salumeria

(215) 592-8150
This Italian cheese and sandwich shop is a Reading Terminal favorite for hoagies, though the toppings can be a little heavy-handed. Devotees swear by the turkey hoagie.

Sang Kee Peking Duck

(215) 922-3930
This lunch-counter sibling to the classic Chinatown duck house is a great spot for wonton noodle soup, Peking duck spring rolls, and crisp General Tso's chicken.

12th Street Cantina

(215) 625-0321
Also at The Food Court Downstairs at the Bellevue, 200 S. Broad St., 19102, (215) 790-1578
A Mexican food stand that goes far beyond the expectations of a food-court vendor with authentically inspired casseroles, torta sandwiches, and salads.

RETAIL

COFFEE AND JUICE

Four Seasons Juice Bar

(215) 925-4448
Even after a hefty pork sandwich lunch at DiNic's, I always feel virtuous after a smoothie spiced with fresh ginger at this bustling juice bar counter in the Terminal. The combinations are endless, but I usually go with the special.

Old City Coffee

(215) 592-1897
Also at 221 Church St., 19106, (215) 629-9292
This local roaster and cafe is a fine place to catch your breath while touring the neighborhood galleries and sip a full-bodied cup of gourmet single-variety coffee or blends ("Balzar's" is a favorite).

PRODUCE

Fair Food Farmstand

This non-profit organized by the White Dog Cafe has been a major addition to the market, reconnecting the Reading Terminal to its roots as one of the country's original city farmers' markets (circa 1892) — a connection that had grown rather tenuous in recent years. Fair Food doesn't grow anything itself, but serves as the outlet and distributor for dozens of local artisan food producers — from exquisite Oley Valley mushrooms to Harmonyville blue cheese to raw goat's milk and double-smoked Lancaster ham. At season's peak, it's like visiting a dozen farm stands in one. This is also my Thanksgiving source for fresh, naturally raised fresh turkey. Thursday, Friday, and Saturday only.

Iovine Brothers Produce

(215) 928-4366
Iovine's offers much of the usual produce (at very good prices), but also one of the better selections of specialty produce, from salsify roots and inexpensive fresh herbs to an amazing selection of wild mushrooms.

Kauffman's Lancaster County Produce

(215) 592-1898
This Amish farm stand is one of Reading Terminal's other great local purveyors, with the sweetest little Brussels sprouts in the fall, luscious tomatoes in summer, and a year-round selection of Pennsylvania Dutch chow-chow and other pickled delights.

BAKERIES

Famous 4th Street Cookie Co.

(215) 629-5990,
www.famouscookies.com
These heavy-duty chip-laden cookies are a famous post-Terminal lunch indulgence. They're so hefty, no wonder they're weighed "by the pound."

Flying Monkey Patisserie

(215) 928-0340, www.flyingmon-keyphilly.com
One of the most recent arrivals to the Reading Terminal, this creative baker offers New American twists to old bake-sale classics, infusing layered cake with South African rooibos tea, pound cake with ginger and lime, and brownies with chile spice. The signature "monkey bars" are a nice twist on the old coconut chocolate chip brownie.

Le Bus

(215) 592-0422
Also at 135 S. 19th St., 19103, (215) 569-8299

One of the first French-style artisan bakeries in the city is still one of the finest destinations for a great crusty baguette, pain d'epi, or especially good croissants. The popular choice for good rolls in city restaurants.

Metropolitan Bakery

(215) 829-9020
Also at
262 S. 19th St., 19103, (215) 545-6655
15 S. 3rd St., at (Farmicia Restaurant), 19106, (215) 627-6274
8607 Germantown Ave, Chestnut Hill, 19118, (215) 753-9001
Ardmore Farmer's Market, Suburban Square, 19003, (610) 649-8395
4013 Walnut St., 19104, (215) 222-1492, www.metropolitanbakery.com
Philadelphia's best French-style artisan baker now has several locations, but this corner shop just south of Rittenhouse Square is always packed with locals clamouring for its crusty baguettes and yeasty rounds of sourdough miche, as well as indulgent sweets, home-made matzo (in season) and a small but fine selection of oils, cheeses, and other locally grown edibles.

Termini Brothers Bakery

(215) 629-1790, www.termini.com
One of the classic Italian bakeries of South Philadelphia has numerous locations, and is famous for its pound cakes, assorted cookies, and cannoli (which aren't as good as Isgro's, but will do just fine for a Terminal dessert).

BUTCHERS AND POULTRY

Godshall's Poultry

(215) 922-7589
My favorite stop for poultry, Godshall's also sell a local curiosity known as a turkey chop, sage-flavored turkey scrapple, as well as plump ducks and geese.

Harry G. Ochs Meats

(215) 922-6870

When you feel like splurging on steak, there's no better destination than this Terminal standby, where they'll hand-cut your order from dry-aged sides of prime-grade beef. It'll cost you, but it's worth it.

L. Halteman Family Meats

(215) 925-3206

This Pennsylvania Dutch butcher in the market is my favorite spot for locally smoked meats — turkey legs for stews, fabulous thick-cut bacon, and double-smoked pork chops that beg for a side of kraut.

Martin's Quality Meats and Sausages

(215) 629-1193

Another classic Terminal butcher, Martin isn't as fancy as Ochs, but still makes a wide variety of excellent Italian sausages.

CHEESE AND DAIRY

Downtown Cheese Shop

(215) 351-7412

Jack Morgan has a talent for bringing the most amazing and rare artisan cheeses to this excellent market stand, which has some other quality condiments, from Tuscan ham to Spanish oils and Greek yogurt.

Lancaster County Dairy

(215) 922-0425

Tucked away near the side door of the Convention Center, this is a great stop for fresh, rich Lancaster cream and buttermilk, unpasteurized goat's milk, yogurts, and fresh-squeezed juice.

COOKING SUPPLIES AND GENERAL PROVISIONS

Cookbook Stall

(215) 923-3170

The city's only bookstore (or stand, as this case may be) completely dedicated to the world of cookbooks. A great source for hard-to-find food tomes.

Foster's Gourmet Cookware

(215) 925-0950

Snug in the back corner of the Reading Terminal, Foster's crams an amazing amount of cooking gadgetry into its space — all of it cutting-edge equipment that is a tribute to owner Ken Foster's nose for the latest in urban style. If you're looking for the latest Ken Onion knife or hottest hue of BYO bag, or just a really cool cookie cutter, this is a great place to start.

The Pennsylvania General Store

(215) 592-0455

Yes, it's a handy tourist stop, but this is also where hardcore Pennsylvanians come to stock up on certain items when they're heading out of town for extended periods, from bags of Wilbur Buds (the original chocolate kiss) to extra-dark pretzels, to the sweet dried Cope's corn that is a staple at every Pennsylvania Dutch holiday table.

Rembrandt's

🎏🎏 VERY GOOD

MENU HIGHLIGHTS Wood-fired pizzas; spicy clam chowder; crabcake; cornmeal-crusted calamari; burger; spinach crepes; Parmesan-crusted pork chop; cedar-planked salmon; rack of lamb; bouillabaisse; porcini-dusted striped bass; ricotta cheesecake.

WINE LIST Small but smart selection of good wines, most under $50, including Ojai chardonnay ($48) and Seghesio zinfandel ($42). But surprisingly weak beer selection has shown some improvement.

WEEKEND NOISE Lively

IF YOU GO Lunch M-Sa 11:30 a.m.-2:30 p.m. Dinner M-Th 5:30-10 p.m.; F and Sa 5:30-11 p.m.; Su 5-9 p.m. Sunday brunch 10:30 a.m.-2:30 p.m. Bar's lunch and tavern menu Su-Th 11:30 a.m.-10 p.m.; F and Sa 11:30 a.m.-midnight. Coffee shop open M-Sa 2:30 p.m. to 10 p.m.; Su 10 a.m. to 9 p.m. Late night menu M-Th 10 p.m.-1a.m.; Sa and Su 11 p.m.-1 a.m.; Su 9 p.m.-1 a.m.
- **M** Dinner entrees, $13.95-$24.95
- Reservations recommended
- Wheelchair-accessible
- Parking on street, nearby lots (no discounts)

Rembrandt's is known for its regular tarot card nights, but had someone read the restaurant's own future when it opened in 1985, its current ambitions might have seemed improbable. After all, the 12 partners who put in $10,000 apiece to acquire the 70-year-old taproom had little experience. Most were executives at nearby SmithKline Beckman who simply wanted a watering hole of their own.

More than 20 years later, with the acquisition of three adjacent buildings and a major expansion completed, Rembrandt's has become an all-purpose neighborhood megalith. A large new kitchen is making fabulous wood-fired pizzas, an upstairs banquet room offers a view of Center City, and there's even a jam-packed bar and cafe next door.

Rembrandt's has always played its primary role of friendly neighborhood tavern well, with weekly Quizzo and live jazz, and great char-grilled burgers. In fact, most locals never eat in the white-tablecloth confines of the dining room, which caters more to crowds visiting the nearby Philadelphia Museum of Art.

That's understandable. The dining room is pleasant enough, with ornate Dutch lights hanging from the exposed wood rafters and faux windows fitted with elegant Belgian stained glass. But managing partner Jan Zarkin and chef Peter McAndrews have imposed some odd menu restrictions there to distinguish it from the bar, including when you can order a burger (at lunch only).

Such rigidity isn't reflected in the friendly service. But it does betray a restaurant trying to puff up its more upscale efforts, which, in my mind, have pulled even with (and maybe beyond) its neighbor and rival, London Grill.

The food could be more consistent. But I was constantly surprised by the creativity and quality delivered for less than $20 an entree.

McAndrews, who studied in Turin, brings a clear Italian bent to Rembrandt's wide-ranging menu. Delicate

GASTRO-PUB / CONTEMPORARY ITALIAN • FAIRMOUNT

741 N. 23rd St., 19130

215-763-2228 • www.rembrandts.com

crepes stuffed with mascarpone and spinach come folded over truffled pecorino cream. A porcini-dusted cod played against risotto darkened with tangy balsamic.

The pizzas are easily among the best in town, thin-crusted, free-form ovals that bake so quickly they must be lightly dressed. My favorite was a special called the fresca, which brought arugula and tomato salad over a cracker-thin crust topped with salty cheese.

McAndrews has a penchant for salty flavors. And he overdid it with the white clam pie. The simple margherita, though, was fabulous. And usually, McAndrews's love of big flavors was a plus.

The creamy clam chowder was pixie-dusted with homemade Old Bay. Cornmeal lent earthiness to the tender fried calamari. Richly sauced escargots tumbled over a zesty pedestal of provolone bruschetta. And a straightforward crabcake was complimented by a citrus butter sauce and apple-fennel slaw.

A good seafood-fennel broth was the backbone of a fine bouillabaisse brimming with scallops, shrimp, striped bass, clams, and mussels. Perfectly cooked rack of lamb was also a delight beneath a reduction of sweet figs.

Some of the kitchen's experiments worked, as in the cedar-planked salmon that exuded a hint of cinnamon. Sometimes (the chewy cedar-planked filet mignon) they didn't.

A couple dishes were just one small stroke away from great. A Parmesan-crusted pork chop was slightly overcooked. The garbure stew begged for more beans. The gnocchi were so light and airy that they were overwhelmed by the hearty duck ragout.

The desserts were also mixed. The creme brulee was made soggy by fruit. But I loved the maple rice pudding, the dense chocolate tart, and the light ricotta cheesecake.

Of course, the tarot card reader probably could have told me all this before I even ordered. But sometimes it's more fun to just be pleasantly surprised.

— OR TRY THESE —

London Grill 🍴🍴
2301 Fairmount Ave., 19130, (215) 978-4545
Strikes an appealing balance between neighborhood pub and fine-dining spot. Creative New American menu, ranging from fabulous burgers to Asian duck spring rolls. Some nagging inconsistencies of late nudged it off the favorites list.

Illuminare 🍴🍴
2321 Fairmount Ave., 19130, (215) 765-0202
One of the city's prettiest dining rooms — including a gorgeous back patio with trickling fountain. The Italian cuisine has varied, but showed improvement at a recent lunch. Brick-oven pizzas remain superb.

Bridgid's
726 N. 24th St., 19130, (215) 232-3232
This Fairmount nook earns points for creativity with inexpensive ingredients. But the big beer list is first-rate, from a chalice of La Chouffe to a bottle of rare, sublimely refreshing organic Foret Saison ale.

Restaurant Alba

⚜⚜ VERY GOOD

MENU HIGHLIGHTS Caprese; fish chowder; foie gras torchon; agnolotti; rabbit and gnocchi; whole daurade; hanger steak; pork Milanese; lamb and polenta; king salmon; fruit crostata; lemon meringue.

BYOB The wine-friendly menu tastes even better with a good bottle, so bring something nice, preferably Italian — a great Barbaresco or dolcetto d'Alba.

WEEKEND NOISE Noisy to Deafening

IF YOU GO Dinner Tu-Th 5:30-9 p.m.; F and Sa 5:30-10 p.m.
- **E** Entrees, $16-$28
- Reservations recommended
- Most major cards
- No smoking
- Wheelchair-accessible
- Free parking, bank lot across street or SEPTA lot behind restaurant after 4 p.m.

As the name Restaurant Alba might suggest, the Northern Italian capital of wine and truffles, where Sean Weinberg lived and worked for two years, is a major inspiration for his BYOB in downtown Malvern.

But Weinberg insists there is no strict theme here at all. The menu counts homemade pastas like spinach agnolotti and wild mushrooms and slow-braised game meats among its highlights. But Weinberg's infatuation with Mexico also makes some tasty cameos, in the shrimp-and-watermelon ceviche and in the succulent king salmon over guacamole with chile-dusted jicama slaw.

Even the 55-seat space inside this low-slung building is deliberately vague — evocative of a country auberge somewhere, but slyly obscure in provenance. The persimmon-colored walls are wrapped in glass-jar candlelight, and rows of antique shutters are stacked like bellows inside the windows. The air is strummed with both the sound of flamenco and the scent of woodsmoke from the live-fire grill in the open kitchen. And here, it seems, the truest inspirations flow from the rhythms of the seasons and local produce.

In early fall, thick rounds of luscious Caspian Pink heirloom tomatoes made perfect pedestals for the milky slices of homemade mozzarella in the Caprese salad. Tart pomegranate seeds and quince fruit scented with cardamom and clove balanced the sublime richness of his stock-simmered foie gras "torchon." A simple dessert of dough folded in over peaches made the ideal pastry frame for the roasted essence of late-season fruit.

Weinberg is a searcher in the kitchen, constantly experimenting and refining his palette as the seasonal ingredients scroll by, and the menu changes often. It's an honest process that's vulnerable to inconsistency — chewy octopus; an ill-advised mayonnaise sauce for the otherwise delicious pork chop Milanese. But Weinberg, who previously ran his parents' Rose Tattoo Cafe in

NEW AMERICAN • WESTERN SUBURBS (Chester County)
7 W. King St., Malvern, Pa. 19355
610-644-4009 • www.restaurantalba.com

Center City with his wife, Kelly, has since made tangible progress, occasionally hitting a higher level altogether. The service is already showing a seasoned grace.

On a later visit, my guests had dug deep into their cellars for some truly great bottles — and Weinberg's food responded impressively, gaining depth and greater complexity from these wines rather than meekly bowing down.

With a honeyed glass of 2001 Riesling Auslese from Germany's Wwe. Thanisch, Weinberg's torchon of foie gras was a lyric poem to liver. The braised rabbit with gnocchi and chanterelle mushrooms would have been a treat with only water to drink. But with a glass of Barbaresco from Sori Paitin, the ragu revealed more profoundly earthy wonders. Barbaresco also worked magic on the finely grilled leg of lamb with olives and polenta. Likewise for the hanger steak with potato-wild mushroom gratin — it was one of the most satisfying $19 beef entrees I've had.

Weinberg's grilled whole daurade was also superb, its luxuriously moist flesh shined with a buttery oil and nicoise olives. Two fish soup starters — one a creamed New England chowder, the other a spicy Sicilian red soup with garlic-smeared crostini — were among the best dishes on the menu.

As at so many chef-driven restaurants, the desserts are a work in progress. The meringue sandwich with lemon curd and huckleberry sauce was a lovely highlight, a delicate explosion of crunch and dark berries. And the seasonal fruit crostatas are also a good bet, as are the cheese platter and the chocolate truffle tart topped with pistachio ice cream.

That tart is just one of a few desserts brought in from the Rose Tattoo for old times' sake. Weinberg may have traveled a long way in his journey from Center City to Malvern, but he hasn't forgotten where he came from.

— OR TRY THESE —

Here are three other great Chester County BYOBs:

BIRCHRUNVILLE STORE CAFE
🍴🍴🍴

Hollow and Flowing Spring Rds., Birchrunville, Pa. 19421, (610) 827-9002. Relaxed country charm combines seamlessly with refined cooking. The French menu was at its game-inspired height recently, ranging from buffalo carpaccio and wild mushroom pastries to pistachio-stuffed rabbit.

MAJOLICA   🍴🍴🍴
258 Bridge St., Phoenixville, Pa. 19460, (610) 917-0962. Phoenixville has a gem in this bistro, one of the area's best BYOBs. Chef Andrew Deery's New American menu showcases vivid combinations of good ingredients; wife Sarah Johnson guides the pleasant staff with grace.

SOVANA BISTRO   🍴🍴🍴
The Willowdale Towne Centre, 696 Unionville Rd., Kennett Square, Pa. 19348, (610) 444-5600. Chef Nick Farrell's gem, with a bright menu — from thin-crust pizzas (with clam chowder?!), to homemade pastas, and hanger steak with three-day frites.

Ritz Seafood

♟♟ VERY GOOD

MENU HIGHLIGHTS Ahi tuna tartare with caviar; Korean calamari with scallion pancake; chicken and andouille spring roll; bacon and wasabi-wrapped shrimp; bi bim bap; devil fish; blackened tuna; hot rock kobe beef; Fuji apple bread pudding; coconut cream pie.

BYOB Bring a crisp white or a chilled sake. Very large selection of fine teas (try the sweet date Korean jujube).

WEEKEND NOISE Noisy

IF YOU GO Lunch Tu-Sa, 11:30 a.m.-2:30 p.m. Dinner Tu-Th and Su 4:30-9 p.m.; F and Sa 4:30-11 p.m.
• **M to E** Dinner entrees, $17-$35
• Reservations required weekends
• No smoking
• Wheelchair-accessible
• Free parking lot

In a South Jersey landscape traced with anonymous strip-malls, the Ritz Center in Voorhees is among the few that can legitimately lay claim to being a gourmet ghetto. It's a stroke of tasty convenience for those heading to the Ritz Sixteen. They can indulge in art films and artful dining without ever leaving the parking lot.

There's surprisingly good tandooried leg of lamb at colorful Coriander Indian bistro, refined Chinese and French menus at pretty Chez Elena Wu, and contemporary wood-oven pizzas topped with lobster at the California-style M/O Cafe. My favorite eatery on this retail strip, though, is a lively pan-Asian BYOB called Ritz Seafood.

Dressed up in silk pillows and trickling waterfall sculptures, this surprising 42-seat seafood bistro created by proprietor Gloria Cho is an oasis of tranquility. But it is the cooking of chef and co-owner Dan Hover that really distinguishes the Ritz.

Hover's wide-ranging cuisine circles through Spain for paella, to Louisiana for andouille and chicken spring rolls. But the heart of his menu is clearly most inspired by Asia, and in particular, Cho's native Korea.

Many of my favorite dishes derive a distinct Korean flavor from an earthy, almost sweet chile paste called gochu jang. It lends a spicy tingle and tenderness to the grilled calamari that tumble over the crisp scallion pancake. It jazzes-up the vinaigrette that enlivens a mixed green salad laced with strips of sushi. It also lends an authentic zap to bi bim bap, a rice bowl topped with vegetables and a fried egg that is one of my favorite Korean comfort foods.

A reconnaissance trip to Asia a few years ago is also responsible for Hover's discovery of devil fish, a delicious snapper-like fish from Malaysia he serves either whole, glazed with fabulous Thai chile-tamarind barbecue

ASIAN FUSION • SOUTH JERSEY

Ritz Center, 910 Haddonfield-Berlin Rd., Voorhees, N.J. 08043
856-566-6650 • www.ritzseafood.com

sauce, or in a sampler alongside lemony grilled escolar and Nobu-style black cod marinated in miso.

Many of Ritz's most memorable dishes have a Japanese flair. The first is Hover's ahi tartare with tobiko — a tall cylinder of minced raw tuna perched dramatically on an upended martini glass. Smeared with whipped cream and layers of wasabi-infused fish eggs, each bite of sweet fish delivers fireworks of popping textures and spice. Wasabi adds a Pacific twist to classic shrimp wrapped in horseradish and bacon. Meanwhile, the pristinely pink flesh of Hover's seared tuna edged with a crust of house-blended blackening spice is one of the best versions of the contemporary standard anywhere.

Ritz's most spectacular entree, however, isn't even seafood at all. It's a bowl of marinated raw kobe beef strips and mushrooms that diners cook themselves on a searing hot 900-degree river rock. At $35, it's by far the most expensive entree (most are low-$20s or less), but the marbled meat is so succulent it's worth it, with fun sides of kimchee, gochu jang-spiced mayo dip, and a steamer basket filled with sweet coconut rice topped with scallions.

Ritz's attentive young servers are impressive for such a casual space, at ease reciting half a dozen specials every night and advising patrons on the restaurant's list of 32 teas. Most intriguing among them is Gloria's jujube dried date tea, a mildly sweet Korean brew layered with ginger, ginseng, and pinenuts that makes a soothing segue into dessert, which you won't want to miss.

There is key lime tart with a real citrus snap, and moist bread pudding ribboned with Fuji apple caramel. But the coconut cream pie made us swoon, its cloud of custard cream and coconut-infused crust so intense with flavor, it stole the show. With a dessert like that, who needs a movie?

— OR TRY THESE —

Here are three other restaurants in or near the Ritz Plaza:

Chez Elena Wu ♟ ♟
910 Haddonfield-Berlin Rd., Voorhees, N.J. 08043, (856) 566-3222
This upscale Chinese restaurant brings a French influence to a largely Cantonese menu, with separate chefs for the superb wonton soup and the escargots.

Coriander Indian Bistro
910 Haddonfield-Berlin Rd., Voorhees, N.J. 08043, (856) 566-4546
This handsomely styled Indian has the feel of a colorful contemporary bistro, and some unusual Indian offerings, from tandooried leg of lamb to tasty yogurt and walnut soups.

The Chophouse ♟ ♟
4 S. Lakeview Dr., Gibbsboro, N.J. 08026, (856) 566-7300
South Jersey's classy local steak house from the owners of P.J. Whelihan's. This sprawling complex with a tony clientele bears little resemblance to the chain of pubs. The fare is standard steak house but well done. Friendly, professional servers take their roles seriously.

Rouge

♟♟ VERY GOOD

MENU HIGHLIGHTS Tomato gazpacho; tuna tartare; oysters; steak tartare; oxtail ravioli; gulf shrimp; veal medallion; chicken breast; scallops with pea puree and risotto; soft shell crab; striped bass with cockles; Rouge burger; carrot cake.

WINE LIST Small but well-chosen list of quality wines, many below $50 a bottle. Numerous wines by the glass and cocktails suit the cafe spirit.

WEEKEND NOISE Deafening

IF YOU GO M-Th 11:30 a.m.-11 p.m.; F 11:30 a.m.-1 a.m.; Sa 10 a.m.-1 a.m.; Su 10 a.m.- 11 p.m. Brunch Sa and Su 10 a.m.-3 p.m.
 • **E to V E** Dinner entrees, $15-$37
 • No reservations
 • Not wheelchair-accessible
 • Street parking only

If a restaurant could wear a Wonderbra, it would look exactly like Rouge.

The glamorous little cafe that launched Philadelphia's sidewalk revolution has always acted much larger than the little nook it is. And when the windows are slung wide open to the flowers and frivolity of Rittenhouse Square, and its Cosmo-sipping denizens spill out onto the sidewalk in glittery urban splendor, everything about Rouge seems more buoyant than real life, from the enormous gourmet cheeseburgers to the coiffed pooches nipping at patrons' heels to some of the best-displayed plastic surgery in the city.

The people watching alone is worthy of a meal — whether you come to bask in the dim glow of Philadelphia glamour, or observe it with a sense of humor. The diminutive bistro boutique that Neil Stein conceived in 1998 remains one of vital social touchstones in Center City. And the food isn't bad, either.

Occasionally, it can be great.

Plump sauteed shrimp pose over ivory butter crackling with crisp prosciutto and sweet dice of mango. Briny West Coast oysters sparkle on the half-shell beneath an icy frozen mignonette tart with vinegar and vodka. Steak tartare glistens with a zippy, red pepper relish. A thick steak of veal ribeye arrives beneath a fried duck egg, sunny-side up.

It's just the ilk of upscaled bistro cooking this kitchen's long string of talented young cooks has always deferred to, including current chef Matt Zagorski. But in recent years, Rouge has become more accurately known as the poshest burger joint in America. And that massive Rouge burger — made nationally famous by Oprah and GQ — is actually worth the hype. It's no wonder every other table seems to be graced with a cone of hand-cut frites and one of these 12 oz. ground beef beauties, towering two-inches high on a toasted challah bun beneath a leaf

CONTEMPORARY FRENCH BISTRO • RITTENHOUSE SQUARE

205 S. 18th St., 19103

215-732-6622

of butter lettuce, caramelized onions, and melted Gruyere cheese.

On a busy day, Rouge sears more than 200 burgers in its cast-iron pans — an astounding number for a place with only 82 seats, many of them occupied by cocktail-swirling boulevardiers who appear never to leave. And that's when the weather is warm enough to line an extra row of rattan cafe chairs along the 18th Street sidewalk.

Zagorski bristles at the mention of the burger phenomenon, hoping the restaurant can also be regarded as a serious fine-dining boite. And Rouge, crafted to flaunt every classy detail by its founder, Neil Stein (currently serving a tax fraud sabbatical in the federal penitentiary), often shows glimmers of its greater aspirations.

And yet, squeezed into the chiffon-draped and gilt-edged boudoir that is its dining room, every inconsistency becomes glaringly obvious. The servers can seem a parody of blase cool, from the waitress with the peek-a-boo g-string to the George Michaels look-alike who wore sunglasses to take our order, to the harried bartender inside Rouge's circular bar who teamed with the kitchen to miraculously botch nearly every course of an entire meal.

Ravioli were filled with cheese instead of the oxtail we'd ordered. Bison paillard was seared well done on both sides, though touted as rare. Lobster spring rolls were forgotten (until we re-ordered). Then I was given the wrong scallop entree, and it was also luke-warm. When the proper dishes were brought, they were undeniably divine, from the truffle-buttered ravioli stuffed with tender shreds of meat to the gorgeous seared scallops that floated over a green puree of peas around a saffron gold risotto.

With the windows open wide and the air abuzz with the tonic of spring, the imperfect-but-resilient world of Rouge had regained its perky demeanor again.

— OR TRY THESE —

Here are three other suggested spots with outdoor seating on 18th Street:

Tria 🍴🍴
123 S. 18th St., 19103, (215) 972-8742. A great beer venue without the usual bar grunge, this chic Rittenhouse cafe has made strides. A recent visit brought more relaxed, less pretentious service and a much-improved cheese board.

Devon Seafood Grill 🍴🍴
225 S. 18th St., 19103, (215) 546-5940. This chain-owned seafooder has a large dining room and a crowd that comes to gobble up its hot sweet biscuits and fresh seafood, though it has slipped from its impressive opening form.

Continental Mid-Town 🍴🍴
1801 Chestnut St., 19102, (215) 567-1800. Stephen Starr's three-story corner playhouse north of Rittenhouse Square is a magnet for trendy seekers of affordable global tapas and girly cocktails. The sensory overload can be irritating, but the food (especially the desserts) lends substance.

Sabrina's Cafe

♟♟ VERY GOOD

MENU HIGHLIGHTS Stuffed French toast; pumpkin-pear pancakes with blueberry compote; Mel's chicken cutlet; polenta-jalapeno fries; "ultimate" Caesar salad; coconut shrimp; calamari; stuffed meatloaf; apple pie.

BYOB

WEEKEND NOISE Lively

IF YOU GO Entire menu M-Sa 8 a.m.-10 p.m.; Su 8 a.m.-4 p.m.
- I Dinner entrees, $10.50-$16
- Dinner reservations for parties of 6 or more. Call-ahead seating available at brunch.
- Most major credit cards
- Not wheelchair-accessible
- Street parking only

A lot can go wrong with a dish like pumpkin-pear pancakes with blueberry compote or a plate of caramelized challah French toast stuffed so thick with farmer's cheese and bananas it could be mistaken for a public-works project. But there's something about brunch at Bella Vista's quirky, whimsical Sabrina's that always makes it work. Just witness the hour-long lines that form each weekend down the Christian Street sidewalk.

Those pancakes, for one, were superb. Blended with pureed pumpkin, they were fluffy and perfectly seasoned, inset with slices of snappy pear and smeared with a blueberry compote that had the texture of apple butter. The French toast brought four tall inches of puffy caramelized bread striped with vanilla maple syrup. Its stuffing of cool cheese and fruit contrasted nicely with the warm bread. A recent variation with apple-orange-molasses caramel and pecans on top was like bread pudding on steroids — but also strangely wonderful.

Owner Robert De Abreu, who named the cafe after his daughter, has allowed the restaurant to evolve organically from the short-lived Molly's Cafe (and before that, the historic Litto's Bakery, whose giant whisks have been electrified and strung into a chandelier). One holdover from the Molly's era is the vegetarian cheesesteak, a saute of seitan, cheese, and roasted hot peppers that's about as good as a veggie steak can be, even if it is a little squishy.

The "ultimate" Caesar salad is a vegetarian bonanza, a gargantuan pile of refreshing romaine ribboned with shredded radicchio, meaty portobello strips, and smoky rings of grilled eggplant. But I am especially addicted to the polenta-cheese fries, thick rails of deep-fried corn pudding flecked with spicy chiles that are certainly one of my favorite things to eat in the entire city.

Some of Sabrina's best dishes, though, are neither breakfasty nor vegetarian. The antipasto is a massive

FUNKY BRUNCH • ITALIAN MARKET

910-12 Christian St., 19147

215-574-1599 • www.sabrinascafe.com

platter of balsamic-streaked prosciutto, roasted vegetables, cheese, and olives. The Mel's chicken cutlet sandwich is one of the few items that places this cafe in its Italian Market context, a polenta-encrusted piece of meat snuggled into a crusty roll with provolone, spinach, and roasted long hot peppers. The buttermilk-soaked calamari are also among the most tender and addictive I've tasted.

The rest of Sabrina's hodgepodge menu, though, recalls the updated comfort food of Judy's Cafe rather than any of its Italian neighbors. The funky pink dining rooms feel like they belong near a college campus. The ever-changing chalkboard of dinner specials brings hearty meatloaf stuffed with something different every week, like spinach and feta cheese, and blanketed with a rich mushroom sauce. A big bowl of pasta with lemon cream was lighter than it sounded, tossed with mushrooms, prosciutto, peas, and optional plump shrimp.

A lot of restaurants botch coconut shrimp, but Sabrina's does it well, frying the giant shrimp in a crust over cool soba noodles dusted with chunky mango salsa like tropical confetti.

This kitchen has a nice touch with seafood in general. A recent salmon burger was moist and tasty, with caramelized onions and horseradish cream. A sesame-crusted tuna steak was perfectly rare, paired with sweet-and-sour butter infused with orange and fennel.

I loved the pumpkin cheesecake baked by De Abreu's mother-in-law, which was far more satisfying than the showy bombe of brought-in fluff called "chocolate bash." But traditional desserts have never been Sabrina's strength, which might seem odd for a place working out of a well-known old bakery. Then again, after a plate of stuffed French toast as big and complex and ever changing as the Italian Market itself, who really needs dessert?

— OR TRY THESE —

Here are three more funky brunch-centric restaurants:

Morning Glory Diner 𝕏 𝕏
735 S. 10th St., 19147, (215) 413-3999. Updated macaroni and other homemade diner favorites, from hefty frittatas to delicious sandwiches, are served in this hip, flower-decked eatery. Over recent years, however, the kitchen and energy here have begun to slip.

Carman's Country Kitchen
1301 S. 11th St., 19147, (215) 339-9613. A quirky corner luncheonette with unlikely but tasty brunch experiments, from waffles with rutabaga and chestnuts to peppery home-made corned beef hash with orange-horseradish mayo. The kitchen's spiciest dish, though, is chef-owner, Carman Luntzel.

Honey's Sit 'n Eat
800 N. 4th St., 19123, (215) 925-1150. The neighborhood's answer to South Philly's Sabrina's for the hipster brunch. The menu is an appealing blend of Jewish (matzo balls), Southern (chicken-fried steak), and Lancaster produce, but the flavors aren't always quite in register.

Sang Kee Asian Bistro

🪓🪓 VERY GOOD

MENU HIGHLIGHTS Peking duck rolls; watercress dumplings; crispy flounder with honey walnuts; shrimp dumpling noodle soup; ginger scallion noodle; sea scallop with XO chile sauce; stuffed eggplant in black bean sauce; beef with eggplant (or green beans) in garlic sauce; General Tso's chicken.

BYOB Bring a crisp Asian lager, like Tsingtao, or '33 Export.

WEEKEND NOISE Deafening

IF YOU GO Entire menu Su-Th 11:30 a.m.-9:30 p.m.; F and Sa until 10:30 p.m.
- **I to M** Entrees, $7-$18
- Reservations limited to 25 percent of dining room capacity; call well in advance
- Most major cards
- No smoking
- Wheelchair-accessible

I've often wondered where, on that long journey from Grandpa's chop suey house to the ersatz mall glamour of P.F. Chang's, does there exist the ideal model of a suburban Chinese restaurant. Something stylish that doesn't pander. Something authentic, minus a duck tongue or two.

To my delight, it resides in Wynnewood at Michael Chow's Sang Kee Asian Bistro.

Chow isn't the first to offer serious Chinese cooking in the suburbs (think Margaret Kuo and fusiony Yangming). What distinguishes Sang Kee is that it is still very much the casual neighborhood haunt, where entrees top out at $18. But the contemporary room has been sleekly outfitted for the 21st century, with an open kitchen wrapped in a cool slate tile bar inset with tiny flat-screen TVs, plush Asian carpets on the wall, and a phalanx of dark-suited young women who run the seating chart with no-nonsense efficiency.

The menu is pretty much straight from Chinatown, with the Hong Kong–style duck house standards that have made Chow's original Sang Kee a favorite for 25 years. Except for the frequent hour-long waits for tables, I actually prefer this one to the original downtown.

The Peking duck, of course, gets top billing, and the honey-crisped bird has a fine balance of tender meat, five-spice crunch, and a thin layer of fat that lathers the meat like cream. I prefer it as an appetizer, rather than an entree, wrapped into pancakes with scallions and hoisin.

Room should definitely be saved for Sang Kee's many other specialties — especially the noodles.

Special thread-thin "wonton" egg noodles anchor the excellent soups, the meal-sized bowls brimming with golden chicken broth and everything from roast pork and Chinese broccoli to dumplings. I particularly loved the thin-skin pork wontons, as well as the subtly different shrimp dumplings. The kitchen uses softer noodles for its

CHINESE NOODLE AND DUCK HOUSE • MAIN LINE

339 E. Lancaster Ave., Wynnewood, Pa. 19096

610-658-0618 • www.sangkeeasianbistro.com

stir-fries, of which I'm partial to the simple ginger and scallion noodles, which tingle with fresh ginger.

Sang Kee isn't perfect. Those TVs are a tacky distraction. And the menu has weak spots, too. Many of the Shanghai juice buns (also known as soup dumplings) had already been pierced and lost their juice. The beggar's purse "money bags" filled with crab were fishy.

Usually, though, this kitchen delivered with a consistency and care that has been lagging at the original the past few years.

Succulent sea scallops come inside a bewitching XO chile sauce of deeply caramelized spices, bacon, and dried seafood seasoning. The stuffed eggplant in black bean sauce is a study of textures — the deep-fried crunch of its crust giving way to pulpy Asian eggplant and springy pork stuffing.

Tender chicken is glazed in dark soy and oyster sauce, then showered with the crunch of snipped chive blossoms. Heat-blistered green beans and super-soft flank steak bask in a sauce that blinks with fresh garlic. A superb General Tso's chicken is rife with sweeter roasted garlic. The watercress dumplings are fabulous precisely because they are not stuffed with too much raw garlic — you taste the vibrant greens.

The five-spice salt-baked shrimp offers one example of Chow tweaking a Chinatown standard for the suburbs — the shells conveniently removed before frying. He has also replaced the usual pork with chicken in a number of standard recipes. But the real compromises are few. You can even, on occasion, spot a downtown delicacy such as steamed giant oysters.

Also true to its roots is the slim dessert selection: only fried bananas and ice cream. But stroll just one door up the strip mall to the soft-serve Carvel, and Sang Kee's new suburban sibling suddenly feels complete.

— OR TRY THESE —

Here are three other suggested Main Line Chinese restaurants:

MARGARET KUO'S 🔺🔺🔺
175 E. Lancaster Ave., Wayne, Pa. 19087, (610) 688-7200
No one presents classic Chinese cuisine with more elegance than Margaret Kuo. Superb Chinese dining on the main floor and excellent sushi upstairs. Service has become professional and polished.

Hunan
47 E. Lancaster Ave., Ardmore, Pa. 19003, (610) 642-3050
This cozy standby, threatened by Ardmore's downtown plans, has a much-deserved, devoted following. The cooking is fairly traditional, and some dishes are better than others, but the hot-and-sour soup and the scallion pancakes are particularly good.

Yangming
1051 Conestoga Rd., Bryn Mawr, Pa. 19010, (610) 527-3200
One of the trailblazers in blending East with West. It's pretty, and reliable, but my meals here rarely have the bright flavors of CinCin, its sister restaurant in Chestnut Hill.

Sansom Street Oyster House

🎗🎗 VERY GOOD

MENU HIGHLIGHTS Raw bar: oysters, clams, smoked mussels, u-peel shrimp; Ipswich clams; oysters Rockefeller; popcorn shrimp; snapper soup; fried oysters with chicken salad; baked clams; crab Imperial; apple Brown Betty.

WINE LIST Modest in size but affordable and well chosen with a focus on crisp, seafood-friendly whites. Good beers (including "oyster stout") on tap.

WEEKEND NOISE Lively

IF YOU GO Lunch M-Sa 11 a.m.-3:30 p.m. Dinner M-Sa 3:30-10 p.m.; Su 3 -9 p.m.
- **M** Entrees, $16.95-$42
- Reservations accepted for parties of 5 or more
- Wheelchair-accessible
- Parking, with $5 discount validation, $11 after 5 p.m., Central Parking garages (15th and Sansom Sts.; 1616 Sansom St.)

The Sansom Street Oyster House is the old leather shoe of local restaurants. It isn't flashy or tailored to the latest trends, and it sometimes feels a little scruffy around the edges. But nothing is quite as familiar — or as Philadelphian — as settling into a wooden banquette beneath a wall of antique seafood plates and tucking into a lunch of fried oysters with chicken salad.

If the brash steak houses of Broad Street are where the power lunchers go to see-and-be-seen, this old-fashioned seafoodery on out-of-the-way Sansom Street is where the blue blazer crowd comes to eat its snapper soup in relative peace. They'll perch at the granite raw bar near the front cafe windows for a solo meal on the half-shell, or wade back into the low-key wooden elegance of the dining rooms where the real business gets done amongst the prosecutors and defense attorneys, the City Hall pols, and Market Street moguls. Many of them frequent the oyster house at least once a week for oyster crackers dabbed with horseradish followed by a taste of classic Philadelphia cookery that has become increasingly hard to find.

In fact, Sansom Street, the descendant of the Kelly's on Mole Street that was founded in 1901, almost single-handedly saved the oyster house tradition from extinction while its once abundant competition dwindled to a pair of uninspired Bookbinder restaurants that pandered to the tourist trade and eventually closed. (The more famous of the two, Old Original Bookbinder's on 2nd Street, made an impressive return in 2005.)

Sansom remains one of the most reliable raw bars in town, and oyster lovers who can't decide among salty Chincoteagues, sweet Kumamotos or briny European Belons can have them all with the seafood plateau. For $24, a wide tray comes piled with oysters, raw cherrystones, u-peel shrimp, crab legs, and marvelous house-smoked mussels. A forkful of the vinegary cabbage pepper hash will wipe your palate clean.

CLASSIC FISH HOUSE • AVENUE OF THE ARTS DISTRICT
1516 Sansom St., 19102
215-567-7683 • www.sansomoysters.com

Many of the cooked seafood appetizers were just as good. The oysters Rockefeller are among the best I've found outside of New Orleans, the silky green pureed topping tinted with anise Pernod. Fried rock shrimp with an Old Bay–scented crust and bleu cheese dip are impossible to stop eating.

The crab imperial was a wonder of old-time richness, mounded into clamshells and dressed to the original Kelly's recipe, a creamy glaze of sherry, dry mustard, and mayo. The wonderful soups are ladled from the cauldrons of history. The rusty brown snapper, deeply flavored yet delicately spiced, turned nutty with a splash of sherry. The oyster stews are milky and intense.

Sansom Street occasionally has had modern pretensions under current owner, Cary Neff, who first arrived several years ago as the chef tasked with freshening-up the menu. This hasn't always been successful. A trendy appetizer of grilled octopus was so badly charred, it was inedible. Simply broiled bluefish or shad is occasionally cooked to careless oblivion.

A special po-boy sandwich piled high with deep-fried popcorn shrimp, meanwhile, was a true hit (not to mention more authentic than the menu's skimpy sauteed version). Then again, one can always count on the deep fryer here — especially for the great Southern-fried oysters and chicken salad, the classic oyster house combination that sounds strange but is uncannily good.

The desserts are also relics of a bygone era, but the hot apple brown Betty spiced with nutmeg and clove, the sweet potato pie, and the eggy creme caramels are decidedly homemade. Sansom Street's best flavors may be far from chic. But they fit the Philadelphian appetite with such tastily broken-in comfort, they would be impossible to replace.

— OR TRY THESE —

Here are three other classic places to get a bowl of snapper soup:

Old Original Bookbinders
♟ ♟
125 Walnut St., 19106, (215) 925-7027
With a serious chef and a pleasant attitude, the new Bookie's is a vast improvement. Service can still be hard-sell, but this once-neglected classic is relevant again.

The Blue Bell Inn
601 Skippack Pike, Blue Bell, Pa. 19422, (215) 646-2010
Some contemporary flavors have appeared here of late, but this classic remains one of the region's best old-time establishments, with staples such as fried oysters, creamed spinach, great wines, and butter-fried prime steaks.

Snockey's Oyster and Crab House
1020 S. 2nd St., 19147, (215) 339-9578
This 90-plus-year-old Queen Village institution has kept its dining room bright and spiffy, and maintained workmanlike renditions of classics such as snapper soup and milky oyster stew.

Savona

✦✦✦ EXCELLENT

MENU HIGHLIGHTS Lobster "lasagne"; quail; hamachi and tuna; Dover sole; black trumpets-crusted elk; branzino a la plancha; cheese cart; coconut-macadamia cake with pineapple carpaccio; pistachio, pear, mascarpone tart; souffle.

WINE LIST One of the area's outstanding wine programs, with a huge international cellar of 900 high-quality wines ranging from multiple-vintage selections of big-name labels to quirky, lesser-known gems. Even better, the staff knows how to serve, with expert guidance from the sommelier, beautiful glassware, and dramatic tableside decanting.

WEEKEND NOISE Lively to Noisy

IF YOU GO Dinner Monday-Saturday, 5:30-10 p.m. Sunday brunch, 11 a.m.-2 p.m.
• **U-E** Entrees, $31-$42
• Reservations highly suggested
• Wheelchair-accessible
• Free valet parking

Losing a star chef can be a nerve-racking trial for any restaurant. But those that survive the trial are often stronger institutions for the experience.

This may well be the case for Savona, the elegant Main Line seafood palace that saw its celebrated French chef, Dominique Filoni, leave nearly two years ago. Any worries I had were put at ease at my last visit. The kitchen, now under long-time Savona veteran, Andrew Masciangelo, has barely missed a beat, turning out the copper pans bearing buttery Dover sole and mini-lobster lasagnes that helped earn its gastronomic reputation to begin with.

Of course, a restaurant as beautiful as Savona always has ambience as insurance. The bones of this fieldstone building erected in 1765, the former home of patriot Aaron Burr, are historic Pennsylvania. But the atmosphere inside is pure South of France, from the terra-cotta-colored walls, glassed-in porch, and tiled floors to the lilting French accents of the enthusiastic young staff that greets you in the gorgeous dining room.

Savona's greatest asset, though, is undoubtedly in its cellar — a collection that is among the finest in Pennsylvania both in breadth (900 selections) and quality. It's stocked with vertical selections of big name labels, from premier cru Bordeaux and Burgundy's Romanee-Conti to California stars like Araujo, Opus One, Dalla Valle, and Harlan. But there are also plenty of New World finds (like the exotic Terrunyo sauvignon blanc from Chile, $57), and bargains from less-hyped corners of France, Italy, and Spain.

Whatever your budget, Savona's outgoing staff will not let you go thirsty, and they'll serve it with crystal pomp. Masciangelo's kitchen also does its part, from the first frothy sip of complimentary soup offered as an amuse-bouch to the inventive Riviera-inspired cuisine that followed.

CONTEMPORARY FRENCH SEAFOOD • MAIN LINE

100 Old Gulph Rd., Gulph Mills, Pa., 19428
610-520-1200 • www.savonarestaurant.com

The restaurant's existing culinary repertoire has been maintained with aplomb. The whole Dover sole is still the height of opulence, lavished tableside with spoonfuls of lemony butter studded with English peas, scallions, asparagus tips, artichokes, and pine nuts. The meat is so fresh you can taste the English Channel. A roasted quail is stuffed with truffled farro and squash and posed over a warm celery root-potato puree. A stunning loin of rare cervena elk is ringed by a dark crust of black trumpet mushrooms, and served alongside melted Brussels sprouts and a creamy salsify gratin — an earthy winter combination that was perfect with a glass of gamey South African pinotage.

What is not yet apparent, however, is whether Masciangelo has the touch to finally push Savona to the next lofty level. An appetizer trio of crab would have been spectacular had one of the three preparations not been a boring salad (the pot de creme and crab-and-honeydew napoleon were the winners.) The lobster in the lasagne could have been more delicately cooked. A beautiful dish of seared branzino should also have made more of its sparsely painted pistachio sauce.

And yet, there were already so many qualities alongside the branzino to admire, from the bittersweet endive marmalade to the ragout of thick-necked asparagus and woodsy blue-foot mushrooms, that I could hardly complain.

Likewise, I was less bothered that our young server didn't know his taleggio from his robiola simply because the substance of Savona's cheese cart was so magnificent, from the pungent Epoisses to the creamy bleu de Basque. As the cart's Christofle glass dome rolled open to release the exquisite fragrance of cheese, it was clear that Savona — even without its star — is still a restaurant that knows how to serve true luxury in a flattering light.

— OR TRY THESE —

Here are three other French-centric Main Line fine-dining restaurants:

Georges'
Spread Eagle Village, 503 W. Lancaster Ave., Wayne, Pa. 19087, (610) 964-2588. Georges Perrier's gorgeous French farmhouse has struggled to find the perfect identity. A recent lunch with Dijon mustard-Gruyere pizza, spectacular Iberian clams, and refined-but-unstuffy service felt just right.

Pond/Bistro Cassis
🍴 🍴 🍴
175 King of Prussia Rd., Radnor, Pa. 19087, (610) 293-9411. A garden-trimmed restaurant and bistro complex. The new owner and chef, Abde Dahrouch, formerly at Taquet, has added a French tone (with Moroccan accents) to a dual-venue concept — a welcome and sophisticated addition.

Restaurant Taquet 🍴 🍴
Wayne Hotel, 139 E. Lancaster Ave., Wayne, Pa. 19087, (610) 687-5005. Clark Gilbert, the new chef at this posh perch, has updated the French cuisine, but the place still exudes Main Line stuffiness.

Siam Lotus

🛆🛆 **VERY GOOD**

MENU HIGHLIGHTS Coconut chicken soup; chicken satay; mieng caam; grilled beef salad; glass-noodle salad; spicy stir-fried rice (kow pahd kee mow); masamun curry; duck in red curry; mahi-mahi in yellow curry; whole red snapper in garlic-chile sauce; chu chee cod special; taro pearls; cream caramel.

WINE LIST Small but smart selection of affordable, Thai-friendly wines, including quenchingly off-dry whites (try Valentin Fleur Vouvray) and spicy, plush reds (Kenwood "Old Vines" zinfandel and Chile's Errazuriz cabernet sauvignon).

WEEKEND NOISE Lively

IF YOU GO Lunch Tu-F 11:30 a.m.-2:30 p.m. Dinner Tu-Th 5:30-10:30 p.m.; F and Sa 5:30-11 p.m. Closed M.
• **M** Dinner entrees: $11.95-$18.95
• Most major cards
• Wheelchair-accessible
• Street parking only

Siam Lotus blooms like an exotic flower against the gunmetal-gray backdrop of Spring Garden Street's Firearms Row, pulsing from its narrow storefront with tones of fuchsia and celadon.

The surprising rebirth of this old Thai favorite, which sat empty for a decade, has brought the restaurant's original chef, Chavivun "Pat" Nanakorn, back from an extended stay in Bangkok.

New owner Hiran Yii, meanwhile, has given the room a contemporary look, with a gorgeous multicolored quilt of Thai silk cushions that lines one wall, and elegant orchids on the other above a long leather banquette.

Philadelphia's Thai scene is relatively weak. But Nanakorn presents the cuisine in all of its dynamic vibrance: a creamy kiss of coconut here, a twang of tamarind there, a zip of lime, and a confident kick of chile spice. Just take one bite of the mieng caam, which mounds a swirl of dodging flavors on a leaf, from toasted shredded coconut to dried shrimp, peanuts, and a tiny wedge of lime tipped with a crimson dot of incendiary chile.

Much of the menu is classic, and some of the standards aren't stellar, including the overly sweet pad Thai and the consistently overcooked squid.

But mostly, dishes were carefully crafted. The chicken satay was sublimely tender, permeated with a char-grilled curry marinade and tamarind peanut sauce. The coconut tom ka kai (chicken soup) was not just sweet, but gingery with galangal and sour with lime.

The nam tok is a plate of crunchy greens with sliced filet mignon whose grilled edges are crusty with a garlicky oyster-sauce marinade. A spicy sour vinaigrette with crumbled ground pork made the cold glass noodles in the sai roong impossible to stop eating. At lunch, the "drunkard-style" stir-fried rice with shrimp and basil

THAI • SPRING GARDEN (Near Loft District, Northern Liberties)
931 Spring Garden St., 19123
215-769-2031 • www.siamlotuscuisine.com

called kow pahd kee mow has an assertive heat basil that is said to cure a hangover.

Dinner offers a selection of coconut milk–based curry entrees made with chicken, beef, or shrimp. I loved all of them, from the mild, creamy masamun studded with roasted peanuts and potatoes to the panang with kefir lime and the fiery red curry with sliced roast duck and juicy cubes of sweet pineapple.

Nanakorn's greatest talent, though, is with seafood. Her deep-fried snapper, or pla lad prig, is a thing of beauty, its red tail curling over a mysteriously complex dark slick of hot-and-sour garlic sauce. The milder chu chee cod tops a pair of crisp fillets with a red chile cream ribboned with fried lime leaf.

But if it's authentic Thai spice you want, Siam Lotus's chile-packed pahd talay seafood medley has enough firepower to give the neighboring gun shop a run for its money. Diners should be licensed and registered before being allowed to eat it.

I opted for a three-chile-pepper heat rating (out of five), since our perky, 90-pound Thai waitress recommended it. ("I don't really like it spicy," she explained.)

The brimming bowl of seafood was so thick with peppers and garlic that its capsaicin tickled my nose with a pleasurable pain. At first. Soon, every mussel, shrimp, and morsel of crab felt like another coal stoking a roaring furnace.

Yes, the Thais know spicy. But they also know sweet. And the sticky rice dessert with coconut custard brings soothing comfort to the taste buds. The taro pearls bobbing in warm coconut milk are another delight. Yet nothing cools the chile fire quite like a scoop of homemade ice cream, snowy with tender chunks of coconut or floral with the tropical pulp of jackfruit that is as exotic as Siam Lotus itself.

— OR TRY THESE —

Here are three more recommended Thai restaurants.

NAN ✗✗✗
4000 Chestnut St., 19104, (215) 382-0818
Venerable chef Kamol Phutlek produces an elegant amalgam of French and Thai cooking at this affordable and consistent University City BYOB. East meets West in sublime Shaxi-vinegared duck breast and lemongrass-crusted fish.

Chabaa Thai Bistro
4371 Main St., 19127, (215) 483-1979
This handsome, multi-level eatery brings a taste of Thai to Manayunk. The food is on the mild side, but the fabric-draped two-story space is a serene haven for a spot of pad Thai.

Little Thai Singha Market
Reading Terminal Market, 12th and Arch Sts., 19107 (215) 873-0231
One of the tastiest spots in the Market, as evidenced by lunchers waiting for grilled fresh salmon, basil chicken, and the crab dumplings topped with crunchy garlic.

Southwark

♟♟♟ EXCELLENT

MENU HIGHLIGHTS Veal cheeks with fettuccine; fried smelts; sweetbreads with blue cheese bread pudding; smoked pork chop with cranberry beans; cornmeal-crusted trout; roasted chicken; venison chop with risotto; pot de creme; ice cream.

WINE LIST Small but excellent list of affordable, interesting wines. Try porty but dry Portuguese Touriga Nacional from Quinta dos Roques ($54) or balanced chardonnay from California's Clos Julien ($28).

WEEKEND NOISE Noisy to Deafening

IF YOU GO Dinner Tu-Th 5:30-10:30 p.m.; F and Sa 5:30-11:30 p.m. Sunday brunch 11 a.m.-5 p.m.
- **M** Dinner entrees, $15-$20
- Reservations suggested
- Not wheelchair-accessible
- Street parking only

A lot of young chefs would eagerly tout their experiences at places like Django or Striped Bass. But Sheri Waide leaves little doubt in her impressive head-chef debut at Southwark, the Queen Village bistro and bar she opened in 2004 with husband, Kip, that she aims to forge a culinary identity of her own.

Braised veal cheeks are the city's bistro dish of the moment, but Waide distinguishes hers with ribbons of homemade fettuccine so fine, they leaven the hearty dish. Classic sweetbreads find new life with a savory blue-cheese bread pudding and a sweet and sour swirl of raspberry gastrique. Even the humble roast chicken gets a make-over in what may be the city's first roasted-to-order bird. After 25 minutes in the extra-hot oven Waide affectionately refers to as "Hell," the chicken that emerges is pure poultry heaven, a succulent half-bird bronzed to a citrus-butter crisp over a ragout of fresh favas and baby artichokes.

Sophisticated yet affordable dishes like these are the key to Southwark's success because it was, first and foremost, created for a neighborhood crowd. After all, it was named for the historic township off Philadelphia's southern border that became known as Queen Village.

There is a gentle formality to the service and slender white linen–tabled dining room, but the spirit is that of a casual bistro. A large rear patio where al fresco dining blooms on warmer days is particularly appealing. But the heart of the restaurant clearly beats in the tavern where Kip, a longtime bartender in town, built himself a magnetic, mahogany-colored bar.

The menu also appears to have been built with the bar in mind, with a long list of appetizers perfect for nibbling, from the cloud-like conch fritters to a meal-sized farmhouse platter laden with pungent cheeses, house-made pheasant terrine, and venison carpaccio. Tempura fried

NEW AMERICAN • QUEEN VILLAGE
701 S. 4th St., 19147
215-238-1888

smelts glazed with anchovy brown butter melt in the mouth like little fish puffs. You'll be asking for more beer after a plate of these, and the bar is well stocked with quality brews.

The wine list is also well done, a thoughtful collection of reasonably priced yet intriguing wines. The deep red Touriga Nacional from Quinta dos Roques in Portugal was a perfect match for some of the lustier entrees, such as the juniper-scented venison chop over parsnip risotto or the grilled lamb with fig jus.

You'll need a softer red for the pork loin, a massive double-smoked chop that was amazingly tender and moist. Posed atop baked cranberry beans beneath a bewitching barbecue glaze, it looked like a blue-ribbon champ at the county fair.

If Waide has a weakness, it would seem to be her soups, which rely too much on cream. The homemade bread would be even better served warm. I found a few shells in the crab salad.

Otherwise, I loved her food, especially fish that highlighted a delicate touch. Corn-crusted trout fillets scented with cumin and chile came over a potato salad tossed in herbed oil with green beans. Baked cod dolloped with hazelnut-basil pesto and set over wild rice with celery root was both earthy and light.

Waide's efforts also pay off at dessert. The chocolate pot de creme is as rich as they come. The crisped mini-bundt cake gets a drenching of rum-soaked pineapple.

Best of all, though, were the daily homemade ice creams. It could be silky dark chocolate studded with brandied cherries, stewed local strawberries in white Godiva chocolate, or apricot with almonds. With such unexpected new fugues of frozen whimsy emerging nightly, who wants a chef to dwell on her past?

— OR TRY THESE —

Here are three other suggested Queen Village–Bella Vista restaurants:

Beau Monde 🔪🔪
624 S. 6th St., 19147, (215) 592-0656
Paris in South Philly. Authentic Breton-style buckwheat crepes are served in one of the city's most beautiful rooms, or there's sidewalk seating. Lean toward the simpler offerings, but just being there is half the pleasure.

Hikaru
607 S. 2nd St., 19147, (215) 627-7110
Get your toro tuna fresh and your scallops alive at this reliable Queen Village sushi stand-by, which recently underwent a handsome renovation, with beautiful tatami booths for an intimate group dinner.

Little Fish 🔪🔪
600 Catharine St., 19147, (215) 413-3464
This Queen Village BYOB is one of the smallest nooks in town, but the daily-changing seafood menu has creative, wide-ranging flavors and great desserts.

Sovalo

♟♟♟ EXCELLENT

MENU HIGHLIGHTS
Mushroom minestra; polenta
with Taleggio fonduta; robiola
and artichoke bruschetta; black
trumpet ravioli; torcetti with
lamb; chicken tortelli with
peas; slow-roasted pork; striped
bass with anchovy-chile vinaigrette; pancetta-wrapped
chicken; chocolate torta; ricotta
fritters; homemade sorbetti
and gelati.

WINE LIST Smart, mid-sized
selection of well-priced
Californian and Italian wines,
with a dozen good choices by
the glass. Burgess merlot a
delight ($38), as was Napa san-
giovese from Seghesio ($48).
BYOB on Mondays.

WEEKEND NOISE Raucous

IF YOU GO Dinner M-Th 5:30-
9:30 p.m.; F and Sa 5-11 p.m.
• **M** Entrees, $13.95 to $21.95
• Reservations recommended
• Most major cards
• Wheelchair-accessible
• Street parking only

True, the gritty urban landscape of Northern Liberties is a far cry from the bucolic Napa Valley, where Joseph and Karey Scarpone met while working at Tra Vigne, the famed Italian restaurant in St. Helena. But it wouldn't take long for Philly's hottest neighborhood to work its urban spell on the Scarpones, he of Drexel Hill, she of Thousand Oaks, California.

It helps that they settled on the neighborhood's most elegant space, the handsome cafe-windowed facade and golden-toned dining rooms of the short-lived Pigalle.

"I was looking for that Napa Valley magic space," Karey says.

But within weeks of taking it over, the Scarpones were charmed by the buzz surrounding 2nd Street. And they quickly settled in, naming the restaurant after their young children, Sophia and Valentino.

Now it's time for Philadelphians to be charmed. Sovalo is one of the most exciting new restaurants in the past few years, raising the bar for sophisticated dining in Northern Liberties with a genuinely fresh take on modern Italian cooking.

Joseph spent nearly seven years in the kitchen at Tra Vigne, and has transported the culinary spirit of that wine-country institution with a menu that stresses seasonality, intensely steeped flavors, and simple but inventive combinations. It's affordable, too, with entrees topping out in the low $20s.

Spring has been a prime time for Scarpone's talent with fresh ingredients. Three-cornered tortelli dumplings filled with poached chicken and prosciutto came scattered with sweet peas and a green pool of pea essence. Lemony braised artichokes were everywhere, pureed into dip with white beans, or sliced into meaty chunks to be layered with mint over bruschetta smeared with robiola cheese, or propping up a juicy breast of chicken wrapped in a sheet of crisp pancetta.

Sovalo serves other dishes that transcend season. A

CONTEMPORARY ITALIAN • NORTHERN LIBERTIES
702 N. 2nd St., 19123
215-413-7770 • www.sovalo.com

warm pie wedge of organic polenta was irresistible over a pungently creamy fonduta sauce of melted Taleggio cheese, its richness tempered by arugula leaves dappled with black droplets of tart huckleberry vinaigrette.

The "forever braised" meats that are a hallmark of Tra Vigne's menu — cooked in a 180-degree oven for up to 12 hours — are also a staple here. The roasted pork shoulder is stunning, infused with Calabrian chile spice and garlicky fennel and mounded over giant white bomboloni beans with pancetta. The fatty braised shortribs, however, were one of Sovalo's few disappointments.

Usually, though, Sovalo's food is impressively balanced. Lamb and potatoes with pasta sounds heavy, but it positively flew from our plate — the crisped nuggets of lamb and roasted fingerlings fragrant with pesto. Anchovies and chiles added earthy depth to a vinaigrette that glazed grilled slabs of wild striped bass and meaty swordfish beneath toasted almonds.

Scarpone doesn't ease up when it comes to dessert. His chocolate torta is intense, dolloped with a cloud of cinnamon-spiced mascarpone. Puffy ricotta fritters ring a deep-purple pool of huckleberry sauce. The best desserts, though, are the homemade gelati and sorbetti, which pair duos of contrasting flavors — coffee and mascarpone, or lush black currant with bright, tart shavings of icy Meyer lemon granita.

And there is a nice selection of dessert wines and grappas to wash them down. Karey has trained an impressive young staff to help you choose your glass — friendly and down-to-earth, but also well versed on the menu and wines.

The cellar is already stocked with some well-priced California and Italian labels, but Joseph promises it soon will fill out with more favorites culled from their wine-country days. With Sovalo's impressive debut, Northern Liberties is already starting to evoke that Napa Valley magic space.

— OR TRY THESE —
Here are three other top Italian restaurants:

VETRI 🥢🥢🥢🥢
1312 Spruce St., 19107, (215) 732-3478
Rustic Italian cooking, unique interpretations of authentic ingredients that are often daring but always delicious. Service is sharp and wines top-notch. A handsome new vestibule entrance has improved the tight space.

MELOGRANO 🥢🥢🥢
2201 Spruce St., 19103, (215) 875-8116
One of our best Italian BYOBs. The boisterous dining room exudes minimalist chic. But it's the authentic Italian fare of chef-owner Gianluca Demontis that entices guests to wait hours for a table — and like it.

RADICCHIO 🥢🥢
314 York Ave., 19106, (215) 627-6850
Much-needed soundproofing at one of our most authentic Italian BYOBs (think: Melograno East), where the pastas are simple but satisfying, and expertly prepared whole fish have become some of the city's signature fine-dining bargains.

Sovana Bistro

♚♚♚ EXCELLENT

MENU HIGHLIGHTS Pizzas: Margherita, prosciutto, chowder; tuna tartare; homemade mozzarella; cavatelli with short ribs; shrimp orecchiette; pappardelle with chorizo Bolognese; scallops with spaetzle; hanger steak; duck with risotto; balsamic-marinated halibut; cheese plate; fruit crisp-of-the-moment; housemade ice creams.

BYOB Bring something nice.

WEEKEND NOISE Raucous

IF YOU GO Lunch M-Sa 11 a.m.-3:30 p.m. Dinner M-Sa 5-10 p.m. Su 4:30-9 p.m.
• **E** Dinner entrees, $19-$30; pizzas, $9.25-$11
• Reservations not accepted
• Most major cards
• No smoking
• Wheelchair-accessible
• Free parking lot

Nick Farrell's surprising BYOB has been hiding for eight years beneath the tin roof of a suburban strip mall nearly an hour from Center City, so deep into Kennett Square horse country that you can smell the pastures from the parking lot.

But when I first settled onto a tufted suede banquette in the airy dining room of Sovana Bistro and took a bite of Margherita pizza, I had to ask myself: "Where have I been?"

The heat-blistered crust was cracker-crisp. The sauce was bright essence of tomato. The patches of mozzarella were so milky sweet and delicately stretchy, I was not surprised to learn it had been made in-house. Could this be the best brick-hearth pizza in the entire region? Quite possibly.

And these fabulous pies are only part of Sovana's appeal. I chased that Margherita with a first-class cassoulet, then a silky scoop of house-churned toasted almond ice cream.

This is obviously not news to the Chester County gentry who endure the no-reservation waits to pack this stylish 100-seat room, its cathedral ceiling and chocolate-brown decor illuminated by a wall of votives.

Farrell has crafted an appealing vision of updated French bistro and Italian cooking rooted in good ingredients and the notion that everything tastes better homemade, from mozzarella to frites that take three days — soaking, par-cooking, air-drying, frying to the finishing crisp. If you've tried (but failed) to resist eating all of these salt-flecked fries alongside the excellent hanger steak, you know that effort was worthwhile.

The recent arrival in the kitchen of ex-Django owner and chef, Bryan Sikora, has only added an extra layer of polish.

The house-made pastas were memorable. Hand-cut pappardelle ribbons folded around meaty crumbles of an amazing chorizo Bolognese singed with cuminy spice and the warmth of cinnamon and clove. Toothsome cavatelli were mounded with tender short rib and tart

CONTEMPORARY ITALIAN/FRENCH BISTRO • WESTERN SUBURBS (Chester County)

The Willowdale Towne Centre, 696 Unionville Rd., Kennett Square, Pa. 19348

610-444-5600 • www.sovanabistro.com

slow-roasted tomatoes. Orecchiette cradled shrimp and baby octopus in a bouillabaisse gravy fragrant with anise Pernod and a tingle of heat.

The lightly dressed pizzas, as mentioned, are another highlight — especially seasonal creations like the chowder pie with fingerling potatoes, chopped clams, and crisped bacon over a creamy smear of bechamel.

The yet-to-be-refrigerated mozzarella was so good, I wish the appetizer brought big slices instead of little knots. But it was one of only a few complaints. The French onion soup was showy but dull. The suckling pig needed a better garnish (the pasta carbonara has since been sensibly replaced with polenta).

The rest of my meals were splendid. Succulent sea scallops came over spaetzles studded with baby Brussels sprouts and asparagus tips. Striped bass was meaty enough to handle a piquant roast pepper–prosciutto ragout ringed by creamy brandade.

A balsamic marinade gave halibut the trompe l'oeil gray exterior of tuna, but the inside was white and flaky, a vivid contrast to tomato-basil risotto with roasted garlic butter. An equally fine risotto with duck confit and sweet squash was an ideal garnish for a beautiful duck breast. Rose-colored lamb loin came fanned over polenta and pulled lamb shank cacciatore.

Sovana's servers vary, but our baby-faced waiter was so impressive, we began referring to him as "Doogie Howser, MD" after he even did justice in presenting Sovana's great cheese plate.

There are some fine desserts, from the "crisp-of-the-moment" with seasonal fruit to the chocolate tart with chocolate praline gelato. But those perfectly ripe cheeses, a concise but wonderfully diverse selection that ranged from rosemary-rubbed Romao to smoky Rogue Oregon blue, were simply outstanding.

I wasn't surprised. Because after three meals at Sovana, I definitely knew where I had been: one of my new favorites.

— OR TRY THESE —

Here are three other suggested Chester County restaurants:

DILWORTHTOWN INN
♟ ♟ ♟
1390 Old Wilmington Pike, West Chester, Pa. 19382, (610) 399-1390
Still the model for what a Colonial-era country inn should be, with a first-class menu that melds continental with contemporary ideas, one of the region's deepest cellars, and gracious service.

RESTAURANT ALBA   ♟ ♟
7 West King St., Malvern, Pa. 19355, (610) 644-4009
Chef Sean Weinberg and his wife, Kelly, have put Malvern on the culinary map with an ambitious BYO warmed by a seasonal menu inspired by Italy, Mexico, and local ingredients.

The Orchard   ♟ ♟
503 Orchard Ave. (at Rt. 1), Kennett Square, Pa. 19348, (610) 388-1100
The BYO movement has arrived in mushroom country in style. Owner-chef James Howard (formerly of Le Bec-Fin) presents an intriguing New American menu with Spanish and French accents.

Standard Tap

🔔🔔🔔 EXCELLENT

MENU HIGHLIGHTS Beet salad; duck salad; heirloom tomato salad; pork sandwich; burger; venison bratwurst and sauerkraut; chicken pot pie; venison over brandied cherry sauce; tuna tartare; fried oysters; hanger steak; softshell crabs; seared snapper with corn-sausage stew; bread pudding.

WINE LIST Small selection of affordable wines, but focus on local draft beers from Yards, Victory, Stoudt's, Troegs, and others.

WEEKEND NOISE Deafening

IF YOU GO Dinner served every day, 5 p.m.-1 a.m. Brunch Sa and Su 11 a.m.-3:30 p.m.
• **M to E** Entrees, $10-$27
• No Reservations
• Wheelchair-accessible — side entrance
• Street parking only

Few restaurants have managed to define a new neighborhood or lead a culinary movement. But the Standard Tap has convincingly done both, staking a claim for emerging Northern Liberties as the nexus of Philadelphia's best gastro-pubs.

Already a taproom for most of its two centuries, the corner building was given a welcome renovation that transformed it into a moody, gas-lit wooden space. It's ideal for the neighborhood's hipster crowd, a mix of artsy salt-and-pepper bohemians, restaurant industry insiders, and tattooed thirtysomethings who make the Old City–goers to the south look like trendy wannabes.

Of course, Northern Liberties was on the northernmost border of the urban fringe when this bar opened five years ago. The border has edged a bit farther north in more recent years, as gentrification has tightened the neighborhood more firmly in its embrace. But the Tap has matured well as it became a destination rather than strictly a local spot, with expansions to its upstairs space (including the restaurant's only fresh air: an outdoor deck) that can handle serious crowds.

What keeps them coming, though, are the qualities that made the Standard Tap so special to begin with — its status as a premier showcase for local beers, a great juke box, and a sophisticated menu that sets the bar high for gastro-pubs.

This commitment to fresh draft-only beers (13 always on tap from no farther than 60 miles away) is no surprise since one of the two owners, William Reed, spent five years as a brewmaster. But the focus on local goes beyond beer, from the cherry wood that Reed and partner Paul Kimport used to build the bar to the ingredients in the surprising food, which has continuously improved under chef Carolynn Angle.

The Tap does make one of the city's better burgers, not to mention a great pork sandwich with roasted hot pep-

GASTRO-PUB • NORTHERN LIBERTIES
901 N. 2nd St., 19123
215-238-0630 • www.standardtap.com

pers. But this kitchen can also put the "gastro" into the "pub" better than any bar I've ever visited. The minimalist blackboard menu is deceiving.

I've yet to find a better duck confit than the one served here over salad. Angle's choucroute stewed with juniper and Stoudt's ale topped with venison bratwurst was soulfully good. Game has been a prominent cold-weather feature on the frequently changing menus, and I've enjoyed a beautifully seared venison beneath brandied cherry gravy, a massive boar shank braised with bacony broth, and a towering frittata filled with venison sausage served at the popular weekend brunch. I also devoured biscuits and creamy country sausage gravy at that meal, not to mention a half-dozen fresh stone crab claws. But that morning was most memorable for the powerful horseradish bite of the Tap's super-bloody pint-sized "Macho Mary."

Angle's chicken pot pie, topped with ornately decorated puff pastry, is also not to be missed. But given the chef's former jobs at Fishmarket and Striped Bass, it's understandable that fish dishes are among her strongest. There's fabulous tuna tartare tossed with spicy Asian mayo, crisply fried tender oysters with whole grain mustard cream, luxuriously thick cuts of striped bass with truffled butter and wild mushrooms, and meaty seared grouper served over a gutsy ragout of hominy corn, pickled okra, and tasso ham.

When it comes to dessert, the selection is brief but effective: a classic creme brulee and various wacky variations on bread pudding. Recently, it turned out to be a hunk of pudding veined with molten chocolate, mint, and ribbons of melted marshmallow, and it was cosmically good. It wasn't your standard bar dessert, I suppose, but this is one great tap room that has proven to be anything but standard.

— OR TRY THESE —

Here are three other neighborhood bars with good food:

N. 3RD ♟ ♟
801 N. 3rd St., 19123, (215) 413-3666
One of the city's best gastro-pubs, with a crowd who come for chef Peter Dunmire's appealing menu, which roams effortlessly from tuna burgers and soulful soups to high-toned striped bass.

Royal Tavern
937 E. Passyunk Ave., 19147, (215) 389-6694
This South Philly spot has character and a menu of updated comfort food — stuffed meat loaf, great burgers, tangy short ribs, mac-n'-cheese — to go with its smoked-duck club sandwich and other creations.

New Wave Cafe ♟ ♟
782/784 S. 3rd St., 19147, (215) 922-8484
Chef Ben McNamara cooks up one of the best gourmet bargains in town with a menu that ranges from Pernod-scented escargots to great buffalo wings and surprisingly refined desserts.

Striped Bass

★★★★ SUPERIOR

MENU HIGHLIGHTS Shellfish tasting; crab with apple caviar; "shrimp toast"; striped bass ceviche; Thai snapper with chorizo and mussel broth; wild hiramasa; spice-crusted lobster; Philadelphia "cheeseskate"; peach tatin; chocolate peanut butter cake; caramel tasting.

WINE LIST 500-plus selection cellar touches all major regions and price points, with 15 good wines by the glass; markups steep. Try exotic, non-chardonnay white from Rhone Valley, Austria, or southern Italy, or, with meatier dishes, lush Sonoma pinot noir ($82 Siduri was great).

WEEKEND NOISE Lively

IF YOU GO Dinner M-Th 5-10 p.m.; F and Sa 5-11 p.m.; Su 5-9 p.m.
• **U-E** Entrees, $32-$45
• Reservations strongly recommended
• Most major credit cards
• Wheelchair-accessible
• Valet parking $15; 20 percent discount with validation, Parkway Garage, 15th St. between Walnut and Locust (about $15 for 2 hours)

There's no such thing as a remote-control four-bell restaurant, even with legendary New York chef Alfred Portale pushing the buttons from Gotham Bar & Grill.

Portale was certainly much more than a figurehead in Stephen Starr's relaunch of the soaring seafood palace that defined the '90s glitz of Walnut Street's Restaurant Row. But it would take the emergence of his Philly-based protege, Christopher Lee, to finally brand Striped Bass with the distinctive personality it deserves and restore the beloved big fish to the summit of Philadelphia dining.

With Lee's sudden departure recently back to Manhattan, just as this guide was going to press, Striped Bass must yet again find the right chef to fill big shoes. Lee, a young New Yorker brimming with cutting-edge ideas who won rising-star accolades from the James Beard Foundation and *Food & Wine* magazine, combined the polish of Manhattan's best kitchens with a rare sense of wit and daring.

This was obvious early on with his creation of an instant classic: the "Philadelphia cheeseskate." Lee sandwiched braised short ribs, wild mushrooms, and caramelized pearl onions inside the white folds of skate encrusted with bread crumbs. On the plate, a swirl of Parmesan cream streaked with homemade hot sauce flexed the muscle of spice where other, hokier haute cheesesteaks wilted under empty froufrou flourishes.

It was just one of many clever creations that balanced complexity, technical prowess, and pristine seafood. A luscious salad of crab, for example, becomes transcendent beneath a glistening green layer of apple "caviar" — tiny beads of sour apple essence jelled with an experimental Spanish technique.

Another starter called "shrimp toast" encrusts buttery Alaskan spot prawns with thin squares of grilled toast dabbed with exotic poufs of lemongrass foam. Succulent

NEW AMERICAN SEAFOOD • RESTAURANT ROW
1500 Walnut St., 19102
215-732-4444 • www.stripedbassrestaurant.com

lobster is split and bronzed with Moroccan spice over tiny vegetables in a crustacean broth that rings with ginger, orange, and sour tamarind.

I've gotten used to the decor changes that made Starr's new Bass a little more corporate than Neil Stein's sexier original. But the service, a bit stiff at the 2004 reopening, is better than ever, a smooth ballet of detailed presentation. The substantial and pricey wine cellar, now at more than 520 bottle selections (and an excellent variety by the glass), even has a superb ambassador in sommelier Lauren Bernardini, whose elegant consultations recall the grace that brought former Bass sommelier Marnie Old to fame.

The food has always worthy of a great bottle. An exotic Austrian grüner veltliner was perfect for the seared hiramasa, a rare wild yellowtail that took on Asian tones with pickled turnips and a yuzu edamame coulis. It also matched a luxurious halibut posed over sweet corn with a spicy Thai coconut sauce punctuated by the crunch of deep fried quinoa.

Crispy Thai snapper came with a saffron-chorizo broth that had enough Mediterranean spice to match a red tempranillo. A porcini orecchiette was my lone disappointment, and only because the shaved white truffles were too dull for the steep $50 supplement. Usually, though, Striped Bass's entrees merited their high-$30s prices.

Pastry chef Carrie Chavenson follows with equally impressive desserts: a triple caramel tasting; a luscious tatin of caramelized peaches; and a layered chocolate peanut butter indulgence that comes with concord grape sorbet and an adorable miniature vanilla shake. Sip it until the straw slurps empty. The latest Striped Bass has been worth savoring until the last drop. Hopefully, as it undergoes yet another major transition, it will remain that good.

— OR TRY THESE —

Here are three other seafood palaces:

SAVONA 🔱 🔱 🔱
100 Old Gulph Rd., Gulph Mills, Pa. 19428, (610) 520-1200
This Main Line jewel remains one of the region's best fine-dining destinations, from its terra-cotta dining rooms to its refined Euro-service to the elegant Riviera-inspired cuisine and spectacular wine cellar.

MORIMOTO 🔱 🔱 🔱
723 Chestnut St., 19106, (215) 413-9070
Masaharu Morimoto's original venue remains the region's premier Japanese experience, from the rare and exquisite raw fish and blowout omakase tastings to creative fusion cooking served in a beautiful, undulating bamboo dining room.

Estia 🔱 🔱
1405-07 Locust St., 19102, (215) 735-7700
An elegant Greek seafood palace with a display of imported Greek fish, the kitchen's signature. The whole fish are exquisite, but high prices and a limited menu have kept the vast dining room feeling empty.

Susanna Foo

♟♟♟♟ SUPERIOR

MENU HIGHLIGHTS Wild mushroom dumplings; hundred-corner crab cakes; veal dumplings with ancho chile sauce; lobster dumplings; Mongolian lamb pillows; tuna spring roll; goat cheese–beet salad; wonton soup; hot and sour soup; scallops with mushrooms; wok-shaking filet mignon and scallops; mu-shu pork; tea-smoked duck; crispy duck; spicy Mongolian venison; Mongolian lamb; coconut panna cotta; lychee mousse charlotte; Asian pear terrine.

WINE LIST Good international cellar, slightly smaller than before (her Suilan's Atlantic City list has grown); greater focus on American wines. Rhone-style reds match spicier meat dishes; crisp whites (Insolia, $48, from Sicily; Sancerre, $65, from the Loire) dim sum and seafood.

WEEKEND NOISE Lively

IF YOU GO Lunch M-F 11:30 a.m.-2:15 p.m. Dinner Su 5-9 p.m.; M-Th 5-10:30 p.m.; Sa and Su 5-11 p.m.
• **V E** Dinner entrees, $16-$33; 5-course tasting menu, $65
• Reservations recommended
• Most major cards
• Wheelchair-accessible
• Valet parking $15, front of Sharper Image (dinner only)

It would be easy to underestimate Susanna Foo. After all, she set the benchmark nearly two decades ago for the kind of Asian fusion cooking that has since become mainstream.

But every time I return to the silk and orchid-fringed elegance of her Walnut Street dining room, I'm reminded by both her limitless inspiration and her attention to the tiniest details why she is one of the city's great chefs.

Foo was one of the first chefs to produce "French-Chinese" cuisine when she opened her eponymous restaurant on Walnut Street in 1987. And she remains one of the best. Very few others spin authentic flavors with such ease into a seamless modern blend of personal expression and refined technique. Foo, in her early sixties, is still a presence in the kitchen alongside chef-de-cuisine, Ann Cole, sending forth a stream of new ideas through her vivid repertoire of East-West standards.

The "hundred corner" crunch of her famous crab cakes and the truffled luxury of her chaterelles-chicken dumplings remain irresistible. But you can also taste the earthy Mongolian "lamb pillows" inspired by a recent trip to her family's home region in Northern China. The bon-bon-shaped dumplings have ginger-scented lamb stuffings that bask in bold ancho spice with moons of Asian eggplant. Saturn-shaped dumplings filled with sweet lobster are ringed with a green edamame-lobster puree, then misted with coconut foam.

I've seen many a tuna spring roll, but Foo perfects it, wrapping ruby fish inside a sheer wrapper crisp. A garnish of tuna tartare, spiced with tobiko and wasabi creme fraiche, plays against the tartness of green apple chutney.

Anyone who has savored Foo's stellar wonton soup or kung pao chicken knows that rehabilitating the mun-

ASIAN FUSION • RESTAURANT ROW
1512 Walnut St., 19102
215-545-2666 • www.susannafoo.com

dane is one of the chef's greatest tricks. She does it again for mu-shu pork with an upgrade of ingredients, blending the most tender pork loin, chewy mushrooms with tiger lilly buds, and pressed bean curd glazed in a hoisin souped-up with brandy.

At $20, it's one of the best values on a menu that, hovering below $30 an entree, remains reasonable for Restaurant Row. And old complaints about petite portions no longer apply. The scallops that came on my entree were huge and succulent, paired with a milky puree of cauliflower and parsnip and a woodsy sautee of hedgehog and maitake mushrooms. A Mongolian venison with cauliflower risotto and honeycap mushrooms was not just hearty, it was beguilingly complex, the tender game spiced with anchos and jalapenos, but also layered with the sweet tang of orange.

My only disappointment was a slightly overfried sweet and sour–sauced bass that, compared to rest of our meal, was a bit dull.

But it's not a sentiment that arises often at Susanna Foo, especially with the impressive service team (personable and smooth, but not cloying), or the well-stocked international wine cellar.

Even the dessert course is served here with creative elegance. Panna cotta is sweetened with coconut milk and passion fruit gelee. Pastry rolls form a dome-shaped charlotte around lychee mousse. Asian pear is confected into a silky fall terrine with nougatine and a scoop of pear sorbet.

Each one was exquisite. But I should have known, long before the iron teapots arrived with fragrant oolong to announce dessert, not to expect anything else.

— OR TRY THESE —

Here are three other Asian Fusion restaurants:

NECTAR 🍴🍴🍴
1091 Lancaster Ave., Berwyn, Pa. 19312, (610) 725-9000
This pan-Asian palace with its big Buddha and seriously talented chef draws scene-makers and serious eaters alike. The menu from former Susanna Foo chef Patrick Feury is an exciting French-Asian blend.

BUDDAKAN 🍴🍴🍴
325 Chestnut St., 19106, (215) 574-9440
Stephen Starr's Asian-fusion palace with a giant golden Buddha that still draws the chic crowds. It's hardly changed since it opened in 1998, but that may be a risk for a restaurant that once set the trends.

Ly Michael's 🍴🍴
101 N. 11th St., 19107, (215) 922-2688
The suburbanized pan-Asian fare feels slightly out of place in Chinatown, but that's also the draw. The menu ranges from duck dumplings to sauteed wild boar and relies on solid cooking and good ingredients.

Sweet Lucy's Smokehouse

♟♟ VERY GOOD

MENU HIGHLIGHTS Spice-steamed shrimp; rotisserie chicken; ribs; pulled pork; smoked kielbasa; chicken wings; collard greens; carrot cake.

BYOB Crisp beer or rustic Rhone red wine is ideal. Otherwise, sweet iced tea is the house drink of choice.

WEEKEND NOISE Lively

IF YOU GO Open Su and Tu-Th 11 a.m.-8 p.m.; F and Sa until 9 p.m.
• **M** Entrees, $5.55-$19.25
• Reservations for groups of 10 or more
• MasterCard, Visa only
• Wheelchair-accessible
• Free parking lot

There is power in the smell of true barbecue, and Sweet Lucy's Smokehouse is the ultimate proof. How else to explain the success of a venture born inside a used truck parked in an obscure corner of Northeast Philadelphia?

Perhaps it was simply a reflection on the scarcity of authentic Southern barbecue in our region. But word of a real pit prospect spread as surely as the dulcet billows of hickory smoke settled over the land. And after two years, Jim and Brooke Higgins's truck had such a following, they were able to carve a real restaurant out of a section of a store owned by Brooke's dad, Larry Gershel. Ever since, this industrial stretch of State Road just north of the Cottman Avenue exit off I-95 doesn't seem so obscure anymore.

True barbecue has that kind of power, to stick a bright pin on a map of previously uncharted territory. But when you walk through Sweet Lucy's door and the ambrosial warmth wafting from the big Southern Pride smoker literally weakens your knees, there is no mystery as to why it's well worth the drive.

So few restaurants actually slow-smoke their ribs that it is always a treat to eat someplace that takes the process seriously. Lucy's has a straightforward roadhouse appeal that seems neither trite nor overly funky. The room itself is casual, a friendly counter-service operation with a spacious dining space ringed by picnic-table booths and upside-down wash-bucket lights. Pig paraphernalia, a cold tank of sweetened Southern tea, and a country music soundtrack lend the converted warehouse a convincing down-home motif.

But really, all I need for great barbecue is good smoked pork and a handy roll of paper towels. To my surprise, however, it is the chicken that stops me cold.

Jim Higgins gives his brined roasters a five-hour tour

BBQ • NORTHEAST PHILADELPHIA

7500 State Rd. (just north of Cottman), 19136
215-331-3112 • www.sweetlucys.com

through the oven where they are constantly basted by the fat drippings of ribs and pork butts that share the rotisserie carousel. The result is a bronzed bird so completely succulent and tender that your teeth glide in slow-motion pleasure through its juicy flesh. Is there better barbecued chicken in the city? I think not.

Sweet Lucy's finest pig dish is the hand-pulled butt, cooked for 16 hours over green hickory, then splashed with a spicy vinegar in the style of the eastern Carolinas, where Jim went to college. I savored those tender strands of tangy meat, but can't fathom why that porcine treasure is buried inside a bulky egg bun.

I liked the ribs here quite enough — extra-large baby loin backs that clung to the bone just enough to show their smoke. And yet, the flavors were a little restrained. A sauce, for once, adds meaningful value to the meat. Higgins's deep red brew is stylistically somewhere between western Carolina and Tennessee, tomatoey but not too tart, with a delicate sweetness and present-but-subtle spice that finally gets those wallflower ribs to dance.

Even more sauce is needed for the bland brisket. But smoke is all that's needed for the kielbasa, whose snappy brown casings take on a savory burnished shine.

Sweet Lucy's also plays by the book with solid sides. The mashed sweet potatoes are silky and rich. The vegetarian braised collards are braised for hours to tenderness. The corn bread is light and fluffy. "Grandmaw's macaroni" salad is tweaked with green olives.

But it's the baked beans that linger in my memory most, cooked from scratch with molasses and garlic, then studded with nuggets of shredded pork and beef. Real smoked meat, true barbecue, can even add power to a pot of beans.

— OR TRY THESE —

Here are three other suggested barbecue restaurants:

Abner's Authentic Barbecue
505 Old York Rd., 19046, (215) 885-8600
7155 Ogontz Ave., 19138, (215) 224-8600
This take-out does a credible job of smoking its meats, especially the beef brisket. The big, meaty spare ribs, however, were less tender.

Tommy Gunns
4901 Ridge Ave., 19128, (215) 508-1030
4146 Pechin St., 19128, (215) 508-1002 (catering only)
630 South St., 19147, (215) 627-6160
At the original location outside Manayunk's Main Street entrance, the smoked meats are decent, especially the pulled pork, but sides still need work.

Famous Dave's Barbeque
Columbus Commons, 1936 S. Columbus Blvd., 19148, (215) 339-0339
104 Rt. 70 E., Cherry Hill, N.J. 08034, (856) 857-1520
This chain actually does a fairly decent job smoking its meat, even if sauces are overly sweet. Try the wild-rice chicken soup.

Chinatown Tips

IF YOU EAT OFTEN IN CHINATOWN, you have seen the All-Knowing Menu. That list of 300-plus items offering everything from chicken feet to chow fun appears virtually everywhere, an encyclopedia of Cantonese flavors with an occasional tingle of Hunan, Szechuan, and Mandarin.

Of course, precious few restaurants can deliver all the dishes with equal skill. So the real trick to navigating the pleasures of Chinatown hinges on discovering which place best cooks which part of the All-Knowing Menu. I've been exploring the topic for years, but it seems like an eternal pursuit. And it has become all the more fun as Chinatown continues to add more restaurants with specific regional specialties — most recently Szechuan and Malaysian — to its existing coterie of large-ly Cantonese generalists. Here are some of my favorites so far:

- Salt-baked seafood and steamed dumplings with ginger sauce at **Shiao Lan Kung**
- Peking duck rolls, E-Fu "long life" noodles, and wonton soup at **Sang Kee**
- Sichuan turnip soup with shredded pork, the deep-fried Buddha's Delight roll, crispy noodles with beef, and all of the hot pots (especially the chicken with black pepper sauce) at **Lee How Fook**
- Turnip patties, fui qi fei pian (kidney and tongue), ma pao tofu, three-pepper chicken, and golden coins at **Szechuan Tasty House**

- The hand-pulled soy sauce noodles at **Nan Zhou Hand-Drawn Noodle House**
- Roti canai pancakes with chicken curry dip, Malaysian spring rolls, and prawns in house special sauce, and the shaved-ice ABC dessert at both **Penang** and **Banana Leaf**
- Fiery satay beef soup and fried squid at **Ong's**
- Made-to-order dim sum at **Lakeside Chinese Deli**
- Noodle soup with soy sauce chicken, Chinese broccoli, and roast pork at **Ting Wong**
- Emerald 3 Mix soup, winter melon soup with golden-needle mushrooms, and mock Dynasty shrimp at **Cherry Street Chinese Kosher Vegetarian Restaurant**
- The barbecue platter, spring rolls, and broken rice with charred pork at **Vietnam**
- Char-broiled shortribs, marinated raw beef, salt-fried soft-shell crabs, and lemongrass clams at **Vietnam Palace**
- Spicy crisped lentil cakes, flaky thousand-layer bread, fresh ginger salad at **Rangoon**
- The best (and most expensive) cup of coffee in the city (just go for Jamaican Blue Mountain) at **Ray's Cafe & Tea House**

Szechuan Tasty House

VERY GOOD

MENU HIGHLIGHTS Turnip patties; fui qi fei pian (kidney and tongue); cheng-du cold noodles; Szechuan hot and sour soup; ma pao tofu; pork with garlic sauce; Szechuan twice-cooked pork; three-pepper chicken; hua jiao chicken (not on menu); golden coins; prawns with Grand Marnier sauce; fried bananas.

BYOB Consider a cold, brisk lager beer to quench the fire.

WEEKEND NOISE Lively

IF YOU GO Entire menu M-Sa 11 a.m.-midnight; Su 11 a.m.-11 p.m.

- I Entrees, $6-$13.95
- Reservations not required
- Not wheelchair-accessible
- Street parking only

There is spice, and then there is Szechuan spice. It's the difference between a simple burn and feeling the fire dance. It may blaze your tastebuds, but it will also have you wanting more. And when the tiny "Szechuan peppercorn" responsible for this magic — actually the dried pod of the prickly ash tree —snaps between your teeth, you'll discover what the Chinese mean when they describe Szechuan cooking as "ma la." Alone, "la" means spicy. But "ma la" means numbing heat.

This may not sound pleasurable. But it can be thrilling when it's done right. And at the colorful little Szechuan Tasty House in Chinatown, chef Zeng Mi Chen has an authentic Szechuan touch that, until recently, was almost nonexistent in Philly.

So when you dig into the marvelous three-pepper chicken, the heat comes at you in addictive swirls, moving from the sweet fruit of fresh green chiles to the musky spice of small dried reds to the ethereal anise notes stoked by the peppercorn itself.

In the more intense hua jiao chicken (not on the printed menu), fresh chiles are eliminated altogether for more fiery longer red pods and a heaping dose of peppercorns that left my ears buzzing like cicadas in summer. Pair that heat with some startling textures — like big cubes of soft ma po tofu that melt in the mouth like custard — and it's all the more effective.

Such masterful use of spice can even add intrigue to fu qi fei pian, which I knew was going to be scary because it was one of the few untranslated items on the menu. Turns out cold kidneys and beef tongue in fiery oil isn't bad at all.

Unless you speak Chinese, dinner in this pleasant orange 48-seat nook is bound to be full of surprises.

But it's also more than a chile-freak show. The pork in garlic sauce, for example, has the mellow sweetness of

CHINESE SZECHUAN • CHINATOWN
902 Arch St., 19107
215-925-2839

caramelized ginger and garlic goosed by a fermented punch of Szechuan hot bean sauce. But the precise slicing also makes the dish, with uniform threads of tender pork flecked with morsels of chewy shiitake.

Pea leaves are wilted but still crunchy enough to taste the pea's natural sweetness. Heat-blistered green beans snap with the sparks of salty shallots. And turnip patties are actually delicate buns, whose sesame-speckled crusts are filled with fluffy white turnip shavings. Even kitschy Grand Marnier prawns are delightful, the big shrimp perfectly fried beneath an ivory glaze of sweetened mayonnaise.

You will need a few mild dishes to buffer the burn. This is especially true if you begin with a bowl of Szechuan hot and sour soup that stokes a slow but steady fire. Or Szechuan shrimp that arrive beneath scarlet chile pepper glitter.

Patrons can bring their own drink (preferably beer) to Szechuan Tasty. But you might also bring a garden hose to put out the fire.

A handful of dishes didn't excite, like the dang-dang noodles (all orange oil, too little ground meat), and a whole carp incinerated by the liquid fire of its chile-singed gravy.

The twice-cooked pork, though, is not to be missed, its tender slices of belly meat refried with hot bean sauce and fresh green peppers. The "golden coins" are another winner, pillowy rounds of eggplant stuffed with pork then deep-fried to a perfect crunch.

Szechuan Tasty's deep fryer also comes through for dessert, with some of the best fried bananas I've had. Supremely crisp on the outside and dusted with sugar, the insides are a sweet flow of molten fruit. And it is here, at last, that the burn subsides.

— OR TRY THESE —

Here are three other places to discover Szechuan cooking:

Chung King
915 Arch St., 19107, (215) 627-3792. A recent Szechuan entry into Philly's largely Cantonese repertoire. It's too soon for a verdict, but an early meal brought decent ma pao tofu, and an adventurous cold buffet of spicy pig ears, tongue, and addictive chicken hearts.

Yue Kee   📌📌
238 S. 38th St. (between Walnut and Spruce), 19104, (610) 812-7189. A gem disguised as a dingy food truck, where some of the best Chinese food — from fiery Beijing hot noodles and ma pao tofu to ginger chicken — is cooked with fresh ingredients and vivid sauces at bargain prices.

MARGARET KUO'S   📌📌📌
175 E. Lancaster Ave., Wayne, Pa. 19087, (610) 688-7200. No one presents classic regional Chinese cuisine with more elegance than Margaret Kuo. Superb Chinese dining on the main floor and excellent sushi upstairs. Szechuan specialties include spicy lamb stew, dumplings, and dishes from Chengdu.

Tangerine

♟♟♟ EXCELLENT

MENU HIGHLIGHTS Meze (house-made salumi); tuna tartare; calamari; megquz; shortrib spanikopita; chickpea crepes; harissa gnocchi; arugula salad; halibut Espana; grilled fish al limone; shrimp and scallops afrique; pistachio-crusted duck; lamb or chicken tagines; pomegranate pork chop; baklava rolls.

WINE LIST Nice list focused on Mediterranean (Spain, Italy, south of France), with most selections under $75. Good selection of wine by the glass.

WEEKEND NOISE Noisy

IF YOU GO Dinner M-Th 5-11 p.m.; F and Sa 5-midnight; Su 5-10 p.m.
• **V E** Entrees, $18-32
• Reservations highly suggested
• Wheelchair-accessible
• Valet parking $14; $17 weekends

The danger with theme restaurants is that they usually lose steam the minute the fad is over. But the fabric-draped casbah of Tangerine is an exception to the rule, proving that some spaces are so magnetic they can survive their own passing trend, and even embrace a new culinary direction.

At the heart of Tangerine's allure is the sultry design that made it the city's sexiest dining room. Stephen Starr converted an old hardware store into a sultan's lair draped in gauzy red scrims, kilim floors, and hanging filigreed lamps that spray the ceiling with a stardust of dappled lights. A shimmering wall of votives edged by a crepuscular blue glow lends it the mood of a grand caravan.

While the room still feels like nouveau Morocco, much of the menu has edged away, circling back around to the Northern Mediterranean to dabble more in the flavors of Greece, Spain, and Italy.

This transition seemed a tad desperate at first, when a few sure-bet Asian dishes even crept into the repertoire. But in the past two years, the talented young current chef, Todd Fuller, has struck an ideal balance between Tangerine's initial North African flair and its new pan-Mediterranean ambitions.

Of course, many of the brilliant signature dishes that original chef Chris Painter created still anchor the menu. There are the tender gnocchi blushing with harissa spice in a rich cream steeped with celery root and dates. There are chickpea crepes folded around chicken and chanterelles mushrooms; giant arugula salads scattered with honeyed almonds; pistachio-crusted duck; and calamari fragrant with Mahgreb spice. The classic Moroccan tagine stews of chicken with olives and preserved lemons and cinnamon-perfumed lamb are also still ably done.

Fuller's Northern Med inspirations, though, are becoming equally memorable. Greek spinach pie is given more

NEW MEDITERRANEAN • OLD CITY

232 Market St., 19106

215-627-5116 • www.tangerinerestaurant.com

heft with the addition of braised shortribs. Spain is evoked by a gorgeous seared halibut perched over crisped paella rice ringed by Basque roasted pepper sauce.

Fuller's primary influence, however, comes from Italy. His experiments with pork have resulted in some excellent house-made salumis, from tangy wine-infused Genoas to soppressattas rife with rosemary, all-spice, or harissa. Braised Berkshire pork belly was one of the more impressive features of a special called "pork three ways," which presented a thick slab of the tender meat over lentils infused with homemade rosemary-smoked bacon.

Tangerine's pork chop is also a spectacular dish, the meat tenderized by a pomegranate molasses brine, grilled and served over a corn fritter infused with chorizo. But Fuller also showed a nice touch with fish, grilling a succulent daurade whole with lemon and basil, and presenting it with a long boat of clever contorni — whole piquillo peppers sprinkled with slivered almonds, roasted beets, z'atar-dusted asparagus, and potato salad filled with house-cured lardon bacon (the housemade falafel, however, were doughy).

The servers are well informed and outgoing. But Tangerine is also one of a number of Starr restaurants that still present meals "family style," which annoyingly brings food to share in random order, regardless of whether the table is crowded by big plates beyond comfort. Fuller says he plans to focus the menu more on small plates in the future.

But desserts are so enormous, sharing is the only reasonable approach. I still miss some of the original sweets (like the snake and ibrik of chocolate pot de creme), but the chocolate polenta financier and baklava fruit rolls topped with fig gelato were fine consolations.

And as long as this evocative space and its ambitious kitchen continue to be so transporting, Tangerine will remain too magnetic to resist.

— OR TRY THESE —

Here are three other suggested Old City restaurants:

AMADA ✗ ✗ ✗
217 Chestnut St., 19106, (215) 625-2450
Discover your inner flamenco (and the city's hottest new spot) at this sexy tapas haven, where Jose Garces presents stunning updates to classic Spanish flavors in an evocative, 135-seat space in Old City. The service is impressive and the menu well tuned, but those small plates add up quickly.

Cafe Spice ✗ ✗
35 S. 2nd St., 19106, (215) 627-6273
This hip Indian bistro has contemporary decor, but classic dishes prepared with quality ingredients and sharp flavors.

Ristorante Panorama
Penn's View Hotel, 14 N. Front St., 19106, (215) 922-7800
Luca Sena's marble- and mural-clad Italian grill is a reliable destination for good home-made pastas and one of the largest wine-by-the-glass selections in the country.

Tierra Colombiana

🎭🎭 VERY GOOD

MENU HIGHLIGHTS Arepas; Colombian tamale; empanadas; chorizo in white wine; octopus salad; Cubano sandwich; red beans; moro rice; ropa Vieja; Cuban arroz con pollo; muchacho relleno; fried yucca; maduros; tres leches; flan.

WINE LIST Small but affordable list of Spanish and South American wines. Also try Dominican beer, batido fruit shakes, and cafe con leche.

WEEKEND NOISE Lively

IF YOU GO Entire menu M-Th 7 a.m.-11 p.m.; F and Sa 7 a.m.-12:30 a.m.
- **M** Entrees, $7-$31 (paella for two)
- Reservations not required
- Wheelchair-accessible
- Street parking around restaurant supervised by guard at night

The sexy flavors of Nuevo Latino cooking have made their mark on trendy downtown kitchens over the last decade. But those who crave a taste of the original source still head north to the Viejo Latino bastions of North 5th Street's "Golden Mile." There you'll find a number of worthy corner joints, like El Bohio, Shining Star, and Porky's Point, not to mention a chic nuevo lounge in Isla Verde. Reliable Tierra Colombiana, however, is undoubtedly still the institution that draws the widest audience, from Latino power lunchers and foodies on field trips to salsa dancers heading upstairs to the second-floor mambo club.

For those who crave down-home Cuban and Colombian cooking — the corn-scented steam of a banana leaf-wrapped tamale; the pork and pickle crunch of a hot-pressed Cuban sandwich; a dense spoonful of caramel custard flan — this is certainly your best bet for the relatives when they visit from Miami.

Tierra offers a stark contrast to the scrappy streetscape that surrounds it at the southeast corner of 5th and Raymond Streets, just a few blocks south of Roosevelt Boulevard. Inside, its dining rooms are as inviting as any Center City restaurant (including Mixto, Tierra's less-inspired Pine Street sibling), with rustic lanterns, white brick archways, varnished wood ceilings, and walls the color of a passion fruit batido shake.

The servers are sweet and attentive, and are always eager to offer suggestions from the dauntingly large menu. Owner Jorge Mosquera's family is actually from Ecuador. The principally Cuban, Puerto Rican, and Colombian menu, though, reflects the neighborhood clientele and the cooks in the kitchen.

The giant Colombian tamales are the restaurant's unique specialty. Unfold the banana-leaf wrapper and behold a meal in itself, fluffy steamed corn flour with fistfuls of roasted pork, chicken, beef, and vegetables hidden

LATINO • NORTH PHILADELPHIA

4535 N. 5th St., 19140

215-324-6086 • www.tierracolombianaphilly.com

inside like buried treasure. The shrimp soup is another favorite, its golden saffron broth brimming with the pop of peas, the snap of tender shrimp, and flowery blooms of rice cooked to almost-porridge softness.

Among the best entrees are the stewed ropa vieja, brisket cooked so long its name means "old clothes," transformed into a tangy mince of beef as soft as silk threads. The muchacho relleno, or "stuffed boy," is another slow-cooked favorite, a beef roast stuffed with coriander-ground sausage and vegetables smothered in an irresistibly piquant tomato gravy of onions and peppers.

I've enjoyed the giant paellas here in the past, but a recent version was overcooked and expensive. The Cuban arroz con pollo, though, is always a delight filled with tender morsels of chicken, its rice tangy with a splash of beer.

Rice and beans are at the heart of Latin cooking, and Tierra's are generally superb, a hearty side that comes with every entree. You can get them separate, mixed, and cooked together as moro (also known as congri). Or you can have the Colombian-style red beans that were pillowy soft and gently sweetened with chunks of calabaza pumpkin.

The ubiquitous starches, crisply fried yucca strips or green tostone plantain disks, as well as the sweet dark plantain maduros, are also top-notch. Tierra's plantain mofongo, meanwhile, is consistently a bland disappointment compared to the garlicky gold standard at Shining Star.

There are several beers and frothy batido fruit shakes to complement the exotic flavors. But a meal wouldn't be complete here without one of Tierra's stunningly rich desserts, like the tres leches cake that oozes cream and sweetened milk, or the sublimely creamy flan. All you need is a fresh mug of potent cafe con leche, and you'll be ready to dance it off upstairs.

— OR TRY THESE —

Here are three other suggested Latino restaurants in North Philadelphia:

Isla Verde   🎌 🎌
2725 N. American St., Plaza Americana (at Lehigh Ave.), 19133, (215) 426-3600
At this sleek restaurant and lounge, where the salsa crowd pulses across the weekend dance floor, chef Juan Carlos Rodriguez delivers an upscale Nuevo Latino menu.

El Bohio
2746 N. 5th St., 19133, (215) 425-5991
This eatery has anchored the Golden Mile, the commercial strip of Philadelphia's Puerto Rican neighborhood, for more than two decades, with spicy fried chicken, adobo-smothered pork chops, and perhaps the best flan in town.

Shining Star
2460 N. 5th St. (at Cumberland), 19133, (215) 423-8506
At this modest diner the Puerto Rican fare is among the neighborhood's best, especially the mofongo al pilon (mashed green plantains fried with pork and garlic) and crunchy chicharrones (fried pork skins).

Vetri

♟♟♟♟ SUPERIOR

MENU HIGHLIGHTS Antipasto; spinach gnocchi; onion crepe; shaved artichoke salad; cauliflower flan; rabbit casoncelli; pappardelle with venison and pears; chestnut fettuccine with boar ragu; Italian onion soup; rigatoni Bolognese; turbot; whole branzino; roasted goat; stuffed guinea hen; chocolate polenta souffle; lavender ice cream with chocolate lid and hot olive oil.

WINE LIST Major collection of Italian wines, handful of international prestige labels, and surprising list of Belgian beers. Italian selections like Solaia, Giacoasa, and Gaja; Southern cult wines like Montevetrano. Numerous sub-$100 choices include great values like Armecolo ($40) from Puglia.

WEEKEND NOISE Raucous

IF YOU GO Dinner M-F 6-10 p.m.; Sa, one tasting menu seating only, 7 p.m. Summer hours: M-Th 6-10 p.m.; F, one tasting menu seating only, 7 p.m. Closed Sa and Su.
- **U-E** Dinner entrees, $25-$48; tasting menus, $90 (6 courses), $115 (8 courses)
- Reservations recommended, accepted up to 60 days in advance of numerical date
- Not wheelchair-accessible
- Street parking only

In a city already smothered by trattoria fever and retro red gravy, Marc Vetri's intimate townhouse dining room hovers above the rest with a magnetic vision for Italian cooking that melds rustic authenticity with a bold individual swagger.

Something as common as an antipasto becomes a thrilling showcase for his ideas, from sherry-charred Brussels sprouts and saffron-poached cauliflower, to bitter arugula mixed with sweet persimmon, grilled wedges of smoked mozzarella, and silky sheets of prosciutto peeled by the chef himself from the antique slicer beside your table.

It's hard to resist such bounty, even if it is a $28 starter splurge. Likewise, I can rarely pass up any number of Vetri classics — the ethereal spinach gnocchi; the cocoa-dusted chestnut fettuccine with boar ragu; the sublime turbot over crisp potatoes; the caramelized onion galette; the chocolate-polenta souffle; or the lavender gelato with a chocolate lid that melts beneath drizzled hot olive oil. These are the powerfully good creations that have earned Vetri national recognition, from the James Beard Award to a nod from *Bon Appetit* as perhaps the nation's best Italian restaurant.

Those who venture into Vetri's ever-changing seasonal menus, however, will discover a chef at the height of his personal expression, whose effortless creativity is bolstered by the hearty flavors of Lombardy, where he lived and trained for several years.

His pit-roasted baby goat is the ultimate souvenir of the rustic Northern Italian cooking that inspires him. A hunk of it arrives on the bone over polenta on a wooden platter, the skin burnished to a mahogany crisp from hours of turning over smoldering mesquite wood.

And then there are the flights of whimsy. An Italian

CONTEMPORARY ITALIAN • AVENUE OF THE ARTS
1312 Spruce St., 19107
215-732-3478 • www.vetriristorante.com

deconstruction of French onion soup tucks tangy Gruyere cheese into ricotta ravioli beneath brothy caramelized onions. Crumbles of venison sausage tumble with delicately sweet pears over pappardelle. Sweetbread ravioli are sauced with a silky puree of veal shoulder. Cannelloni come wrapped around a mousse of gently smoked capon. And hot cauliflower flan harbors a heart of warm egg yolk that runs across the plate like sunshine flecked with black truffle.

If you are fortunate enough to happen by during white truffle season, you will find them treated also royally (and for a pretty price), shaved like alabaster ambrosia over bowls of risotto or polenta drizzled with creamed robiola cheese.

But Vetri can also transform a humble Bolognese with a key ingredient or two. So, what makes that simple ragu irresistible?

"Lard," he says, "and lots of head meat from the pig."

Never mind. It's good.

If the cooking defies cliches, so, too, does the rest of the restaurant, which removes the starch from fine dining. The Vetri experience is by most measures grand gastronomy (just check your bill), from the beautiful stemware to the great Italian cellar to the stellar service orchestrated by Jeff Benjamin, Vetri's co-owner and maitre d'. There are few reservations more coveted in the city than one of these 36 seats.

And yet there is a natural informality to the simple yellow room, which recently annexed a handsome new vestibule. It is not uncommon to see diners in jeans (probably some famous director) laughing boisterously around the corner six-top as if they were in their own home.

But Mamma never cooked like this.

— OR TRY THESE —

Here are three other upscale Italian restaurants:

SOVALO 𝕏 𝕏 𝕏
702 N. 2nd St., 19123, (215) 413-7770
Joseph and Karey Scarpone have brought a taste of Napa Valley's famed Tra Vigne to Northern Liberties. Joseph's vibrant Cal-Italian menu — seasonal, intensely flavored, inventive, and simple — really turns heads.

La Famiglia 𝕏 𝕏
8 S. Front St., 19106, (215) 922-2803
A bastion of luxury with great Italian specialties, from homemade pasta to rack of lamb, and a world-class wine cellar. But for the astronomical prices, food and service should offer much more.

KRISTIAN'S RISTORANTE 𝕏 𝕏
1100 Federal St., 19147, (215) 468-0104
This handsomely renovated butcher shop is one of South Philadelphia's finest upscale Italian eateries, although the service can't match the finesse of chef Kristian Leuzzi's sophisticated takes on risotto and osso buco.

Vietnam

♟♟ VERY GOOD

MENU HIGHLIGHTS BBQ platter; raw flank steak appetizer; rice vermicelli bowls with spring rolls and char-grilled meats; broken rice with country style beef or pork chop; wonton soup; bun bo hue; cold needle noodles with pork; coconut ice cream.

WINE LIST Stick with refreshing '33' Vietnamese beer, or try high-octane tropical cocktails served in tiki cups.

WEEKEND NOISE Lively

IF YOU GO Entire menu Su-Th 11 a.m.-9 p.m.; F-Sa 11 a.m.-10 p.m.
- ♟ Entrees, $6-$14.95
- Reservations for banquets only
- Most major cards
- Not wheelchair-accessible
- Street parking only

As rivalries go, the cross-street competition between Vietnam and Vietnam Palace isn't quite the Hatfields and the McCoys. But it's the Vietnamese version of Pat's vs. Geno's — with impassioned camps of ethno-foodies splitting Internet chat rooms over spring rolls and bowls of pho.

If I had to choose a favorite, it would be Vietnam. But after several investigative visits, I'd have to say the Palace is nearly as worthy — hardly deserving of the indifference that Vietnam's disciples heap upon it.

Most diners, myself included, were entranced by the physical transformation Vietnam made several years ago when it was renovated from a fluorescent-lit Chinatown joint into a sultry, multi-floor complex evocative of French colonial Saigon. Then the Palace quietly completed its own impressive makeover, with a pleasant open dining room (and upstairs banquet hall) complete with a waterfall mirror and a curvy, cutaway ceiling that reveals an undulating wave of bamboo.

The food is more or less a wash, which shouldn't be surprising given that Palace co-owner, Nhon Nguyen, was one of Vietnam's chefs before she opened the Palace in 1987.

Ultimately, the competition has been a good thing, resulting in a welcome boon of upgrades for 11th Street (nearby Lee How Fook has also upscaled) to answer the newer, parking-friendly Vietnamese contenders on Washington Avenue. How can too much great Vietnamese home cooking be a problem?

Each restaurant has its charms. Vietnam has its barbecue sampler platter, the flaming tiki drinks, and fabulous vermicelli bowls topped with char-grilled pork and tangy nuoc mam. Meanwhile, I'd come to the Palace any day for a number of its specialties, from the fragrant cold salad of raw beef in spicy lime juice and herbs to the gingery char-grilled short ribs to deep-fried spring rolls that are probably the best in town, their blistered skins delicately crisped from the heat, their chicken-and-noodle stuffings noticeably light.

VIETNAMESE · CHINATOWN
221 N. 11th St., 19107
215-592-1163 · www.eatatvietnam.com

Vietnam Palace is slightly weaker on service. Then again, Vietnam's amiable owner and maitre d', Benny Lai, inspires such uncommon loyalty in his customers that many simply feel guilty for dining elsewhere. Vietnam's handsomely moody decor, clad in tall dark wainscoting and sepia-toned photos of the old country, is probably just as responsible for its popularity as the attentive hospitality.

But even before its renovation, Vietnam's consistently excellent menu sealed its claim as one of the city's ethnic gems. The BBQ platter is a snapshot of its best bites — crackly spring rolls, skewers of meat-stuffed grape leaves, and particularly tender meatballs. The shaved raw flank-steak appetizer was like Vietnamese carpaccio marinated in sweetened lime, dusted with nuts and potent peppermint.

Rice flake noodles were wrapped like slippery ravioli around a fine mince of sauteed pork and mushrooms. Wonton soup, brimming with tiny balls of crinkle-wrapped dumplings, scented the air with fried garlic. Another favorite noodle soup, bun bo hue, is a spicy red lemon grass twist on the typical brisket pho.

Cold "needle noodles" brought chewy twines of thick rice noodles tossed in cool coconut milk, shredded pork, and the subtle texture of roasted rice powder. And "broken rice" — with the texture of couscous and the flavor of jasmine rice — is fabulous beneath a sweetly marinated grilled pork chop.

Stir-fried entrees have never been Vietnam's forte, though the lemongrass shrimp and basil chicken have benefited from lighter sauces in the past year. For these, however, I must defer to Vietnam Palace, whose gingery chicken, lemongrass clams, and tender salt-baked squid take the stir-fry prize.

Good thing it's conveniently located right across the street. Perhaps a true eater's loyalties were meant to be divided.

— OR TRY THESE —

Here are three other suggested Vietnamese restaurants:

Vietnam Palace ♟♟
222 N. 11th St., 19107, (215) 592-9596
It's often overshadowed by an ever-popular rival across the street, but Chinatown's "other" big Vietnamese restaurant is worthy itself, with a good menu of traditional Vietnamese cooking and a chic bamboo dining room.

NAM PHUONG ♟♟
1100-1120 Washington Ave., 19147, (215) 468-0410
Very good renditions of traditional Vietnamese cuisine — seafood-studded crepes; country beef with broken rice; tangy green papaya salads — are served to the crowds that flock to this growing Asian shopping zone.

Pho 75
1122 Washington Ave., 19147, (215) 271-5866
Dive into a satisfying meal-in-a-bowl at the city's best (and most utilitarian) Vietnamese pho hall, where the menu's focus (soup, soup, and soup) is a clue to its specialty.

Villa di Roma

⚜⚜ VERY GOOD

MENU HIGHLIGHTS Garlic bread; fried asparagus; steamed clams; shrimp scampi; quattrocini alfredo; baked ziti with asparagus; sausage — broiled, cacciatore, or Genovese; chicken Sicilian; veal parmigiana with eggplant; veal bella bucca; cannoli.

WINE LIST Tiny list of low-end wines. Stick with Peroni beer.

WEEKEND NOISE Noisy

IF YOU GO Entire menu M-Th 4-10:30 p.m.; F and Sa noon-11 p.m.; Su 2-10 p.m.
- **M** Entrees, $7.95-$24.95
- Reservations accepted every day but Sa
- Cash only
- Not wheelchair-accessible — one step outside; bathrooms accessible
- Street parking only; Italian Market parking lot $2, on 900 block of Carpenter St.

In the days before balsamic hit South Philly, when virgin had nothing to do with olive oil and arugula sounded more like a condition than a salad green, Italian restaurants felt like this.

The baskets of garlic bread were so hot and butter-crispy, they disappeared before their fragrance left the room. There were steel bowls brimming with clams, and platters heaped with sausage cacciatore. And when the waitress led our family to the table through the joyously bustling room, she dropped the atty-tude just long enough to confide: "Your kids are getting so big! "

And that's just in the two weeks since we ate there last.

It sounds like the hokey script so many national chains have co-opted. But it still exists in its purest form in South Philadelphia. And in few places does it thrive more genuinely than at Villa di Roma, the unpretentious De Luca family spaghetti hall in the heart of the Italian Market. Its polished brick facade reflects the deep crimson hue of its tomato gravies. The green neon sign glows like a beacon from the 1960s.

And there is very little inside to bring you up to date, from the bentwood chairs to the brick walls with Italian Market paintings, to the wagon-wheel chandeliers and bar where a poster of Rocky jogging sets the mood.

Villa's menu may seem anachronistic alongside the truffled risottos and whole fish of our many upscale Italian eateries. But there's something magnetic about the century-old version of Italian immigrant cooking when it's done with honest care. And that's what you'll find here, where the five De Luca brothers and sisters still give their full attention to the restaurant their parents, Domenic and Carmela, bought in 1963.

Affable Pip (short for Epiphany) runs the dining rooms. Mariann works the bar, and Anna works alongside the veteran servers. Frank cooks a couple nights a week, perfecting indulgences like deep-fried asparagus ladled

ITALIAN RED GRAVY • ITALIAN MARKET

936 S. 9th St., 19147

215-592-1295

with a stick's worth of tangy scampi butter. Meanwhile, brother Basil lays the foundation each morning, setting the giant pots of tomato gravy to simmer and meticulously hand-rolling the meatballs.

Much of this menu was handed down from Vince "Cous" Pilla, the legendary cook who was Villa's original chef. Chief from his repertoire is chicken Sicilian, a zesty saute with cherry peppers, capers, cured olives, and butter that vibrates with spice. It was also Angelo Bruno's final meal (at Cous' Little Italy) before the mob boss was gunned down.

The garlic bread is another classic, with pecorino butter-dipped rounds of airy bread that develop the perfect crunch and puff. Top them with sliced sirloin and garlicky wine butter for Domenic's steak "My Way."

Among the best of the homey pastas is ziti with asparagus tossed in ricotta-blushed marinara. The creamy quattrocini blends Alfredo with prosciutto and fresh spinach. Villa also has a nice touch with meats, including great sausage broiled into horseshoes with peppers and onions, tossed in soulful cacciatore, or simmered Genovese-style with cannellini and escarole.

The veal parmigiana is tender enough (though not as crisp as Ralph's). But the bella bucca was perfect, two veal medallions sandwiching provolone and ham over gravy ribboned with spinach.

The lobster francese was generous, but suffered from a sauce rife with low-end wine. Bad wines, it happens, are among the few old-time legacies here I don't love. Our server boiled the selection down to: "red" or "white."

Go with a Peroni.

The same waitress erupted in laughter at the mere suggestion of an espresso machine: "Everything here is standard!" she laughed. "We don't have anything special!"

How wrong she was.

— OR TRY THESE —

Here are three other suggested red-gravy stalwarts near the Italian Market:

Ralph's
760 S. 9th St., 19147, (215) 627-6011. This 106-year-old institution is still the real deal for lively ambience and flavorful old-time cooking, from greens-and-pastina soup to gravy-stewed squid, crisp-bottomed veal parmesan, soulful cacciatores, and creamy chicken Sorrento.

Dante & Luigi's
762 S. 10th St., 19147, (215) 922-9501. The city's oldest Italian (circa 1899), though not with continuous ownership, is a bit more upscale than the rest, and still a destination for veal braciola, tender gnocchi, and spaghetti with chicken livers. A recent meal was fine, but lacked some spark.

Criniti
2611 S. Broad St., 19145, (215) 465-7750 . This classic red-gravy Italian moved down the block not long ago to a more spacious dining room in a former church. The decor is a step up, but this old favorite seems to have lost a homey edge to its food.

XIX Nineteen

🍺🍺🍺 VERY GOOD

MENU HIGHLIGHTS Raw bar: oysters; tuna sashimi; scallops. Baby octopus; softshell crabs; beef carpaccio; cured king salmon; crab cake; wild striped bass with vidalias; veal cheeks with pappardelle; lamb with curried potatoes; 42-day aged sirloin; deconstructed carrot cake; blackberry study; strawberry-rhubarb cobbler.

WINE LIST Appealing 300-label cellar: French whites and New World bottles. Nearly 40 wines by the glass offer great values (Burgans, Movia, Qupe, St. Urbans-Hof, El Felino, Sena). Cool central bar has fabulous list of premium spirits.

WEEKEND NOISE Quiet

IF YOU GO Breakfast daily, 6:30 a.m.-11 a.m. Lunch daily, 11 a.m.-5 p.m. Dinner M-Th 5:30-10 p.m.; F and Sa 5-11 p.m. Sunday brunch, 11 a.m.-2 p.m.
 • **M to V E** Cafe, $12-$20; entrees, dining room, $21-$45
 • Reservations suggested
 • Wheelchair-accessible
 • Validated self-parking $9.50, valet $21, Bellevue Garage (entrance, Broad or Locust Sts.)

Philadelphia has not been kind to its grandes dames of dining. For such a venerable city, we have precious few century-old classics that really matter anymore.

So I was thrilled to hear about XIX, Park Hyatt's latest attempt to energize the elegant domed dining rooms atop the old Bellevue-Stratford, the 102-year-old Broad Street landmark. Despite its spectacular 19th-floor city views and a string of talented chefs, the former Founders room there felt like an ode to past glories weighed down with heavy curtains and robotic hotel service.

But when the elevator door glides open onto the recently unveiled XIX (a.k.a. Nineteen), it's as if someone finally drew the draperies to reveal the sunny aerie of contemporary dining this space was waiting to be. The two monumental 50-foot domes are still there. But designer Meg Rodgers has modernized and brightened the rooms, with silk curtains and orchids in the front cafe and sleek leather couches in the intriguingly moody central bar. Just beyond a chef's table ringed by glassed-in wine cellar walls, the space opens onto the jaw-dropping circular dining room with a raw bar ensconced at its hub.

Only the giant resin "pearl" necklace here rings a false note, dangling from the ceiling like plastic costume beads. Hyatt should know better than to dress its grande dame for her big coming-out in anything shy of glamorous jewels.

So much else about her comeback is first-class. The servers are soft-spoken but helpful, particularly with the list of 350 well-chosen, fairly priced international wines, and nearly 40 quality choices by the glass.

The cooking from talented newcomer Marc Plessis is worthy of more than one good glass. The French-born, Southern-raised chef blends a polished technique with top-notch seasonal ingredients into gorgeous plates.

Beautiful tempura-fried soft-shell crabs tangle over cucumber raita ringed by cuminy Turkish tomato soup.

NEW AMERICAN SEAFOOD • AVENUE OF THE ARTS DISTRICT

Park Hyatt at the Bellevue, Broad and Walnut Sts., 19102

215-790-1919 • www.nineteenrestaurant.com

Sheets of beef carpaccio are crimped into bundles over a brushstroke of purple mustard. And pristine slices of tuna sashimi are rolled around matchsticks of Asian pear that add an echo of crunchy sweetness to the buttery fish.

That raw bar is one of XIX's obvious pleasures, and few luxuries are more indulgent than gazing across the cityscape through those grand arched windows while downing a platter of icy Cape May Salts.

Seafood is also the dominant theme of the cooked menu. Plump sea scallops come alongside wild mushrooms over silky cauliflower puree. Tender octopus is paired with truffled potato salad. The house-cured King salmon plays against nutty slivers of purple artichokes.

Overcooked halibut was one of the few lesser efforts, though I loved the Southern inspiration of its black-eyed pea garnish studded with country ham.

Some of Plessis's meat dishes, though, were especially worthy. The strip steak is dry-aged for an almost unheard of 42 days, and the result is intense and complex. Braised veal cheeks are so soft, they melt off the fork. Rack of lamb takes a surprising Indian flair with curried potatoes and fresh peas streaked with coriander yogurt.

Pastry chef Jason Etzkin follows with beautifully composed seasonal desserts. His blackberry study distilled the fruit into three shades of intensity. Warm strawberry-rhubarb cobbler exuded the ambrosial perfume of June.

The most startling, though, was the deconstructed carrot cake. A disc of traditional spice cake was set beneath lemon mousse, a wafer-thin walnut praline, and Philadelphia cream cheese sorbet doused tableside with a glass of carrot juice.

All the familiar flavors were there, but they were lighter and startlingly vivid. Much like the century-old grande dame now known as XIX, it was a classic kindly redefined for a new era of glory.

— OR TRY THESE —

Here are three other fine-dining restaurants with a view:

MOSHULU 🏮 🏮 🏮
Penn's Landing, 401 S. Columbus Blvd., 19106, (215) 923-2500
The storied tall ship has been gloriously revived as a worthy destination for exciting food, elegant ambience, and one of the city's best views. The service handles crowds less reliably than the impressive kitchen.

Lacroix at the Rittenhouse
🏮 🏮 🏮
210 W. Rittenhouse Sq., 19103, (215) 790-2533
Chef Jean-Marie Lacroix has stepped-down, but talented successor Matthew Levin has a good track record. It's too soon to know if he can maintain the city's best brunch, and a luxury dining room that has never quite achieved four-bell status.

Bistro St. Tropez 🏮 🏮
Marketplace Design Center, 2400 Market St., 19103, (215) 569-9269
An upbeat bistro with a fantastic Schuylkill view, St. Tropez has a stylish, retro decor befitting its location and a creative take on French cuisine at reasonable prices.

Splurges

I LIKE A GOOD BARGAIN AS MUCH AS ANYONE, but some occasions simply demand a splurge, whether you're trying to wow a client or bring a foodie friend to their knees. Philadelphia, like any big city, has more than a few places to blow the budget. But some big-ticket indulgences are more than just expensive — they can be memorable.

Here's a short list of some of my favorite high-priced pleasures, both large and small:

- The whole suckling pig at **Amada** for $32 a person, minimum four people
- The $165 eight-course chef's tasting (with matching $80 wine flight) at **Le Bec-Fin**
- The $120 omakase at **Morimoto**
- The $44 dry-aged 20 oz. rib eye steak at **Barclay Prime**
- The white truffle supplement for risotto or polenta at **Vetri** (count $50 per dish)
- The gigantic $15 burger at **Rouge**
- The ceviche tasting platter (five for $49) at **¡Pasion!**
- The chocolate buffet at the **Ritz-Carlton**
- The "Heavy Hitters" flight (No. 803) of top-notch red wines by-the-glass at **Ristorante Panorama**, $44
- The $36 whole Peking duck at **Margaret Kuo's** (love that gong)
- The $42 whole Dover sole at **Savona**
- The $8 cup of real Jamaican Blue Mountain coffee at **Ray's Cafe and Tea House** in Chinatown
- A $5 scoop of dark chocolate gelato from **Capogiro**
- The seafood plateau at **XIX Nineteen**

Capsule Reviews

Capsule Reviews

This index contains every restaurant mentioned in the book, except for those on the specialized lists for Cafes and Tea Houses, Retailers, and The Jersey Shore, which follow. The 76 favorites are denoted by ALL CAPS. Restaurants that have been formally reviewed are shown with their bell ratings. If city and state are not listed, the restaurant is located in Philadelphia.

A

The Abbaye
637 N. 3rd St., 19123, (215) 627-6711, www.abbaye.com
Yet another gastro-pub for Northern Liberties, the Abbaye's inconsistent kitchen can't quite rival the neighborhood's best, but still delivers one of the better beer lists in town, with a particular focus on Belgian brews.

Abner's
38th and Chestnut Sts., 19104, (215) 662-0100, www.abnerscheesesteaks.com
The Big Five sports memorabilia leaves little doubt where allegiances lie at this University City institution where the pizza steak was the biggest hit. *Take-out.*

Abner's Authentic Barbecue
505 Old York Rd., 19046, (215) 885-8600, www.abnersbbq.com
7155 Ogontz Ave., 19138, (215) 224-8600, www.abnersbbq.com (take-out only)
This neat little strip-mall take-out (now with a second location on Ogontz Avenue) does a credible job of smoking its meats, especially the beef brisket, which was meltingly tender with an awesome garlicky sauce. The big, meaty spare ribs, however, were less tender. *Take-out.*

Abyssinia
229 S. 45th St., 19104, (215) 387-2424
Probably the best of the West Philly Ethiopians, this night club-cum-restaurant serves spicy stews over spongy injera bread. The kitfo, an Ethiopian steak tartare that blends ruby cubes of raw beef with a potent blend of cardamom and musky cayenne, ranks high on my list of dangerous dining thrills.

Aladdin
33d and Spruce Sts.
This tiny Middle Eastern food cart in front of the University of Pennsylvania Hospital is a favorite for its platters of couscous (or lentil rice) with grilled kofta and chicken kabobs.

Alfa
1709 Walnut St., 19103, (215) 751-0996
Come for a tempura-fried hot dog (the "Ichiro") or a fish taco and a craft beer at this cool and casually sleek gastro-pub near Rittenhouse Square. It's still too new for a verdict, but the international bar food nibbles are fun and affordable, a mellow prelude to the serious lounge scene at the Walnut Room upstairs.

Alisa Cafe   🔔🔔
112 Barclay Farm Shopping Center, Route 70 E., Cherry Hill, N.J. 08034, (856) 354-8807, www.alisacafe.com

After two decades as an Upper Darby mainstay, this French-Thai BYOB has moved across the river to a strip mall in Cherry Hill. The green room is comfortable and the service outgoing, and the chef uses good ingredients, but the cooking can feel too dated and inconsistent for the price. Some modest improvement since opening earned the restaurant its second bell.

ALISON AT BLUE BELL   🍴🍴🍴
721 Skippack Pike, Blue Bell, Pa.19422, (215) 641-2660, www.alisonatbluebell.com
Philly's kitchen-diva-turned-New-Yorker, Alison Barshak, has made a major comeback with her eponymous suburban BYOB, cooking stylish personal fare — from ginger-spiced calamari to Turkish lamb dumplings and chile-spiced chocolate pots de cremes — that opts for substance over flash. *Take-out.*

Alma de Cuba   🍴🍴
1623 Walnut St., 19103, (215) 988-1799, www.starr-restaurant.com
Douglas Rodriguez, the nation's godfather of Nuevo Latino cuisine, has paired with Stephen Starr to bring culinary fireworks, from ceviches to flaming chocolate cigars, to light this chic but dark Walnut Street space. *Take-out.*

AMADA   🍴🍴🍴
217 Chestnut St., 19106, (215) 625-2450, www.amadarestaurant.com
Discover your inner flamenco (and one of the city's hottest new reservations) at this sexy tapas haven, where Jose Garces presents stunning updates to classic Spanish flavors in an evocative, 135-seat space in Old City. The service is impressive and the menu well-tuned, but those small plates add up quickly. *Take-out.*

An Indian Affair
4425 Main St., 19127, (215) 482-8300
This cozy spot has a polished style suited to Manayunk's tony strip. While I found much of the food inconsistent (and a tad

greasy), the Bengal-style lamb chops sauced with cashew-coconut curry were unique and wonderful. *Take-out.*

Anastasi Seafood   🍴🍴
1101 S. 9th St., 19147, (215) 462-0550
A glassed-in dining room sits inside this South Philly fish market where fresh, fairly priced seafood is served up with a neighborhood Italian flair. Straight-forward seashore preparations are better than the fussier entrees. *Take-out.*

Anjou   🍴
206 Market St., 19106, (215) 923-1600; www.anjouphilly.net
Old City's first Korean-fusion restaurant also has decent sushi and an interesting sake lounge. Service has been shaky. *Take-out.*

ANSILL   🍴🍴🍴
627 S. 3rd St., 19147, (215) 627-2485, www.ansillfoodandwine.com
The small-plate phenomenon meets strange meats at David Ansill's daring Queen Village wine and "snack" bar in the former Judy's. But set your inhibitions aside, because while the offerings may be exotic, chef Kibett Mengech spins them into exquisite bites served with style and one of the city's smartest wine-and-beer lists. No reservations. *Take-out.*

Apamate
1620 South St., 19146, (215) 790-1620
This intriguing new tapas BYO has brought an intriguing taste of Spain to its paprika-colored room on South Street, with tortilla Española omelets, plancha-grilled sandwiches with authentic Iberian chorizo, and crispy churros stuffed with rich, dark, bitter chocolate. Too new for a verdict. *Take-out.*

Ariana
134 Chestnut St., 19106, (215) 922-1535
This rug-draped nook is one of the city's few Afghan restaurants. The yogurt-

sauced pumpkin, steamed scallion dumplings, and the kabobs, of course, are highlights. *Take-out.*

Aromatic House of Kebob

113 Chestnut St., 19106, (215) 923-4510, www.gokabob.com
Sip a glass of sour yogurt soda and savor tasty Middle Eastern fare beside a trickling fountain and the mural of a desert dream fortress at this sunny Persian grill. The soda is an acquired taste, but the delicately flavored kabobs and dill-laced pilafs are easy to love. *Take-out.*

Astral Plane

1708 Lombard St., 19146, (215) 546-6230, www.theastralplane.com
Few destinations have the quirky charm of this Restaurant Renaissance classic, where the time-capsule decor and charismatic owner, Reed Apaghian, have drawn loyalists to the tented dining rooms for more than three decades. The kitchen strives for updated flavors, but is too inconsistent to carry it off. Service also lags. *Take-out.*

Audrey Claire

276 S. 20th St., 19103, (215) 731-1222, www.audreyclaire.com
This is the bistro that launched the contemporary BYO boom with its unique urban style — and still draws Rittenhouse loyalists to its breezy corner dining room and sidewalk seating. The simple neo-Med menu, though, has slipped a bell in quality — especially compared with the new wave of BYO competition. *Take-out.*

August

1247 S. 13th St., 19147, (215) 468-5926, www.augustbyob.com
Partners MaryAnn Brancaccio and Maria Vanni have revitalized a South Philadelphia corner space with a dose of contemporary BYO style. The room has a polished, dark-toned ambience, and the service is warm and outgoing. The New

Italian menu is appealing, too, but needs more consistency and finesse to reach its potential.

August Moon

300 E. Main St., Norristown, Pa. 19401, (610) 277-4008
This ambitious Korean-Japanese is an unexpected surprise in downtown Norristown, serving good sushi and a broad menu of Korean specialties in a well-appointed room. *Take-out.*

Augusto's

530 Madison Ave., Warminster, Pa. 18974, (215) 328-0556
This surprising spot brings a sophisticated BYOB to the Northern 'burbs, with a pretty room and an ambitious chef-owner in Augusto Jalon turning out a contemporary menu with Mediterranean accents, from polenta-crusted fish to creamy "Creole" bisque flecked with crab.

Ava

518 S. 3rd St., 19147, (215) 922-3282, www.avarestaurant.com
This pretty Society Hill BYOB, from Le Castagne veteran Michael Campagna, offers some contemporary twists on Northern Italian cooking, from home-made pappardelle with rabbit ragu to shrimp sauteed with limoncello, and ravioli stuffed with eggplant and Taleggio cheese. *Take-out.*

Aya's Cafe

2129 Arch St., 19103, (215) 567-1555, www.ayascafe.net
One of the few interesting options in Logan Square, a former pizzeria was converted into this simple but pleasant Mediterranean BYO where the strongest dishes have a Middle Eastern flair, from the sesame-speckled Egyptian falafel to the excellent lamb shawarma. *Take-out.*

Azure

931 N. 2nd St., 19123, (215) 629-0500

An airy cafe and bar, Asure is a spacious and accessible neighorhood hang-out rather than a destination, but a reliable bet for lunch, brunch, occasional live music and patio seating beside a trickling fountain. The menu offers fairly cooked renditions of modern comfort food with a tropical twist — beef tips with tortillas and chipotle aioli, a pretty good crab cake, and polenta fries (a la Sabrina's).

B

Ba Le Bakery
606 Washington Ave., 19147, (215) 389-4350
A Vietnamese take-out bakery that serves traditional Southeast Asian pastries and savory steamed buns, as well as an excellent Vietnamese chicken hoagie with spicy pickled vegetables.

Bacio
2806 Rt. 130 N., Cinnaminson, N.J. 08077, (856) 303-9100, www.baciorestaurant.com
Former Harrah's casino chef Robert Minniti has wowed South Jersey diners with an upscale BYOB that delivers sophisticated ambience (great glassware), polished service, and stylish updates on Italian cuisine, from crab-stuffed crespelle to pork Milanese and fried artichokes.

Balkan Express Restaurant   🔔🔔
2237 Grays Ferry Ave. (at 23rd and Kater Sts.), 19146, (215) 545-1255
This surprising spot off reviving South Square is a solid American luncheonette by day and a treasure trove of authentic Serbian comfort foods by night. It still has awkward edges to smooth, but the room is pleasant and owner Radovan Jacovic is an outgoing host whose passion for the home-smoked flavors of his native land is satisfyingly evident. *Take-out.*

Banana Leaf
1009 Arch St., 19107, (215) 592-8288
Former Penang employees have opened Chinatown's second Malaysian restaurant to rival their former haunt. The big menu is virtually identical (plus sushi), and is also well-prepared, from roti to the chicken satay. *Take-out.*

Bar Ferdinand
1030 N. 2nd St., 19123, (215) 923-1313
The latest in a wave of Spanish offerings, this Northern Liberties tapas bar from designer Owen Kamihira in the Liberties Walk development features authentic Iberian flavors from chef Blake Joffe (ex-El Vez, Akellare) and an extensive Spanish wine list with 25 available by the glass. Too new for a verdict.

BARCLAY PRIME   🔔🔔🔔
237 S. 18th St., 19103, (215) 732-7560, www.barclayprime.com
More than just a $100 cheesesteak gimmick, this swanky hot spot off Rittenhouse Square redefines the dated steak house genre with a deft contemporary touch and a plush, modern look for a historic dining room. Only egregious markups on wine and liquor hold this Stephen Starr-let back from four-bell glory.

The Bards
2013 Walnut St. 19103, (215) 569-9585
Great brown bread, shepherd's pie and stuffed chicken anchor the updated Irish menu, and live Celtic music fills the Sunday morning air at this pleasant, wood-trimmed pub.

Bassetts Ice Cream
Reading Terminal Market, 12th & Arch Sts., 19107, (215) 925-4315, www.readingterminalmarket.org
An old-fashioned ice cream stand dedicated to America's oldest ice cream company, a Philadelphia classic founded in 1861.

Beau Monde   ✗✗

624 S. 6th St., 19147, (215) 592-0656,
www.creperie-beaumonde.com
Paris in South Philly begins at this
bustling cafe. Authentic Breton-style
buckwheat crepes, which seem to always
get better, are served in one of the city's
most beautiful rooms, with gilt paneling
and a mosaic hearth, or there's sidewalk
seating. Lean toward the simpler offerings, but just being there is half the
pleasure. *Take-out.*

BIRCHRUNVILLE STORE CAFE
✗✗✗

Hollow and Flowing Spring Rds.,
Birchrunville, Pa. 19421, (610) 827-9002,
www.birchrunvillestorecafe.com
Few destinations combine relaxed country charm with refined cooking as seamlessly as this bucolic general-store-
turned-BYO. The seasonal French menu
was at its game-inspired height recently,
ranging from buffalo carpaccio and wild
mushroom pastries to fabulous pistachio-stuffed rabbit. *Cash only.*

Bistro di Marino

492 Haddon Ave., Collingswood, N.J. 08108,
(856) 858-1700, www.bistrodimarino.com
Collingswood is stocked with notable
Italians, but this charming BYOB stands
out for its sleekly austere, exposed-brick
dining rooms, and personal takes on
Italian classics like homemade gnocchi
and eggplant rolatini stuffed with
smoked mozzarella. It also offers one of
the region's great lunch values, a $10
buffet worth double the price.

Bistro 7   ✗✗

7 N. 3rd St., 19106, (215) 931-1560
This minimalist green slip of a dining
room brings the welcome respite of a
food-focused BYO to the party-lounge
heart of Old City. The room and service
are pleasant, and the New American
menu from ex-White Dog chef Michael
O'Halloran is appealing. Same nagging

details, though, keep the food from
achieving its full potential.

Bistro St. Tropez   ✗✗

Marketplace Design Center,
2400 Market St., 19103, (215) 569-9269,
www.bistrosttropez.com
An upbeat bistro with a fantastic
Schuylkill view, St. Tropez has a stylish,
retro decor befitting its location in the
Marketplace Design Center and a creative take on French cuisine at reasonable prices. *Take-out.*

Bitar's

947 Federal St., 19147, (215) 755-1121,
www.bitars.com
7152 Germantown Ave., 19119, (215) 755-
1121
The original South Philadelphia market
and sandwich shop (it now has branches
in University City) is the innovator of the
grilled falafel sandwich. *Take-out.*

Black Bass Hotel

3774 River Rd., Lumberville, Pa. 18933, (215)
297-5770, www.blackbasshotel.com
There is an undeniable charm to the
rambling rooms of this historic inn (circa
1745). The menu is an odd blend of
Continental (beef Wellington) and New
American with a Southern twist, but the
heavy-handed cooking feels dated for
entrees that are about $10 too high.

The Black Door

629 S. 2nd St. (at Bainbridge), 19147, (215)
574-2958
This muli-level corner space in the
Queen Village 'hood has seen a number
of concepts come and go. The latest is a
gastro-pub with a serious Belgian beer
list and a former-Buddakan line cook in
the kitchen.

The Black Sheep   ✗✗

247 S. 17th St. (at Latimer), 19103, (215)
545-9473, www.theblacksheeppub.com
Don't expect neon shamrocks in this
handsomely upscale Irish pub, which

brings the warmth of an antique hearth, creamy Guinness, and premium whiskeys to a beautifully restored townhouse near Rittenhouse Square. The pub fare is better than average. *Take-out.*

Bleu   ♜♜

227 S. 18th St., 19103, (215) 545-0342
This parkside cafe with the colorful, muraled wall has finally found its lower-key neighborhood niche and moved out from the style-conscious shadow of Rouge with good-value bistro cooking. Has remained open, though there has been talk to transform it into a Stephen Starr project. *Take-out.*

Bliss   ♜♜

220-224 S. Broad St., 19102, (215) 731-1100, www.bliss-restaurant.com
Chef Francesco Martorella's (ex-Brasserie Perrier, Avenue B) contemporary boutique is one of the few locally owned restaurants on the Avenue of the Arts and serves fusion fare with a minimalist look. After a disappointing debut, the kitchen has showed some fresh imagination, from venison with chestnut ravioli and scallops with purple rice to cheesesteak empanadas. But service remains inconsistent. *Take-out.*

The Blue Bell Inn

601 Skippack Pike, Blue Bell, Pa. 19422, (215) 646-2010, www.bluebellinn.com
Some contemporary flavors have appeared here of late, but this classic remains one of the region's best old-time establishments, with staples such as fried oysters, creamed spinach, great wines and prime steaks butter-fried in cast-iron skillets. *Take-out.*

Blue Danube Restaurant

538 Adeline St., Trenton, N.J. 08611, (609) 393-6133
Rustic fabrics festoon the half-timbered dining room of this Hungarian eatery, where a shot of palinka and a plate of paprikash and spaetzles can make a Trenton neighborhood feel like the old country. *Take-out.*

Blue Sage   ♜♜

772 2nd Street Pike, Southampton, Pa. 18966, (215) 942-8888
This casual strip mall bistro remains one of the region's few worthy mainstream veggie alternatives. Chef Michael Jackson's menu (unlike Horizons) is not vegan and eschews mock meats for a vegetable-centric cuisine that offers creative international takes on everything from blue corn-asparagus tacos to goat cheese gnocchi. *Take-out.*

Bluefin

1017 Germantown Pike, Plymouth Meeting, Pa. 19462, (610) 277-3917, www.sushibluefin.com
The little strip-mall storefront doesn't promise much, but Chef Yong Kim turns out some of the suburb's best-cut and most creative sushi. Among the special rolls, the Marlee (tuna over crunchy, spicy yellowtail) is a favorite. *Take-out.*

Boccella's

521 Fayette St., Conshohocken, Pa. 19427, (610) 825-3693
The cheesesteaks at this unpretentious 32-year-old luncheonette are rightly famous, easily some of the best around. But I'm especially partial to the home-made Italian sausage patties smothered in caramelized onions and tomato gravy. *Take-out.*

Bonefish Grill   ♜

1015 Easton Rd. (Rt. 611), Willow Grove, Pa. 19090, (215) 659-5854, www.bonefishgrill.com
This Outback-owned seafooder aims for an upscale feel with the value and consistency of a chain, and the oak-scented grill delivers a few worthy dishes, especially for this particularly restaurant-deprived suburb. But careless cooking, collegiate service, and a tacky sound-

track will remind you that it's just another strip-mall concept. *Take-out.*

Branzino   ♟ ♟
261 S. 17th St., 19103, (215) 790-0103, www.branzinophilly.com
There is an appealing touch of Old World elegance to this Italian BYO that seems ideally suited to the well-heeled Rittenhouse Square crowd that dines here. The menu is stocked with standard dishes, but they are carefully done, from the airy gnocchi to delicate stuffed veal and the signature whole fish. *Take-out.*

BRASSERIE PERRIER   ♟ ♟ ♟
1619 Walnut St., 19103, (215) 568-3000, www.brasserieperrier.com
Georges Perrier's second restaurant offers top-notch upscale contemporary dining in the back, and a more casual brasserie menu in the lively front lounge and sidewalk cafe. Under chef and co-owner Chris Scarduzio, it has quietly remained one of the city's most reliable addresses for nearly a decade. *Take-out.*

Brasserie Perrier at Boyd's
1818 Chestnut St., 19103, (215) 564-1801
This posh little satellite to Georges Perrier and Chris Scarduzio's Walnut Street brasserie is a surprisingly affordable hideaway for a stylish light lunch — frittata du jour, crab cake, panini — the perfect respite from the luxury shopping. *Take-out.*

Brasserie 73
4024 Skippack Pike, Skippack Village, Pa. 19474, (610) 584-7880
With its grand terrace and stately facade, this upscale roadside brasserie looks like a vision out of France. The Gallic menu is pricey but well-executed with style.

Bridget's Steakhouse
8 W. Butler Ave, Ambler, Pa. 19002, (267) 465-2000, www.bridgets8west.com
This upscale addition to Ambler's aspiring downtown offers a martini bar and steak house with a Hawaiian accent. *Take-out.*

Bridgewater's Pub
2955 Market St. (30th St. Station), 19104, (215) 387-4787
Waiting for the train at 30th Street Station has been so much more interesting since this surprisingly ambitious pub arrived in the westside lobby, where there's a wide selection of microbrews to wash down eclectic bar fare made with wild game, from kangaroo chile to elk meatloaf. *Take-out.*

Bridgid's
726 N. 24th St., 19130, (215) 232-3232, www.bridgids.com
The eclectic comfort food isn't gourmet, though this Fairmount nook earns points for getting creative with inexpensive ingredients. But the big beer list is first-rate, from a potent chalice of La Chouffe to a tall bottle of rare and sublimely refreshing organic Foret Saison ale.

Brown Sugar Bakery & Cafe
219 S. 52nd St., 19139, (215) 472-7380
The windows of this tidy Trinidadian bakery/cafe just south of the Market Street El pulse with the rhythms of socca music while customers line up at the steam table window for excellent Caribbean soul food, from fabulous oxtails to sweet currant rolls and freshly made roti pancakes wrapped around a meal of curried chicken. *Take-out.*

Bubble House
3404 Sansom St., 19102, (215) 243-0804, www.thebubblehouse.com
Trendy Asian bubble teas filled with chewy tapioca beads are served up with affordable Asian fusion fare for the Penn crowd. *Take-out.*

Buca di Beppo
258 S. 15th St., 19102, 215-545-2818, www.bucadibeppo.com

The Italian tradition here is treated as a high comedy in garlic, gorging, and red-checked table cloths, but if you order right (lemon chicken, garlic cheese bread), it can be a fun family destination. *Take-out.*

BUDDAKAN 🗡 🗡 🗡

325 Chestnut St., 19106, (215) 574-9440, www.buddakan.com
Stephen Starr's first mega-hit restaurant is an Asian-fusion palace with a giant golden Buddha that still draws the chic crowds to its soaring Old City dining room. It's hardly changed since it opened in 1998, but that consistency may also be a risk for a restaurant that once set the trends. *Take-out.*

Buka-Teria

4070 Lancaster Ave., 19104; 215-222-5216
This modest luncheonette emerged after owner Funke Olashore's lunch truck was stolen. The result is a friendly, bare-bones cafe that is among the city's only Nigerian eateries. Starchy foufou (yam balls) are the centerpiece for spicy egusi (melon-seed paste) stews and fresh fish.

By George

Reading Terminal Market, 12th and Arch Sts., 19107, (215) 829-9391, www.reading-terminalmarket.org
This market standby serves up excellent brick-oven pizza slices, hearty strombolis (including one filled with a cheesesteak), veggie hoagies and tasty homemade pastas.

C

Cadence 🗡

300 S. Broad St., 19102, (215) 670-2388
The hours at this seldom-open French brasserie inside the Kimmel Center have gotten progressively more restrictive rather than more inviting. But stick with

the raw bar (when it's open) and gaze up at City Hall from the spectacular balcony.

Cafe de Laos 🗡 🗡

1117 S. 11th St., 19147, (215) 467-1546
This tidy spot has added Thai and Laotian flavors to the already diverse Asian hub around Washington Avenue. It has a surprisingly handsome dark wood interior, but the sharp flavors of its uncommon Laotian dishes (not the more standard Thai fare) are its best draw. It has changed owners since its review. *Take-out.*

Cafe Fresko 🗡 🗡

1003 Lancaster Ave., Bryn Mawr, Pa. 19010, (610) 581-7070, www.cafefresko.com
The Pappas family's bustling little BYO clad in polished granite and copper brings a surprisingly sophisticated French menu with Greek touches to the Main Line scene. It has changed chefs since its review. *Take-out.*

Cafe Habana 🗡

102 S. 21st St., 19103, (215) 561-2822, www.cafehabana.com
The homestyle Cuban fare has been up and down, but this stylish Latin bar shakes a fabulous mojito.

Cafe Lift

428 N. 13th St., 19123, (215) 922-3031, www.cafelift.com
The city's edgy new loft district between Vine and Spring Garden streets has a promising hangout in this surprising lunch-only cafe, an industrial-chic room of polished concrete and stainless steel that bustles with School District and Inquirer staffers who come for the stylish Italianesque menu of panini, salads, and good pastry. *Take-out.*

Cafe Lutecia

2301 Lombard St., 19146, (215) 790-9557
This pleasant corner cafe in the Fitler Square neighborhood is ideal for a sim-

ple baguette with pate and brie, toasty croque-monsieurs, soups, or a fresh salad. *Take-out.*

Cafe Spice   🔥🔥

35 S. 2nd St., 19106, (215) 627-6273, www.cafespice.com/philadelphia/welcome.html
This hip Indian bistro has contemporary decor, but classic dishes prepared with quality ingredients and sharp flavors. *Take-out.*

Cafe Sud

801 E. Passyunk Ave., 19147, (215) 592-0499, www.sudcakes.com
Exotic and sumptuous breakfasts and pastries with mint tea and a Moroccan touch in a cozy Bella Vista cafe.

Caffe Aldo Lamberti

2011 Rt. 70 E., Cherry Hill, N.J. 08002, (856) 663-1747, www.lambertis.com
The Lamberti family's flagship restaurant is a cut above its less impressive Cucina chain. From the sleek glass modern design to the serious wine list and Northern Italian menu that focuses on good ingredients and such unusual dishes as grilled tuna skewers over pasta with bottarga, I was impressed by a lunch. *Take-out.*

Caffe Casta Diva   🔥🔥

227 S. 20th St., 19103, (215) 496-9677
This storefront Italian BYO near Rittenhouse Square serves carefully wrought homemade pastas (try the spinach fettuccine with walnut pesto), interesting salads, and nice veal dishes in a tranquil little room trimmed with an opera theme. *Take-out.*

Cantina Los Caballitos

1651 E. Passyunk Ave., 19148, (215) 755-3550.
Amidst the authentic no-frills taquerias opening across South Philadelphia, this fun cantina done up in Southwestern orange and rustic wood trim has a polish aimed more at the upwardly mobile young gringos now gentrifying the 'hood. There's a serious tequila selection at the bar, and a menu rooted in authentic dishes, but it's still too new for a verdict.

THE CAPITAL GRILLE   🔥🔥🔥

1338 Chestnut St., 19107, (215) 545-9588, www.thecapitalgrille.com
This clubby steak house is the best of the corporate steak chains, with consistently cooked chops, a first-class bar, outgoing servers, and a power-lunch scene to rival the Palm's. Recent changes in the management and kitchen have been seamless.

Capogiro

117 S. 20th St., 19103, (215) 636-9250, www.capogirogelato.com
119 S. 13th St., 19107, (215) 351-0900
If there is better gelato in America than the sublimely creamy and intensely flavored frozen confections coming from Capogiro, I haven't tasted it yet. The midnight dark chocolate is an addiction. The recently opened second location near Rittenhouse Square is also a stylish cafe, with great panini, coffee, and sweets. *Take-out.*

Carambola   🔥🔥

1650 Limekiln Pike, Dresher, Pa. 19025, (215) 542-0900, www.carambolabyo.com
A strip-mall find in the northern suburbs with fun atmosphere and surprisingly sophisticated eclectic fare, from great grilled pizzas to roast duck, phyllo-wound shrimp Carambola, and homemade gelati. *Take-out.*

Caribou Cafe

1126 Walnut St., 19107, (215) 625-9535, www.cariboucafe.com
This handsome cafe is historically inconsistent, but the current owner, chef Olivier de St. Martin, has satisfyingly redirected the menu back toward its classic French bistro roots. Service, though, can be painfully slow.

Carman's Country Kitchen
1301 S. 11th St., 19147, (215) 339-9613
The changing chalkboard menu at this quirky corner luncheonette has seen its share of unlikely but tasty brunch experiments, from waffles with rutabaga and chestnuts to peppery homemade corned beef hash with orange-horseradish mayo. The kitchen's spiciest dish, though, is the inimitably sassy chef-owner, Carman Luntzel. *Take-out.*

Carmen's Famous Italian Hoagies
Reading Terminal Market, 12th & Arch Sts., 19107, (215) 592-7799, www.readingterminalmarket.org
The former Rocco's remains one of the purveyors of the best traditional Italian hoagie in the Reading Terminal Market, with good crusty bread, meats freshly sliced to order, and a good balance of stuffings.

CARMINE'S CREOLE CAFE   🍴🍴
232 Woodbine Ave., Narberth, Pa. 19027, (610) 660-0160, www.carminescreole.com
Chef John Mims has moved his wildly popular Havertown BYOB to Narberth, and while the dining room has more of an upscale polish, the menu still has the two-fisted gusto that made it the region's best ambassador for Louisiana-inspired cookery. The kitchen is more inconsistent than I'd like, but a good night at Carmine's is worth the one-hour wait. No reservations. *Take-out.*

Casona   🍴🍴
563 Haddon Ave., Collingswood, N.J. 08108, (856) 854-5555, www.mycasona.com
South Jersey has found a surprisingly convincing Latin beat at this sultry newcomer, where traditional Cuban and nuevo Latino specialties, from tender pulled pork and maduros to ceviches, are served in contemporary style at a splendidly redone Haddon Avenue manse wrapped in a grand dining porch that gives the Collingswood breezes a touch of the Caribbean.

Cassatt Lounge and Tea Room
The Rittenhouse Hotel, 210 W. Rittenhouse Sq., 19103, (215) 546-9000
Nibble afternoon sandwiches and scones with Devonshire cream in the civilized tranquility of the tea room and trellised garden at the Rittenhouse Hotel.

Casselli's
7620 Ridge Ave., 19128, (215) 483-6969
Old-time Roxborough natives claim this neighborhood classic has seen better days (est. 1941), but it's still a fun destination for decent family-style, red-gravy Italian fare and ambience that, from the homemade pastas to the karaoke crooner, still evokes retro comfort. *Take-out.*

Catherine's
1701 W. Doe Run Rd. (Rt. 82), Unionville Village, Kennett Square, Pa. 19348, (610) 347-2227, www.catherinesrestaurant.com
An old general store has been turned into an enchanting and popular showcase for chef Kevin McMunn's Southwestern-tinged contemporary fare. The intense seasonings and sauces would benefit from more finesse, but the mushroom-crab soup is tremendous.

Chabaa Thai Bistro
4371 Main St., 19127, (215) 483-1979, www.chabaathai.com
This handsome, multi-level eatery brings a taste of Thai to Manayunk. The food is on the mild side, but the fabric-draped, two-story space is a serene haven for a spot of pad Thai. *Take-out.*

Charles Plaza
234-236 N. 10th St., 19107, (215) 829-4383
This pink-and-black haven for seitan-seekers offers both mock and real versions of fish and meat. The "paradise goose" — bean-curd-wrapped veggies glazed with tangy peanut sauce — is truly inspired. But the crispy mock fish tastes a bit too much like turkey stuffing. *Take-out.*

Chaucer's Tabard Inn

1946 Lombard St., 19146, (215) 985-9663
The new ownership at this Graduate Hospital watering hole has upgraded the pub a bit, with some excellent burgers (try the blue cheesey Rittenhouse or the Old Bay-laced Chesapeake) and a good selection of local craft beers. *Take-out.*

The Chef's Table at the David Finney Inn 🎎🎎

222 Delaware St., New Castle, Del. 19720, (302) 322-6367, www.chefstablerestaurant.com
Former Deep Blue chef Robert Lhulier has revived the colonial-era David Finney Inn in charming old New Castle. With a contemporary menu that stresses seasonal ingredients and reasonable prices (including wine), the inn's warm tavern-style rooms feel as much like a neighborhood spot as a destination. Green service, though, still needs polish. *Take-out.*

CHERRY STREET CHINESE KOSHER VEGETARIAN RESTAURANT 🎎🎎

1010 Cherry St., 19107, (215) 923-3663
This pleasant dining room may be on a quiet street behind Chinatown's bustling main strip, but the kitchen is right on the mark. It defies the stereotypes of deep-fried mock-meat Chinese cooking with creative, well-seasoned dishes that emphasize good ingredients that taste as they should, whether in pure veggie cookery or convincing mock shrimp. *Take-out.*

Chez Elena Wu 🎎🎎

910 Haddonfield-Berlin Rd., Voorhees, N.J. 08043, (856) 566-3222
This upscale Chinese restaurant brings a French influence to a largely Cantonese menu, with separate chefs for the superb wonton soup and the escargots. *Take-out.*

Chickie's & Pete's

(The Original) 4010 Robbins Ave., 19135, (215) 338-3060, www.chickiesandpetes.com
(Stadium District) 15th St. and Packer Ave., 19145, (215) 218-0500
(Boulevard Plaza) 11000 Roosevelt Blvd., 19116, (215) 856-9890
(South Jersey) 183 US Highway 130, Bordentown, N.J. 08505, (609) 298-9182
Pete Ciarrocchi's handsomely converted supermarket-turned-crab-hall in South Philly's stadium district is the city's undisputed sports bar mecca, but the original corner tavern in Northeast Philly is hard to beat for a pre-game feast of garlicky crabs and Iggles-fever. *Take-out.*

Chickie's Italian Deli

1014 Federal St., 19147, (215) 462-8040, www.chickiesdeli.com
This small corner deli in South Philadelphia turns out a fabulous olive oil–roasted vegetable hoagie sprinkled with salty white cheese. *Take-out.*

Chick's Deli of Cherry Hill

906 Township Lane, Cherry Hill, N.J. 08002, (856) 429-2022
The chicken steaks are famous at this back-alley find off Route 70, but the beef steak is also worth noting, a perfect blend of flowing cheese, sweet onions, and tender meat. *Take-out.*

Chink's Steaks

6030 Torresdale Ave., 19135, (215) 535-9405, www.chinkssteaks.com
Step into a time warp at this marvelously preserved soda shop where chocolate egg creams and frothy shakes are the ideal pairing for what may be the most succulent traditional soft-roll American cheese cheesesteak in town. The controversial name is an homage to the late founder's nickname. *Take-out.*

Chloe 🎎🎎

232 Arch St., 19106, (215) 629-2337, www.chloebyob.com

Husband-and-wife chefs Dan Grimes and Mary Ann Ferrie run this homey neighborhood BYO in a tiny Old City space warmed by thistle brooms and votive lights, and a deftly rendered, affordable menu of international comfort food ranging from Indonesian prawns with corn cakes to pork chops and spaetzle.

The Chophouse   🍴🍴
4 S. Lakeview Dr., Gibbsboro, N.J. 08026, (856) 566-7300, www.thechophouse.us
South Jersey has a classy local steak house from the owners of P.J. Whelihan's. This sprawling complex with mission-style wood accents, leather booths, and a tony clientele bears little resemblance to the chain of pubs. The fare is standard steak house but well done. Friendly, professional servers take their role seriously. *Take-out.*

Chris' Jazz Cafe
1421 Sansom St., 19102, (215) 568-3131, www.chrisjazzcafe.com
Tucked into an obscure block across from the Union League, this unpretentious hideaway is a great place to catch jazz stars such as Jimmy Bruno in a late-night jam session. The menu isn't gourmet, but the ribs and crab cakes are respectable. *Take-out.*

Christis's Unnamed Lunch Cart
20th and Market Sts. (N.E. corner)
There's a reason a long line can always be found leading up to this unusual cart bedecked in potted plants, flowers and copper pots. Gregarious owner Konstandinos Christis cooks excellent marinated chicken sandwiches over a charcoal-fired grill, and his crisp falafel — fluffy and herbaceous inside and vibrant with green herbs — is one of the best in town. It's slow, but worth it.

Chung King
915 Arch St., 19107, (215) 627-3792
This large new Chinatown restaurant is one of a handful of recent Szechuan

entries into Philly's largely Cantonese fare. The more spice the better. It's too soon for a verdict here, but early scouts have raved about the pickled pepper lamb.

CinCin
7838 Germantown Ave., 19118, (215) 242-8800
This sunny little sibling of Bryn Mawr's Yangming offers thoughtfully upscale Chinese food with good ingredients and French-accented, wine-infused sauces. The fusion fare is generally more successful than the standard Chinese menu. *Take-out.*

Citron
818 W. Lancaster Ave., Bryn Mawr, Pa. 19010, (610) 520-9100, www.citrongrill.com
The Wakim brothers' upscale Mediterranean is replete with mahogany, wrought-iron gates, and a mural that lends flamenco flair. The menu also has a Spanish theme that has maintained reasonable consistency despite some chef changes in the kitchen. *Take-out.*

Citrus
8136 Germantown Ave., 19118, (215) 247-8188
A tiny bistro-bakery that offers modern seafood and vegetarian dishes with a light Asian touch and a heavy dose of animal-rights activism. *Take-out.*

City Tavern
138 S. 2nd St., 19106, (215) 413-1443, www.citytavern.com
For a place that has waiters in colonial knickers serving tourists pot pies in pewter bowls, this 18th-century re-creation is better than it needs to be, but it also usually lacks the soul to make it feel real. My most recent meal, though, was good, from the pecan biscuits and honeyed Jefferson ale to excellent venison.

Coconut Bay

Echelon Village Plaza, 1120 White Horse Rd., #103, Voorhees, N.J. 08043, (856) 783-8878

This handsome pan-Asian eatery has enlivened its strip-mall space with colorful silk lanterns, a waterfall, and an ambitious pan-Asian menu. The food is appealing, albeit tamed for the mainstream, ranging from Vietnamese lemongrass pork skewers to "Aloha" chicken scattered with macadamias. The sushi was disappointing. *Take-out.*

Coleman Restaurant   ✗

1401 Morris Rd., Blue Bell, Pa. 19422, (215) 616-8300, www.normandyfarm.com

Celebrity chef Jim Coleman's suburban digs anchors an elaborately restored dairy-farm-turned-conference-center. The concept of an all-organic modern twist on Pennsylvania Dutch cooking is fabulous, but the results have been inconsistent. *Take-out.*

The Continental

138 Market St., 19106, (215) 923-6069, www.continentalmartinibar.com

This Old City diner-turned-martini-bar is where Stephen Starr first found his restaurant mojo, serving global tapas and high-style salads to an endless supply of buff swingers in black. *Take-out.*

Continental Mid-Town   ✗ ✗

1801 Chestnut St., 19103, (215) 567-1800, www.continentalmidtown.com

Stephen Starr's three-story corner playhouse north of Rittenhouse Square is a magnet for trendy seekers of affordable global tapas and girly cocktails served in over-the-top surroundings with hanging-basket chairs and a rooftop bar. The sensory overload can be irritating, but the food (especially the desserts) lends this hot spot substance. *Take-out.*

Copabanana; Copa Too

263 S. 15th St., 19102, (215) 735-0848

344 South St., 19147, (215) 923-6180, www.copabanana.com

These cramped bars are known for great burgers, spicy Spanish fries, and addictive margaritas. *Take-out.*

Coriander Indian Bistro

910 Haddonfield-Berlin Rd., Voorhees, N.J. 08043, (856) 566-4546, www.coriandernj.com

This handsomely styled Indian has the feel of a colorful contemporary bistro, and some unusual Indian offerings, from tandooried leg of lamb to tasty yogurt and walnut soups. *Take-out.*

Corinne's Place   ✗ ✗

1254 Haddon Ave., Camden, N.J. 08103, (856) 541-4894

The homey pink dining room comes alive at Sunday brunch with one of the best soul-food buffets around, thanks in no small part to the cast-iron-skillet-fried chicken. *Take-out.*

Cork   ✗

90 Haddon Ave., Westmont, N.J. 08108, (856) 833-9800, www.corknj.com

South Jersey native Kevin Meeker has brought the same sense of approachable style that marks his Philadelphia Fish & Co. in Old City to Haddon Avenue's burgeoning restaurant scene. Cork's sleek room, lively bar scene, and appealing contemporary menu seem right, but the young kitchen struggled.

Cosmi's Market

1501 S. 8th St., 19147, (215) 468-6093

One of the best of South Philly's authentic corner hoagie shops, the sandwich meats here get slapped straight from the slicer to the seeded Sarcone's roll. The cheesesteaks are also quite good. *Take-out.*

Couch Tomato Cafe

102 Rector St., 19127, (215) 483-2233, www.thecouchtomato.com

This cafe does credible renditions of all the schmancy slices that gourmet pizzerias are prone to, including a great barbecue chicken with smoked gouda and scallions and an unusual white-chicken slice with walnuts, gorgonzola, and sage. But the cracker-thin plain earns it a vote as possibly the city's best by-the-slice pizzeria. *Take-out.*

Country Club Restaurant   🗡

1717 Cottman Ave., 19111, (215) 722-0500
A change in longtime ownership has been disastrous for this once-great Northeast institution, a storehouse of Jewish soul food that has become just another mediocre diner. *Take-out.*

The Countryside Market & Deli

514 Yale Ave., Swarthmore, Pa. 19081, (610) 604-4799,
www.countrysidemkt.tripod.com
Lunchers pack the dining room and patio at this excellent Swarthmore sandwich deli. Go for the warm house signature, a delicious muffaletta taste-alike called the Countryside, and a dessert of soft black licorice snips. *Take-out.*

Coyote Crossing

Market and Walnut Sts., West Chester, Pa. 19382, (610) 429-8900, www.coyotecrossing.com
800 Spring Mill Ave., Conshohocken, Pa. 19428, (610) 825-3000
I never loved the Conshohocken original, but this newer West Chester branch is in a stunningly rehabbed bank space. A pleasant lunch brought careful renditions of tequila-soused shrimp, a hearty stuffed pepper, and decent mole. *Take-out.*

The Creperie

13th and Norris Sts.
Owner Vasilios "Bill" Zacharatos ladles out the crispy crepe cones for the Temple crowd at his lunch truck, then heaps them with a pound of fillings ranging from grilled meats with homemade feta spread to "savory pizza" crepes and more traditionally French ones for dessert with Nutella.

Crescent City

600-602 S. 9th St. (at South), (215) 627-6780, www.crescentcityphilly.com
This good-looking Southern newcomer has its cafe windows wide open to the reviving South Street scene. It's still too new for a verdict, but the early buzz has been mixed on its Louisiana-inspired grill. *Take-out.*

Criniti

2611 S. Broad St., 19145, (215) 465-7750
This classic red-gravy Italian moved down the block not long ago to a more spacious dining room in a former church. The decor is a step up, but this old favorite seems to have lost a homey edge to its food. *Take-out.*

Cuba Libre   🗡

10 S. 2nd St., 19106, (215) 627-0666,
www.cubalibrerestaurant.com
Tropicana, The Quarter, 2801 Pacific Ave., Atlantic City, N.J. 08401, (609) 348-6700
A fantasy dining room built to resemble an old Havana streetscape hosts an awesome rum list that makes this Old City nightspot worth a try, though the Nuevo and Viejo Latino cooking has been inconsistent.

Cucina Forte   🗡 🗡

768 S. 8th St., 19147, (215) 238-0778
Ebullient chef-owner Maria Forte has settled into a cozy, gold-ceilinged BYOB across the street from her former roost at Mezza Luna. The simple but pleasant South Philly space emphasizes warm hospitality and elevated Italian home cooking, from cloudlike ricotta gnocchi to sublime leg of lamb. *Take-out.*

D

Dahlak

4708 Baltimore Ave., 19143, (215) 726-6464, www.dahlak.com
5547 Germantown Ave., 19144, (215) 849-0788
This Ethiopian standby isn't fancy, but the spicy stews and spongy injera bread are tasty, and the house-roasted ginger-flavored coffee is not to be missed. *Take-out.*

Dalessandro's

Henry Ave. and Walnut Ln., 19128, (215) 482-5407
The staff couldn't be nicer at this Roxborough classic, but the tall berm of finely chopped, mass-cooked beef tends to make a dry sandwich. *Take-out.*

Dante & Luigi's

762 S. 10th St., 19147, (215) 922-9501, www.danteandluigis.com
The city's oldest Italian (circa 1899), though not with continuous ownership, is a bit more upscale than the rest, and still a destination for veal braciola, tender gnocchi, and spaghetti with chicken livers. A recent meal was fine, but lacked some spark.

The Dark Horse   ♟ ♟

421 S. 2nd St., 19147, (215) 928-9307, www.darkhorsepub.com
The owners of the former Dickens Inn have struggled to keep the English fare here up to the level of their Black Sheep near Rittenhouse Square now that Chef Ben McNamara has returned to the New Wave Cafe. But this handsome, rambling old pub is still a great destination for world-class single-malt scotch, darts, and soccer-heads craving European football on the tube.

Davio's   ♟ ♟

111 S. 17th St., 19103, (215) 563-4810, www.davios.com
This Boston-based Italian chain has a sleek second-floor perch in a former Chestnut Street bank building, and excels with classic steaks.

DeBreaux's

2135 N. 63rd St., 19151, (215) 877-4559
Frances DeBreaux's little soul kitchen next to the Overbrook SEPTA station puts out some of the area's best Southern cooking, from fabulous corn-meal-fried fish to super potato salad, oxtail gravy, and smoked turkey. It's great take-out, but super slow, so be sure to call ahead. *Take-out.*

Deep Blue

111 W. 11th St., Wilmington, Del. 19801, (302) 777-2040, www.deepbluebarand-grill.com
Despite its location in a parking garage, this chic restaurant is a power-crowd destination thanks to its contemporary decor and a modern seafood menu. An impressive raw bar, with briny Canadian Beau Soleil oysters and buttery Hog Islands from California, is the highlight. *Take-out.*

Delilah's Southern Cafe

Reading Terminal Market, 12th and Arch Sts., 19107, (215) 574-0929, www.readingterminalmarket.org
30th St. Station, 30th and Market Sts., 19104, (215) 243-2440.
Before Delilah Winder attempted nouveau soul food at her stylish Bluezette in Old City, these casual food stands set decent local benchmarks of the Southern classics.

Denise's Soul Food

Truck location: Market and 30th Sts. (S.E. corner)
5809 N. Broad St., 19141, (215) 424-7022
The jerk chicken platter with rice and beans is a mouthful of Caribbean flavor, best washed down with a big gulp of sweetened iced tea. *Take-out.*

Derek's
4411 Main St., 19127, (215) 483-9400, www.dereksrestaurant.com
Once the king of Manayunk, chef Derek Davis is down to this eponymous remake of his former Sonoma. The old Cal-Ital vodka bar has been revamped to warmer earth tones and a casual neighborhood feel, with a deep granite bar for eating, and a casual American grill menu that ranges from wood-fired pizzas to big salads and burgers. *Take-out.*

Desi Village Restaurant
15 S. Gulph Rd., King of Prussia, Pa. 19406, (610) 265-8500
This authentic and friendly Indian restaurant is a welcome respite from all the chain restaurants at the mall. Try the chaat and tableside-sizzling tandoori chicken.

Deuce Restaurant and Bar   ♟♟
1040 N. 2nd St., 19123, (215) 413-3822, www.deucerestaurant.com
A slice of Old City has landed in Northern Liberties at this loungey restaurant, which feels like a gastro-pub with a feminine touch, from the red-lit, button-tufted decor to the corny cocktails and homemade ketchup. The kitchen tries hard, with promising success, to deliver affordable and creative upgrades to pub comfort food. But there's been a chef change since the review. *Take-out.*

Deux Cheminees   ♟♟♟
1221 Locust St., 19107, (215) 790-0200, www.deuxchem.com
Turn back the clock to an era of classic French dining in an elegant 19th-century townhouse, beautifully maintained by the jovial and scholarly chef Fritz Blank, whose massive cookbook library upstairs is as famous as the stunningly rich soups served from antique terrines. Master Blank has hinted for a few years at imminent retirement, so enjoy this jewel while it lasts.

DEVI   ♟♟
151 Whiteland Town Center, Exton, Pa. 19341, (610) 594-9250
Dosa lovers should make the trek to this obscure suburban Indian find. Wedged into a strip mall between Route 30 and the Pottstown Pike, it's an adventure diner's gem — a rare example of South Indian vegetarian cuisine (think gunpowder idlys, sambar and coconut chutneys) that is so finely prepared, it transcends the modest steam table buffet format and plain strip-mall decor.

Devon Seafood Grill   ♟♟
225 S. 18th St., 19103, (215) 546-5940, www.devonseafood.com
This chain-owned seafooder has a large, accessible dining room and a slightly less tony crowd than the rest of Rittenhouse's chic cafes, which comes to gobble up its hot sweet biscuits and fresh seafood, though it has slipped over the years from its impressive opening form. *Take-out.*

Di Bruno Bros. House of Cheese
1730 Chestnut St., 19103, (215) 665-9220, www.dibruno.com
Take a lunch break from prosciutto shopping at this sunny self-service cafe atop Di Bruno's Rittenhouse food emporium. The cafeteria-style lay-out and much of the food is still a work in progress. But the casual ambience and variety of high-quality flavors make this a popular stop for a quick and tasty meal, whether for soup, salad or sushi. Anything with cheese is stellar (of course). The oversized sandwiches leave much to be desired. But the pizzas are also surprisingly good.

DILWORTHTOWN INN   ♟♟♟
1390 Old Wilmington Pike, West Chester, Pa. 19382, (610) 399-1390, www.dilworthtown.com
This classic is still the model for what a Colonial-era country inn should be, with a first-class menu and talented young

kitchen that artfully melds continental with contemporary ideas, one of the region's deepest cellars, and gracious Old World service to match the historic candlelit setting.

DiNardo's Famous Crabs

312 Race St., 19106, (215) 925-5115, www.dinardos.com
This old-time seafooder is an unpretentious Old City standby for classic fish house fare, from snapper soup to a pile of steamed crabs. *Take-out.*

DiNic's

Reading Terminal Market, 12th & Arch Sts., 19107, (215) 923-6175, www.readingterminalmarket.org
This lunch counter is a longtime destination for a proper pork sandwich and zesty Terminal banter. However, some recently added sandwiches — juicy brisket and super slow-roasted pork shoulder dressed in spicy long hots, greens, and sharp provolone — have taken DiNic's to an entirely new, lofty level..

Divan Turkish Kitchen   ♦ ♦

918 S. 22nd St. (at Carpenter), 19146, (215) 545-5790
This pretty, new Turkish BYO is a bright surprise in the rapidly gentrifying neighborhood between South Street and Washington Avenue. The affordable menu offers standard Turkish grill fare, from adana and doner kebabs to whole dorado, and a selection of Mediterranean meze. Too new for a verdict.

DJANGO   ♦ ♦

526 S. 4th St., 19147, (215) 922-7151
The cozy BYOB that inspired a generation of ambitious bistros has seen few obvious changes to its ambience and impressive service since it changed hands last year. But the appealingly seasonal New American menu has taken a noticeable step down in its elegance and execution. The new chef may just be trying too hard, and would do well to simplify his plates. *Take-out.*

DMITRI'S   ♦ ♦

3rd and Catherine Sts., 19147, (215) 625-0556
23rd and Pine Sts., 19103, (215) 985-3680
Dmitri Chimes's appealing, simple Greek seafooderies are still a draw. A recent visit to the larger Fitler Square branch was as satisfying as ever, with lemony octopus and whole fish, spicy shrimp pilpil, and grilled lamb served up casually for a nice price. No reservations. *Take-out.*

Domaine Hudson Wine Bar & Eatery   ♦ ♦

1314 N. Washington St., Wilmington, Del. 19801, (302) 655-9463, www.domainehudson.com
Wilmington gets into the small-plate wine-bar craze at this clubby little eatery, where a huge selection of intriguing wines by the glass is paired with ex-Dilworthtown chef Jason Barrowcliff's New American fare. The wines are worthwhile, the service is fine-tuned, and though the menu sometimes lacks focus, it's good enough to help the affordable wines shine.

Domani Star

57 W. State St., Doylestown, Pa. 18901, (215) 230-9100, www.domanistar.com
Look out through the window-paned storefront onto charming downtown Doylestown from this always-packed BYOB, where the Italian menu has an authentic touch, from the generous antipasto platter to the hearty, lightly creamed Bolognese sauce and the excellent tomato-basil soup. *Take-out.*

Donkey's Place

1223 Haddon Ave., Camden, N.J. 08103, (856) 966-2616
7 Tomlinson Mill Rd., Medford, N.J. 08055, (856) 810-0445
10 Asbury Ave., Ocean City, N.J., 08226, (609) 399-9959

Imitated to great acclaim by an eatery in Manhattan, Donkey's specialty is a fistful of flavor on a kaiser roll, as notable for its generous mop-top of onions as it is for its grease-dripping, salty punch. *Take-out.*

Down Home Diner
Reading Terminal Market, 12th and Arch Sts., 19107, (215) 627-1955
Jack McDavid's Reading Terminal outlet for hog-jowl soup and pan-fried chicken could be so good if the food were more consistent.

Drafting Room
635 N. Pottstown Pike, Exton, Pa. 19341, (610) 363-0521, www.draftingroom.com
The eclectic American grill menu ranges from cashew- and coconut-crusted shrimp to gumbo, ribs and grilled ostrich, but the Drafting Rooms are primarily known as major destinations for a huge selection of craft beers and a list of more than 70 single-malt scotches.

Dutch Eating Place
Reading Terminal Market, 12th & Arch Sts., 19107, (215) 922-0425, www.readingterminalmarket.org
Squeeze in at this perpetually busy counter for a taste of simple but authentic Pennsylvania Dutch flavors, from the pork and kraut to tasty sloppy joes. Too bad those homey apple dumplings get nuked soggy.

E

Eclipse Bistro
1020 N. Union St., Wilmington, Del. 19805, (302) 658-1588, www.eclipsebistro.com
This contemporary bistro has a colorful dining room and an open kitchen, with a fun fusion menu to match, from pulled pork–sweet potato spring rolls to excellent wild boar tacos and a dangerous Cosmo sorbet. Entrees could be more carefully cooked. *Take-out.*

Effie's   ♠ ♠
1127 Pine St., 19107, (215) 592-8333, www.effiesrestaurant.com
Classic Greek home foods, from moussaka to baklava, can be savored in the lovely brick patio or the cozy cottage behind Effie's townhouse-turned-taverna. A recent meal, though, was a bit sloppy. *Take-out.*

821
821 N. Market St., Wilmington, Del. 19801, (302) 652-8821, www.restaurant821.com
Across from Wilmington's Grand Opera House, this sophisticated restaurant has been a mainstay of foie gras decadence and wood-roasted gusto for the credit-card city. A change in ownership and in the kitchen since its former three-bell rating has generated an overall positive buzz.

El Bohio
2746 N. 5th St., 19133, (215) 425-5991
This corner eatery has anchored the Golden Mile, the commercial strip of Philadelphia's traditional Puerto Rican neighborhood, for more than two decades, with spicy fried chicken, adobo-smothered pork chops, and perhaps the best flan in town. *Take-out.*

El Fuego
723 Walnut St., 19107, (215) 592-1901
Grab a spicy beef burrito and settle into one of the community wooden tables at this spare but cool hangout for the Jefferson Hospital and Jewelers' Row lunch crowd. The menu is limited but fresh, tasty, and cheap, making this one of the better Tex-Mex spots in town.

El Sarape
1380 Skippack Pike (Rts. 73 and 202), Blue Bell, Pa. 19422, (610) 239-9466, www.elsarapebluebell.com
This Blue Bell cantina eschews the usual Tex-Mex cooking for some authentic and upscale Mexican flavors ranging from

mole poblano to chorizo-topped filet mignon and seared tuna topped with chile de arbol orange glaze. There is also an excellent selection of good tequilas.

El Sol de Peru

57 Garrett Rd., Upper Darby, Pa. 19422, (610) 352-1232

This warm little nook still delivers an intriguing taste of the Peruvian Andes, with weekend chicken roasts and a hominy-scattered Peruvian ceviche flavored with a salty, sour and spicy marinade.

EL VEZ

121 S. 13th St., 19107, (215) 928-9800, www.elvezrestaurant.com

The city's most sophisticated Mexican food is still at Stephen Starr's colorful Tijuana fantasy room, with Mexican-born chef Adrian Leon. A slip in service and too much ice in the margaritas, though, have dropped El Vez a notch from its previous three-bell rating. *Take-out.*

Elements Cafe   ♜ ♜

517 Station Ave., Haddon Heights, N.J. 08035, (856) 546-8840, www.elementscafe.com

Chef-owner Fred Kellermann has created a cozy BYO in this charming downtown storefront, with a creative New American menu built around small plates, all under $10. The food could be more consistent, but the price is right to experiment, the service is outgoing, and this simple room has the warm vibe of a promising neighborhood haunt. *Take-out.*

Emerald Fish

65 Barclay Farms Shopping Center, Route 70 E., Cherry Hill, N.J. 08034, (856) 616-9192, www.emeraldfish.com

This colorful strip-mall BYOB has an internationally inspired kitchen and pate. Recently changed hands. *Take-out.*

Ernesto's 1521 Cafe   ♜ ♜

1521 Spruce St., 19102, (215) 546-1521, www.ernestos1521.com

In the shadow of the Kimmel Center, this pretty trattoria remains a great pre-theater value, with fresh pastas, delicious crabcakes, homemade limoncello, and an affordable list of interesting Italian wines. A lovely new back dining room has added much-needed space and a charming outdoor patio.

Estia   ♜ ♜

1405-07 Locust St., 19102, (215) 735-7700, www.estiarestaurant.com

The grand theater-district space left by Toto is now an elegant Greek seafood palace decked in Jerusalem limestone, rustic wood beams, and a display of imported Greek fish, the kitchen's signature. The whole fish are exquisite, but high prices and a limited menu have kept the vast dining room feeling empty. *Take-out.*

Eulogy

136 Chestnut St., 19106, (215) 413-1918, www.eulogybar.com

The Flemish pub fare has been inconsistent at this amiable Belgian bar in Old City, where you can lay your Corsendonk on a pine box in the upstairs Coffin Room lounge. Stick with the burger or moules and frites — and any number of the 300-plus ales — and a jolly time should be had by all. *Take-out.*

F

Fado Irish Pub

1500 Locust St., 19102, (215) 893-9700, www.fadoirishpub.com

Guinness owns this noisy, Atlanta-based pub chain, which is decorated to the hilt with antiquey Irish kitsch and serves a decent pub-plus menu that offers modern spins on traditional boxty potato pancakes. *Take-out.*

Famous Dave's Barbeque

Columbus Commons, 1936 S. Columbus Blvd., 19148, (215) 339-0339, www.famous-daves.com
104 Rt. 70 E., Cherry Hill, N.J. 08034, (856) 857-1520
This rapidly expanding chain out of Minnesota has a hokey hunting-lodge decor, but actually does a fairly decent job smoking its meat, even if sauces are overly sweet. Try the wild-rice chicken soup. *Take-out.*

FAMOUS 4th STREET DELICATESSEN   🍴🍴

700 S. 4th St., 19147, (215) 922-3274
The Queen Village institution has gotten a much-needed makeover from new owner Russ Cowan, who has completely rehabbed the 83-year-old deli and upgraded the food to the level of his former Kibitz delis. The service and room still feel like a work in progress, but Philadelphia finally has the makings of a great sit-down deli. No reservations. *Take-out.*

The Farmhouse   🍴🍴🍴

1449 Chestnut St., Emmaus, Pa. 18049, (610) 967-6225, www.thefarmhouse.com
This charmingly restored farmhouse has a world-class beer collection to accompany a New American menu bursting with local ingredients and vivid flavor combinations. It's a malt drinker's haven that takes food and ambience seriously. Well worth the hour-plus drive from Center City.

Farmicia   🍴

15 S. 3rd St. 19106, (215) 627-6274, www.farmiciarestaurant.com
The owners of Metropolitan Bakery have teamed with former White Dog Cafe chef Kevin Klause to brighten up the old Novelty space with a New American menu featuring organic and local ingre-

dients. The menu shows an occasional spark with its salads, vegetarian dishes and desserts, but has otherwise been underwhelming. Service has been disorganized. *Take-out.*

Fat Jack's BBQ

1261 Blackwood-Clementon Rd., Commerce Plaza 1, Clementon, N.J. 08021, (856) 309-7427, www.fatjacks.net
The barbecue is legit at this strip-mall smoke pit deep in the heart of Camden County, but I'd stop shy of declaring it a contender for the region's best (as some surveys have proclaimed). The sauce is dark and sweet, and though the meats are clearly smoked, they lack the more profound flavors of the very best. *Take-out.*

Fayette Street Grille

308 Fayette St., Conshohocken, Pa. 19428, (610) 567-0366, www.fayettestreetgrille.com
This casual cafe transforms itself into an ambitiously creative BYOB at dinner, with choices ranging from root beer-glazed pork to scallops with pear chutney in a $31 three-course menu. A lunch brought very good crabcakes, irresistible crab dip, and a surprisingly fine pulled-pork barbecue sandwich. *Take-out.*

Figs

2501 Meredith St., 19130, (215) 978-8440, www.figsrestaurant.com
This Art Museum bistro is a cozy, pumpkin-colored corner room with an intriguing (albeit inconsistent) menu that blends contemporary cooking with North African accents. *Take-out.*

Fish Tank on Main

4247 Main St., 19127, (215) 508-020, www.fishtankonmain.com
This sleek corner room brings a stylish new spot with an Italian bent (and, yes, a fish tank) to Manayunk's Main Street. Too new for a verdict. *Take-out.*

Fitzwater Cafe

728 7th St., 19147, (215) 629-0428
From the owners of the upscale Saloon comes this pleasant Italian BYOB, a sunny yellow room in a former filling station that has a beautiful nickel caffe bar, a loyal breakfast following, and a more ambitious Italian menu at night. A recent lunch brought an excellent chicken cutlet, but disappointingly watery pasta. *Take-out.*

FORK　🍴🍴

306 Market St., 19106, (215) 625-9425, www.forkrestaurant.com
Always reliable for stylish, affordable New American bistro cuisine, Fork may be the definitive Old City bistro. Inconsistencies keep it shy of great, but the addition of the Etc. shop next door has added to its appeal with a great selection of cheeses, prepared foods and house-baked breads, as well as tasting menus for adventurous eaters on Wednesday nights. *Take-out.*

FOUNTAIN RESTAURANT　🍴🍴🍴🍴

Four Seasons Hotel, 1 Logan Sq., 19103, (215) 963-1500, www.fourseasons.com/philadelphia
The Fountain wraps diners in the lavish elegance of a grand hotel with the city's best service and a powerhouse kitchen. Expect to pay big, but the menu delivers stellar international haute cuisine rooted in the finest ingredients and refreshing imagination.

Four Dogs Tavern

1300 W. Strasburg Rd., West Chester, Pa. 19382, (610) 692-4367, www.marshaltoninn.com
Set amid the rolling farmland, just across the parking lot from the fancier Marshalton Inn, this rustic pine-paneled tavern has country ambience to spare. Some grouchy service and careless cooking at a recent visit, though, took away from an otherwise intriguing New American meal with spicy Louisiana accents. *Take-out.*

Four Seasons Juice Bar

Reading Terminal Market, 12th & Arch Sts., 19107, (215) 925-4448, www.readingterminalmarket.org
Even after a hefty pork sandwich lunch at DiNic's, I always feel virtuous after a smoothie spiced with fresh ginger at this bustling juice bar counter in the Terminal. The combinations are endless, but I usually go with the special.

Frenchtown Inn　🍴🍴

7 Bridge St., Frenchtown, N.J. 08825, (908) 996-3300, www.frenchtowninn.com
This historic inn beside the Delaware River has a long tradition of sophisticated dining, with an ambitious menu rooted in seasonal French cooking, fine wines, and cozy fireplace dining rooms. *Take-out.*

FRIDAY SATURDAY SUNDAY　🍴🍴

261 S. 21st St., 19103, (215) 546-4232, www.frisatsun.com
The fluorescent chalkboard still glows brightly alongside some beautiful new murals at this Rittenhouse Square classic, which, with its romantic dining room (and cool upstairs Tank Bar), remains one of the Renaissance's most vibrant spots, with a finely rendered menu ranging from mushroom soup to superb crabcakes, and a great wine list that adds only a $10 markup to each bottle. *Take-out.*

Frusco's Steak Shop

7220 Frankford Ave., 19135, (215) 333-0800
Virtually unknown outside the great Northeast, this Frankford Avenue grill cooks some of the best no-chop cheesesteaks around, as well as a respectable pork sandwich. *Take-out.*

Funky Lil' Kitchen　🍴🍴

232 King St., Pottstown, Pa. 19464, (610) 326-7400, www.funkylilkitchen.com

This surprising Center City-style bistro adds a real spark to Pottstown's downtown revival. With its groovy lava-lamp decor, it has a spunky personality and an adventurous New American menu from chef-owner Michael Falcone that should draw fans from beyond the nearby 'burbs. *Take-out.*

FuziOn

2960 Skippack Pike, Worcester, Pa. 19490, (610) 584-6958, www.fuzionrestaurant.com
The team behind Chinatown's Ly Michaels serves ambitious Asian-fusion cuisine farther west in a pretty little BYOB near Skippack Village. *Take-out.*

G

Gables at Chadds Ford

423 Baltimore Pike, Chadds Ford, Pa. 19317, (610) 388-7700, www.thegablesatchadds-ford.com
Dine in the rustic elegance of a handsomely refurbished 1800s dairy barn and patio, which give new meaning to farmyard chic. The serious contemporary menu ranges from great mushroom soup to Asian-spiced calamari. *Take-out.*

GAYLE 🍴🍴🍴

617 S. 3rd St., 19147, 215-922-3850, www.gaylephiladelphia.com
Former Le Bec-Fin chef Daniel Stern gives unexpected modern twists to familiar foods at this warm new destination in the former Azafran, where soups become sauces, stews are deconstructed, and endive will never be the same. Some experiments work better than others, but the gambles almost always pay off. Service is also superb.

General Sutter Inn

14 E. Main St., Lititz, Pa. 17543, (717) 626-2115, www.generalsutterinn.com

When in Lititz for a visit to the Wilbur chocolate factory and Sturgis pretzelry, try this rambling old hotel (circa 1764), a reliable stop for a quality meal. The upscale dinner menu has a surprisingly adventurous focus on game with a French twist. Our lunch, meanwhile, brought a very impressive broiled crab cake and a tasty weinerschnitzel.

Genji 🍴🍴

1720 Sansom St., 19103, (215) 564-1720, www.genjionline.com
It may have slipped a shade since the tragic death of its owner a few years ago, but this remains one of Center City's most reliable venues for standard sushi. Service is inconsistent. *Take-out.*

Geno's Steaks

1219 S. 9th St., 19147, (215) 389-0659, www.genosteaks.com
I've generally preferred this South Philly institution to its cross-street rival Pat's, especially with a splash of the killer hot sauce. But Geno's has unfortunately become better known lately for owner Joe Vento's ugly English-only grandstanding — a nitwit policy that disqualifies Geno's from my go-list. There are better steaks, so why bother?

Georges'

Spread Eagle Village, 503 W. Lancaster Ave., Wayne, Pa. 19087, (610) 964-2588, www.georgesonthemainline.com
Georges Perrier's gorgeous French farmhouse on the Main Line has struggled to find the perfect identity for its suburban crowd, changing names (remember Le Mas?), concepts, and chefs regularly. A recent lunch with Dijon mustard-Gruyere pizza, spectacular Iberian clams, and refined-but-unstuffy service felt just right. *Take-out.*

GILMORE'S 🍴🍴🍴

133 E. Gay St., West Chester, Pa. 19380, (610) 431-2800, www.gilmoresrestaurant.com

A spectacular revisit to Peter Gilmore's charming townhouse dining room has earned the ex-Le Bec-Fin chef a third bell, with polished French cuisine that shows magical sparks of innovation (try the "corndog" shrimp and "candied apple" chocolate mousse) and service that is personal and poised.

Gioia Mia   ♟ ♟

2025 Sansom St., 19103, (215) 231-9895, www.gioiamiaphl.com
Two La Veranda alums have added yet another Italian restaurant to Rittenhouse Square's wealth of Italian options, but this one is worthwhile, with authentic flavors from chef Fabrizio Pace focusing on seafood, simple pastas, and quality meats. The airy double-floored space (formerly Cibucan) is roomier than much of the competition. *Take-out.*

Giumarello's

329 Haddon Ave., Westmont, N.J. 08108, (856) 858-9400, www.giumarellos.com
This upscale hot spot serves decent but pricey Italian fare (fine veal, lobster mac-n-cheese, spicy calamari) in a sprawling dining room and manicured garden that have the crisp formality of a corporate banquet hall. The handsome martini bar exudes a livelier, more casual vibe. *Take-out.*

Goji Tokyo Cuisine

2001 Hamilton St., 19130, (215) 569-1667
This sleek new Japanese emporium purports to bring authentic Tokyo cooking to Fairmount. The contemporary, glassed-in space next to the City View condos is appealingly upscale, but early meals here have been inconsistent and expensive.

Golden Gates

11058 Rennard St., 19116, (215) 677-9337, www.ggrestaurant.com
Reserve ahead and bring lots of friends and vodka to the Northeast's definitive Russian nightclub, where the tasty banquet menus (from blini and pirozhki to chicken Kiev) and live floor-show disco will make you feel as if you're dancing in Moscow on the Delaware. *Take-out.*

Good Dog

224 S. 15th St., 19102, (215) 985-9600, www.gooddogbar.com
The city's new smoking ban will encourage me to go more often to this funky, multi-level gastro-pub. The inventive bar-food is definitely worth checking out, especially the Cordon Bleu chicken tenders and what may be the most unique cheeseburger in town — it's stuffed with a core of molten Roquefort. *Take-out.*

Good 'n' Plenty

150 Eastbrook Rd., Smoketown, Pa., 17576, (717) 394-7111, www.goodnplenty.com
You'll get your fill of Amish kitsch (and then some more) at this sprawling Lancaster County feed hall. But for a place where tourists arrive by the busload, the country cooking is surprisingly good (from fried chicken and ham loaf to excellent shoo-fly pie). The family-style service is preferable to the competition's free-for-all buffets.

Grace Tavern

2229 Grays Ferry Ave., 19146, (215) 893-9580
The team behind Monk's Cafe has taken over a classic neighborhood bar and restored the antique pressed-tin charm to this appealing, elbow-shaped room. The beer is wonderful (try Nodding Head B.P.A.), and the Creole-centric menu is limited but tastily focused on gourmet sausages, burgers, and deep-fried green beans. *Take-out.*

Great Tea International

1724 Sansom St. 19103, (215) 568-7827, www.great-tea.net
At this new basement tea room just below the Joseph Fox bookstore, the owner serves a classic Chinese tea ceremony with teas imported directly from

Taiwan, along with pastries, steamed buns, and dumplings. *Take-out.*

Greater India Fine Dining

1218 Welsh Rd., Assi Plaza, North Wales, Pa. 19454, (215) 412-3690, www.greaterindiafinedining.com

An exotic surprise deep in the Northern Suburbs, this whimsically decorated and friendly restaurant serves authentically spiced and carefully prepared Indian cuisine, from richly creamed chicken korma, to onion bhaji fritters, puffy deep-fried poori, and excellent dal makhni. It's quite child-friendly — the servers even know to introduce the pakora-fried chicken to kids as "Indian chicken fingers." *Take-out.*

Green Hills Inn

2444 Morgantown Rd., Reading, Pa. 19607, (610) 777-9611

This gracious inn with classic French-inspired cuisine is a Berks County special-occasion standby.

Grey Lodge Pub

6235 Frankford Ave., 19135, (215) 624-2969, www.greylodge.com

A great beer destination, serving a wide array of micro-brews in the Bud-centric Northeast, this ambitious pub recently added a second-floor dining room that serves quality bar food, from spinach salads to mussels and creamy-sauced cheesesteaks. *Take-out.*

The Grill   🎖️🎖️🎖️

Ritz-Carlton Philadelphia, 10 Ave. of the Arts, 19102, (215) 523-8211, www.ritzcarlton.com/hotels/philadelphia/dining

The departure of star-chef Terrence Feury has taken some inventiveness and glamour from the Ritz-Carlton's premier dining room, but you'll still find high-quality updates of American grill cooking and classy service in the well-padded hunt club confines of this classic room.

Grilladelphia

Exxon Station, 2330 Aramingo Ave., 19125, (215) 739-3801, www.grilladelphia.com

It gets points for turning one end of an Exxon station convenience store into a serious steakerie. The hollowed-out round rolls are unusual, but the steaks themselves are satisfying fare. *Take-out.*

H

H & J McNally's Tavern

8634 Germantown Ave., 19118, (215) 247-9736, www.mcnallystavern.com
Citizens Bank Park, left field stands, 19148

Everything is made from scratch at this dark little tavern, from the lunch meat to the soups and desserts. But it's the Schmitter, a salami-cheesesteak fantasy on a kaiser roll, that makes it worth the trip. *Take-out.*

H.K. Golden Phoenix

911 Race St., 19107, (215) 629-4988

One of Chinatown's first big Hong Kong–style dim sum houses in Chinatown isn't quite as good as it used to be, but is still a fair bet for a big assortment of competently done dumplings, heaps of garlicky greens, and a wide-ranging Cantonese menu.

Hank's Place

Baltimore Pike and Rt. 100, Chadds Ford, Pa. 19317, (610) 388-7061

Prepare to stand in line at this popular local hangout for hearty homemade diner fare. It's open for breakfast and lunch only. Omelettes are a specialty. *Take-out.*

The Happy Rooster   🎖️🎖️

118 S. 16th St. (at Sansom), 19102, (215) 963-9311, www.thehappyrooster.com

This quirky bar-cum-restaurant has always been a brass-railed gourmet hideaway for Market Street movers and restaurant insider dish. It's still a fun bet for pasta Bolognese, roast chicken, and chocolate cake, but a chef carousel has drained some finesse from the blackboard menu's greater ambitions. *Take-out.*

Harmony Vegetarian Restaurant
135 N. 9th St., 19107, (215) 627-4520
Delicate veggie dumplings, wafer-thin scallion pancakes, and zippy Hunan-sauced mock beef made from wheat gluten are the highlights at this serene cafe. The service could be warmer. *Take-out.*

The Harvest Moon Inn   🐓 🐓 🐓
1039 Old York Rd., Ringoes, N.J. 08531, (908) 806-6020,
www.harvestmooninn.com
This old stone inn, set in picturesque Hunterdon County, has a talented chef-owner whose complicated but inspired modern cuisine is fueled by heirloom and local ingredients. *Take-out.*

High Street Caffe
322 S. High St., West Chester, Pa. 19382, (610) 696-7435, www.highstreetcaffe.com
This funky purple BYOB has ceiling lights fringed with carnival beads and a gutsy kitchen that indulges in high-octane Cajun flavors. Ignore the gratuitous spice of the flame-throwing voodoo crawfish; the andouille gumbo and fine blackened catfish are authentic. *Take-out.*

Hikaru
607 S. 2nd St., 19147, (215) 627-7110
Get your toro tuna fresh and your scallops alive at this reliable Queen Village sushi standby, which recently underwent a handsome renovation with a riverstone paved entranceway and beautiful tatami booths for an intimate group dinner. *Take-out.*

Honey's Sit 'n' Eat
800 N. 4th St., 19123, (215) 925-1150
This funky breakfast-luncher is the neighborhood's answer to South Philly's

Sabrina's for the hipster brunch, set in an old warehouse-turned-barn dressed up in Green Acres kitsch. The menu is an appealing blend of Jewish (matzo balls), Southern (chicken-fried steak), and Lancaster produce, but the flavors aren't always quite in register. *Take-out.*

HORIZONS   🐓 🐓 🐓
611 S. 7th St., 19147, (215) 923-6117,
www.horizonsphiladelphia.com
You don't have to be a vegan to appreciate what Rich Landau and Kate Jacoby have created at their new location for Horizons in Bella Vista — a pretty, Caribbean-style room that is the city's only serious vegetarian restaurant. Landau's exotic and inventive preparations of seitan and tofu are spectacular, and the ambience, bar, and service are major steps up from their now-closed suburban location. *Take-out.*

Hostaria da Elio
615 S. 3rd St., 19147, (215) 925-0930
This slender storefront in Queen Village has a lovely back patio and a charming owner, veteran chef Elio Sgambati, whose long list of specials — veal cannelloni, risotto Milanese, duck ravioli with truffle sauce — adds interest to a stock trattoria menu. *Take-out.*

Hotel DuPont   🐓 🐓
11th and Market Sts., Wilmington, Del. 19801, (302) 594-3100,
www.hoteldupont.com
The soaring, oak-clad Green Room offers unmatched classical grandeur. The service and the wine cellar are first-class, but the kitchens, while better than average, are rarely as magical as I hope. The weekend brunch is a blowout carved-ice-sculpture classic.

The Howard House Tavern
Main & North Sts., Elkton, Md., 21921, (410) 398-4646, www.howardhousetavern.com
Real Maryland crabs can't be found much closer to Philadelphia than Elkton,

and this unpretentious, pre–Civil War tavern also delivers some of the best hardshells I've had, succulent big guys steamed beneath a thick dusting of Old Bay. The soft pretzel stuffed with crab imperial is an instant classic.

Hunan

47 E. Lancaster Ave., Ardmore, Pa. 19003, (610) 642-3050
This cozy standby, threatened by Ardmore's downtown plans, has a muchdeserved devoted following. The cooking is fairly traditional, and some dishes are better than others, but the hot-and-sour soup and the scallion pancakes are particularly good. *Take-out.*

I

Il Cantuccio

701 N. 3rd St. 19123, (215) 627-6573
The tiny corner room covered with painted vines embodies the funky, handcrafted spirit of Northern Liberties, and regional Italian dishes like white beans and sausage are finally evolving from sloppy to rustic. *Take-out.*

Il Tartufo

4341 Main St., 19129, (215) 482-1999, www.iltartuforestaurant.com
Alberto Delbello's "Roman-Jewish" trattoria is tight inside, but has a lovely sidewalk cafe from which to watch Main Street pass by while you nibble awesome fried artichokes, homemade mozzarella, and truffle-sauced veal scallopini. *Take-out.*

Illuminare   🔥 🔥

2321 Fairmount Ave., 19103, (215) 765-0202, www.illuminare2321.com
One of the city's prettiest dining rooms — including a gorgeous back patio with trickling fountain — provides a pleasant setting. The Italian cuisine has varied, but

has showed improvement. Brick-oven pizzas remain superb. *Take-out.*

Imperial Inn

146 N. 10th St., 19107, (215) 627-5588
This sprawling Chinatown classic is a standby for Cantonese standards and basic dim sum. The dining room menu can be mundane, but the inn has really shined with some excellent banquets. *Take-out.*

Indonesia

1029 Race St., 19107, (215) 829-1400
The spicy peanut curries and multicourse rice table feasts of Indonesia have found a home in this friendly, wellappointed Chinatown dining room. The prices are reasonable, but the flavors are a bit too bland to qualify this as a truly special Indonesian kitchen.

Inn at Phillip's Mill   🔥 🔥

2590 River Rd., New Hope, Pa. 18938, (215) 862-9919
The French country fare is better than average, but the inn's real draw is candlelit ambience that breathes romance, from the fireplace lounge to the lush patio.

Inn at St. Peter's Village

3471 St. Peter's Rd., Elverson, Pa. 19520, (610) 469-2600.
Talented chef Martin Gagne has moved from sleek SoleFood in the Loews Hotel to a country inn in western Chester County (just south of Pottstown), where he's serving upscale New American cuisine with a waterfall view of French Creek. Too new for a verdict.

Iron Hill Restaurant & Brewery

3 W. Gay St., West Chester, Pa. 19380, (610) 738-9600
30 E. State St., Media, Pa. 19063, (610) 627-9000
1460 Bethlehem Pike, North Wales, Pa. 19436, (267) 708-2000

710 S. Madison St., Wilmington, Del. 19801, (302) 472-2739
147 E. Main St., Newark, Del. 19711, (302) 266-9000, www.ironhillbrewery.com
This converted former Woolworth's store makes a dramatic space for a brew pub, with handsome wood paneling, cozy booths, and a friendly staff. The house-brewed beers are fresh but unexciting; the updated pub fare is no better than average. It has been one of the area's fastest-expanding chains. *Take-out.*

Isla Verde ♟♟
2725 N. American St., Plaza Americana (at Lehigh Ave.), 19133, (215) 426-3600
You'll find a surprising slice of South Beach in North Philly at this sleek restaurant and lounge, where the salsa crowd pulses across the weekend dance floor and the young chef, Juan Carlos Rodriguez, delivers an upscale Nuevo Latino menu that pays homage to his training at Alma de Cuba and the Park Hyatt at the Bellevue. *Take-out.*

J

Jack's Firehouse
2130 Fairmount Ave., 19130, (215) 232-9000, www.jacksfirehouse.com
Perhaps new ownership will revive this longtime Fairmount tourist destination, a rehabbed firehouse where Jack McDavid's nouveau hillbilly cooking (lots of BBQ, game, and bourbon) once earned him celebrity status. With the sale, McDavid plans to get back into the kitchen. *Take-out.*

JAKE'S ♟♟♟
4365 Main St., 19127, (215) 483-0444, www.jakesrestaurant.com
A pioneer of Manayunk's fine-dining scene, Jake's is still the neighborhood's best bet, offering the sleek clientele a stylish yellow dining room, polished service, and a creative take on every-thing from mashed potatoes and calves' liver to the signature dessert cookie taco. *Take-out.*

Jamaican Jerk Hut
1436 South St., 19146, (215) 545-8644
With steel drums and tall grass hedging in from the vacant lot next door, this South Street Jamaican has a shaded back patio (and the jerk sauce) to conjure a convincing Caribbean mood. Not as upscale as portrayed on the big screen's *In Her Shoes*, but it's still authentic and fun. *Take-out.*

Jewel of India
53 W. Lancaster Ave., Ardmore, Pa. 19003, (610) 645-5502, www.mainline jewelofindia.com
Wide-ranging menu spans varieties of Indian cooking (including non-vegetarian), but also has decent South Indian specialties like dosa and pizza-like uthappam. Closer to Center City, but the cooking's not as sharp as the others.

Jimmy John's Pipin' Hot
1507 Wilmington Pike, West Chester, Pa. 19381, (610) 459-3083
This classic West Chester hotdog stand serves snappy-skinned, old-style frankfurters in the ambience of a roadside luncheonette festooned with working model trains. *Take-out.*

Jim's Steaks
400 South St., 19147, (215) 928-1911
431 N. 62nd St., 19151, (215) 747-6615
One of the big three of the touristic cheesesteak temples, this South Street mainstay is known for chopping its steaks to hamburger-like crumbles — all the better to mix with a ladle of griddle-heated Whiz. Purists prefer the West Philly original. *Take-out.*

Joe's Pizza
122 S. 16th St., 19102, (215) 569-0898
For its wide variety of mix-and-match toppings and super crust, office-district

workers will rightly stand in line at this bright pizzeria which has recovered from a fire. *Take-out.*

Johnny Brenda's

1201 N. Frankford Ave., 19125, (215) 739-9684, www.johnnybrendas.com
The owners of Standard Tap in Northern Liberties have breathed new life into this vintage dive in up-and-coming Fishtown. It still looks like a '60s watering hole, but the local beers and tasty Mediterranean-style tapas — from grilled octopus to fried mushroom "cigars" — reflect an exciting new spirit in the neighborhood. *Take-out.*

JOHN'S ROAST PORK

14 E. Snyder Avenue, 19148, (215) 463-1951
This relatively unknown South Philly lunch shack survived 70 years in delicious obscurity until it was suddenly discovered a few years ago by the crowds as the definitive practitioner of the sloppy roast pork and cheesesteak tradition. Don't expect tablecloths, but the picnic tables have great city views, and it's also now convenient to South Philly's big-box shopping district. *Cash only. Take-out.*

Jolly's

Jolly's Piano Joint, 135 S. 17th St., 19102, (215) 563-8200
Jolly's Sporting Saloon, 39 S. 19th St., 19103, (215) 564-4800
This casual sibling of the Prime Rib sits just below the Walnut Street sidewalk, offering a black-lacquer, piano lounge hideaway for top-notch American fare, from steaks and burgers to artichoke dip, at fair prices. One new Jolly's offshoot has added a sports bar (with good burgers) to nearby 19th St. *Take-out.*

Jones

700 Chestnut St., 19106, (215) 223-5663, www.jones-restaurant.com
Stephen Starr's groovy take on Dick Van Dyke's living room serves up grilled

cheese with tomato soup and excellent fried chicken and waffles in one of the noisiest rooms in town. *Take-out.*

Jong Ka Jib Soft Tofu Restaurant

6600 N.5th St., 19120, (215) 924-0100
This serenely handsome restaurant in North Philly's Koreatown, decorated with book paper and carved wooden booths, specializes in spicy tofu soups that arrive bubbling in hot stone pots. There is a limited selection of other classic Korean specialties, but they are well prepared. Staff speaks very little English.

Jose's Tacos

469 N. 10th St., 19123, (215) 765-2369
This unassuming little market-turned-taqueria on an obscure corner behind the Spaghetti Warehouse is a lunch favorite of *Inquirer* staffers, who walk here for the simple but authentic Mexican platters, topped with tequila-marinated shrimp, and ginger-chicken soup. *Take-out.*

Joy Tsin Lau

1026 Race St., 19107, (215) 592-7228, www.philachinatown.com
This Chinatown classic is still decent for standard dim sum, but the well-worn dragon-red dining room could use a sprucing-up. *Take-out.*

K

Kabobeesh

4201 Chestnut St., 19104, (215) 386-8081
The former American Diner at 42nd and Chestnut Streets has been converted to a Pakistani kabob house where especially vibrant flavors from the subcontinent arrive in the form of spicy skewered meats, and fragrant curries come with puffy, homemade naan. *Take-out.*

Kami Sushi Express
1526 Sansom St., 19102, (215) 751-9195,
www.kamisushiexpress.com
This no-frills Japanese nook (above the
Afghan kebab house) is probably the
best of Center City's many express sushi
take-out counters. Chef-owner Gunawan
Wibisono spent time at Morimoto and it
shows in the quality of the fish and careful preparation. Try the red dragon roll
(spicy tuna and eel) or sashimi salad.
Take-out.

Karina's
*1520 E. Passyunk Ave., 19147, (215) 218-
0455*
This diminutive corner spot is draped
with red velvet curtains and filled with
gaggles of BYOB groupies sampling chef
Pedro Beltrano's hybrid Italian-Latino
menu. The South American specialties
(goat stew, breaded veal, shrimp soup)
are most interesting. *Take-out.*

KARMA   ♟ ♟
114 Chestnut St., 19106, 215-925-1444,
www.thekarmarestaurant.com
2015 Burlington Mt. Holly Rd., Mt. Holly, N.J.
08060, (609) 914-0800
Old City has a colorful new Indian spot
that fills a satisfying niche between the
city's cheaper buffets and chic Cafe Spice
nearby. The menu uses good ingredients,
and the service is diligent. It remains to
be seen whether consistency can be
maintained as owner Munish Narula
clones the restaurant into a chain, including a South Jersey location convenient
to the turnpike.

Khajuraho   ♟ ♟
Ardmore Plaza, 12 Greenfield Ave.,
Ardmore, Pa. 19003, (610) 896-7200,
www.khajurahoindia.com
The ancient arts of exotic food and sen-
suality are tastefully linked at this Main
Line ethnic, where some of the region's
finest Indian cuisine is served under the
gaze of erotic sculptures from ancient
Khajuraho. *Take-out.*

Kibbitz Room
Shoppes at Holly Ravine, Springdale and
Evesham Rds., Cherry Hill, N.J. 08003, (856)
428-7878
This suburban deli convenient to the
JCC has long had some of the best hot
corned beef in the region, not to men-
tion garlicky Romanian steak and short
ribs for the old-time flanken crowd.
Take-out.

Kim's
5955 N. 5th St., 19120, (215) 927-4550
This friendly North Philly standby
remains one of the region's best destinations for true Korean barbecue cooked
tableside on charcoal grills. The converted diner is starkly decorated, but the flavors are vivid.

King of Falafel
16th St. and JFK Blvd. (S.E. corner)
This little food cart parked across from
Love Park at 16th and JFK fires up one of
the most reliable falafels in town, as well
as a delicious weekly special of oniony
lentil rice called mjadra.

Kisso Sushi Bar
205 N. 4th St., 19106, (215) 922-1770
A sleek, earth-toned sushi bar in Old City
where inventive ideas such as the
cooked tuna-wrapped raw tuna roll and
the BYO-sake policy have been a hit.
Take-out.

Koch's Deli
4309 Locust St., 19104, (215) 222-8662,
www.hollyeats.com/Kochs.htm
Devotees swear by the garlic-infused
corned beef special at this cramped
take-out deli as the definitive Philly-
style (cold, thin-sliced) corned beef. But
the colorful counter-side banter and
complimentary cold-cut noshes are also
a draw, though ebullient owner, Bob
Koch (who died in 2005) is missed.
Take-out.

Koja

38th and Walnut Sts. (N.W. corner)
Along with notably friendly service, this truck serves extremely tasty Korean fare, including a hearty mound of sesame-tinged beef bulgogi, refreshing cubes of kimchee radish, and an addictive stir-fried tofu tossed with a chile sauce that glows like fire.

Konak   ♟♟

228 Vine St., 19106, (215) 592-1212, www.konakturkishrestaurant.com
This cavernous Old City room (once Marco's) has been pleasantly trans-formed into a kilim-draped hideaway meant to evoke the courtyard of a Turkish manor. But it is the flavorful kabobs and Ottoman home cooking that give this spot the authentic taste of Istanbul. *Take-out.*

Krazy Kats   ♟♟

Rt. 100 and Rockland Rd., Montchanin, Del. 19710, (302) 888-2133, www.montchanin.com
A wacky animal motif somehow fits in at this beautifully refurbished inn with adventurous New American cooking and a fine wine list.

KRISTIAN'S RISTORANTE   ♟♟

1100 Federal St., 19147, (215) 468-0104, www.kristiansrestaurant.com
This handsomely renovated butcher shop is one of South Philadelphia's finest upscale Italian eateries, although the service can't match the finesse of chef Kristian Leuzzi's sophisticated takes on risotto and osso buco.

L

La Boheme

246 S. 11th St., 19107, (215) 351-9901
This little storefront BYOB near Jefferson Hospital serves up bistro fare with a North African accent. It has changed chefs often, but this space has an irre-sistible charm.

La Calebasse

4519 Baltimore Ave., 19143, (215) 382-0555
This no-frills dining room is a favorite among African cabdrivers who come for authentic Ivory Coast cuisine, including grilled guinea hen with jolof rice, roasted lamb shank with onions, and creamy peanut-butter-sauced mafe chicken. *Take-out.*

La Cava

60 E. Butler Pike, Ambler, Pa. 19002, (215) 540-0237
Ambler's resurgent main street has an intriguing entry in this cheery storefront cafe, where authentic Mexican flavors are tweaked into "haute" renditions of pasilla-sauced chicken stuffed with chorizo and homemade griddled sopes. *Take-out.*

La Collina

37 Ashland Ave., Belmont Hills, Pa. 19004, (610) 668-1780
You'll pay big for a seat by the windows of this classic Italian perch overlooking the Schuylkill River. It isn't quite as stale as one might suspect, with good ingredi-ents (from garlicky soft-shells to thick veal chops) presented in old-fashioned simplicity. But if you're a youngster, pre-pare for a cool reception from the veter-an staff. *Take-out.*

La Esperanza

40 E. Gibbsboro Rd., Lindenwold, N.J. 08021, (856) 782-7114, www.mexican-hope.com
Even if this restaurant lays on the mole a bit too thick, it's a pleasant surprise to discover an authentic Mexican restau-rant in a converted house in the middle of Camden County. Mashed-to-order guacamole, chicken stewed with green pumpkin-seed sauce, spicy pork arabe, and tender beef tongue tacos are among the highlights. *Take-out.*

La Famiglia   🍸🍸

8 S. Front St. 19106, (215) 922-2803,
www.lafamiglia.com
The Sena family's Old City institution is a bastion of classic luxury with a handful of great Italian specialties, from home-made pasta to rack of lamb, and a world-class wine cellar. But for the astronomi-cal prices, the food and service should offer much more. Recently underwent renovations.

La Fourno Trattoria

636 South St., 19147, (215) 627-9000,
www.lafourno.com
This casual South Street standby has a broad trattoria menu, but it's best known as one of the better wood-fired pizza ovens in town. *Take-out.*

La Locanda del Ghiottone

130 N. 3rd St., 19106, (215) 829-1465
The wacky chef Giuseppe who brought notoriety to this charming trattoria — one of the city's first Italian BYOs — is no longer with us, but his spirit lives on in the unpretentious, rustic dining room and the two-fisted flavors of the menu, which includes one of the city's notable osso bucos. *Take-out.*

LA LUPE   🍸🍸

1201 S. 9th St., 19147, (215) 551-9920
The city's best taqueria brings a fiesta of authentic Mexican cooking to 9th Street's Cheesesteak Central. The service is painfully slow, but the made-to-order tortillas are worth the wait, as is most of the broad menu. The roll-up glass walls (and fair-weather picnic tables) have a view onto this bustling South Philly hub. *Take-out.*

La Terrasse

3432 Sansom St., 19104, (215) 386-5000
This standby University City French bistro has been an upscale dining option for Penn's campus since the days of the Restaurant Renaissance — but my meals have always been slightly underwhelm-ing. It recently changed hands, so the jury's still out. *Take-out.*

La Veranda   🍸🍸

Pier 3, N. Columbus Blvd., 19106, (215) 351-1898, www.laverandapier3.com
A large selection of whole fish and a wood-burning Tuscan grill (also good for meats) are the best reasons to visit this pricey Italian spot with a pier-side view of the Delaware River. The succulent, 2-pound salt-crusted fish of the day is a treat but reports have been mixed since the most recent ownership change. *Take-out.*

La Viola

253 S. 16th St., 19102, (215) 735-8630
There's nothing particularly unusual about the standard trattoria menu at this little storefront Italian BYOB near the Avenue of the Arts, but it has proven a solid recommendation for an affordable pre-theater meal.

Laceno Italian Grill

1120 White Horse Rd., #3, Voorhees, N.J. 08043, (856) 627-3700
This is the South Jersey counterpart to Old City's Radicchio, and though it's in a suburban strip mall, it's a great destina-tion for whole fish, authentic pastas, and crusty, house-baked bread. *Take-out.*

Lacroix at the Rittenhouse   🍸🍸🍸

210 W. Rittenhouse Sq., 19103, (215) 790-2533, www.lacroixrestaurant.com
Chef Jean-Marie Lacroix (ex-Fountain) has stepped down from his gorgeous green velvet perch overlooking the park from the Rittenhouse Hotel. Talented successor Matthew Levin has a good track record at Moonlight and North Jersey's Pluckemin Inn, but it's too soon to know if he can maintain the city's best cutting-edge brunch, and a luxury dining room that has always flirted — but never quite achieved — elite four-bell status. *Take-out.*

LAKESIDE CHINESE DELI   🍴🍴
207 N. 9th St., 19107, (215) 925-3288
Don't walk past the gritty broken facade. Chinatown's best dim sum is made to order here, along with heaping platters of garlicky baby bok choy, clams with ground pork, and steam-salted chicken. Extremely low prices and consistently high quality make it easy to ignore the bare-tile decor. *Cash only. Take-out.*

L'ANGOLO   🍴🍴
1415 W. Porter St., 19145, (215) 389-4252
This cozy corner grotto deep in the heart of South Philly's red-gravy zone is always jammed with diners seeking out simple, deftly prepared trattoria fare, from the unusual antipasti to homemade pastas to the wonderful desserts. Service has become superb. *Take-out.*

Las Cazuelas   🍴🍴
426-28 W. Girard Ave., 19123, (215) 351-9144, www.lascazuelas.net
This charming and colorful BYO on Northern Liberties' northern border is a nice step up from most bare-bones taquerias, but the food is classic Puebla home cooking, ranging from mole-sauced enchiladas to fresh sopes and Veracruz-style whole snapper. *Take-out.*

The Latest Dish
613 S. 4th St., 19147, (215) 629-0565, www.latestdish.com
A gastro-pub that has endured for the South Street hipster crowd, with copper tables, occasional DJ's spinning tunes (with a nightclub upstairs) and an ambitiously eclectic menu ranging from duck spring rolls to wild mushroom lasagne and seared tuna with wasabi whipped potatoes.

LaVa Cafe
2100 South St., 19146, (215) 545-1508
The undercaffeinated Graduate Hospital neighborhood has fallen for this handsome new Mediterranean coffee house, which transformed a former blues club into a chandeliered living room cafe with an Israeli touch, including authentic "upside down" Nespresso cafe au lait, panini, and flaky bureka pastries filled with feta and spinach.

Lazaro's Pizza House
1743 South St., 19146, (215) 545-2775
When it comes to the search for cheap-but-decent pizza, the massive, slightly sweet pizzas at Lazaro's have become a staple for neighbors of Graduate Hospital. *Take-out.*

Le Bar Lyonnais
1523 Walnut St., 19102, (215) 567-1000, www.lebecfin.com
The no-reservation downstairs bar at Le Bec-Fin is still one of the city's best gourment deals, where the a la carte menu of refined bistro classics, from steak and frites to the excellent cheese plate, more than compensates for the claustrophobic room.

LE BEC-FIN   🍴🍴🍴🍴
1523 Walnut St., 19102, (215) 567-1000
The multi-course, budget-busting French feast may be a dying art, but Georges Perrier's gastronomic jewel remains an experience unlike any other. From the lavishly gilded room to the tuxedoed minions and a kitchen that produces both classic and contemporary French cuisine at its highest level, this institution still delivers ultimate luxury after 35 years. Lunch (and downstairs at Le Bar Lyonnais) are great bargains.

Le Castagne   🍴🍴
1920 Chestnut St., 19103, (215) 751-9913, www.lecastagne.com
This contemporary Northern Italian spot from the owners of La Famiglia serves some unusual fresh pastas (that I prefer to the more expensive, less consistent entrees) in sleek surroundings of imported marble and cherry-paneled walls. *Take-out.*

Lee How Fook   🍴🍴

*219 N. 11th St., 19107, (215) 925-7266,
www.leehowfook.com*
The family-owned Chinatown veteran
has been handed down to the family's
next generation and is still one of the
neighborhood's most dependable standbys for great hot pots, restorative soups,
crispy Buddha rolls, and delicious whole
fish at affordable prices. *Take-out.*

A Little Cafe

*Plaza Shoppes, 118 White Horse Rd. E.,
Voorhees, N.J. 08043, (856) 784-3344,
www.alittlecafe.com*
This tiny strip-mall space has been transformed into a charmingly personal, hand-
painted room. The dinner menu is a little
pricey, but lunch hit the spot, with homemade asparagus ravioli, indulgent onion-
gorgonzola soup, and panko-crusted fish
with Thai chile sauce. *Take-out.*

Little Fish   🍴🍴

600 Catharine St., 19147, (215) 413-3464
This Queen Village BYOB is one of the
smallest nooks in town, but the daily-
changing seafood menu has creative,
wide-ranging flavors and great desserts.
Take-out.

Little Thai Singha Market

*Reading Terminal Market, 12th and Arch
Sts., 19107, (215) 873-0231, www.read-
ingterminalmarket.org*
This stand has become one of the tastiest spots in the market, as evidenced by
reliably long lines of lunchers waiting for
grilled fresh salmon, basil chicken, and
the crab dumplings topped with crunchy
garlic.

Loie Brasserie

128 S. 19th St., 19103, (215) 568-0808
This youthful Rittenhouse hotspot has
always straddled the line between hipster lounge and French bistro, with more
success as a lounge. Perhaps new chef
David Gilberg (ex-Novelty, Matyson) will

be able to give this kitchen more than
just a great burger to brag about. Too
soon for a verdict.

LOLITA   🍴🍴

*106 S. 13th St., 19107, (215) 546-7100,
www.lolitabyob.com*
The BYO boom takes a Mexican turn at
this charming storefront cafe. Chef-owner
Marcie Turney (ex-Audrey Claire, Valanni)
serves affordable fare that feels more
New American bistro than authentic
Mexican. But it succeeds often enough,
aided by genuinely warm service and
killer mix-your-own margarita punch that
make this mellow spot worth trying.

Lombardi's Specialty Hoagies

1226 Ritner St., 19148, (215) 389-2220
A corner deli in deep South Philly that
serves hefty, flavorful Italian hoagies that
are easily among the city's best. *Take-out.*

London Grill   🍴🍴

*2301 Fairmount Ave., 19130, (215) 978-
4545, www.londongrill.com*
This Art Museum–area institution strikes
an appealing balance between neighborhood pub and fine-dining spot with a
creative New American menu that
ranges from fabulous burgers to Asian
duck spring rolls. Some nagging inconsistencies of late, though, nudged it off
the favorites list. *Take-out.*

Lorenzo's Pizza

900 Christian St., 19147, (215) 922-2540
This corner pizzeria and steak shop sits
in the heart of the Italian Market, dis-
pensing wide slices of prototypical
Philly-style pizza. *Take-out.*

LOS CATRINES RESTAURANT
& TEQUILA'S BAR   🍴🍴

*1602 Locust St., 19103, (215) 546-0181,
www.tequilasphilly.com*
The elegant room is graced with beautiful Mexican art, charming servers, and an
amazing collection of fine tequilas. The
menu aims for polished authenticity

rather than creativity, but has real high-lights, from the tortilla soup to langosti-nos in tequila sauce. The new house-label tequila, Siembra Azul, is top-notch.

Los Taquitos de Puebla
1149 S.9th St., 19147, (215) 334-0664
The latest taqueria to pop up in the growing Puebla-delphia on the Italian Market's south end, this cheery orange storefront specializes in spit-roasted tacos al pastor seasoned with pineapple and chiles, as well as some more daring fillings like cabeza (head) and ojos (eye-balls). *Take-out.*

Lourdes Greek Taverna
50 N. Bryn Mawr Ave., Bryn Mawr, Pa. 19010, (610) 520-0288
This sunny, white room with sky-blue trim evokes the pleasant, casual mood of a Greek taverna. The menu offers a list of Hellenic classics, too, from moussaka to souvlaki and spinach pie, but the flavors lack the zip of a little opa! to energize the fare. *Take-out.*

Lou's Restaurante
305 N. 33d St., 19104, (215) 386-5687
Powelton Village has a cheery little Tex-Mex spot in this charming storefront duded up with Southwestern pastels, a big burrito menu, a low-key cactus theme and that's Lou cooking in the cowboy hat. The big burrito menu has potential, but would benefit greatly from better cheese. *Take-out.*

Ludwig's Garten
1315 Sansom St., 19107, (215) 985-1525, www.ludwigsgarten.com
The German fare at this quirky Sansom Street brauhaus can be way too heavy (especially the lunch buffet). But the selection of yeasty, potent German brews, served by frauleins dressed like Heidi, is among the best around. *Take-out.*

Ly Michael's
101 N. 11th St., 19107, (215) 922-2688, www.lymichaels.com
The suburbanized pan-Asian fare that is a hit for the owners' FuziOn in Worcester, Montgomery County, feels slightly out of place in Chinatown, but that's also the draw. The menu ranges from duck dumplings to sauteed wild boar and relies on solid cooking and good ingredients. The modern yellow space is austere, but should warm up once the Convention Center crowds discover it. *Take-out.*

M

Maccabeam
128 S. 12th St., 19107, (215) 922-5922
One of the city's very few glatt kosher meat restaurants, this casual, no-frills grill focuses on Israeli-style sandwiches like turkey shawarma and falafel.

Maggiano's Little Italy
1201 Filbert St., 19107, 215-567-2020, www.maggianos.com
With its retro dining room, Sinatra nostal-gia, and jumbo-sized Italian-American fare, this is probably the best of the ersatz Little Italy chains, but it's still no replacement for the real thing in South Philly. *Take-out.*

Mahogany on Walnut
1524 Walnut St., 19102, (215) 732-3982, www.phillycigarbar.com
Cigar lovers can puff their smokes and sip their brandies, too, at this posh stogie bar above the Holt's Cigar Co. There is light fare, but the real draws here are the clubby room (big chairs, fireplace, great ventilation), a stellar cigar list and one of the region's top collections of premium scotches and cognacs. The owner expects to survive and thrive with an exception under the new smoking ban.

Mainland Inn ✗✗

17 Main St. (Sumneytown Pike), Mainland, Pa. 19451, (215) 256-8500, www.main-landinn.org
This pleasant Montco inn delivers candlelit rooms, classy service, fine wines, and New American cooking that thrives on quality seasonal ingredients and straightforward, traditional ideas.

MAJOLICA ✗✗✗

258 Bridge St., Phoenixville, Pa. 19460, (610) 917-0962, www.majolicarestaurant.com
Resurgent Phoenixville has a gem in this charming, husband-and-wife bistro, which has transformed a derelict tavern into one of the area's best BYOBs. Chef Andrew Deery's elegant New American menu showcases vivid combinations of good ingredients; wife Sarah Johnson guides the pleasant, front-of-the-house staff with grace.

Makiman

7324 Oxford Ave., 19111, (215) 722-8800
A surprising oasis in a sushi desert, this unassuming storefront hides a jazzy little dining room where the chef-owner turns out a long list of creative maki rolls from superbly fresh fish. Of course, many of the best — McNabb, T.O. NoMo — pay homage to Iggles-land. *Take-out.*

Mama Palma's

2229 Spruce St., 19103, (215) 735-7357
This casual Fitler Square Italian corner undoubtedly serves some of the best brick-hearth pizza in town, not to mention amazingly addictive "polenta bread." We've had mixed experiences with service, though, ranging from sweet and accommodating to downright grouchy. *Take-out.*

Mama's Vegetarian

18 S. 20th St., 19103, (215) 751-0477
Haviz David and his sons bake the pita breads fresh for their Israeli-style sandwiches. But the real secret is in their falafel balls, fried to a delicate crisp on the outside, with an herby, ground chickpea center that is still fluffy and soft. An extra round of fried eggplant makes it deluxe. *Take-out.*

Mandoline ✗✗

213 Chestnut St., 19106, (215) 238-9402, www.mandolineoldcity.com
Restaurants don't get much smaller than this corner cranny, but Old City locals will be pleased to land another low-key spot that takes its food seriously. It's a nice city debut for chef Todd Lean's thoughtful contemporary fare, but awkward service and the uncomfortably tight room limit the restaurant's potential. *Take-out.*

Mantra

122 S. 18th St., 19104, (215) 988-1211
The latest tenant of the perpetually changing space of the former Fishmarket is an Asian small-plate lounge from Al Paris, the exec-chef from Zanzibar Blue, whose opening "Asian bistro–soul food" menu looks to be a Rittenhouse-d version of his former South Street Guru. Too new for a verdict.

Maoz

248 South St., 19147, (215) 625-3500
This Middle Eastern vegetarian take-out chain serves some of the area's most authentic falafel sandwiches with wonderfully soft, house-baked pitas. The awkwardly placed take-out salad bar (in front of the register), slow waits, and occasionally rude service are drawbacks, but it's still a worthy, healthy option amidst South Street's junk food temptations.

Marathon Grill

40th and Walnut Sts., 19104, (215) 222-0100
2001 Market St., 19103, (215) 568-7766
1617 JFK Blvd., 19103, (215) 564-4745
1818 Market St., 19103, (215) 561-1818
121 S. 16th St., 19102, (215) 569-3278
1338 Chestnut St., 19107, (215) 561-4460, www.marathongrill.com
The sleek, glass-and-wood prow jutting off the Bridge Cinema in University City

is a stylish step up for this casual chain of lunch-centric eateries, melding Marathon's updated take on affordable grill fare, which often seems like Caesar salad fusion, with the collegiate lounge scene of the Marbar upstairs. *Take-out.*

Marathon on the Square

1839 Spruce St., 19103, (215)-731-0800, www.marathongrill.com
This slightly more upscale branch of the lunch-centric local chain literally has a corner on the brunch scene just south of Rittenhouse Square. It's a reliable neighborhood destination for a casual meal from fresh ingredients, but the cooking's never quite as good as it could be, and the service is painfully slow. *Take-out.*

Marco Polo

8080 Old York Rd., Elkins Park, Pa. 19027, (215) 782-1950, www.mymarcopolo.com
Ignore the old fern-bar decor and strip-mall location; this Jenkintown mainstay serves a reliably decent Italian menu specializing in whole fish. A recent change in owner has brought few obvious changes. *Take-out.*

MARGARET KUO'S ♟♟♟

175 E. Lancaster Ave., Wayne, Pa. 19087, (610) 688-7200, www.margaretkuos.com
No one presents classic Chinese cuisine with more elegance than Margaret Kuo at her eponymous suburban restaurants. Her gorgeous outpost in Wayne has superb Chinese dining on the main floor and a sleek Japanese lair for excellent sushi upstairs. Service has become professional and polished. *Take-out.*

Margaret Kuo's Peking ♟♟

Granite Run Mall, 1067 W. Baltimore Pike, Media, Pa. 19063, (610) 566-4110, www.margaretkuo.com
Shockingly elegant for a mall restaurant, this Chinese-Japanese stalwart highlights lesser-known regional cuisines from Shanghai and Beijing, as well as sushi. A recent meal was not up to its for-

mer three-bell form, with slips in service and sushi craftsmanship (perhaps drained by Kuo's newer venue in Wayne). But it's still a hidden gem. *Take-out.*

MARIGOLD KITCHEN ♟♟♟

501 S. 45th St. (at Larchwood), 19104, (215) 222-3699, www.marigoldkitchenbyob.com
This contemporary remake of the homey Marigold townhouse has become one of the city's most exciting BYOBs. Opening chef Steven Cook is still an owner, but has passed the pans to an equally talented successor in former Vetri sous Michael Solomonov, an Israeli-born chef who has warmed the modern menu with some Mediterranean flavors.

Marrakesh

517 S. Leithgow St., 19147, (215) 925-5929
This venerable Moroccan hidden on a tiny street just off South has been a longtime destination for pillow-propped North African tasting meals that move predictably from a rote menu ranging from b'stilla to tagines and pastries. It's a fun night out, but the kilim-covered rooms could use a good cleaning.

Marra's

1734 E. Passyunk Ave., 19148, (215) 463-9249
It doesn't get much more old-time South Philly than this red-gravy classic with black-tiled facade, well-worn wooden booths, and salt-of-the-earth service. Stick with such basics as the sizzling clams casino and crisp-crusted pizzas which are at their best when cooked with fresh mozzarella. *Take-out.*

MARSHA BROWN ♟♟

15 S. Main St., New Hope, Pa. 18938, (215) 862-7044, www.marshabrownrestaurant.com
Marsha Brown, who also owns the local Ruth's Chris franchise, has transformed a former Methodist church into a dramatic, Southern-inflected grill where the best dishes reflect her New Orleans roots. It's

an impressive and reliable destination for a New Hope splurge, but some of the Louisiana flavors still need fine-tuning. *Take-out.*

MATYSON   🍴🍴🍴
37 S. 19th St., 19103, (215) 564-2925, www.matyson.com
This charming storefront bistro from Matt and Sonjia Spector has become one of the best BYOs in the city. He cooks, she's a pastry whiz, and their creative New American fare has matured by leaps and an extra bell after my most recent visit. The weekday theme tastings are fun, but the coconut cream pie alone is worth a visit. *Take-out.*

Maya Bella
119 Fayette St., Conshohocken, Pa. 19428, (610) 832-2114
This appealing spot from longtime Le Bec-Fin sous chef Ken Shapiro and his wife, Angela, brings a Center City–style BYO to downtown Conshohocken. The room is stylish but dark, and the menu is a shade expensive. But Shapiro's New American cooking, on the whole, delivers good ingredients with a satisfying Mediterranean flair. *Take-out.*

Mayfair Diner
7373 Frankford Ave., 19136, (215) 624-8886
This stainless-steel classic rimmed with green neon still draws a devoted Northeast crowd for homey '50s-era diner fare. *Take-out.*

McCormick & Schmick's   🍴
1 S. Broad St., 19107, (215) 568-6888, www.mccormickandschmicks.com
This Portland-based chain brings an upscale dining room to a prime power lunch spot across from City Hall, although the reasonably priced seafood menu has been inconsistent. *Take-out.*

McMenamin's Tavern
7170 Germantown Ave., 19119, (215) 753-9911

Mount Airy has a true neighborhood haunt in this corner bar with WXPN on the radio all day, 17 excellent beers on tap, a superb collection of whiskeys, and pub fare that is thoughtfully prepared, if not always great. Homemade beef stew and the chili over wild rice were highlights. *Take-out.*

Mediterranean Grill
870 W. Lancaster Ave., Bryn Mawr, Pa. 19010, (610) 525-2627
A taste of Persian cuisine comes to the Main Line in this simple, affordably priced BYOB, with house-baked flatbreads that wrap kebabs, tahdig ("crispy rice" from the bottom of the pot), Persian meatballs with pomegranate sauce, and aromatic vegetable stews. *Take-out.*

Megu Sushi
Village Walk, 1990 Rt. 70 E., Cherry Hill, N.J. 08003, (856) 489-6228, www.megusushi.com
Grab a bottle of sake at Corkscrewed across the strip mall and take a seat at this surprisingly good sushi BYO (formerly Kyoto), where the chef offers well-cut, pristine fish, from white tuna to buttery toro, and creative maki rolls that go crunch. *Take-out.*

Melange Cafe   🍴🍴
1601 Chapel Ave., Cherry Hill, N.J. 08002, (856) 663-7339, www.melangecafe.com
Chef Joe Brown's increasingly upscale restaurant is South Jersey's best bet for a Mardi Gras fete, with a menu inspired by Louisianan and Italian ideas, from the creamy smoked tomato crab bisque to the tasty mixed-grill jambalaya. *Take-out.*

MELOGRANO   🍴🍴🍴
2201 Spruce St., 19103, (215) 875-8116
This tiny, no-reservations trattoria near Fitler Square is one of the best of our Italian BYOBs. The boisterous dining room exudes minimalist chic. But it's the authentic Italian fare of chef-owner Gianluca Demontis that entices guests to

wait hours for a table — and like it. No reservations.

Melrose Diner
1501 Snyder Ave., 19145, (215) 467-6644, www.melrose-diner.com
This 24-hour South Philly standby with the coffee-cup clock and horseshoe booths has been beautifully restored, but the menu consists of typically mundane diner fare. *Take-out.*

Mercato   ♟ ♟
1216 Spruce St., 19107, (215) 985-2962, www.mercatobyob.com
The windows are swung wide open at this handsome little theater-district bistro, an old market-turned-corner-BYOB. The minimalist decor has the right neighborhood vibe, and R. Evan Turney's contemporary Italian menu offers appealing ideas rooted in seasonal ingredients. It could use more finesse, though, to reach its full potential. *Take-out.*

Meritage Philadelphia   ♟ ♟ ♟
500 S. 20th St. (at Lombard), 19146, 215-985-1922,
www.meritagephiladelphia.com This quirky yet charming restaurant is a fine-dining throwback, with a serious wine cellar and a beautifully rendered menu of regional European classics presented with personal service. It recently changed ownership, though the kitchen remains the same. *Take-out.*

Mexico Lindo   ♟ ♟
3521 Federal St., Camden, N.J. 08105, (856) 365-9004
This tidy bungalow on the outskirts of Camden serves some of the area's most genuine Mexican cooking, from quesadillas made with hand-pressed tortillas to my favorite mole poblano. The decor is modest, but the homey cooking is worth a trip across the border (to New Jersey, that is). *Take-out.*

Mezza Luna   ♟ ♟
763 S. 8th St., 19147, (215) 627-4705
This crisp, contemporary space has one of South Philly's more upscale dining rooms, and an affordable Italian wine list to go with airy ricotta gnocchi in gorgonzola sauce, rabbit stew, and fine seafood are worth the trip. *Take-out.*

Mezze
Reading Terminal Market, 12th and Arch Sts., 19107, (215) 922-2707, www.readingterminalmarket.org
This stylish prepared food stand from the owners of By George is one of the more recent (and more upscale) additions to the Market, serving great Mediterranean sandwiches, soups, and thin-crust pizzas with unusual toppings.

Miel Patisserie
1990 Rt. 70 E., Marlton, N.J. 08053, (856) 424-6435
204 S. 17th St., 19103, (215) 731-9191
Robert Bennett has left the pastry atelier he created, but it remains a premier destination for sublime chocolate truffles, exquisitely crafted cakes, gelati and artisan breads. *Take-out.*

Mikado
2370 Rt. 70 W., Cherry Hill, N.J. 08002, (856) 665-4411
This Route 70 Japanese is giving local powerhouse Sagami a run for the South Jersey sushi crowd, but I'm not as enthusiastic as many about Mikado's wildly busy maki rolls. *Take-out.*

Mikimoto's
1212 Washington St., Wilmington, Del. 19801, (302) 656-8638, www.mikimotos.com
The flashy decor is as Americanized as the oversweetened Asian-fusion fare and jumbo-cut sushi, both of which were hit-or-miss during my visit. The atmosphere, though, is fun, and the tempura was a surprising standout. *Take-out.*

Miraku

1326 Spruce St., 19107, (215) 732-1110,
www.mirakusushi.com
Try some sushi before the show at this handsome new Japanese tucked into a former tanning salon just a half-block from the Kimmel Center. It's still too new for a verdict, but a promising early lunch at the black granite sushi bar brought excellent tempura, well-crafted rolls, and a yummy yellowtail ceviche.

Miran

2034 Chestnut St., 19103, (215) 569-1200
This relative newcomer offers some of the only Korean cooking in Center City, with a broad menu of well-done traditional dishes ranging from dolsot bi bim bap, good mandu potststickers, and marinated shortribs cooked on your in-table grill. *Take-out.*

Mixto   🍴

1141 Pine St., 19107, (215) 592-0363,
www.mixtophilly.com
The owners of North Philadelphia's Tierra Colombiana have salsa-ed into Center City with this handsome two-story, dark-wood haven of exposed brick and sky-lights. It's an ideal spot to sip a mojito and savor arroz con pollo. The authentic Latino menu, initially a pale shadow of Tierra's vibrant flavors, has been generating a more positive buzz of late. *Take-out.*

M/O Cafe

910 Haddonfield-Berlin Rd., Ritz Plaza,
Voorhees, N.J. 08043, (856) 566-4225,
www.mocafeandgrill.com
Chef-owner Michael O'Mara has opened an airy, California-style grill for the South Jersey cinema crowd, serving up playful fare like lobster wasabi pizza, root beer pork chops, and blue cheese burgers. Portions are a little small for the fee, and service can be pokey. *Take-out.*

MONK'S CAFE   🍴🍴

264 S. 16th St., 19102, (215) 545-7005,
www.monkscafe.com
This likable and influential Belgian bistro is the region's undisputed beer paradise. There are surprises beyond the famous burgers and mussels, including stellar octopus and gueuze-stewed rabbit. But the beer-cuisine theme occasionally feels forced and is often drowned in the deafening noise of what is still essentially a jam-packed bar. No reservations. *Take-out.*

Monte Carlo Living Room

150 South St., 19147, (215) 925-2220,
www.montecarlolivingroom.com
This classic Northern Italian has a tradition of exquisite continental cuisine and expert service but has had numerous chef changes in recent years since its last three-bell review. The kitschy decor and upstairs nightclub were updated a few years ago.

MORIMOTO   🍴🍴🍴

723 Chestnut St., 19106, (215) 413-9070,
www.morimotorestaurant
Masaharu Morimoto's attention may be focused on a second location in New York, but his original remains the region's premier Japanese experience, from the rare and exquisite raw fish and blow-out omakase tastings to creative fusion cooking served in the beautiful, undulating bamboo dining room.

Morning Glory Diner   🍴🍴

735 S. 10th St., 19147, (215) 413-3999
Updated macaroni and other home-made diner favorites, from hefty frittatas to delicious sandwiches, are served in this hip, flower-decked eatery. Over recent years, however, the kitchen and energy here have begun to slip. *Take-out.*

MORO   🍴🍴🍴

1307 N. Scott St., Wilmington, Del. 19806,
(302) 777-1800, www.mororestaurant.net
This seductive spot in Trolley Square offers a stunning stage for talented young chef-owner Michael DiBianca. From his freewheeling New American

cuisine to the awesome wine list and intimate atmosphere, this restaurant has only gotten better with time. *Take-out.*

Mosaic Cafe

50 Glocker Way, Suburbia Shopping Ctr., Rt. 100, North Coventry, Pa. 19465, (610) 323-9120, www.cafemosaic.info

The bland suburban strip mall gets an intriguing splash of color from this ambitious BYO, where an upscale menu ventures from kobe burgers to lavender-glazed salmon. My meal brought an excellent crabcake but awkward service. *Take-out.*

Moshi-Moshi-18th

108 S. 18th St., 19103, (215) 496-9950

This little Japanese storefront is easy to pass by. But the cozy, tatami-booth-lined dining room is a tranquil neighborhood hideaway serving fresh, well-priced sushi (try the volcano roll), deep-fried sawa-gani crabs, and popular bento-box lunch specials, including tasty Korean barbecued beef. *Take-out.*

MOSHULU   🗡🗡🗡

Penn's Landing, 401 S. Columbus Blvd., 19106, 215-923-2500, www.moshulu.com

The storied tall ship has been gloriously revived in the past few years, not just for tourists, but as a worthy destination for locals seeking exciting food, elegant ambience, and one of the city's best views. The service occasionally handles crowds less reliably than the impressive kitchen.

Ms. Tootsie's Soul Food Cafe   🗡🗡

1314 South St., 19147, (215) 731-9045, www.kevenparker.com

Traditional soul food finds a stylish home in this little Center City bistro, where brushed-copper walls add modern attitude, and the cheery staff sets a welcoming tone for great yams and rich, gravy-smothered turkey chops. A major expansion of the space has been in the works. *Take-out.*

Murray's Deli

285 Montgomery Ave., Bala Cynwyd, Pa. 19004, (610) 664-6995

In the battle of titans for Bala's deli soul, I tend to side with the old-fashioned mood in Murray's dining room (over snazzier Hymie's), where one can taste one of the best examples of a Philly-style (cold, thin-cut) corned beef special.

Museum Restaurant

Philadelphia Museum of Art, 26th St. and Benjamin Franklin Pkwy., 19130, (215) 684-7990, www.philamuseum.org

The silk scarf crowd pops by for lunch at this tranquil oasis of chiffon-draped civility, where chef Tracey Hopkins's menus draw inspiration from the latest blockbuster exhibit upstairs. But whether it's Moroccan, Indian, or Catalan, the only word you need to remember is this: crabcakes. They're more reliable than the overly ambitious theme menus. The "artists' table" buffet is also worthwhile.

Mustard Green

622 S. 2nd St., 19147, (215) 627-0833

This pleasant and pretty Queen Village standby has a fiercely loyal clientele for its outgoing service and cleanly updated Chinese cuisine. I've always found the food a little too Americanized and bland, but its many fans rave about the soft-shell crabs and signature greens. *Take-out.*

N

N. 3RD   🗡🗡

801 N. 3rd St., 19123, (215) 413-3666, www.norththird.com

This neighborhood bar has evolved into one of the city's best gastro-pubs, with a funky decor (check out the blowfish lamp) and a crowd ranging from local hipsters to Rittenhouse sophisticates who come for chef Peter Dunmire's appealing menu, which roams effortlessly from tuna burgers and soulful soups to high-toned striped bass. No reservations. *Take-out.*

NAM PHUONG   ♟♟

1100-1120 Washington Ave., 19147, (215) 468-0410, www.namphuongphilly.com
This large, pleasantly appointed space serves some very good renditions of traditional Vietnamese cuisine — seafood-studded crepes; country beef with broken rice; tangy green papaya salads — to the crowds that flock to Washington Avenue's growing Asian shopping zone. *Take-out.*

NAN   ♟♟♟

4000 Chestnut St., 19104, (215) 382-0818
Venerable chef Kamol Phutlek produces an elegant amalgam of French and Thai cooking that far exceeds the starkly understated packaging of this affordable and consistent University City BYOB. East meets West in sublime Shaxi-vinegared duck breast and lemongrass-crusted fish.

Nan Zhou Hand-Drawn Noodle House

927 Race St., 19107, (215) 923-1550
The menu is very limited at this little Chinatown nook, but the specialty — noodles that are expertly hand-spun into threads before your eyes — is definitely worth a visit. The "soy sauce noodles," more like a Chinese Bolognese, is a personal favorite.

Nanee's Kitchen

Reading Terminal Market, 12th and Arch Sts., 19107, (267) 918-0786, www.readingterminalmarket.org
This friendly lunch counter, with mildly spiced but homey renditions of Indian and Pakistani cuisine for the Reading Terminal lunch crowd, has improved over time. And there's also delicious house-labeled mango lassi shakes bottled to go.

NECTAR   ♟♟♟

1091 Lancaster Ave., Berwyn, Pa. 19312, 610-725-9000, www.tastenectar.com
This high-style pan-Asian palace has become the Buddakan of the 'burbs with its big Buddha and a seriously talented chef, drawing scene-makers and serious eaters alike. The menu from former Susanna Foo chef Patrick Feury is an exciting French-Asian blend that easily ranks among the most ambitious dining experiences the suburbs have to offer. *Take-out.*

New Wave Cafe   ♟♟

782/784 S. 3rd St., 19147, (215) 922-8484, www.newwavecafe.com
Chef Ben McNamara has returned to the bar where he helped launch the gastropub trend. Once known as the unofficial waiting room for Dmitri's, it's now one of the best gourmet bargains in town, with a menu that ranges from Pernod-scented escargots to great buffalo wings and surprisingly refined desserts. *Take-out.*

Next   ♟♟

223 South St., 19147, (215) 629-8688, www.nextbyob.com
Walk a few steps down from the sidewalk to discover an industrial-chic room with inventive New American food that offers reasons to reconsider South Street as a dining destination. The room is warmer than it looks, but it's the emergence of young talents — in both the dining room and the kitchen — that makes this more than just the next BYO.

Nick's Roast Beef

2149 S. 20th St., 19145, (215) 463-4114
The original independent Nick's is still the best, a dark corner taproom where regulars pick their own cuts of the sublime roast beef, which comes served over a kaiser roll with deep, dark gravy. *Take-out.*

NINETEEN. *See* **XIX NINETEEN**

Nodding Head Brewery & Restaurant

1516 Sansom St., 2nd fl., 19102, (215) 569-9525, www.noddinghead.com

One of the few micro-breweries left in Philadelphia proper, this quirky second-floor restaurant brews some legitimately tasty beers that go beyond the brew-chain norm (the B.P.A. is a favorite). The pub fare is also recommendable, including good smoked ribs and pulled pork, plus a surprisingly zesty crab cake.

Nonna's

211 Berlin Rd., Cherry Hill, N.J. 08034, (856) 795-1778

There is a vine-covered Tuscan mood to this charming BYO. Good ingredients and massive portions give the busy Italianate dishes — from Parmesan-crusted scallops a to giant raviolo stuffed with chicken mousse and wild mushrooms — a satisfying touch. Recently changed hands.

Nunzio's Ristorante Rustico   🍴🍴

706 Haddon Ave., Collingswood, N.J. 08108, 856-858-9840, www.nunzios.net

Chef Nunzio Patruno has created a sprawling South Jersey space that looks like an Italian village and has a reasonably priced menu focused on trattoria fare rather than the upscale alta cucina that marked his two decades at South Street's Monte Carlo Living Room. *Take-out.*

O Sandwiches

1205 S. 9th St., 19147, (215) 334-6080, www.osandwiches.com

A taste of Vietnam has been added to the menu of Passyunk's cheesesteak row, where this pleasantly appointed bakery and cafe specializes in Southeast Asian hoagies. Not as much headcheese as the more authentic hoageries on 8th Street (Cafe Huong Lan), but a good place for gringos to start.

Ocean City

234 N. 9th St., 19107, (215) 829-0688

This big Hong Kong dim sum palace has become popular for big banquets and multi-dumpling feasts served from rolling steam carts from lunch until 3 a.m. *Take-out.*

Oh Yoko!

1428 Rt. 70 E., Pine Tree Plaza, Cherry Hill, N.J. 08002, (856) 857-9050

This contemporary Japanese BYO from John Lennon lovers Jin Sung and In Mi Jang offers a serene ambience for high-quality sushi — try the undulating green caterpillar roll or the giant shrimp (with the deep-fried head) — as well as the intriguing okonomiyaki Japanese pizza. *Take-out.*

Old Guard House Inn   🍴🍴🍴

953 Youngsford Rd., Gladwyne, Pa. 19034, (610) 649-9708, www.guardhouseinn.com

A Main Line haunt for 24 years, Albert Breuers' restaurant remains a destination for the blue-blazer crowd that craves his German-accented continental fare and log-cabin dining rooms. It's devoid of flash, and somewhat pricey, but this is an Old World spot that still performs at a high level. *Take-out.*

Old Original Bookbinders   🍴🍴

125 Walnut St., 19106, (215) 925-7027, www.bookbinders.biz

With a major renovation that tastefully blends past and present, and with a serious chef and a pleasant attitude, the new Bookie's is a vast improvement over its past incarnation as a tourist trap. Service can still be hard-sell, but this once-neglected classic is relevant again. *Take-out.*

Olympic Gyro

Reading Terminal Market, 12th and Arch Sts., 19107, (215) 629-9775, www.read-ingterminalmarket.org

I regularly crave a warm pita sandwich filled with shaved gyro meat and tzatziki yogurt at this simple Greek lunch counter. If I'm feeling indulgent, I'll add in a spinach pie and sweet baklava.

Ong's

1038 Race St., 19107, (215) 625-8393

This bustling Chinatown noodle house completed an upscale face-lift and name change (formerly Nice Chinese Noodle House), but remains a good bet for a no-nonsense variety of hearty, flavorful noodle dishes served either "dry" in stir-fries, or floating in giant soups. The beef satay noodle is a personal favorite, as is the fried squid. *Take-out.*

Ooka Japanese Sushi and Hibachi Steak House

1109 Easton Rd. (Rt. 611), Willow Grove, Pa. 19090, (215) 659-7688
110 Veteran's Ln., Doylestown, Pa. 18901, (215) 348-8185, www.ookasushi.com

Don't let the goofy griddle-top slapstick in the hibachi room fool you. This sleekly designed Japanese steak house offers some of the most interesting sushi in the region, with excellent ingredients and real creativity. Try the special haru nohana roll topped with crunchy smoked salmon skin. *Take-out.*

The Orchard   ✗✗

503 Orchard Ave. (at Rt. 1), Kennett Square, Pa. 19348, (610) 388-1100

The BYO movement has arrived in mushroom country in style in this elegantly minimalist dining room. Owner-chef James Howard (formerly of Le Bec-Fin, Buddakan) presents an intriguing New American menu with Spanish and French accents that shows promise and originality, though at these prices it could be more consistent. It's also one of the few local BYOs to charge a corkage fee.

Osaka   ✗✗

8605 Germantown Ave., 19118, 215-242-5900

This handsome Japanese sibling of Osaka in Wayne has become one of Chestnut Hill's best restaurants, winning fans with its high-quality sushi (live scallop, Hong Kong dragon roll) as well as creative cooked items, from the massive crabcake to an indulgent appetizer of Kobe beef with foie gras.

Otto's Brauhaus

233 Easton Rd., Horsham, Pa., 19044, (215) 675-1864

Don your lederhosen at this German outpost for schnitzel, brats, and snapper soup. The big beer garden hops during Oktoberfest. *Take-out.*

Overtures   ✗✗

609 E. Passyunk Ave., 19147, (215) 627-3455

There is an old-fashioned sense of romance to this stalwart BYO off South Street, from the florid trompe l'oeil dining-room murals to the charming black-tie service to chef-owner Peter Lamlein's classic French menu. Despite some inconsistencies, it still satisfies with the timeless appeal of good ingredients cooked with simple care.

P

Pagano's Market

Market Place East, 701 Market St., 19106, (215) 925-4700, www.paganos.com

You'll find cops and defendants alike catching a lunch-break on cheesesteaks and hot Italian sandwiches at this surprisingly good counter-service cafeteria in the subterranean food court below Market Place East. *Take-out.*

Pagoda Noodle Cafe

125 Sansom Walk, 19106, (215) 928-2320
This spacious sibling of the Sang Kee
duck house is tucked into a courtyard
behind an Old City parking lot, but is a
reliable destination for affordable and
tasty Chinese fare, with a focus on Hong
Kong–style noodles, salt-baked seafood,
greens, and Peking duck. *Take-out.*

The Palm

*Park Hyatt at the Bellevue, 200 S. Broad St.,
19102, (215) 546-7256, www.thepalm.com*
If you're not one of the elite hobnobbers
caricatured on the wall of this recently
expanded national chain, prepare to be
underwhelmed by hard-sell servers and
pricey but artless chop-house cooking.
Take-out.

Paloma ✗✗

6516 Castor Ave., 19149, (215) 533-0356
Chef Adan Saavedra's French-influenced
"haute Mexican" is one of the more
intriguing menus in the city — let alone
Northeast Phillly. Persistent issues with
inattentive service have held the restaurant back from the next level.

Paninoteca

120 S. 18th St., 19103, (215) 568-0077
Chic Italian sandwiches come hot off the
grill (with a side of great olives) at this
simple but stylish wood-panelled lunch
caffe, which was among the city's first
panini emporiums. It's still easily one of
the best.

Paradigm

*239 Chestnut St., 19106, (215) 238-6900,
www.paradigmrestaurant.com*
Would-be voyeurs come for the famous
peek-a-boo frosted-glass bathroom
doors. But this comfortably chic neighborhood mainstay also makes an effort
in the kitchen, with decent homemade
pastas and a great prosciutto-wrapped
fried mozzarella. The addition of the
adjoining Dolce next door has added
more sleek, loungey dining. *Take-out.*

Paradise Restaurant

8336 Bustleton Ave., 19152, (215) 742-9811
Slightly smaller banquet-style club than
Golden Gates, but with great Siberian
dumplings and live music.

PARADISO ✗✗

*1627-29 E. Passyunk Ave., 19148, (215) 271-
2066, www.paradisophilly.com*
South Philly's resurgent restaurant row
just got hotter with the addition of this
ambitious restaurant and wine bar. The
large yellow room exudes modern elegance, and the appealing contemporary
fare from chef-owner Lynn Marie Rinaldi
shows strong potential. With more consistency, it could become a magnetic
new draw for the old neighborhood.
Take-out.

¡PASION! ✗✗✗

*211 S. 15th St., 19102, (215) 875-9895,
www.pasionrestaurant.com*
The brilliant ceviches and chile-kissed
flavors of Nuevo Latino cooking blossom
in this beautifully tropical tented dining
room. Chef Guillermo Pernot still creates
some of the city's most inventive and
personal cuisine; however, both the
kitchen and service have slipped a notch
in consistency of late.

Pastrami and Things

24 S. 18th St., 19103, (215) 405-0544
This bustling little cafeteria deli still slices
one of the best New York–style hot
corned beef sandwiches in town
(though, ironically, the pastrami's just
OK). It has also held up better than most
of founder Russ Cowan's other former
delis. Take-out.

Pat's King of Steaks

*1237 E. Passyunk Ave., 19147, (215) 468-
1546, www.patskingofsteaks.com*
The inventor of the steak has coasted on
its reputation, serving up puny sandwiches at its famous corner. A recent
facelift, though, has shown some welcome effort. *Take-out.*

Pearl's Oyster Bar

Reading Terminal Market, 12th and Arch Sts., (215) 627-7250, www.readingterminal-market.org
This fried-fish counter in the Reading Terminal Market is pretty ordinary, except for its big fried oysters and the fact that it is among the last of a dying breed. *Take-out.*

PENANG   🍴🍴

117 N. 10th St., 19107, (215) 413-2531
This Malaysian chain from New York serves authentic Southeast Asian fare in Chinatown's most stylish dining room, from the signature roti pancakes to pungently sauced house shrimp and exotic Malaysian water ice (called "ABC"). *Take-out.*

Penne   🍴🍴

The Inn at Penn, 3611 Walnut St., 19104, (215) 823-6222, www.pennerestaurant.com
The Italian concept is a vast improvement over the former Ivy Grille, with pastas being hand-crafted in the dining room to order, thin-crust pizzas, and an Italian wine bar with more than 30 wines to choose from. Some of the non-pasta cooking, though, has been sloppy.

People's Pizza

1500 Chapel Ave., Cherry Hill, N.J. 08002, (856) 665-6575
The no-cheese tomato pies of Trenton are famous, but People's makes a fine one (as well as hefty stuffed pizzas) just across the Ben Franklin Bridge. *Take-out.*

Pho Cali

1000 Arch St., 19107, (215) 629-1888
This Chinatown branch of the Atlantic City pho house is a pleasantly appointed corner room that offers a wide menu of classic Vietnamese fare. A nice option, but not distinguishably better than Chinatown's other Viet standbys.

Pho Ha

600 Washington Ave., 19147, (215) 599-0264
For soup alone, I'm partial to nearby Pho 75. But the menu at this bustling cafe is broader (with the bonus of bun noodle bowls and fried spring rolls), so it's a frequent take-out stop for my family on the way back from weekend shopping on Columbus Boulevard. *Take-out.*

Pho 75

1122 Washington Ave., 19147, (215) 271-5866
Dive into a satisfying meal-in-a-bowl at the city's best (and most utilitarian) Vietnamese pho hall, where the menu's focus (soup, soup, and soup) is a clue to its specialty. *Take-out.*

Picanha Brazilian Grill   🍴🍴

6501 Castor Ave. (at Hellerman), 19149, (215) 743-4647
A Northeast diner has been transformed into a genuine Brazilian rodizio grill, with an authentic buffet leading to a back counter where the grill chef slices salt-crusted meats from the skewer to your plate. The owner's taxidermy collection adds a little churrasco touch to the coffee shop decor. *Take-out.*

Pietro's Coal Oven Pizzeria

121 South St., 19147, (215) 733-0675, www.pietrospizza.com
1714 Walnut St., 19103, (215) 735-8090
140 W. Rt. 70, Marlton, N.J. 08053, (856) 596-5500
I've often thought of this local brick-oven pizza chain as a "poor man's Lombardi's." The pies are decent but definitely superior to the mundane Italian fare, and the service can be slow. The big cafe location in Rittenhouse Square, however, serves a useful niche as a casual and accessible destination for families in an otherwise upscale neighborhood. *Take-out.*

PIF ✗✗✗

1009 S. 8th St., 19147, (215) 625-2923
David Ansill's enchanting little BYO, now earning its third bell, has matured into one of the city's special corners, with a simple but warm decor and an ever-changing market menu that elevates French bistro cooking through fine ingredients, clever twists and adventurous ideas, from crispy pig's feet to ice cream scattered with bergamot candy. Bring your best bottle. *Cash only.*

Pikkles Plus

1801 Market St., 19103, (215) 751-1914
This Market Street standby is a perfect example of the Philly-style corned beef — cold, lean and thinly sliced — that is carefully built with quality ingredients. *Take-out.*

PJ Whelihan's Pub and Restaurant

700 Haddon Ave., Haddon Township, N.J. 08108, (856) 427-7888, www.pjwheli-hanspub.com
These popular Jersey-based pubs are a solid notch above national fern bar chains and a great place to watch the game with spicy wings, a meaty burger, a decent crab cake, or a grilled turkey reuben. *Take-out.*

Plough and the Stars

123 Chestnut St., 19106, (215) 733-0300; www.ploughstars.com
Sit on a low stool near the fireplace and sip some great Guinness in this dramatically rehabbed bank space. The Frenchified Irish menu has some hits (mussels) to balance its misses (fish and chips).

Pod ✗✗

3636 Sansom St., 19104, (215) 387-1803, www.podrestaurant.com
Conveyor-belt sushi and light-changing booths are part of the gimmick at this cool, futuristic spot, but reliably good Japanese fusion fare is one of the better reasons to return. *Take-out.*

Pompeii ✗✗

1113 Walnut St., 19107, (215) 829-4400, www.pompeiirestaurant.com
Some of the best renditions of upscale South Philadelphia cooking in Center City can usually be found at this sleek Italian, though prices are slightly lower since it moved from Broad Street a few years ago (including a three-course, $25 pre-theater deal). There's also been a recent change in chef. *Take-out.*

Pond/Bistro Cassis ✗✗✗

175 King of Prussia Rd., Radnor, Pa. 19087, (610) 293-9411, www.pondrestaurant.com
There are still swans in the pond and a storybook allure to the garden-trimmed restaurant and bistro complex that used to be Passerelle. The new owner and chef, Abde Dahrouch, formerly at nearby Taquet, has added more of a French tone (with Moroccan accents) to a dual-venue concept that is a welcome and sophisticated addition to the Main Line scene. *Take-out.*

Ponzio's

7 W. Rt. 70, Cherry Hill, N.J. 08002, (856) 428-4808, www.ponzios.com
This stone- and flower-faced institution has been overshadowed lately by flashier (but also lesser) ersatz diners. A recent meal, though, was pleasant in every way, from the outgoing service to the fairly priced veal entrees and a well-kept showcase of classic diner desserts. *Take-out.*

Porcini ✗✗

2048 Sansom St., 19428, (215) 751-1175, www.porcinirestaurant.com
One of the first in a wave of no-frills trattorias, this closet-sized BYOB remains one of the most consistent, with a simple but well-prepared menu of delicate, homemade pastas, grilled chicken with

balsamic sauce, and exuberant hospitality from the brothers Sansone.

Porky's Point

3824 N. 5th St., 19140, (215) 221-6243
This North Philadelphia take-out stand is the Latino equivalent of Tony Luke's, where cars triple-park and the line grows long into the night with people hungry for homemade blood sausage, red beans with chopped pig ears, and one of the city's most tender and tasty pork sandwiches. *Take-out.*

Posh

584 Rt. 38, Maple Shade, N.J. 08052, (856) 222-1128, www.poshbistro.com
This sleek new martini bar for South Jersey has an airy contemporary decor, trimmed with water walls, metal bead curtains and stylish, bone-colored banquettes. The pricey Thai-French menu, meanwhile, has a bit of a retro-fusion feel. Too new for a verdict. *Take-out.*

POSITANO COAST BY ALDO LAMBERTI   🍴🍴

212 Walnut St., 19106, (215) 238-0499, www.lambertis.com
The old pasta depot (Lamberti's Cucina) has gotten an impressive upgrade in concept and look. Splashed with deep blue tiles and giant photos of Positano, the airy room evokes the Amalfi coast. A good wine bar and an appealing small-plate Italian menu (try the mahi crudo) make for a smart pre-movie meal. *Take-out.*

Prima Donna

1506 Spruce St., 19102, (215) 790-0171
This friendly trattoria behind the Kimmel Center does a decent job with a wide menu of Italian standards, and has earned a devoted following for fairly priced pre-theater dining.

The Prime Rib   🍴🍴🍴

1701 Locust St. (in Radisson Plaza Warwick Hotel), 19103, (215) 772-1701, www.the primerib.com

Step back into the era of the steak house supper club, where leopard-print carpeting, live jazz, and comfy leather chairs offer the ideal retro setting for a prime rib that is one of the region's single best slices of beef. *Take-out.*

Pudge's

1530 Dekalb Pike, Blue Bell, Pa. 19422, (610) 277-1717
This longstanding sandwich shop serves some of the best cheesesteaks in the suburbs. *Take-out.*

PUMPKIN   🍴🍴

1713 South St., 19146, (215) 545-4448
This charming shoebox eatery has brightened a block of South Street near Graduate Hospital. Owner Hillary Bor and fiance Ian Moroney, former Little Fish chef, present a menu that turns on simple and satisfying Mediterranean combinations (as well as some surprises like a blue-cheese cake), a casual ambience, and service that is warm, if not always smoothly paced. *Cash only.*

Pura Vida

527 Fairmount Ave., 19123, (215) 922-6433
Guatemalan-born chef Charles Alvarez delivers tasty and authentic pan-Latin specialties at this cheery, unpretentious corner spot, from Mexican tostadas to banana leaf–wrapped Guatemalan tamales, pupusa corn cakes, and his signature ginger-chicken soup. *Take-out.*

Q

Queen of Sheba Pub II

4511 Baltimore Ave., 19143, (215) 382-2099
From all appearances (beaten-up long bar, pool table, beer banners), this is an ordinary, gritty neighborhood tavern. But at the far rear is an open kitchen window through which patrons can order some of the best Ethiopian home cooking in town, including spicy stews of lamb and

beef served atop spongy sourdough crepes called injera. *Take-out.*

R

Race Street Cafe

208 Race St., 19106, (215) 627-6181
Exposed brick and rafters and a wood-burning stove lend this refurbished blacksmith shop the warmth of a neighborhood tavern. The beers are excellent, and the menu — from mushroom ravioli to fish tacos — has modest gastro-pub ambitions. *Take-out.*

RADICCHIO   🔔🔔

314 York Ave., 19106, (215) 627-6850, www.radicchio-cafe.com
Much-needed soundproofing has softened the din at one of our most authentic Italian BYOBs (think: Melograno East), a contemporary corner cafe where the pastas have that simple but satisfying special touch and the expertly prepared whole fish have become some of the city's signature fine-dining bargains. No reservations. *Take-out.*

Ralph's

760 S. 9th St., 19147, (215) 627-6011, www.ralphsrestaurant.com
This 106-year-old institution is still the real deal for lively ambience and flavorful, old-time cooking, from greens-and-pastina soup to gravy-stewed squid, crisp-bottomed veal parmesan, soulful cacciatores, and creamy chicken Sorrento. *Take-out.*

Rangoon   🔔🔔

112 N. 9th St., 19107, (215) 829-8939
This modest but pleasant dining room has remained a worthy Chinatown standby for more than a decade. It's still the city's only destination for Burmese food, a unique and vividly flavored hybrid of Indian, Thai, and Chinese cuisines that brings fabulous cold ginger

salad, spicy lentil patties, and thousand-layer bread. *Take-out.*

Rat's   🔔🔔

16 Fairgrounds Rd., Hamilton, N.J. 08619, (609) 584-7800, www.ratsrestaurant.org
J. Seward Johnson Jr.'s Giverny-like sculpture park outside Trenton offers one of the region's most fantastical settings for ambitious French cuisine and a tremendous wine cellar. Only steep prices and pretentious service hold it back. A new chef has taken over since my last visit.

Raw Sushi and Sake Lounge   🔔🔔

1225 Sansom St., 19107, (215) 238-1903, www.rawlounge.net
The entertainment crossroads of 13th and Sansom has another cool nightspot in this stylish sushi and sake bar (with over 50 choices) slipped into the narrow bamboo-fringed storefront of the old Stetson building. It's promising for a drink and a sushi nibble, but the cooked fusion fare rarely tastes as good as it looks. *Take-out.*

Ray's Cafe & Tea House

141 N. 9th St., 19107, (215) 922-5122
Excellent Chinese dumplings and delicate French pastries are but a prelude to the amazing (and amazingly expensive) coffee that emerges from Ray's elaborate vacuum brewing rig of beakers and Bunsen burners. It's worth the price. *Take-out.*

Red Hot & Blue

Rt. 70 and Sayer Ave. (at Holiday Inn), Cherry Hill, N.J. 08002, (856) 665-7427, www.redhotandblue.com
Though it bears many of the uninspired traits of a corporate chain restaurant attached to a hotel (slow service, tacky room), the surprising barbecue redeems it with a reasonably authentic rendition of dry-rubbed Memphis ribs. *Take-out.*

Red Sky   ♟ ♟

224 Market St., 19106, (215) 925-8080,
www.redskylounge.com
This stark white box of a room seems at
first glance to be just what the neighborhood didn't need: another martini
bar/restaurant. The New American menu
from (ex-Audrey Claire) chef Michael
Salvitti, however, offers thoughtful cooking at fair prices and stands above most
other Old City lounge fare.

REMBRANDT'S   ♟ ♟

741 N. 23rd St., 19130, (215) 763-2228,
www.rembrandts.com
Open nearly two decades, this Fairmount
tavern/restaurant continues to mature
with an expansion that has added a
large kitchen, a banquet room, and a
smoke-free bar/cafe. A new wood-burning oven brings fabulous, thin-crust pizzas to an Italian-inflected menu that is
surprisingly ambitious at less than $20
an entree, but could be more consistent.
Take-out.

Restaurant Acapulco

1144 S. 9th St., 19147, (215) 465-1616
Another authentic newcomer to Baja
Filadelfia, this simple Mexican cafe specializes in seafood cocktails from the
Acapulco coast, as well as tender barbacoa tacos and Thursday special posole
stews that come flavored with red or
green chiles. *Take-out.*

RESTAURANT ALBA   ♟ ♟

7 West King St., Malvern, Pa. 19355, (610)
644-4009, www.restaurantalba.com
Former Rose Tattoo chef Sean Weinberg
and his wife, Kelly, have put Malvern on
the culinary map with their ambitious
BYO, an evocative, auberge-like space
warmed by the open wood grill and a
seasonal menu inspired by Italy, Mexico,
and local ingredients. *Take-out.*

The Restaurant at Doneckers   ♟ ♟ ♟

333 N. State St., Ephrata, Pa. 17522, (717)
738-9501, www.doneckers.com
Former Le Bec-Fin chef Greg Gable
blends French haute cuisine with regional flavors at this upscale Lancaster
County shopping complex. The dinners
are considerably more interesting than
the shopper-friendly lunches.

Restaurant Taquet   ♟ ♟

Wayne Hotel, 139 E. Lancaster Ave., Wayne,
Pa. 19087, (610) 687-5005,
www.taquet.com
Clark Gilbert is the new man behind the
stove at Jean-Francois Taquet's posh
perch in the Wayne Hotel, an elegant
room and grand outdoor porch overlooking Wayne's main drag. Gilbert has
done a nice job updating the French cuisine, but still has room for improvement.
The restaurant also exudes Main Line
stuffiness. *Take-out.*

Rib Stand

Reading Terminal Market, 12th and Arch
Sts., 19107, (215) 925-3155, www.read-
ingterminalmarket.org
Who knew the Pennsylvania Dutch did
good pork barbecue? The tasty boneless
rib sandwiches at this steady little lunch
stand are proof.

Rick's Philly Steaks

Reading Terminal Market, 12th and Arch
Sts., 19107, (215) 925-4320,
www.rickssteaks.com
The Reading Terminal steakerie descends
from the Olivieri family that founded
Pat's, but the water-steamed meat is
served in small, unseasoned portions. It's
better than the original, but far from the
best. Word is Spataro's will be making
steaks at its new location across from
DiNic's — it's about time the Market had
a good steak.

Ristorante La Buca ♟♟

711 Locust St., 19106, (215) 928-0556,
www.ristlabuca.com
This downstairs grotto off Washington
Square is an often-forgotten hideaway
with black-tie service and classic Italian
specialties, such as grilled langostinos,
whole fish, and ribollita, executed with
perfect understatement. *Take-out.*

Ristorante Panorama

Penn's View Hotel, 14 N. Front St., 19106,
(215) 922-7800, www.pennsviewhotel.com
Luca Sena's marble- and mural-clad
Italian grill is a reliable destination for
good homemade pastas and one of the
largest wine-by-the-glass selections in
the country.

Ristorante Pesto ♟♟

1915 S. Broad St., 19148, (215) 336-8380,
www.ristorantepesto.com
This handsome nook from the owners of
Io e Tu is one of the more polished
entries in a crop of new South
Philadelphia BYO trattorias. The kitchen
isn't perfect, but Neapolitan-style pizzas
from the imported wood-fired oven are
a highlight, as are several homemade
pastas and veal dishes.

Ristorante Valentino

1328 Pine St., 19106, (215) 545-6265,
www.valentinoonthesquare.com
A charmingly decorated Italian BYOB
with distressed walls and cherubs, it has
been inconsistent, but try the gnocchi
and simple grilled fish. *Take-out.*

RITZ SEAFOOD ♟♟

Ritz Center, 910 Haddonfield-Berlin Rd.,
Voorhees, N.J. 08043, (856) 566-6650,
www.ritzseafood.com
This diminutive BYO wraps diners in a
natural ambience of waterfalls and koi.
It's a homey setting for chef Daniel
Hover's innovative pan-Asian seafood,
ranging from fabulous Korean calamari
pancakes and tuna tartare to Thai fried

devil fish and killer coconut cream pie.
Take-out.

Roberto Cafe

2108 South St., 19146, (215) 545-0793
Yet another new Italian BYOB, but with a
worthy pedigree. Former employees of
Old City's Radicchio have brought a similar concept to a simple room with a back
patio in the burgeoning Graduate
Hospital neighborhood, focusing on
whole fish and pastas with an authentic
touch. Too new for a verdict.

Rock Lobster

221 N. Columbus Blvd., 19106, (215) 627-
7625, www.rocklobsterclub.com
The chef changes each year at this seasonal outdoor seafood grill in the shadow of the Ben Franklin Bridge, so quality
always varies. But if you stick with the
basics (steamed lobster's a good bet),
few terraces have a more pleasant riverside view. *Take-out.*

Roller's

8142 Germantown Ave., 19118, (215) 242-
1771, www.rollersrestaurant.com
Paul Roller last year moved his long-
standing Chestnut Hill favorite, a reliable
destination for updated comfort food,
from the top of the hill down to his former Flying Fish. *Take-out.*

Rose Tattoo Cafe ♟♟

1847 Callowhill St., 19130, (215) 569-8939,
www.rosetattoocafe.com
The flower- and vine-draped iron gallery
remains a pleasant balcony perch for a
lunchtime rendezvous spiced with jambalaya and Texas chili. The cooking,
though, has lost a little finesse since the
departure of ex-chef (and the owners'
son) Sean Weinberger for his own place
in Malvern. *Take-out.*

Roselena's Coffee Bar

1623 E. Passyunk Ave., 19148, (215) 755-
9697, www.restaurant.com/roselenas

The quirky Victorian coffee parlor offers multi-course dinners upstairs, but the main attractions are the after-dinner desserts by lamplight in the charming Old World parlor rooms downstairs. *Take-out.*

ROUGE   🍴🍴

205 S. 18th St. (Rittenhouse Claridge), 19103, (215) 732-6622
The glamour crowd (and their pets) come to bask in the good life of Rittenhouse Square at the open-windowed boutique that launched the city's sidewalk cafe revolution. There's an ambitious and pricey modern bistro menu, but the famously big Rouge burger has lately stolen the show. No reservations. *Take-out.*

Roux 3   🍴🍴

4755 West Chester Pike, Newtown Square, Pa. 19073, (610) 356-9500, www.roux3.com
This ambitious contemporary restaurant with stained-glass walls and plush circular booths has survived well despite a series of chef changes that seem to have settled down. The New American menu highlights the natural flavors of good ingredients, with occasional Asian and Mediterranean accents. The eclectic wine list is also strong. *Take-out.*

Royal Tavern

937 E. Passyunk Ave., 19147, (215) 389-6694
With its tin ceiling and spectacular carved wooden bar, this South Philly spot has character and a menu of updated comfort food — stuffed meat loaf, great burgers, tangy short ribs, upscaled mac-n'-cheese — to go with its smoked-duck club sandwich and other nouveau creations. *Take-out.*

Roy's   🍴

124-34 S. 15th St., 19102, (215) 988-1814, www.roysrestaurant.com
An old bank has been beautifully transformed into a branch of this upscale

Hawaiian-fusion chain, but the creative fare, from wasabi spaetzle to pork chops with plum sauce, is a bit too inconsistent for these prices, and service has been iffy.

Rustica

903 N. 2nd St., 19123, (215) 627-1393
This funky Northern Liberties pizzeria turns out crispy thin-crust pies with unusual ingredients that are a solid cut above your average neighborhood joint, from barbecued chicken to my personal favorite, pancetta and smoked mozzarella. *Take-out.*

Rx   🍴🍴

4443 Spruce St., 19104, (215) 222-9590
The Spruce Hill neighborhood owes its restaurant rebirth to this pioneer, an apothecary turned casual corner spot that has matured nicely over the last few years. The creative New American menu doesn't always taste as good as it sounds, but a commitment to local ingredients and fair prices keeps it on the go-list. *Take-out.*

S

Sabor Latino

33 Garrett Rd., Upper Darby, Pa. 19082, (610) 352-8414
This friendly new restaurant brings a quadruple dose of Latin flavors — Ecuadorian, Colombian, Cuban, and Mexican — to ethnically diverse Upper Darby. The menu is too broad for its own good, so stick with its strengths — Ecuadorian dishes and meat and shrimp entrees — for maximum felicidad.

SABRINA'S CAFE   🍴🍴

910 Christian St., 19147, (215) 574-1599
This funky, multi-room cafe has evolved into one of Bella Vista's hottest brunch destinations, with an artsy young crowd and an eclectic menu that ranges from stuffed French toast to gutsy chicken

cutlet sandwiches. The affordable dinner menu is a worthwhile non-Italian option for the neighborhood. *Take-out.*

Sagami
37 W. Crescent Blvd., Collingswood, N.J. 08108, (856) 854-9773
One of the area's first and finest sushi haunts, this dark, wood-paneled restaurant keeps closely to tradition, resisting overly trendy maki rolls in favor of pristine fish (and perfect tempura) served in classic but artful ways.

Saigon Maxim Restaurant
612-632 Washington Ave., 19147, (215) 271-8838
This massive banquet hall has changed names several times but remains a reliable spot for decent Chinese dim sum and a wider menu of Vietnamese favorites. *Take-out.*

The Saloon   🍴🍴
750 S. 7th St., 19147, (215) 627-1811, www.saloonrestaurant.net
This manly, wood-clad South Philadelphia power-dining spot serves expensive (and occasionally unspectacular) Italian cuisine, but it is rightly best known for its awesome garlic-infused chops that make it one of the area's most distinctive local steak houses.

Salt & Pepper Cafe
746 S. 6th St., 19147, (215) 238-1920
This tiny Bella Vista BYO has been winning raves since a change in ownership for simple but carefully prepared New American cuisine. *Take-out.*

Salumeria
Reading Terminal Market, 12th and Arch Sts., 19107, (215) 592-8150, www.readingterminalmarket.org
This Italian cheese and sandwich shop is a Reading Terminal favorite for hoagies, though the toppings can be a little heavy-handed. Devotees swear by the turkey hoagie.

Sang Kee   🍴🍴
238 N.9th St., 19107, (215) 925-7532
Long a favorite for Peking duck and noodles, this humble institution underwent an ambitious renovation several years ago, doubling and renovating its dining rooms. It's looking worn again lately, but the food is still great. *Take-out.*

SANG KEE ASIAN BISTRO   🍴🍴
339 E. Lancaster Ave., Wynnewood, Pa. 19096, (610) 658-0618, www.sangkeeasianbistro.com
Chinatown has landed with double happiness on the Main Line at this casual, stylish sibling of Michael Chow's ever-popular downtown duck house. The decor is crisp and modern, but the food is true to the fresh, crisply cooked Hong Kong–style noodles and roasted meats that made Sang Kee a favorite to begin with. *Take-out.*

Sang Kee Peking Duck
Reading Terminal Market, 12th and Arch Sts., 19107, (215) 922-3930, www.readingterminalmarket.org
This lunch-counter sibling to the classic Chinatown duck house is a great spot for wonton noodle soup, Peking duck spring rolls, and crisp General Tso's chicken.

Sansom Street Kabob House
1526 Sansom St., 19102, (215) 751-9110, www.sansomkabobhouse.com
This friendly, subterranean Afghan grill specializes in juicy, heat-charred lamb and chicken kabobs served over brown basmati pilaf. Scallion dumplings and pumpkin sauced with yogurt and mint are also great. *Take-out.*

SANSOM STREET OYSTER HOUSE   🍴🍴
1516 Sansom St., 19102, (215) 567-7683, www.sansomoysters.com
The best of the old-time seafood houses has maintained a waning Philadelphia tradition, beautifully restored dining

rooms and a menu that offers good examples of seafood classics. The cooking hasn't been as sharp since chef Cary Neff bought it from longtime owner David Mink, but it still fits the Center City lunch crowd like an old shoe. *Take-out.*

Sapori

601 Haddon Ave., Collingswood, N.J. 08108, (856) 858-2288, www.sapori.info
The updated medieval-dungeon look — complete with spiky, ball-and-chain chandeliers — may be odd, but the service is warm. And with a little extra polish, the rustic regional Italian menu at this trattoria has become a nice alternative to the splashier Nunzio's across the street.

SAVONA   ♟ ♟ ♟

100 Old Gulph Rd., Gulph Mills, Pa., 19428, (610) 520-1200, www.savonarestaurant.com
This Main Line jewel survived the departure of its star chef nicely, and remains one of the region's best fine-dining destinations, from the warmth of its terra-cotta dining rooms to its refined Euro-service to the elegant and inventive Riviera-inspired cuisine. It's biggest draw, though, is still one of the state's greatest wine cellars.

Seafood Unlimited

270 S. 20th St., 19103, (215) 732-9012, www.seafoodunlimited.com
A handsome renovation has transformed this bare-bones, little fish house and market into a neighborhood spot with real charm. But don't get too fancy when you order: Stick with simple fare such as the steamed lobster and crab-stuffed flounder. *Take-out.*

Seo Ra Bol

2nd and Grange Sts., 19120, (215) 924-3355
This relative newcomer from the former owner of Sam Won Garden in the Northeast gives Kim's a serious run for the region's best Korean barbecue, with

old-style charcoal in its tabletop braziers, a complex spicing to its grilled meats, and a pleasantly appointed dining room trimmed with wood rafters and paper screens.

Sergeantsville Inn   ♟ ♟

601 Rosemont-Ringoes Rd., Sergeantsville, N.J. 08557, (609) 397-3700, www.sergeantsvilleinn.com
This cozy 18th-century stone inn has ambitious young owners and an adventurous fine-dining menu that ranges from game to great tomato soup. The wine list is also excellent. *Take-out.*

Serrano

20 S. 2nd St., 19106, (215) 928-0770, www.tinangel.com
With one of the city's best folk clubs upstairs (the Tin Angel) and a romantic downstairs dining room warmed by a fireplace and art, Serrano offers an affordable evening of entertainment, even if the globe-hopping menu has traditionally been erratic. *Take-out.*

Shank's and Evelyn's Roast Beef

932 S. 10th St., 19147, (215) 629-1093
The all-woman staff at this tiny luncheonette dishes out counter-side sass with the big flavors of cutlet sandwiches topped with hot roasted peppers, everything omelets for two, and excellent roast beef. *Take-out.*

Shiao Lan Kung   ♟ ♟

930 Race St., 19107, (215) 928-0282
The busy, no-frills room has grown a bit worn around the edges since my last visit, but the kitchen still turns out some of the city's brightest Cantonese cooking, with awesome salt-baked seafood, made-to-order wontons, and memorable orange beef that draws crowds into the early morning hours. Not open for lunch. *Take-out.*

Shining Star

2460 N. 5th St. (at Cumberland), 19133, (215) 423-8506
You're likely to wait a while for your meal at this modest diner in the heart of the Centro de Oro, but the Puerto Rican fare is among the neighborhood's best, especially the mofongo al pilon (mashed green plantains fried with pork and garlic) and crunchy chicharrones (fried pork skins). *Take-out.*

Shouk

622 S. 6th St., 19147, (215) 627-3344
The South Street lounge crowd has found a sultry new haunt for puffing on hookahs and savoring some clever Israeli-themed, small-plate "mezza," from saffron chicken croquettes to veggie kofta, and variations on couscous.

Shundeez

8305 Germantown Ave., 19118, (215) 242-0665, www.shundeez.com
The former Roller's space at the top of the hill has been converted into a Persian grill. A recent meal was pleasant, though the food was a bit too mildly seasoned. *Take-out.*

SIAM LOTUS   ♟ ♟

931 Spring Garden St., 19123, (215) 769-2031, www.siamlotuscuisine.com
After a decade-long hiatus, this Thai spot has bloomed again on Spring Garden Street with surprising style, decked out in a rainbow quilt of gorgeous Thai silk and orchids. The cooking by Siam's original chef, Chavivun "Pat" Nanakorn, is just as vibrant, easily ranking among the city's best examples of authentic Thai cuisine. *Take-out.*

Sidecar Bar and Grille   ♟

2201 Christian St., 19146, (215) 732-3429, www.thesidecarbar.com
The long-promised gentrification of the neighborhood south of Graduate Hospital gets a boost from this stylish corner bar, which has transformed an old-style taproom into an aspiring gastro-pub with microbrews, Quizzo nights, grilled "toastie" sandwiches, and arugula salads with blood orange vinaigrette. If only the food were a notch better, this pioneer could be a hit. *Take-out.*

Sila Turkish Restaurant   ♟ ♟

Park Plaza, 4313 Rt. 130 S., Edgewater Park, N.J. 08010, (609) 835-7300
Hidden in the back of an obscure strip mall, this surprisingly well-appointed Turkish dining room is worth discovering for an authentic taste of yogurt-laced grilled meats and steam-puffed bubble bread. It has changed owners since the review.

Silk City Diner

1640 N. Reading Rd., Stevens, Pa. 17578, (717) 335-3833
Not to be confused with the recently closed Northern Liberties diner, this Lancaster County standby is a favorite lunch stop on our westbound turnpike roadtrips. It's a family-friendly venue that is one of the last bastions of old-time Dutch country and diner cooking, from noodle-topped chicken pot pies and smoked pork chops with kraut to meatloaf and good house-baked pastries. *Take-out.*

Simon Pearce on the Brandywine
♟ ♟

1333 Lenape Rd., West Chester, Pa. 19382, (610) 793-0948, www.simonpearce.com
Watch the artisan glass-blowing, then head upstairs for creative regional American cooking, with some Irish accents, that has improved over time.

Singapore

1006 Race St., 19107, (215) 922-3288
Peter Fong's long-standing kosher-vegetarian restaurant has moved from the space now occupied by Indonesia to a smaller room on the south side of Race Street. The mock-meat Chinese specialties have the added flair of Southeast

Asian curry. Unfortunately, the kitchen often hides many of its fresh flavors inside big puffs of deep-fried dough. *Take-out.*

Siri's Thai French Cuisine

2117 Rt. 70, Cherry Hill, N.J. 08002, (856) 663-6781, www.siris-nj.com
The racetrack's gone, but this longtime neighbor survives as one of South Jersey's favorite fusion spots. I've had mixed success here over the years. My latest lunch showed it in fine form, from the rich and tangy coconut milk–shiitake soup to an excellent shrimp-stuffed salmon with pungent green curry. *Take-out.*

Sitar India

60 S. 38th St., 19104, (215) 662-0818
The best of the University City buffets keeps the bargain steam-table of tandoori chicken and curried stews reasonably fresh and cheap. *Take-out.*

Slate Bleu   ✗ ✗

100 South Main St., Doylestown, Pa. 18901, (215) 348-0222, www.slatebleu.com
Mark and Susan Matyas have brought a classic French bistro to downtown Doylestown's historic Agriculture Works building. The menu is upscale and features well-crafted retro standards drawn from Mark's years as chef at Manhattan's La Grenouille. The low-energy service staff and weak wine list, though, need serious attention.

Sly Fox Breweries

312 N. Lewis Rd., Royersford, Pa. 19468, (610) 948-8088
519 Kimberton Rd, Pikeland Village Sq., Phoenixville, Pa. 19460, (610) 935-4540, www.slyfoxbeer.com
This mini-chain of the brewpubs turns out some of the best local craft beers, especially the impressively Guinness-like O'Reilly's stout. *Take-out.*

Smith & Wollensky

Rittenhouse Hotel, 210 W. Rittenhouse Sq., 19103, (215) 545-1700, www.smithandwollensky.com
The clubby New York steak house chain in the Rittenhouse Hotel has outgoing service and parkside views, but has been inconsistent for the prices. The more casual downstairs grill makes a particularly tasty burger. *Take-out.*

The Smoked Joint   ✗ ✗

Academy House, 1420 Locust St., 19102, (215) 732-7500, www.smokedjoint.com
Happy smoke signals are finally coming from this long-cursed restaurant space in the Academy House, because real barbecue has landed in Center City at last. The name and karaoke nights are goofy, but the room is comfortable and the kitchen does it right, slow-smoking everything from the tender spareribs to the awesome homemade pastrami. *Take-out.*

Snockey's Oyster and Crab House

1020 S. 2nd St., 19147, (215) 339-9578, www.snockeys.com
This 90-plus-year-old Queen Village institution has kept its dining room bright and spiffy, and maintained workmanlike renditions of classics such as snapper soup and milky oyster stew.

Society Hill Hotel

301 Chestnut St., 19106, (215) 923-3711, www.phillyhotelbar.com
The old bar has been upscaled into a casual-but-cool gastro-pub, with great wines and beers by the glass and a new menu ranging from fennel-dusted scallops to verbena-grilled shrimp. Ambitions here sometimes exceed abilities. The tall tables can also be numbingly uncomfortable over the course of a meal. *Take-out.*

SoleFood

Loews Philadelphia Hotel, 1200 Market St., 19107, (215) 627-1200, www.solefoodrestaurant.com

The posh contemporary dining room at the Loews hotel has always aspired — but never quite joined — the local pantheon of luxury hotel dining. Perhaps newly arrived chef Thomas Harkins (ex-Moshulu, Circa, Plate) will give it a boost. *Take-out.*

Sonny's Famous Steaks
228 Market St., 19106, (215) 629-5760, www.sonnysfamoussteaks.com
The owner of this Old City sandwich shop takes her traditional steak seriously, slicing the never-frozen domestic beef to order, and insisting on real Cheez Whiz (imagine!). But stick with the basic steaks — variations were disappointing. *Take-out.*

South Philadelphia Tap Room
1509 Mifflin St., 19145, (215) 271-7787, www.southphiladelphiataproom.com
A gastro-pub for Deep South Philly, with a stellar selection of local craft brews and an ambitiously eclectic menu that ranges from deep-fried asparagus to wild boar burritos.

South Street Souvlaki
509 South St., 19147, (215) 925-3026
This stalwart South Street taverna still serves a respectable selection of classic Greek fare, from massive moussaka platters to yogurt-laced souvlaki pita sandwiches to a delicious dinner special called exohiko, which wraps lamb and cheese stew in a crunchy phyllo package. *Take-out.*

SOUTHWARK ✗✗✗
701 S. 4th St., 19147, (215) 238-1888
Talented couple Sheri and Kip Waide have transformed the old Tartine into a Queen Village gem, with a lively eat-at-the-bar scene in front and a slender rear dining room that opens onto a large patio. An impressive debut for Sheri (ex-Django, La Terrasse), whose creative New American fare blends seasonality and a

light touch. Kip makes perhaps the best Manhattan in town.

SOVALO ✗✗✗
702 N. 2nd St., 19123, (215) 413-7770, www.sovalo.com
The husband-wife team of Joseph and Karey Scarpone have brought a taste of Napa Valley's famed Tra Vigne to Northern Liberties. The former Pigalle space is as elegant and romantic as ever, but it's Joseph's vibrant Cal-Italian menu — seasonal, intensely flavored, inventive and simple — that really turns heads.

SOVANA BISTRO ✗✗✗
The Willowdale Towne Centre, 696 Unionville Rd., Kennett Square, Pa. 19348, (610) 444-5600, www.sovanabistro.com
Chef Nick Farrell's horse-country strip-mall gem has grown into one of the suburbs' best BYOBs, with a casual contemporary room and bright menu that elevates European bistro fare in creative ways, from awesome thin-crust pizzas (with clam chowder?!) to superb homemade pastas and great hanger steak with three-day frites. No reservations. *Take-out.*

Spice Mexican Food
400 block of North Broad St. (west side, in front of The Inquirer *building)*
You know it's a tight deadline day when I'm standing in line at this cheery Mexican cart, but the hearty, black-bean–laden platters are honestly cooked and deliver satisfying flavors, from the open-faced, belly-busting enchiladas (chicken and spinach is a fave) to the occasional special of excellent mole tamales. Beware the "hot" salsa — it'll make you breathe fire.

Spring Mill Cafe
164 Barren Hill Rd., Conshohocken, Pa. 19428, (610) 828-2550, www.springmill.com
There is a bucolic charm to this converted general store and BYO, where French

country classics such as rabbit prune stew mingle with North African flavors such as spicy lamb tagine and flaky chicken b'stilla pie. *Take-out.*

STANDARD TAP   🍺🍺🍺

901 N. 2nd St., 19123, (215) 238-0630, www.standardtap.com
This moody Northern Liberties tavern is the premier showcase for the best local beers, a rocking jukebox, and an ever-ambitious kitchen serving food worthy of any white-tablecloth eatery, from sublime duck confit to soulful sauerkraut with venison sausage. The only drawbacks are the crowds and noise. No reservations.

Steve's Prince of Steaks

2711b Comly Rd., 19154, (215) 677-8020
This outpost of the Northeast chain just off Roosevelt Boulevard is a stainless-steel food bar where you can watch them cook thick-cut pads of excellent steak behind a bulletproof glass viewing window. Very tasty, with a particularly oozy white American cheese and good, spicy condiments. *Take-out.*

Strawberry Hill   🍺🍺🍺

128 W. Strawberry St., Lancaster, Pa. 17603, (717) 393-5544, www.strawberryhillrestaurant.com
This warm tavern offers a surprising slice of California wine country in historic Lancaster, with an extraordinary cellar of 1,400 wines and a creative contemporary menu that uses excellent local ingredients.

STRIPED BASS   🍺🍺🍺🍺

1500 Walnut St., 19102, (215) 732-4444, www.stripedbassrestaurant.com
Striped Bass has made a major comeback as the city's premier destination for contemporary seafood under its latest owner, Stephen Starr. The recent departure of star chef Christopher Lee will be a challenge to overcome, but the soaring

space remains one of the city's most spectacular settings for a special meal.

SUSANNA FOO   🍺🍺🍺🍺

1512 Walnut St., 19102, (215) 545-2666, www.susannafoo.com
Susanna Foo's exquisite French-Chinese cuisine sets the city's benchmark for creative but natural fusion cooking in a dining room dressed in silk and orchid elegance. Foo's kitchen does a nice job melding new ideas with her classic repertoire, and the service is impressively polished. *Take-out.*

Sushikazu   🍺🍺

920 Dekalb Pike, Blue Bell, Pa. 19422, (610) 272-7767, www.sushikazu.com
The smartly renovated little bungalow is home to a surprisingly creative sushi counter, where premium ingredients, from toro to live scallops, are sliced with great skill. Try off-the-menu specials such as the spicy tuna over crunchy rice or the Area 51 roll. Ownership has changed since the review. *Take-out.*

Swann Lounge

1 Logan Sq., 19103, (215) 963-1500, www.fourseasons.com
The Four Seasons' casual dining room cafe offers the hotel's grand luxury at bargain prices, with an excellent price-fixed lunch buffet, formal tea, a Viennese dessert table, and one of the city's best-outfitted bars. The cheesesteak spring roll is a signature dish.

SWEET LUCY'S SMOKEHOUSE   🍺🍺

7500 State Rd. (just north of Cottman), 19136, (215) 331-3112, www.sweetlucys.com
If you like true 'cue, it's worth the quick detour off I-95 to this cheerily converted warehouse in the Northeast, where the smoker turns out some of the city's finest ribs, pulled pork, and especially tender chicken in a simple but pleasant counter-service dining room that has a nice country flair. *Take-out.*

Syrenka

3173 Richmond St., 19134, (215) 634-3954
The steam-table service can be gruff, but
the Polish specialties are pure comfort,
from the delicious breaded pork chops,
sweet-and-sour stuffed cabbage, and
bigos stew to the addictive side of sweet
mashed beets.

SZECHUAN TASTY HOUSE ♟♟

902 Arch St., 19107, (215) 925-2839
Get a rare and fiery taste of authentic
Szechuan cooking at this Chinatown
newcomer. The colorful little room is
pleasant enough, but it's the vibrant
dishes that make the meal, with careful
preparations and a peppercorn-flared
chile heat that is both stinging and
seductive. *Take-out.*

T

Tacconelli's Pizzeria

*2604 E. Somerset St., 19134, (215) 425-
4983, www.tacconellispizzeria.com*
Reserve your dough for the white pies,
but request them without the granulat-
ed garlic, and meat-lover pizzas laden
with prosciutto and sausage that are
pulled from the immense brick oven.
This Port Richmond institution is no
longer affiliated with the South Jersey
store by the same name. *Take-out.*

Tacconelli's Pizzeria (New Jersey)

*450 S. Lenola Rd., Maple Shade, N.J. 08052,
(856) 638-0338*
The younger generation of the legendary Port Richmond pizza family has
opened an independent branch across
from the Moorestown Mall. It's already
turning out some of the region's best
pies from its big oven with crispy, thin-
crusted pizzas topped with good cheese,
fresh sausage, and prosciutto (though, as
in Port Richmond, I'm no fan of the gran-

ulated garlic). With the bonus of bright
decor, pleasant service, and no pre-
ordered dough hassles, I prefer this one
to the original. *Take-out.*

Taco Riendo

1301 N. 5th St., 19122, (215) 235-2294
This colorful little taqueria from
Armando Castro, father of Las Cazuelas
chef Alfredo Aguilar, brings authentic
and affordable Pueblan street food —
tamales, tacos dorados, stuffed poblanos,
posole stew — to a casual but cheery
corner room. Can be very slow. *Take-out.*

Tampopo

104 S. 21st St., #A, 19103, (215) 557-9593
719 Sansom St., 19106, (215) 238-9373
The larger new Jeweler's Row location is
a sleek urban lunchroom that elaborates
on the satisfyingly simple Japanese grill
concept of the original Rittenhouse
nook. The affordable focus is on donburi
rice bowls topped with teriyaki or kim-
chee-spiced meats, bi bim bap in hot
stone bowls, and surprisingly good sushi
(try the volcano roll). *Take-out.*

TANGERINE ♟♟♟

232 Market St., 19106, (215) 627-5116,
www.tangerinerestaurant.com
This fabric-draped and votive-lit casbah
of a restaurant is still the city's sexiest
dining space. The menu still has a nouveau Moroccan bent with harissa gnocchi and great tagine stews, but also has
added more pan-Mediterranean accents,
from Spanish-inflected fish to some
excellent house-cured salumi from talented chef Todd Fuller. *Take-out.*

Tangier Restaurant

1801 S. 18th St., 19146, (215) 732-5006
It's hard to find a great burger for around
$5 or less anymore, but it comes char-
broiled and juicy at this reliable neighborhood bar. Also known for their wings
and a good beer selection on tap. *Take-
out.*

Taqueria La Michoacana

310 E. Main St., Norristown, Pa. 19401, (610) 292-1971

This corner cantina in downtown Norristown did a major renovation a few years ago, securing its reputation with both the lunchtime courthouse crowd and the local Mexican population who come seeking a taste of Michoacan-style carnitas tacos, sopes, punchy salsas, and potent margaritas.

Taqueria La Veracruzana

908 Washington Ave., 19147, (215) 465-1440

South Philadelphia's authentic Mexican revolution began at this bare-bones taqueria in the Italian Market. It's no longer quite the best of the neighborhood, but devotees love the tamales and tacos al pastor.

Tashkent

842 Red Lion Rd., 19116, (215) 464-0106

This intimate spot specializes in the distinctive shish kebabs of Uzbekistan.

Taste   🛪 🛪

161 W. Girard Ave., 19123, (215) 634-1008

Jovial Billy Wong (ex-Mustard Greens) has teamed with talented young Fountain vet Jimmy Ng to open this intriguing BYO on the urban frontier just beyond Northern Liberties. The rarely busy corner room is bare-bones, except for the funky paintings on the ceiling, but the crowds should come once word of Ng's artful French bistro cooking spreads.

Taste of Portugal

718 Adams Ave., 19124, (215) 535-8700, www.tasteofportugal.net

There's a sports bar tavern upstairs but a surprisingly nice dining room downstairs at this Northeast destination for authentic Portuguese cooking, including flaming chorizo, bountiful paella, stewed pork, and clams — and Brazilian feijoada on weekends. *Take-out.*

Teca

38 E. Gay St., West Chester, Pa. 19380, (610) 738-8244, www.teca-r.com

Italo-philes say this light-bite caffe from the son of Alberto's serves up authentic panini, antipasti, and salads to go with an extensive wine bar. *Take-out.*

Ted's Montana Grill   🛪

260 S. Broad St. (at Spruce), 19102, (215) 772-1230, www.tedsmontanagrill.com

You can bet on the bison at Ted Turner's casual new steak chain on the Avenue of the Arts, but not much else. The western saloon decor is appealing, as is the notion of affordable pre-theater dining, but the food is mundane at best, even the touted burgers. For such a high-profile corner (formerly Avenue B), this newcomer is shootin' low. *Take-out.*

Teikoku   🛪 🛪

5492 West Chester Pike, Newtown Square, Pa. 19073, (610) 644-8270, www.teikokurestaurant.com

This stylish restaurant combines Thai and Japanese flavors in a stunningly handsome space evocative of an Asian lodge. The kitchen uses superb ingredients, from Kobe beef to fine sushi, but could be more consistent. *Take-out.*

Ten Stone

2063 South St., 19146, (215) 735-9939, www.tenstone.com

This pleasant corner bar near Graduate Hospital is a handsome space for great brews and billiards. If only the inconsistent kitchen could put a little more "gastro" into the "pub" (my last brunch here was almost inedible), this spot could fulfill its considerable promise as a casual neighborhood grill.

TEQUILA'S BAR. *See* LOS CATRINES RESTAURANT & TEQUILA'S BAR

Teresa's Cafe Italiano

124 N. Wayne Ave., Wayne, Pa. 19087, (610) 293-9909

This lively trattoria has a chic, modern look that hardly compensates for the noise level. But decent brick-oven pizzas and affordable pastas make it an appealing destination for a casual, family-friendly meal on the avenue. Has plans to open a bar next door, but won't change its BYO-friendly policy. *Take-out.*

333 Belrose 🚩🚩

333 Belrose Ln., Radnor, Pa. 19087, (610) 293-1000, www.333belrose.com
Carlo de Marco's New American grill in Radnor has some vibrant tropical flavors and one of the Main Line's liveliest bar scenes.

TIERRA COLOMBIANA 🚩🚩

4535 N. 5th St., 19140, (215) 324-6086, www.tierracolombianaphilly.com
Mambo up to North 5th Street, where this restaurant-nightclub remains the neighborhood's most reliable destination for traditional Latino cooking. The large menu is at times too broad, but stick with such specialties as the Colombian tamale, Cuban-style arroz con pollo, and flan. *Take-out.*

Ting Wong

138 N. 10th St., 19107, (215) 928-1883
This bustling, utilitarian noodle house serves great bowls of golden soup topped with everything from roast duck to sweet barbecue pork or, my favorite, silky white pads of sliced soy-sauced chicken with vibrant green Chinese broccoli. Ideal for a restorative Chinatown lunch. *Take-out.*

Tir Na Nog 🚩

The Phoenix, 1600 Arch St., 19103, (267) 514-170, www.tirnanogphilly.com
This handsome Irish chain out of New York brings a sprawling, upscale ole Dublin decor and traditional pub menu to the ground floor of one of Center City's toniest new apartment buildings. Stick with the Guinness and burgers. *Take-out.*

Tommy Gunns

4901 Ridge Ave., 19128, (215) 508-1030
630 South St., 19147, (215) 627-6160,
www.tommygunns.net
All old gas stations should be converted into cheery yellow barbecue pits like the original location of this expanding local mini-chain, which sits just outside the Main Street entrance to Manayunk. The smoked meats here are decent, especially the pulled pork, but sides still need work. *Take-out.*

Tony Luke's

39 E. Oregon Ave., 19148, (215) 551-5725,
www.tonylukes.com
The homemade rolls elevate the broccoli rabe–topped steak Italian and pork sandwich at this Oregon Avenue take-out (which also has an open-air seating shelter), making this branch the best of the famous big-crowd steak emporiums. With a huge clientele from nearby law enforcement paramilitary agencies, this may also be the best-armed lunch crowd in town. The terrible Rittenhouse Square branch is no longer affiliated. *Take-out.*

Tony Luke's Beef & Beer Sports Bar

26 E. Oregon Ave., 19148, (215) 465-1901,
www.tonylukes.com
Set across from TL's landmark cheese-steakery, the Beef & Beer Sports Bar looks like a battleship dressed in South Beach deco. Inside, you'll find the pure gusto of South Philly sandwiches, a wall of giant screens and ice-cold brews, and a platter of cheese fries topped with fresh bacon that is the city's cardiac danger champ. *Take-out.*

Trattoria Lucca

1915 E. Passyunk Ave., 19148, (215) 336-1900, www.trattorialucca.com
It's not hard to imagine sitting in the Italian piazza painted on the wall in this friendly trattoria. The affordable menu is classic South Philly — veal and chicken parm, fettuccine Bolognese, tiramisu — but updated with good ingredients and

an authentic touch. Regulars say it has continued to improve. *Take-out.*

Trax Cafe

27 W. Butler St., Ambler, Pa. 19002, (215) 591-9777, www.traxcafe.com
This bright little dining room has the charm of a small-town junction converted into a pleasant cafe, with trackside outdoor eating and an ambitious menu that ranges from house-smoked ribs to porcini-dusted salmon. *Take-out.*

Tre Famiglia Ristorante

403 N. Haddon Ave., Haddonfield, N.J. 08033, (856) 429-1447, www.trefamiglia.com
The former Little Tuna space has been transformed into a simple South Philly–style BYOB that delivers a satisfying taste of homey Italian, from the pasta e fagiole with homemade noodles to the Chip's antipasto salad and the house-filled cannoli. *Take-out.*

Tre Scalini   ✗ ✗

1533 S. 11th St., 19147, (215) 551-3870
Authentic Central Italian home cooking, from fresh pasta al la chitarra to grilled polenta with broccoli rabe and veal with mushrooms, is served with familial warmth in a bi-level BYOB. The menu almost never changes.

Tria   ✗ ✗

123 S. 18th St., 19103, (215) 972-8742, www.triacafe.com
A great beer venue without the usual bar grunge, this chic Rittenhouse cafe with Italianesque nibbles has made strides since opening. Some recent visits brought more relaxed, less pretentious service and a much-improved cheese board with riper, powerful cheeses.

Trio   ✗ ✗

2624 Brown St. (at Taney), 19130, (215) 232-8746, www.triobyob.com
This pleasant Asian venture from three Siri's alums is one of Fairmount's first

new restaurants in a while, offering affordable and fairly well-prepared Thai-fusion cuisine in a pretty, multi-level space featuring an airy deck with a sky-line view. The service is friendly but is uneven, and the place feels more like a welcome neighborhood haunt than a destination. *Take-out.*

12th Street Cantina

Reading Terminal Market, 12th and Arch Sts., 19107, (215) 625-0321, www.readingterminalmarket.org
The Food Court Downstairs at the Bellevue, 200 South Broad St., 19102, (215) 790-1578
A Mexican food stand that goes far beyond the expectations of a food-court vendor with authentically inspired casseroles, torta sandwiches, and salads.

Twenty Manning   ✗ ✗

261 S. 20th St., 19103, (215) 731-0900, www.twentymanning.com
Audrey Taichman's corner magnet for the urban chic blends solid Asian bistro fusion fare with a loungey decor of black leather couches for trendy people who don't mind the deafening noise. *Take-out.*

Twenty21   ✗ ✗

2005 Market St., 19103, (215) 851-6262, www.twenty21.com
The old Cutter's was purchased by its former managers and redesigned into a soaringly upscale American grill that caters to the Market Street corporate crowd with good service and an excellent bar. It's too soon for a verdict on the latest chef, Townsend Wentz, but a recent lunch showed an impressive upgrade in the cooking since my two-bell review. *Take-out.*

U

Uduppi Dosa House
2163 Galloway Rd., Bensalem, Pa. 19020, (215) 638-4008, www.uduppidosa.com
This casual spot in the Northern 'burbs is a destination for less common South Indian specialties, such as dosa made from rice and lentil-flour crepes with coconut chutney, steamed idly rice dumplings, hot pickles, Madras coffee, and a wide-ranging, affordable buffet of other vegetarian offerings.

Umbria
7131 Germantown Ave., 19119, (215) 242-6470
This contemporary bistro serves some of the best food on Germantown Avenue, with a New American menu that offers appealing Italian twists — sweet sausage roasted with figs, swordfish "chops" marinated in rosemary, and juicy roast duck with currants. The service, though, can be snippy.

V

Valanni
1229 Spruce St., 19107, (215) 790-9494, www.valanni.com
This liquor-license sibling to popular Mercato across the street has lacked some focus to its "Medi-Latin" fusion menu, but Washington Square West locals and pre-theater goers alike have embraced it as a comfortable and convenient "restau-bar." *Take-out.*

Valentino on the Square
267 S. 19th St., 19103, (215) 545-0441, www.valentinoonthesquare.com
With a player piano in the open window and giant white banquettes in the little room, this overdressed branch of the underwhelming Valentino's group (sharp

on looks, but dull on flavors) wins points for outgoing service and a sophisticated little bar convenient to Rittenhouse Square. *Take-out.*

VETRI
1312 Spruce St., 19107, (215) 732-3478, www.vetriristorante.com
Marc Vetri's townhouse homage to rustic Italian cooking continues to mature as the city's most personal and intimate gastronomic experience. The chef revels in unique interpretations of authentic ingredients that are often daring but always delicious. The service is uncannily sharp. The wines are top-notch. And a handsome new vestibule entrance has improved the tight space.

Vientiane Cafe
4728 Baltimore Ave., 19104, (215) 726-1095
This cheery Asian cafe provides a welcome oasis for striving Baltimore Avenue, a simple but pleasant destination for crisp but basically prepared Thai and Laotian cuisine. The ground chicken laab salad dressed in spicy-tangy vinaigrette was a hit. *Take-out.*

VIETNAM
221 N. 11th St., 19107, (215) 592-1163, www.eatatvietnam.com
The evocative French-colonial ambience of this Chinatown favorite is hard to top, as are the polished service, flaming tiki cup cocktails, and satisfying Vietnamese home cooking, from the BBQ platter to the noodle soups and broken-rice entrees. Some of the stir-fry entrees, though, can be inconsistent. *Take-out.*

Vietnam Palace
222 N. 11th St., 19107, (215) 592-9596, www.vietnampalacephilly.com
It's often overshadowed by an ever-popular rival across the street, but Chinatown's "other" big Vietnamese restaurant is a worthy destination itself, with a good menu of traditional Vietnamese cooking and a nicely remod-

eled dining room done in bamboo chic. Service is pleasant, too, but less than snappy. *Take-out.*

VILLA DI ROMA   🎖🎖

932-36 S. 9th St., 19147, (215) 592-1295
The DeLuca family's red-gravy classic may look and taste like a '60s time capsule, but it remains an essential part of the Italian Market experience, with some of the most genuine Southern Italian-American home cooking in town, a lively, unpretentious dining room, and a motherly staff that makes sure you polish off every last bite. *Cash only. Take-out.*

Vintage

129 S. 13th St. (at Sansom), 19107, (215) 922-3095, www.vintage-philadelphia.com
This appealing new wine bar with simple French bistro eats is yet another addition to developer Tony Goldman's growing entertainment crossroads just a block off Broad. Still too new for a verdict. *Take-out.*

W

Wally's Wiener World

High and Market Sts. (N.W. corner), West Chester, Pa. 19380
Scott Vassil has been serving tasty wieners for nearly two decades from his cart outside the Chester County Courthouse, in the shadow of the statue of "Old Glory." He closes on the early side and takes the winter months off, but his dog topped with excellent homemade chili is one of the best ways I can think of to spend $1.50. Vassil, by the way, made a splash on David Letterman's "stupid human tricks" by stopping a fan with his tongue.

Warsaw Cafe

306 S. 16th St., 19102, (215) 546-0204, www.warsawcafephilly.com
The tiny, window-paned bistro that sits behind the Kimmel Center is a charming old spot, even if the pan–Eastern European menu is often hit or miss.

Washington Square

210 W. Washington Sq., 19106, (215) 592-7787, www.washingtonsquare-restaurant.com
The umbrella-topped outdoor cocktail lounge remains a hip slice of urban paradise, even though celebrity opening chef Marcus Samuelsson is long gone. His "global street food" has also been replaced by a decent but more familiar New American menu (great lobster roll) with Mediterranean accents. *Take-out.*

Water Works Restaurant & Lounge

640 Water Works Dr., 19130, (215) 236-9000, www.thewaterworksrestaurant.com
After nearly a quarter century in the making, a fine-dining restaurant has finally opened in the historic Water Works with a terraced view of Boathouse Row. Manager Ed Doherty (ex–Capital Grille) has a stellar track record, and young chef Adan Trinidad (El Vez) has created an intriguing Mediterranean menu ranging from small plates (seared watermelon; tuna cruda) to vanilla-poached lobster. But it's still too new for a verdict.

White Dog Cafe   🎖🎖

3420 Sansom St., 19104, (215) 386-9224, www.whitedog.com
Judy Wicks is the force behind this trail-blazing University City institution, which blends social activism with creative organic cooking and a funky, homey atmosphere. There have been a number of chef changes in recent years. *Take-out.*

The Wild Onion

900 Conestoga Rd., Rosemont, Pa. 19010, (610) 527-4826, www.thewildonion.com
This sprawling Rosemont haunt near Villanova is more like three restaurants in one: a big-screen sports bar on the second floor, a more formal downstairs dining room for rack of lamb and home-

made ravioli (with a surprisingly sophisticated wine list), and an intimate wooden booth tavern for home-cooked pub classics. *Take-out.*

Winnie's Le Bus Manayunk
4266 Main St., 19127, (215) 487-2663, www.lebusmanayunk.com
The eclectic comfort fare at this bakery-cafe is a family-friendly lunchtime favorite. Hopefully, a change in ownership has smoothed out the occasionally snippy service. *Take-out.*

The Wooden Iron
118 N. Wayne Ave., Wayne, Pa. 19087, (610) 964-7888
This downtown Wayne chop house and bar is a destination for the brass-button-and-pinstripe crowd. The upscale space is swathed in clubby mahogany and a none-too-subtle golf motif. The conservative chop house menu makes attempts to update some classics with modest success.

Word of Mouth
729 Haddon Ave., Collingswood, N.J. 08108, (856) 858-2228
The intriguing New American menu and over-the-top chandelier-lit decor set a plush mood for this ambitious anchor of Collingswood's busy dining scene. Try the crabcakes and gnocchi with shrimp. *Take-out.*

World Cafe Live
3025 Walnut St., 19104, (215) 222-1400, www.worldcafelive.com
The WXPN crowd can now do dinner with their favorite live music acts at this ambitious new multi-venue performance complex in University City. Unfortunately, the kitchen has been out of tune with a menu that hints at pretension but food that is carelessly cooked and poorly paced to mesh with performances. *Take-out.*

X

XIX NINETEEN
Hyatt Bellevue, Broad and Walnut Sts., 19102, (215) 790-1919, www.nineteen-restaurant.com
Hyatt recently completed a stellar renovation for the dining rooms high atop its grand hotel, dangling pearl-like baubles from the domed ceilings and swapping a modern look for fusty old Founders. The raw bar and wines-by-the-glass are a treat. The contemporary menu from new chef Marc Plessis, meanwhile, is often spectacular.

Y

Yangming
1051 Conestoga Rd., Bryn Mawr, Pa. 19010, (610) 527-3200
This Bryn Mawr standby from Nectar co-owner Michael Wei has been one of the trailblazers in blending East with West. It's pretty, and reliable, but my meals here rarely have the bright flavors of CinCin, its sister restaurant in Chestnut Hill. *Take-out.*

Yue Kee
238 S. 38th St. (between Walnut and Spruce), 19104, (610) 812-7189
This University City mainstay is a gem disguised as a dingy food truck, where some of the city's best Chinese food — from fiery Beijing hot noodles to fragrant ginger chicken — is cooked with fresh ingredients and vivid sauces at bargain prices. No wonder its devoted, largely Asian, clientele puts up with the ridiculously long waits that require phoning in orders in advance.

Z

Zanzibar Blue 🗡🗡

200 S. Broad St., 19102, (215) 732-4500,
www.zanzibarblue.com
The Bynum brothers' slick downstairs
jazz club has upped its standing as a
fine-dining venue since addition of chef
Al Paris, who delivers some inspired
global cuisine — though responsibilities
at other restaurants (TSOP, Mantra) may
be a distraction. The club must still rec-
oncile noise conflicts between serious
food and music. *Take-out.*

Zeke's Mainline Bar B Que

6001 Lancaster Ave., 19151, (215) 871-7427
This converted McDonald's near
Overbrook High School has been one of
the better destinations for real slow-
smoked ribs. (The fluffy mac-and-
cheese is great, too.) But it has struggled to maintain consistency, tidiness,
and pleasant service. Perhaps, a recent
renovation will give it new energy.
Take-out.

Zen Tea House

225 N. 11th St., 19107, (215) 629-4848,
www.zenteahouse.net
Nibble Italian pastries with your
Technicolor bubble tea shakes at this
tiny cafe, which brings a pint-sized stroke
of cool, modern design and youthful
lounge culture to Chinatown.

Zocalo 🗡🗡

3600 Lancaster Ave., 19104, (215) 895-
0139, www.zocalophilly.com
This colorful, contemporary Mexican in
Powelton Village was one of the first
local spots to attempt contemporary
updates on authentic flavors from South
of the Border, with house-made tortillas,
Puebla mole, fresh guacamole, and one
of the best tequila bars in town. There
have been chef changes over the years,
but a recent lunch was as good as ever.
Take-out.

Zorba's Taverna

2230 Fairmount Ave., 19130, (215) 978-
5990
7930 Bustleton Ave., 19152, (215) 742-8558,
www.zorbastavern.com
A Fairmount neighborhood standby
with its steam table stocked full of
steady Hellenic favorites like braised
lamb shank, now has another location in
the Northeast. *Take-out.*

Cafes and Tea Houses

Like most American cities, Philadelphia has at times seemed in danger of drowning in Starbucks Coffee. But the last few years have also seen a refreshing backlash crop of independent cafes appear to create some unique spaces with a local flair where people can hang out, surf Wi-Fi and caffeinate on something other than the ubiquitous Big S corporate brew. Philly's La Colombe coffee tends to dominate the pots in most of the better cafes (not to mention virtually every restaurant), and that's a pretty good thing as far as I'm concerned. But there are some other good small local roasters to keep your eyes on — like Norristown's Fonseca and Phoenixville's Kimberton Coffee Roasting Co. As a card-carrying coffee-holic, I consider this important information.

Here's a good starter list of some of the more intriguing cafes the region has to offer:

Ambler Coffee Co.
14 W. Butler Ave., Ambler, Pa. 19002, (215) 542-9330
A spacious-yet-cozy anchor to Ambler's downtown revival, with occasional live music. *Open late. Serves food. Wi-Fi.*

Anthony's Italian Coffee
903 S. 9thSt., 19147, (215) 627-2586, www.italiancoffeehouse.com
Pause from your Italian Market shopping for a biscotti and cappuccino at the first caffe to put sidewalk tables onto 9th Street. *Open late. Serves food. Wi-Fi.*

Ants Pants Cafe
2212 South St., 19146, (215) 875-8002, www.antspantscafe.com
Residents near the Gray's Ferry end of South Street got a major boost with the opening of this funky cafe, which has become a popular stop for casual breakfast and light lunch. *Serves food. Wi-Fi.*

The Bakery at the Mills
The Mills at East Falls, 3510 Scotts Ln., 19129, (215) 754-1111
This intriguing bakery cafe anchors the recently rehabbed Dobson Mills complex. It's hard to find but worth a visit, especially for the crusty loaves of bread, which are less beautiful but more consistent than the pastries. *Open late. Serves food. Wi-Fi.*

Bonte
130 S. 17th St., 19103, (215) 557-8510, www.bontewaffles.com
922 Walnut St., 19107, (215) 238-7407
This downstairs refuge just off the Walnut Street glitz is a reliable spot for good coffee and a Belgian-style waffle crusted with coarse sugar. *Serves food. Wi-Fi.*

Cafe Loftus
3649 Lancaster Ave., 19104, (215) 382-2143; www.cafeloftus.com
136 S. 15th St., 19102, (215) 988-9486

These stylishly minimalist nooks provide a sleek perch onto Powelton Village and 15th Streets. *Serves food. Wi-Fi.*

Cafe Lutecia

2301 Lombard St., 19146, (215) 790-9557
This pleasant corner cafe in the Fitler Square neighborhood is ideal for a simple baguette with pate and brie, toasty crocque-monsieurs, soups, or a fresh salad. *Serves food.*

Capogiro

117 S. 20th St., 19103, (215) 636-9250
119 S. 13th St., 19107, (215) 351-0900,
www.capogirogelato.com
If there is better gelato in America than the sublimely creamy and intensely flavored frozen confections coming from Capogiro, I haven't tasted it yet. The midnight dark chocolate is an addiction. The recently opened second location (the first is at 13th and Sansom) is also a stylish cafe, with great panini, coffee, and sweets. *Open late. Serves food. Wi-Fi.*

The Chapterhouse Cafe and Gallery

627 S. 9th St., 19147, (215) 238-2626
A rambling space with artsy decor and a large patio out back. *Open late. Serves food. Wi-Fi.*

Darling's

404 S. 20th St. (at Pine), 19149, (215) 545-5745
The friendly owners have done a lot with their tiny storefront coffeehouse, focusing on superb house-baked cheesecakes and simple but satisfying lunches (pork sandwiches and the signature Tex-Mex bowl). *Serves food.*

Gleaners Cafe Gallery

917 S. 9th St., 19147, (215) 923-3205,
www.thegleanerscafegallery.com
An Italian Market haunt — where the coffee's good — for Bella Vista's arty grunge set, frequently seen composing songs at the tables. *Serves food.*

Great Tea International

1724 Sansom St., 19103, (215) 568-7827,
www.great-tea.net
At this new basement tea room just below the Joseph Fox bookstore, the owner serves a classic Chinese tea ceremony with teas imported directly from Taiwan, along with pastries, steamed buns, and dumplings. *Serves food.*

Green Line Cafe

4239 Baltimore Ave., 19104, (215) 222-3431, www.greenlinecafe.com
Settle in next to Penn grad students at this handsome cafe looking out onto Clark Park through beautiful stained glass windows. *Open late. Serves food.*

Ground Floor

209 Poplar St., 19123, (215) 627-1420
This Northern Liberties nook is tiny, but has a dreamy coffee garden that looks out onto the Second Street action. The owner also sources one of the better alternative coffees I've tasted to the ever-present La Colombe, a series of micro-batch coffees from Crooked River in Ohio. Warm weather Thursdays are also al fresco movie nights, with films projected on the wall in the garden. *Serves food. Wi-Fi.*

Hausbrandt Caffe

207 S. 15th St., 19102, (267) 971-8954,
www.hausbrandtusa.com
This sharp addition to the downtown cafe scene is the first U.S. branch of a venerable Italian coffee roaster from Trieste (not far from espresso powerhouse, Illy). It's comfortable and friendly, for the flagship of a new corporate presence (and the coffee's preferable to nearby Starbucks and Cosi). Their espresso is also beginning to make inroads into La Colombe's and Illy's hold on the restaurant trade. *Serves food. Wi-Fi.*

High Point Cafe
602 W. Carpenter Lane, 19119, (215) 849-5153
A meeting place for the Weaver's Way Co-op crowd of West Mount Airy, who come for the Seattle coffee, as well as crepes, black pepper cheddar biscuits, and truffled quiche. *Serves food.*

Higher Grounds
631 N. 3rd St., 215-922-3745, www.higher-groundscafe.com
A groovy living room cafe for Northern Liberties, with shabby velvet couches, the occasional live music act, and late weekend hangout hours.

The House of Tea
720 S. 4th St., 19147, (215) 923-8327, www.houseoftea.com
This is the city's best store devoted to serious loose teas, where everything from toasted Ecuadorian yerba mate to fancy oolongs are scooped out of oversize tins.

Joe Coffee Bar
1100 Walnut St., 19107, (215) 592-7384, www.joecoffeebar.com
Jefferson docs can get their caffeination with a side of P.C. at this conscientious coffee bar, where the beans are fair trade, shade-grown, and organic (of course). It's also well brewed. *Wi-Fi.*

La Colombe Torrefaction
130 S. 19th St., 19103, (215) 563-0860, www.lacolombe.com
2600 E. Tioga St, 19134, (215) 426-2011
The hip Euro-Rittenhouse crowd lounges around the chessboards at this smoky, chic cafe where the baristas really know how to pull the best single shot of espresso in town. *Serves food.*

Last Drop
1300 Pine St., 19107, (215) 893-9262
One of the originals of Philly's independent cafes, this smoky corner with the ornately painted classical façade

still exudes a Bohemian mood fitting for Antiques Row. *Open late. Serves food. Wi-Fi.*

Latte Lounge
816 N. 4th St., 19123, (215) 629-9808
This amiable little nook is a reliable stop for good java in Northern Liberties that also features the occasional poetry reading and knitting circle. *Serves food.*

LaVa Cafe
2100 South St., 19146, (215) 545-1508
The undercaffeinated Graduate Hospital neighborhood has fallen for this handsome newcomer, which transformed a former blues club into a chandeliered living room cafe with an Israeli touch, including authentic "upside-down" Nespresso cafe au lait, panini, and flaky bureka pastries filled with feta and spinach. *Open late. Serves food. Wi-Fi.*

Le Petit Mitron
207 Haverford Ave., Narberth, Pa. 19072, (484) 562-0500
Some of the best croissants in the region are baked at this charming cafe in darling downtown Narberth. *Serves food.*

MilkBoy Coffee
2 E. Lancaster Ave., Ardmore, Pa. 19003, (610) 645-5269, www.milkboycoffee.com
Downtown Ardmore has landed its own hipster coffeehouse, a spacious converted art gallery where Lower Merion teens come to hear poetry slams, open-mics and garage bands that have been wandering the Main Line since the closure of the Point in Bryn Mawr. The West Coast–roasted coffee is serious, but so is the music scene — the owners also run the nearby MilkBoy recording studio. *Wi-Fi.*

Mug Shots
2100 Fairmount Ave., 19130, (267) 514-7145, www.mugshotscoffeehouse.com
This hip hangout across from the prison has become Fairmount's unofficial living

room, with good light fare, excellent coffee, and the ever-essential Wi-Fi. *Serves food.*

Old City Coffee
221 Church St., 19106, (215) 592-1897
Reading Terminal Market, 12th and Arch Sts., 19107, (215) 629-9292
This local roaster and cafe is a fine place to catch your breath while touring the neighborhood galleries and sip a full-bodied cup of gourmet single-variety coffee or blends ("Balzar's" is a favorite). *Serves food. Wi-Fi.*

Philadelphia Java Company
518 S. 4th St., 19147, (215) 928-1811
This rambling Society Hill cafe goes head to head with the South Street Starbucks and wins hands-down for exposed-brick, wooden-pew ambiance, pastries from Le Bec-Fin, and thick-lipped espresso cups filled with one of the better short shots in town. *Open late. Serves food. Wi-Fi.*

Premium Steap
111 S. 18th St., 19103, (215) 568-2920, www.premiumsteap.com
This tea retailer just north of Rittenhouse Square sells some of the finest loose teas in the city, as well as a beautiful selection of tea pots and brewing paraphernalia.

Ray's Cafe & Tea House
141 N. 9th St., 19107, (215) 922-5122
Excellent Chinese dumplings and delicate French pastries are but a prelude to the amazing (and amazingly expensive) coffee that emerges from Ray's elaborate vacuum brewing rig of beakers and Bunsen burners. It's worth the price. *Open late. Serves food.*

Remedy Tea
1628 Sansom St., 19103, (215) 557-6688, www.remedyteabar.com
One of the first cafe-style tea houses, this Sansom Street newcomer offers cups of steeped-to-order loose teas to go and a machine that is the tea equivalent of a cappuccino maker. *Serves food. Wi-Fi.*

Spoons Coffeehouse
8919 Ridge Ave. (near Bell's Mill Rd.), 19128, (215) 482-0907, www.spoonscoffee.com
An ambitious new coffee house for Andorra, this cafe serves good Kimberton Coffee and sandwiches — just what weekenders might need after hiking along the nearby Wissahickon trails. *Serves food. Wi-Fi.*

Three Beans Coffee Co.
140 N. Haddon Ave., Haddonfield, N.J. 08033, (856) 354-2220
This comfy, couch-filled coffee shop hang-out is the local alternative to the corporate crowd at the downtown Starbucks a few blocks away. *Open late. Serves food.*

Twenty Two Gallery Cafe
236 S. 22nd St., 19103, (215) 772-1911
This simple corner cafe near Fitler Square is a popular weekend homework spot for Penn students, but also maintains one of the better quality art galleries to be found among the local cafes. *Serves food. Wi-Fi.*

Walnut Bridge Coffee House
2319 Walnut St., 19103, (215) 496-9003, www.walnutbridgecoffeehouse.com
Pause on some of the designer couches on your way to Penn for a perfect demitasse of Illy espresso and one of the finest collections of designer chocolates and pastries in town. *Serves food.*

Zen Tea House
225 N. 11th St., 19107, (215) 629-4848, www.zenteahouse.net
Chinatown's hip young crowd comes to this stylish cafe next to Vietnam for trendy bubble teas. *Open late. Serves food. Wi-Fi.*

Retailers

WHERE TO SHOP

There are benefits to eating out all the time. But there are also downsides, chief among them that I also love to cook at home. Thankfully, when I do get a chance to cook, this region has an amazing array of markets to visit, from the Reading Terminal to the Italian Market. Here are some of the great places I've patronized over the years:

BAKERIES

Cacia Bakery
1526 W. Ritner St., 19145, (215) 334-1340, www.caciabakery.com
One of the under-appreciated gems of Ritner Street, this classic bakery specializes in puffy Italian loaves and airy pan pizzas.

Carangi Baking Co.
2655 S. Iseminger St., 19148, (215) 462-6991
The crusty, seeded long loaves of this pleasant Oregon Avenue bakery are often mistaken for Sarcone's, since they are often used as the sturdy vessels for some of the area's best cheesesteaks.

Famous 4th Street Cookie Co.
Reading Terminal Market, 12th and Arch Sts., 19107, (215) 629-5990, www.famouscookies.com
These heavy-duty, chip-laden cookies are a famous post-Terminal lunch indulgence. They're so hefty, no wonder they're weighed "by the pound."

Faragalli's Bakery
1400 St. 13th St. (at Reed), 19147, (215) 468-5197
I've recently become addicted to the rustic, flour-dusted Italian loaves that come from the venerable South Philly corner bakery. It's also a great source for fresh, unseasoned bread crumbs and raw dough great for bake-at-home pizzas, as well as uncooked dough-by-the-pound for stellar bake-at-home pizza crusts. Take a peek at the ancient, wood-fired brick hearth in back — it's a classic. Friday afternoons, the loaves are still hot.

Fisher's Soft Pretzels and Ice Cream
Reading Terminal Market, 12th and Arch Sts., 19107, (215) 592-8510, www.readingterminalmarket.org
For my money, this Pennsylvania Dutch pretzel stand makes the best soft twists in the city. The "smoky cheesers" — little cheese-stuffed pigs in soft pretzel blankets — are one of my guilty pleasures. The ice cream side of the stand also makes a nice shake — especially when its Lancaster County strawberries are fresh.

Flying Monkey Patisserie
Reading Terminal, 12th and Arch Sts., 19107, (215) 928-0340, www.flyingmonkeyphilly.com
One of the most recent arrivals to the Reading Terminal, this creative baker offers New American twists to old bake-sale classics, infusing layered cake with South African rooibos tea, pound cake with ginger and lime, and brownies with chile spice. The signature "monkey bars"

are a nice twist on the old coconut chocolate chip brownie.

Haegele's Bakery

4164 Barnett St., 19135, (215) 624-0117
A favorite of my colleague, Rick Nichols, this German bakery in Mayfair still bakes real cinnamon buns, butter cake, fantastic seasonal donuts, and German Christmas cookies.

Isgro Pastries

1009 Christian St., 19147, (215) 923-3092, www.bestcannoli.com
There is no better Italian pastry shop than this century-old Italian Market benchmark. The cannolis are unparalleled (the shells have a shattering crunch), and Isgro's cake makers are among the city's most skilled at decorating birthday cakes. Give them a picture, and they'll make it sing in icing.

Kaplan's New Model Bakery

901 N. 3rd St., 19123, (215) 627-5288
Very similar in crumb and flavor to Lipkin's, but not risen quite as uniformly. The crust had a nice crisp, egg-wash shine. The challah here also makes great French toast.

Le Bus

135 S. 19th St., 19103, (215) 569-8299
Reading Terminal Market, 12th and Arch Sts., 19107, (215) 592-0422, www.read-ingterminalmarket.org
One of the first French-style artisan bakeries in the city is still one of the finest destinations for a great crusty baguette, pain d'epi, or especially good croissants. The popular choice for good rolls in city restaurants.

Lipkin Bakery

8013 Castor Ave., 19152, (215) 342-3005
Made to the original Polish recipe from a 50-year-old natural starter, this loaf had the most appealing rustic crust and hearty crumb of local ryes, with a mild and toasty flavor that was as much sourdough as rye.

Metropolitan Bakery

262 S. 19th St., 19103, (215) 545-6655
Reading Terminal Market, 12th and Arch Sts., 19107, (215) 829-9020
15 S. 3rd St., at Farmicia Restaurant, 19106, (215) 627-6274
8607 Germantown Ave., Chestnut Hill, 19118, (215) 753-9001
Ardmore Farmer's Market, Suburban Square, 19003, (610) 649-8395
4013 Walnut St., 19104, (215) 222-1492, www.metropolitanbakery.com
Philadelphia's best French-style artisan baker now has several locations, but this corner shop just south of Rittenhouse Square is always packed with locals clamoring for its crusty baguettes and yeasty rounds of sourdough miche, as well as indulgent sweets, home-made matzo (in-season), and a small but fine selection of oils, cheeses, and other locally grown edibles.

Miel Patisserie

1990 Rt. 70 E., Marlton, N.J. 08053, (856) 424-6435
204 S. 17th St., 19103, (215) 731-9191
Robert Bennett has left the pastry atelier he created, but it remains a premier destination for sublime chocolate truffles, exquisitely crafted cakes, gelati, and artisan breads.

Night Kitchen Bakery

7725 Germantown Ave., 19118, (215) 248-9235, www.nightkitchenbakery.com
If old-fashioned baked goods are what you crave, few shops deliver them with the homespun indulgence of this Chestnut Hill standby. I can still taste their strawberry shortcake. The candy-baubled Willy Wonka cake is another show-stopping dessert.

Petit 4 Pastry Studios

160 N. 3rd St., 19106, (215) 627-8440
An Old City pastry shop with coffee-shop style, the confections here are beautiful and indulgent (rather than elegant and

refined à la Miel). The bread pudding is particularly renowned.

Sarcone's Bakery

758 S. 9th St., 19147, (215) 922-0445, www.sarconesbakery.com
The crusty, sesame-seeded loaves of this legendary Italian Market bakery are one of the city's signature flavors — the premier choice for most of the area's top-line hoagies.

Stock's Bakery

2614 E. Lehigh Ave., 19125, (215) 634-7344
This River Ward classic is Polish pound cake heaven. The butter cakes are also recommended.

Termini Brothers Bakery

Reading Terminal, 12th and Arch Sts., 19107, (215) 629-1790, www.termini.com
One of the classic Italian bakeries of South Philadelphia has numerous locations, and is famous for its pound cakes, assorted cookies, and cannoli (which aren't as good as Isgro's, but will do just fine for a Terminal dessert).

BUTCHERS

Cappuccio's Meats

1019 S. 9th St., Philadelphia, Pa. 19147, (215) 922-5792
Old-timers stand in line for the tripe, pig's feet, spring goat and liver sausage at this classic Italian Market butcher. But the veteran meat-cutters also make some of the best renditions of straight-ahead sausage in South Philly. The thin coils of cheesey cervellata are a personal favorite.

D'Angelo Brothers

909 S. 9th St., 19147, (215) 923-5637, www.dangelobros.com
Sonny D'Angelo may be the city's finest individual butcher, and is a reliable source for exotic game meats, special request cuts, and unique sausages. But

be forewarned, customer service isn't always as cheery as it could be.

Fiorella Brothers

817 Christian St., 19147, (215) 922-0506
This beautifully preserved Italian pork store does excellent renditions of the classics — plain sausage, cheese sausage, and liver sausage. They also sell superbly tender pork cutlets and marvelously seasoned roasts.

Godshall's Poultry

Reading Terminal Market, 12th and Arch Sts., 19107, (215) 922-7589, www.readingterminalmarket.org
My favorite stop for poultry, Godshall's also sells a local curiosity known as a turkey chop, sage-flavored turkey scrapple, as well as plump ducks and geese.

Harry G. Ochs Meats

Reading Terminal Market, 12th and Arch Sts., 19107, (215) 922-6870, www.readingterminalmarket.org
When you feel like splurging on steak, there's no better destination than this Terminal standby, where they'll hand-cut your order from dry-aged sides of prime-grade beef. It'll cost you, but it's worth it.

L. Halteman Family Meats

Reading Terminal Market, 12th and Arch Sts., 19107, (215) 925-3206, www.readingterminalmarket.org
This Pennsylvania Dutch butcher in the market is my favorite spot for locally smoked meats — turkey legs for stews, fabulous thick-cut bacon, and double-smoked pork chops that beg for a side of kraut.

Martin's Quality Meats and Sausages

Reading Terminal Market, 12th and Arch Sts., (215) 629-1193, www.readingterminalmarket.org
Another classic Terminal butcher, Martin isn't as fancy as Ochs, but still makes a wide variety of excellent Italian sausages.

Rieker's Prime Meats

7979 Oxford Ave., 19111, (215) 745-3114
The city's once-thriving German commu-
nity has dwindled, but this classic
Northeast butcher is still the go-to
wurst-master for German specialties.
Many of their sausages are also carried at
Di Bruno's near Rittenhouse Square.

Simon Glatt's Kosher Meat Products

6926 Bustleton Ave., 19149, (215) 624-5695
One of the few great kosher butchers in
town, the little shop is mobbed during the
High Holy Days for those seeking Israeli-
style cuts of lamb shoulder stew, chicken
schnitzel, and some marvelously spiced
ground meat kebabs (beef or turkey) that
taste just like a Middle Eastern grill.

SEAFOOD

*A lack of great fish and seafood markets is
currently one of Center City's main retail
shortcomings. There is none I'd consider to
be superb on the level of, say, Ochs for meats
— though the recently unveiled Di Bruno's
seafood case shows great promise. But here
are your best bets:*

Anastasi

1101 S. 9th St., 19147, (215) 462-0550
At the heart of the Italian Market,
Anastasi's has a nice selection of seafood
basics, and a surprisingly good Italian
seafood cafe set behind glass at the center of the market.

Capt. Thomas Trading Co.

933 Race St., 19107, (215) 574-1328
I'm generally not a fan of the Chinatown
fish markets, but this plastic-curtained
nook is supposedly one of the region's
largest purveyors of lobster and exotic
Asian sea delicacies. It's a fascinating
warren of fish tanks to browse, even if
you're not shopping.

Groben Sea Food Market

*6833 Germantown Ave., 19119, (215) 843-
4717*
Mt. Airy residents rave about this long-
standing Germantown fish fixture. And
for good reason.

Ippolito's Seafood Co.

1300 Dickinson St., 19147, (215) 389-8906
It isn't in Center City, but this recently
spruced-up South Philly classic (circa
1929) is pretty close. And it's worth the
drive for the best fish market in town —
a great destination for all kinds of clear-
eyed whole branzinos, luscious Jersey
scallops, live crabs and lobsters, prepared
seafood, and specialty finds like ground
cracker crumbs.

Whole Foods Market

*20th and Callowhill Sts., 19130, (215) 557-
0015*
929 South St., 19147, (215) 733-9788
Expensive, but probably Center City's
most reliable in terms of freshness and
quality. They should all be the same, but
in Center City, I've preferred the selection
at the South Street location to the larger
store at 20th and Callowhill.

CHEESES, CHARCUTERIE, AND DAIRY

Claudio Caseificio

922 S. 9th St., 19147, (215) 238-0435

Claudio's King of Cheese

926 S. 9th St., 19147, (215) 627-1873
Long the stay-at-market rival of its
expansion-minded neighbor, Di Bruno's,
Claudio's excels in all the usual Italian
goods, especially house-label bargains
like its fabulous aged balsamic vinegar.
I'm a fan of their aged provolone, but
there is no better mozzarella in the city
than the milky white cheeses they make
fresh every day at the Caseificio annex
next door. I'm addicted.

Di Bruno Bros. House of Cheese

930 S. 9th St., 19147, (215) 922-2876,
www.dibruno.com
1730 Chestnut St., 19103, (215) 665-9220
Purists still prefer the cramped quarters of
the ancient downtown original, but Di
Bruno's massive specialty foods emporium just north of Rittenhouse Square is
the answer to this Philadelphia foodie's
dreams. The incredible selection of
cheeses, charcuteries, and specialty ingredients is more comparable to the food
palaces of Manhattan than anything this
city has had. Service is friendly and knowledgeable, and the quality is top-notch.
The prepared foods operations, both in
the airy cafe upstairs and the take-out
counters on the ground floor, are still
somewhat disappointing, but are a work
in progress. No matter, I have to set strict
spending limits before entering these
doors — otherwise I lose control. As of
July 2006, Di Bruno's expanded again, re-
annexing their former 18th Street space
and connecting it to the main store to
feature a butcher case with high-end
meats and a fresh fish market — two
amenities Rittenhouse Square was sorely
lacking. It's expensive, but worth it.

Downtown Cheese Shop

Reading Terminal Market, 12th and Arch
Sts., 19107, (215) 351-7412, www.read-
ingterminalmarket.org
Jack Morgan has a talent for bringing the
most amazing and rare artisan cheeses
to this excellent market stand, which has
some other quality condiments, from
Tuscan ham to Spanish oils and Greek
yogurt.

Fork, Etc.

308 Market St., 19106, (215) 625-9425,
www.forkrestaurant.com/forketc.htm
The take-out market attached to Fork
has a wide selection of appealing salads
and provisions, including excellent
house-baked breads and the finest collection of artisan cheeses east of Broad.

Lancaster County Dairy

Reading Terminal Market, 12th & Arch Sts.,
19107, (215) 922-0425, www.readingterminalmarket.org
Tucked away near the Convention
Center–side door, this is a great stop for
fresh, rich Lancaster cream and buttermilk, unpasteurized goat's milk, yogurts,
and fresh-squeezed juice.

PRODUCE

The farmers' market scene has been a late
bloomer in Southeast Pennsylvania, which
may seem odd for such a fertile agricultural
crescent. But in recent years it has finally
begun to hit stride, becoming a major
warm-weather boon to residents near
some of the best city markets in Headhouse
Square, Rittenhouse Square, and Clark Park
in West Philly, as well as some of the better
suburban markets in West Chester and
Phoenixville. There are so many great farmers you'll encounter, but some of my
favorites have been North Star Orchards
(awesome heirloom apples), Country Time
Farm (amazing antibiotic-free pork), Spiral
Path Farm (organic produce), Somerton
Tank Farms (heirloom veggies from North
Philly), B&L Grassland Farm (spectacular
lamb), and Livingood's (great organic produce, including local paw-paws). The hours,
vendors, and locations change every year,
but the two organizations responsible for
the majority of these markets — The Food
Trust and Farm to City — maintain updated schedules on their handy websites:
www.thefoodtrust.org and www.farmtocity.org.

Fair Food Farmstand

Reading Terminal Market, 12th and Arch
Sts., 19107, (215) 627-2029, www.readingterminalmarket.org
This non-profit organized by the White
Dog Cafe has been a major addition to
the market, reconnecting the Reading
Terminal to its roots as one of the coun-

try's original city farmers' markets (circa 1892) — a connection that had grown rather tenuous in recent years. Fair Food doesn't grow anything itself, but serves as the outlet and distributor for dozens of local artisan food producers — from exquisite Oley Valley mushrooms to Harmonyville blue cheese to raw goat's milk and double-smoked Lancaster ham. At season's peak, it's like visiting a dozen farm stands in one. This is also my Thanksgiving source for fresh, naturally raised fresh turkey. Open Thursday, Friday, and Saturday only.

Iovine Brothers Produce

Reading Terminal Market, 12th and Arch Sts., 19107, (215) 928-4366, www.readingterminalmarket.org
Iovine's offers much of the usual produce (at very good prices), but also one of the better selections of specialty produce, from salsify roots and inexpensive fresh herbs to an amazing selection of wild mushrooms.

Kauffman's Lancaster County Produce

Reading Terminal Market, 12th and Arch Sts., 19107, (215) 592-1898, www.readingterminalmarket.org
This Amish farm stand is one of Reading Terminal's other great local purveyors, with the sweetest little Brussels sprouts in the fall, luscious tomatoes in summer, and a year-round selection of Pennsylvania Dutch chow-chow and other pickled delights.

Michael Anastasio Produce, Inc.

911 Christian St., 19147, (215) 627-2807
In general, Italian Market produce is cheap but ordinary. Anastasio is the exception, selling specialty items — from mushrooms to baby artichokes, chestnuts, and green olives — to restaurants and locals alike.

Sue's Fruit & Produce

115 S. 18th St., 19103, (215) 569-0985 (phone is rarely answered)
The ultimate Center City corner produce stand — small, stocked with ripe treasures, and charmingly personal. Their specialty selection has boomed since a recent cross-street move to larger quarters, with particular finds in micro-greens from Branch Creek Farms (otherwise found only in restaurants), Claudio's mozzarella, and Pequea Valley yogurts.

PREPARED FOODS, PROVISIONS

Bacchus Market

2300 Spruce St., 19103, (215) 545-6656
This prepared foods store is a tiny corner shop near Fitler Square that offers homey cooking with a sophisticated touch. Fabulous soups, excellent fish, indulgent sides (creamed Brussels sprouts), and bake-sale-style desserts add up to a satisfying dinner.

Bobby Chez

The Village Walk, 1990 Rt. 70, Cherry Hill, N.J. 08003, (856) 751-7575
8007 Ventnor Ave., Margate, N.J. 08402, (609) 487-1922, www.bobbychezcrabcakes.com
Prepare to stand in line at this immensely popular South Jersey seafood take-out chain — and not just because the service is painfully slow. The famous lump-filled crab cakes are worth the wait (and only $6.95), but they do need some sauce for pizzazz. The shrimp puffs, BBQ shrimp, and chicken potpies are also great.

Carlino's

2616 E. County Line Rd., Ardmore, Pa. 19003, (610) 649-4046, www.carlinosmarket.com
This Main Line prepared-foods institution specializes in excellent house-made pastas and sauces, pizzas, and a wide assortment of fine vinegars, oils, and other specialty products.

Caviar Assouline

Liberty Place, 1625 Chestnut St., 19103, (215) 972-1616, www.caviarassouline.com
The retail presence for this specialty wholesaler has shrunk over the past few years, but Joel Assouline's boutique in Liberty Place remains the city's best destination for caviar.

The Chef's Market

231 South St., 19147, (215) 925-8360, www.chefsmkt.com
This Queen Village institution was one of Center City's first specialty foods retailers and prepared foods markets, and it remains a reliable standby — especially for catered parties. The smoked whitefish salad is a classic.

Claudio Specialty Foods

926 S. 9th St., 19147, (215) 627-1873, www.claudiofood.com
Long the stay-at-market rival of its expansion-minded neighbor, Di Bruno's, Claudio's excels in all the usual Italian goods, especially house-label bargains like its fabulous aged balsamic vinegar, creamy green pesto, roasted peppers, and long-stemmed artichokes. I'm a fan of their aged provolone, but there is no better mozzarella in the city than the milky white cheeses they make fresh every day at the Caseificio annex next door.

Dad's All Natural Stuffings

1615 W. Ritner St., 19145, (215) 334-1934
312 S. Black Horse Pike, Blackwood, N.J. 08012, (856) 228-7744
This prepared foods market in Deep South Philly has some of the best crab cakes in town (perhaps better than Bobby Chez), excellent meat loaf, and a surprisingly good cheesesteak.

Dienner's Bar-B-Q Chicken

Reading Terminal Market, 12th and Arch Sts., 19107, (215) 925-8755, www.readingterminalmarket.org

One of the city's best stops for whole roasted chickens basted to a BBQ crisp in their own fat on large rotisseries.

Essene Market & Cafe

719 S. 4th St., 19147, (215) 922-1146, www.essenemarket.com
This crunchy Queen Village institution predates Whole Foods as a destination for organic products, from flax oil to locally made seitan, bulk mung beans, and anything else you might need to survive as a vegan. There is also a cafe in back serving so-so vegetarian meals. For the most part, it's a throwback to the old co-op days that has been kept nicely up to date.

Mancuso & Son

1902 E. Passyunk Ave., 19148, (215) 389-1817
An old-time Italian cheese shop on resurgent East Passyunk Avenue, Mancuso's makes its own mozzarella, outstanding ricotta impastata, and authentic lemon water ice in the summer.

Matteo Italian Food Products

12th & Ritner Sts., 19148, (215) 467-7644, www.matteositalianfood.com
One of the hidden markets of Deep South Philly has some of my favorite marinated mozzarella knots and a wide selection of frozen Italian meals (including excellent manicotti and sausage cacciatore).

The Pennsylvania General Store

Reading Terminal Market, 12th and Arch Sts., 19107, (215) 592-0455, www.pageneralstore.com
Yes, it's a handy tourist stop, but this is also where hardcore Pennsylvanians come to stock up on certain items when they're heading out of town for extended periods, from bags of Wilbur Buds (the original chocolate kiss) to extra-dark pretzels, to the sweet, dried Cope's corn that is a staple at every Pennsylvania Dutch holiday table.

Picnic, Inc.

3131 Walnut St., 19104, (215) 222-1608

A prepared foods oasis in the Left Bank from the former founding chef of Fork.

Talluto's Authentic Italian Food
944 S. 9th St., 19147, (215) 627-4967
6101 Elmwood Ave., 19142, (215) 727-9704
530 Foundry Rd., Norristown, Pa. 19401,
(610) 630-6788
This busy corner shop sells a wide selection of quality Italian goods, but is best known for its superb ravioli and frozen meatball dinners, as well as some very good handmade mozzarella.

Taste Buds Market
2400 Lombard St., 19146. (215) 546-6900,
www.tastebudsonlombard.com
This relatively new market has quickly become a fixture near Fitler Square for its good sandwich board, pastries and tasty coffee.

ETHNIC MARKETS
Bell's Market
8330 Bustleton Ave., 19152, (215) 342-6016
You'll feel like you're visiting Moscow when you enter this Russian supermarket in Northeast Philly. There is a fabulous selection of Eastern European dairy products (including tubs of delicious Bulgarian feta), but I'm also thrilled to shop the deli cases filled with smoked fish and sausage, cheap caviar, ready-to-heat chicken Kiev, pickled mushrooms, and a wide selection of superb Russian chocolates (dark Korkunov is a personal fave). The frozen pierogi and pelmeni dumplings are also worth a try.

Bitar's
947 Federal St., 19147, (215) 755-1121,
www.bitars.com
7152 Germantown Ave., 19119, (215) 755-1121
One of the few Middle Eastern markets in Philadelphia. Grab a falafel and a baklava at the grill next door before

stocking up on tabouli, cardamom-scented coffee and pitas.

Chung May Chinese and American
1017 Race St., 19107, (215) 625-8883
One of the area's original Asian markets, this Chinatown institution is a standby for Asian condiments, Chinese greens, and cooking gear. Need a clay hot pot, fermented bean paste, or Chinese anise? This is your place.

Han Ah Reum Supermarket
7320 Old York Rd, Elkins Park, Pa. 19027,
(215) 782-1801
1720 Rt. 70 E., Cherry Hill, N.J. 08003, (856)
751-6659
These impressive Korean supermarkets are bright, clean and sprawling, with noisy machines popping out fresh rice crackers, hand-slathered kimchee on weekends, huge fresh fish counters, and an amazing array of spicy pickled vegetables.

Hung Vuong
1122 –1138 Washington Ave., 19147, (215)
336-2803
This is my favorite of Washington Avenue's mega-Asian markets. It has a Vietnamese bent, but there is every variety of Asian green imaginable, fresh-bagged noodles, dried fungus mushrooms, chicory coffee, and freezers full of great dim-sum dumplings.

Krakus Market
3150 Richmond St., 19134, (215) 426-4336,
www.krakusmarket.com
There are several nice Polish markets in Port Richmond, but Krakus is your best one-stop bet, with an awesome selection of kielbasa and locally made pierogi.

La Tienda Wholesale, Inc.
227 Washington Ave., 19147, (215) 334-8168
A great spot to prepare for a fiesta, La Tienda pioneered the Mexican market in South Philadelphia, with a wide selection of fresh and dried chiles, salty Mexican

cheese, tortillas, and fresh-made tamales on the weekend.

Maido!

36 N. Narberth Ave., Narberth, Pa. 19072, (610) 747-0557, www.maidookini.com
Stock up on your natto, miso, and tofu at one of the area's only authentic Japanese markets, an enterprising community hub that runs a shuttle bus to the Japanese Language School at Friends Central, and also doubles as a luncheonette serving home-style comfort snacks like yakisoba, onigiri rice balls, and okonomiyaki everything "pizzas."

Mandi Subzi

Street Road Plaza, 2610 Street Rd., Bensalem, Pa. 19020, (215) 244-2028
1400 Berlin Rd., Cherry Hill, N.J. 08003, (856) 354-5061
These Jackson Heights–based supermarkets cater to the region's suburban Indian communities, with bins of exotic produce (like bumpy-skinned karelas), walls piled high with sacks of basmati, and everything from jars of lime pickle to bulk spices and chappati flour. The subcontinent sweets at the front are worth a nibble.

Rice-n-Spice International Grocery Store

4205 Chestnut St., 19104, (215) 387-5250
Situated in the West Philly Curry Zone next to the city's best Pakistani kebab house (Kabobeesh), this aromatic store is a trove of Indian curries and bulk spices — not to mention Bollywood videos.

Variedades Veracruzanas

914 Washington Ave., 19147, (215) 271-2991
Considerably smaller than La Tienda, but more conveniently located to Italian Market shopping, this little store has all the standard provisions of the Mexican pantry, from great queso fresco to bulk barrels of mulatto chiles.

COOKING SUPPLIES

Philadelphia has its share of high-end kitchenware chains like Williams-Sonoma and Kitchen Kapers. But it also has a few worthy independent stores that provide their own unique spin on the world of kitchen gadgets. Here are three of the best:

Cookbook Stall

Reading Terminal Market, 12th and Arch Sts., 19107, (215) 923-3170, www.readingterminalmarket.org
The city's only bookstore (or stand, as this case may be) completely dedicated to the world of cookbooks. A great source for hard-to-find food tomes.

Fante's Cookware

1006 S. 9th St., 19147, (215) 922-5557, www.fantes.com
Set into the heart of the Italian Market, Fante's is a sprawling (and somewhat cluttered) emporium crammed with high-quality kitchen wares and a knowledgeable staff to advise. The store has all the major brands, but also a good share of esoterica, from Neapolitan flip-pot coffee makers to African soapstone cooking pots for the fire pit, Abruzzese pasta chitarras, pizzelle irons and an entire room dedicated to specialty baking.

Foster's Gourmet Cookware

Reading Terminal Market, 12th and Arch Sts., 19107, 215-925-0950, www.shopfosters.com
Snug in the back corner of the Reading Terminal, Foster's crams an amazing amount of cooking gadgetry into its space — all of it cutting-edge equipment that is a tribute to owner Ken Foster's nose for the latest in urban style. If you're looking for the latest Ken Onion knife or hottest hue of BYO bag, or just a really cool cookie cutter, this is a great place to start.

WINE AND SPIRITS

At first glance, Philadelphia appears to be smack in the heart of the drinker's purgatory that is a state-controlled wine and spirits system. But major progress has been achieved to improve the bureaucracy of the Pennsylvania Liquor Control Board over the past few years, including better selections in the newer high-end "superstores," serious deals on serious "Chairman's Selections" wines, and a handy website that puts the entire state inventory at your finger tips. (Go to www.lcb.state.pa.us, and then follow the link "For Consumers" to arrive at the most helpful browsers.)

That said, not all state stores are created equal. Even the best ones look like gussied-up supermarkets with only sporadic (and often helpless) help. In my wine adventures, however, I've found these state stores to be among the best:

In Philadelphia
Columbus Commons N., 1940 S. Columbus Blvd., 19148, (215) 271-1908
1218 Chestnut St., 19107, (215) 560-4380
Society Hill Shopping Ctr., 326 S. 5th St., 19106, (215) 560-7064
1913 Chestnut St., 19103, (215) 560-4215

On the Main Line
922 Lancaster Ave., Bryn Mawr, Pa. 19010, (610) 581-4560
143 S. Gulph Rd., King of Prussia, Pa. 19406, (610) 768-3060

In Chester County
Devon Village Shoppes, 821 W. Lancaster Ave., Ste. 110, Wayne, Pa. 19087, (610) 964-6516

The best news for local drinkers, of course, is that some excellent wine stores are just across the bridge or south down I-95 in the free-market states of New Jersey and Delaware. With interstate wine-shipping laws in tumult, Pennsylvania acknowledged last year it was no longer criminally pursuing those who crossed the border with out-of-state-purchased wines. Most avid wine drinkers in Philly, though, have been making Jersey and Delaware runs for years regardless, and with good reason. Here's my short list of some of the best stops "across the border":

Buy-Rite Liquors
1811 W. Rt. 70, Cherry Hill, N.J. 08002, (856) 317-1234, www.buyriteliquor.com
The space still bears the discount mart feel of the former auto parts store it was, but I've found a surprising number of well-priced bottles here, including one of the area's better selections of single-malt scotches and Belgian beers.

Canal's Discount Liquor Mart (a.k.a. The Bottlestop)
10 W. Rt. 70, Marlton, N.J. 08053, (856) 983-4991, www.wineaccess.com/store/canals-marlton
This is one of my true favorites for a broad mainstream selection, helpful service, and great prices — especially with one of the store's discount cards.

Canal's Discount Liquor Mart

5360 Rt. 38, Pennsauken, N.J. 08109, (856) 665-4202

One of the closest decent stores to the Ben Franklin Bridge, this Canal's (there are a number of unaffiliated others) has an excellent selection of quality wines and spirits. The prices are pretty good, though it's one of the more disorganized stores to browse in. Serious collectors will want to wander up the wooden ladder in back to the attic cache of premium bottles.

Circle Liquor Store

1 MacArthur Blvd., Somer's Point, N.J. 08244, (609) 927-2921, www.wineaccess.com/store/circleliquors

When we're down the Shore, I always stock up at this venerable store, which has an awesome selection of quality wines (especially strong on California), great Belgian beers, and some outstanding deals when you sign up for their discount card.

Corkscrewed

1990 Marlton Pike East, Cherry Hill, N.J. 08003, (856) 874-1090

This quirky but worthwhile store is hidden at the rear of a Cherry Hill strip mall, and has the austere look of a bargain-hunter's garage sale, with unpacked boxes of wine. The prices aren't always bargains, and the service can often be indifferent, but I've found this shop to have superb taste in selecting some unusual quality wines, from one of the area's best premium sake collections to excellent kosher Rioja.

Frank's Union Wine Mart

1206 N. Union St., Wilmington, Del. 19806, (302) 429-1978, www.frankswine.com

This store features quality stuff, but has a decided focus on high-end wine buyers. I find it a bit disorganized, and the staff isn't always hip to helping bargain hunters. The prices, accordingly, are on the high side — unless you indulge in one of Frank's worthwhile sample packages. There's also an excellent selection of beers.

Kreston Liquor Mart

904 Concord Ave., Wilmington, Del. 19802, (302) 652-3792, www.krestonwines.com

Another of my most favorite shops, this store offers a wide variety of quality wines, experienced and helpful help, and a discount card program that saves serious bucks. Among many other things, Kreston's has one of the better local selections of German Rieslings and collector spirits.

Moore Brothers Wine Co.

7200 N. Park Dr., Pennsauken, N.J. 08109, (856) 317-1177, www.wineaccess.com/store/moorebrosnj 1416 N. Dupont St., Wilmington, Del. 19806, (302) 498-0360

Nobody sells the story of their wines as convincingly as the staff at these marvelous stores from the former sommelier at Le Bec-Fin, Gregory Moore. Every one of them is as knowledgeable as a sommelier, and they have some fabulous wines to sell — well-priced, smaller-label artisan wines from France, Italy, Germany and Japan (the sake selection is great). My only frustration here is that the selection is quite limited to Moore Brothers finds, most of which are exclusives you've never heard of. But if you spend $15 or more a bottle, the success rate has been stellar.

Phillips Fine Wines

17 Bridge St., Stockton, N.J. 08559, (609) 397-0587

It's a hike from Center City, but a connoisseur's treat to browse the cozy rooms upon rooms of incredible wines at this rambling old residence-turned-wine shop in scenic Stockton (just up the Delaware from Lambertville and New Hope). The prices are uniformly high, but the selection of high-end bottles is among the region's best.

Total Wine & More

The Plaza at Cherry Hill, 2100 Rt. 38, Cherry Hill, N.J. 08002, (856) 667-7100, www.total-wine.com
Northtowne Plaza, 691 Naamans Rd., Claymont, Del. 19703 (302) 792-1322, www.wineaccess.com/store/totalwine-claymont/

These mega-wine stores are the closest we have to wine supermarkets, and they're stocked with good bottles (among them, one of the best selections of Champagnes). That said, finding a helpful staff member here is a constant challenge and, given the huge inventory, I'm often amazed by how often I don't find what I'm looking for.

BEER RETAILERS

Beer Yard

218 E. Lancaster Ave., Wayne, Pa. 19087, (610) 688-3431; www.beeryard.com

If you're buying Belgian by the case, there are few destinations near the city with a better selection. The store's website is also a superb source for general information on almost any beer.

The Foodery Market

10th and Pine Sts., 19107, (215) 928-1111

This corner market is the place to go for that obscure can of Trappist ale; they stock nearly every beer known to man.

The Foodery Northern Liberties

2nd and Poplar Sts., 19123, (215) 238-6077

The Foodery recently opened a spectacular new branch of its original Pine Street beer heaven in brew-centric Northern Liberties. It's larger, with nearly 700 individual beers to choose from.

There's also a deli, Capogiro ice creams, and a dining area where you can crack that Belgian brew open for a taste.

Latimer Delicatessen, Inc.

255 S. 15th St., 19102, (215) 545-9244

It isn't quite the Foodery, but it easily sells the largest variety of high-end six-packs west of Broad Street.

Shangy's

40 E. Main St., Emmaus, Pa. 19049, (610) 967-6793

Welcome to specialty beer heaven. It's a serious brewhead road-trip, and you must buy by the case (so go with a group). But Shangy's is one of the biggest specialty beer importers in the country — and the distributor to many Philadelphia retailers. So you'll get better prices here — not to mention an amazing selection of beer glassware for purchase. Stop over for dinner at the nearby Farmhouse (a stellar beer restaurant), then make a beeline for your Philadelphia fridge.

The Six-Pack Store

7105 Roosevelt Blvd., 19149, (215) 338-6384

A quality beer store in blue-collar Northeast Philly is a cause worth supporting. There are also a number of local craft beers on tap used to fill "growler" jugs to go.

Voorhees Liquor Store

6 Berlin Rd., Voorhees, N.J. 08043, (856) 429-5273

This store does sell wine, but it's the amazing beer selection that draws me back. It's considerably cheaper than its Pennsylvania counterparts.

Taste of Youth —

An Inhaling of the Wildwood Boardwalk's "Culinary" Delights Brings Back Some of the Fondest Memories of Youth

I HOLD A DROOPING SLICE OF MACK'S PLAIN cheese pizza up to Howard Trachtman's nose, and his eyes drift shut.

"This is the smell that I think of," he says, breathing deeply, his nostrils just above the molten sheen of salty cheese. "If I were in Kansas City and you put this slice under my nose, I think: Wildwood."

If Marcel Proust had visited the Boardwalk, this obviously would have been his madeleine. Trachtman, the real estate lawyer, is suddenly transported to his youth.

It is summer in the 1970s, and little Howard is pressing Kiss logos and Elks lodge decals onto T-shirts at Pegasus, the Boardwalk trinket store owned by his Grandpa Ruby and Grandma Gert. There were afternoons on the wide beach buying ice cream from men carrying freezers on their backs, yelling, "Cream-sicle! Fu-dgy wudgy!"

There were rides galore in the evening, stuffed animals to win for his high school sweetheart. And, of course, there was a steady inhaling of the Boardwalk's "culinary" delights, usually in this order: pizza, fries, custard cones, "and pizza again."

"You remember your fondest memories from childhood? Mine are here," he says. "I don't know if it makes the taste buds more active, or if the salt air gives your appetite a little extra boost, but everything tastes better here."

The question we set out to answer on this beautiful weekend afternoon was whether the taste of memories can endure the test of decades. Can big Howard's neighborhood nostalgia tour survive my scrutiny? Can it be updated with a few new favorites? ("Corn dogs?" he says incredulously. "Never had one.")

Nate's hot dog shop is gone. The Planter's Peanut store is now a Dairy Queen. And the old Taylor's Pork Roll place, where Howard's uncle used to send him for a sandwich with cash from the Pegasus register, is nowhere to be found.

Many of the names have changed, perhaps. But Wildwood is thriving, its great wooden way still an explosion for the senses. Roller coasters rattle by, trailing screams that mingle with the huckster's calls ("Everybody wins!"). The giant piers to our left are a massive jumble of rides, the storefront facades to our right a seemingly endless stream of flashing honky-tonk arcades. How to choose where to eat?

Mack's rightly remains Howard's touchstone, its happy pink and purple room uncompromised by the years. From its long formica counter, you can watch a carousel turn in the distance. But it is the pizza in front of us that holds my attention. Its cheese is addictively sharp. The sauce has an herby, orange flavor that eats just right. And the thin crust leaves a tricky dusting of flour that clings to my finger tips as we head out. I pause once again and lick them clean.

Next destination: the zig-zag counter at **Curley's Fries.**

The original stand at 26th Street opened in 1974 and was named not for the shape of the thick, ruffle-cut fries, but for the curl-topped head of its founder, Joseph Marchiano. My guide likes the fact that they serve vinegar here as a condiment, but it would be nothing without the spuds, which are a monument to the dying art of fresh-cut french fries. Idahoes are sliced through a hand-cranked chunker into a water bath, deep-fried, then piled into buckets and barrels for the suntanned hoards.

How could anyone cover them with cheesy-orange cheese goo? Plenty do. But these fries are worth a solo flight, as fine a rebuke to the standard frozen fry as I've ever tasted. They are not mealy and soft inside from the freezer, but light and fluffy, like crisp little sticks of baked potato.

Curley's treats lemonade in the same rewardingly natural way — shaking just-squeezed lemons, shaved ice, water, and sugar in a cup — and it is startling just how refreshing it can be.

All is not bliss on the Boardwalk menu. I have to duck out of the way of a giant pretzel, a cinnamon-dusted twist so large it looks more like a catcher's mitt than something to be digested. We take some free samples of fudge and they are rubbery, even in the afternoon sun. And while Howard's experiment with a corn dog is intriguing — the sweet cornmeal crust is a sensation — we are unable to identify the substance of the pale meat inside.

TLC's Polish Water Ice is a pleasant surprise. The manager lures us in with a tray of Technicolor freebies and the promise that they are "creamier" than Italian water ice. The flavor isn't dairy, but the texture, in fact, is quite smooth, churned in a soft-serve machine to the consistency of custard. The flavors are sharp and true. Bracing lemon. Root beer with a woody edge. We'll pass, thanks, on the ice that is atomic blue.

A stop at **Kohr Bros. Custard** is required, as it is hard to find a creamier, two-tone swirl than theirs. My little cone has a peak that bends toward me in the softening heat and melts across my tongue at the lazy pace of richness.

Now where do we stop for funnel cakes? Howard has no favorite in this category, so we look up and simply walk into the nearest door: **Giovanna's Goodies I**.

How lucky we are to find owner Mary Difranco, whose thickly painted eyelids and gravity-defying hair lend a quirky note of legitimacy to her boastful pitch:"I make the best funnel cakes on the Boardwalk! You taste it now! I'm the best. Now! ...You tell me."

Behind her, husband John pipes a thin stream of batter into a metal ringform that floats in the deep fryer. Back and forth, he makes a careful criss-cross lattice of dough that inflates and turns brown in the oil. A shower of powdered sugar is cranked over the finished product, and Difranco slides it over, so hot I can barely touch it at first.

Still, I'm feeling pressure to taste, as a stern-faced Difranco awaits the verdict. With a napkin, I break off an edge and pop it in my mouth. The powdered sugar is liquefied from the heat; the crust burns my lip. But inside, it all simply melts — a perfect harmony of crunch and puff.

Unable to speak, I give Difranco thumbs up.

As we leave, we find ourselves standing, coincidentally, before the storefront that used to be Pegasus. Howard's grandparents' old store is now an arcade called Fat Daddy's Games.

"Step right up and spin the Fat Daddy candy wheel!" shouts the huckster."Po-kemon! Stuffed animals! "

The store may be different, but Howard is having another flashback. It is summer in the 1970s again. This time, it is 9 at night. He and his brother have been sent to bed in the little apartment behind this facade. Shadows of the carnival rides flash on the walls. Sounds of the crowds outside fill their room.

"We were wiped out from the beach and the rides," he says."But it was hard to fall asleep when you were hearing all the excitement on the Boardwalk. You wanted to be in it."

So much for sleep. At least their bellies were full.

• **Mack's**, 3218 Boardwalk, (609) 522-6166; 4200 Boardwalk, (609) 729-0244
• **Curley's Fries**, 2509 Boardwalk
• **TLC's Polish Water Ice**, 1068 Boardwalk, (609) 399-2662
• **Kohr Bros. Custard**, 4001 Boardwalk, (609) 523-6792
• **Giovanna's Goodies I**, 2416 Boardwalk, (609) 729-3131

The Jersey Shore

THERE IS SOMETHING ABOUT THE SALT AIR that makes me hungry at the Shore. OK . . . so I'm always hungry.

But there is something about strolling the Boardwalk, running through the sand and surf, and soaring through the nighttime sky on a Ferris wheel that makes those summer meals taste even better. And after eight years of scouring the Jersey coast from Long Beach Island down to Cape May, I know there's more to my enthusiasm than the powers of suggestion.

The Jersey Shore is stocked with great places to dine, whether you're looking for top-notch contemporary cooking, a classic fish house, a surprising variety of great ethnic flavors, or a belly-busting breakfast. And Atlantic City's long-promised casino-dining boom has finally begun to deliver, from the first true Vegas-style luxury spots in the Borgata to a slew of promised new arrivals in late summer '06 for The Pier at Caesar's and other casinos from the likes of Stephen Starr (Buddakan and Continental). As is typical in seasonal restaurant scenes, many favorites change ownership or close from year to year. But here are more than 40 fondly remembered survivors that have delivered reliably for a number of seasons — plus a few new entries you'll probably be hearing about soon.

Allen's Clam Bar

5650 Rt. 9, New Gretna, 08224, (609) 296-4106
This old-time clam shack at the fringe of the Pinelands is a classic destination for fresh seafood in unpretentious surroundings. The cold, salty clams, homemade clam pies, and french-fried lobster tails provide all the class this no-frills sea shanty needs. *Take-out.*

Athenian Garden

619 S. New York Rd. (Rt. 9 S.), Galloway, 08205, (609) 748-1818
A friendly and pleasantly appointed spot just north of A.C., featuring traditional Greek taverna fare, with a notable skill for whole fish on the grill. *Take-out.*

Basilico's

27 43rd St., Sea Isle City, 08243, (609) 263-1010
A cozy trattoria that serves pizzeria favorites and well-done trattoria fare, from fig polenta to soulful braciole. Moderate.

Beach Creek Oyster Bar & Grille

500 West Hand Ave., Wildwood, 08260, (609) 522-1062
Tucked into a marina at the base of the Rio Grande bridge, this ambitious restaurant offers one of the island's few fine-dining options, with a surprisingly ambitious menu to accompany its spectacular sunset view, including a super raw bar, deep-fried soft-shell crabs, and a martini to watch to sun go down.

The Black Duck on Sunset
1 Sunset Blvd., West Cape May, 08204, (609) 898-0100, www.blackduckonsunset.com
J. Christopher Hubert has made the former Peaches his own with a bright, modern room and an appealing New American menu that lends a contemporary touch to good local seafood. *Take-out.*

Bobby Flay Steak
Borgata Hotel & Casino, 1 Borgata Way, Atlantic City, 08401, (866) 692-6742 (MY BORGATA) or (609) 317-1000, www.theborgata.com
Celebrity chef Bobby Flay adds a bit of Southwestern fusion spice to a steak house concept at this splashy, sleek space, where the "Philadelphia-style" strip gets a provolone sauce and onions, and non-carnivores can dig in to creatively done crustaceans at the "lobster bar." Too new for a verdict.

Brass Monkey
900 W. Brigantine Ave., Brigantine, 08230, (609) 266-8520, www.brassmonkeygourmet.com
This funky spot does it all for isolated Brigantine with an appealing casual style. Cafe hang-out and gourmet market by day, the Monkey also has an ambitious, globe-hopping and affordable menu that runs from Caprese salads with homemade mozzarella to Asian duck noodle stir fries, Italian pasta bowls, and mixed satay grills.

Brennan's by the Bay
50th and Landis Ave., Sea Isle City, 08243, (609) 263-8881
The owner of popular Nick's Chatawhile Inn in Reading made a splash in Sea Isle last summer with this surprisingly sophisticated (yet laid-back) contemporary Italian, featuring fabulous BBQ clams with provolone and pancetta, super softshell crabs, and grilled pizzas. Breakfasts are also featured, with corn flake-battered French toast. *Take-out.*

Brown's Restaurant
110 Boardwalk, Ocean City, 08226, (609) 391-0677
Watch the hot doughnuts being made for breakfast at this seasonal Boardwalk institution at St. Charles Place, then come back after a morning at the beach for a BLT or the ultimate simple hamburger (ground fresh daily, never frozen, and hand-formed with care), and discover why this no-frills, screened-in room may be the Shore's definitive beachside grill. *Take-out.*

Brulee
The Quarter at the Tropicana, 2801 Pacific Ave., Atlantic City, 08401, (609) 344-4900, www.bruleedesserts.com
Celebrate your winnings with a multi-course chocolate jackpot at this glittery, all-dessert boutique. It may be the most innovative boite in the splashy Quarter, with exquisite, composed confections painting the plates and service captains that deliver the "meals" with often-fiery tableside flair. There's even a special luxe menu for high-rollers. *Take-out.*

Busch's Seafood Restaurant
8700 Anna Phillips Lane, Sea Isle City, 08243, (609) 263-8626, www.buschsseafood.com
This vast, traditional fish house isn't trendy, but at more than 120 years old, it remains one of the Shore's most reliable old-time kitchens, with lovely deviled crabs, creamy she-crab soup, and excellent broiled lobsters.

Cafe Beach Club
Beach Club Hotel, 13th and the Boardwalk, Ocean City, 08226, (609) 398-7700, www.cafebeachclub.com
This unpretentious Boardwalk eatery serves one of the Shore's best breakfasts, from the puffy waffles to the creamiest creamed chipped beef. Open only in season. *Take-out.*

Claude's

Anglesea Village, 100 Olde New Jersey Ave., North Wildwood, 08260, (609) 522-0400, www.claudesrestaurant.com
Claude and Mary Pottier have added a little French panache to North Wildwood with their cheery yellow clapboard bistro, serving up delightful Gallic fare such as lobster in hollandaise, coq au vin, and sublime strawberries "Japanaise."

Curley's Fries

2509 Boardwalk, Wildwood, 08260
The original stand at 26th Street opened in 1974 and was named not for the shape of the thick, ruffle-cut fries, but for the curl-topped head of its founder, Joseph Marchiano. Still, these hand-crank-cut french fries are among my favorite in the world (especially with malt vinegar). The fresh-squeezed lemon juice is also one of the signature tastes of summer.

Daddy O

4401 Long Beach Blvd., Brant Beach, 08008, (609) 494-1300, www.daddyorestaurant.com
The latest project from the crew behind the Plantation and Moshulu, this sprawling restaurant, to-go store, and boutique hotel with 22 rooms feature comfort food with a modern twist. Still too new for a verdict. *Take-out.*

Dock's Oyster House

2405 Atlantic Ave., Atlantic City, 08401, (609) 345-0092, www.docksoysterhouse.com
A handsomely preserved Atlantic City classic that offers a fine atmosphere for steaks and updated seafood, with an excellent raw (and piano) bar. *Take-out.*

410 Bank Street

410 Bank St., Cape May, 08204, (609) 884-2127
Ebullient veteran chef Henry Sing Cheng anchors this Cape May standby, where the tented room and glassed-in porch are crowded with diners who crave his New Orleans and Caribbean-inspired fare, including specialties such as crab terrine and the mesquite-grilled tuna steak.

4th Street Cafe

400 Atlantic Ave., Ocean City, 08226, (609) 399-0764
This funky neighborhood cafe is known for its creative scones. But it also transforms itself by night into a gem of casual-yet-adventurous dining, with memorable dishes such as coffee-brined pork with goat cheese macaroni and grilled fish with mango salsa over crisp soba noodles. (The drawback: no alcohol allowed in Ocean City.)

Gallagher's Steakhouse

Resorts, 1133 Boardwalk, Atlantic City, 08401, (609) 340-6555, www.arkrestaurants.com
You can watch the meat age in the glassed-in cold room at the latest brand-name steak house to land in AC. It's loosely related to the Manhattan classic, with a decidedly more upscale bent, but shares the original's focus on dry-aging beef to a sublime complexity. The food is good, but considering the prices, the service isn't quite up to snuff.

Harvey Cedars Shellfish Co.

7904 Long Beach Blvd., Harvey Cedars, 08008, (609) 494-7112
Going strong for more than three decades, this LBI institution has perfected the steamed lobster–sweet corn dinner, homemade chowders, and blistered steamer clams of the classic seashore repertoire in a casual, screened-in dining room where diners dig in at picnic benches, and waits can sometimes extend an hour or more. Take-out is a popular alternative. It's BYOB, but there's an excellent wine store next door.

The Hula Grill

Betw. 9th and 10th Sts. on the Boardwalk, Ocean City, 08226, (609) 399-2400, www.hulagrilloc.com

It's always a bonus to find real food amidst the Boardwalk honky-tonk, but this Hawaiian grill is a real find for great fresh salads, crab cakes, and grilled ahi tuna lunches slicked with sweet, teriyaki-like "huli-huli" sauce, as well as pineap-ple-y pulled pork and banana-and-Guinness-battered fish. *Take-out.*

Island Grill
311 Mansion St., Cape May, 08204, (609) 884-0200
This casual BYOB sibling to nearby Daniel's on Broadway has a laid-back tropical feel and light fare (big salads, grilled Cuban sandwiches), but also ren-ditions of chef Harry Gleason's vividly rendered tropical flavors, from molasses-glazed coconut shrimp to pork chops beneath corn salsa and macadamia-crusted chicken in Thai curry. *Take-out.*

Joe Pesce
5206 Atlantic Ave., Ventnor, 08406, (609) 823-6500
A new seafood-centric venue with a South Philly flair from ex-Pompeii (and Joseph's Seafood Italiano) chef Joseph Tucker, who also owns Tucker's in Somers Point. Much simpler than Tucker's, this cash-only BYO focuses on straightfor-ward seafood dishes like fried calamari and fish grilled or served beneath piquant tomato gravy, as well as excel-lent pork Milanese. *Take-out.*

Jonathan's on West End
672 N. Trenton Ave., Atlantic City, 08401, (609) 441-1800
Tucked into the neighborhood, this ambi-tious spot is a local favorite thanks to per-sonable service and an eclectic, creative menu that dabbles in some unexpected combinations (with mixed results) like raspberries with filet mignon.

Karen & Rei's
1882 Rt. 9, Clermont, 08210, (609) 624-8205, www.karenandrei.com

Chef Karen Nelson and her husband, Rei Prabhakar, have settled into a sprawling property off Route 9 after moving from their popular nook in Avalon. Expect the same garlic-powered, globe-hopping fare, from mojo pork to Goan curried duck, in a pleasant, fine-dining ambience.

Kibbitz Down the Shore
846 Central Ave., Ocean City, 08226, (609) 398-0880
A former Russ Cowan deli, this corner lunch spot in Ocean City's downtown is still a great place for a gigantic sandwich of steaming hot corned beef and other Jewish deli standards.

Knife & Fork Inn
Atlantic and Pacific Aves., Atlantic City, 08401, 609-344-1133, www.knifeand-forkinn.com
The owners of longtime rival Dock's have taken over this beautiful A.C. landmark and restored it to high-end glory, pre-serving the building's distinctive Flemish look and speakeasy feel (especially at the flapper bar upstairs), but redirecting the focus to an updated steak house con-cept with a serious cellar. It's a worthy independent in a land of casino giants.

LoBianco Coastal Cuisine
8409 Ventnor Ave., Margate, 08402, (609) 822-0600
Nicholas and Stephanie LoBianco's 68-seat BYOB has a simple but chic khaki look and splendid contemporary cook-ing, which ranges from Italianesque mushroom agnolotti to Asian-inflected Arctic char glazed in hoisin and tender shortribs as big as broom handles.

Lobster House
Fisherman's Wharf, 906 Schellenger's Landing Rd. (Rt. 109), Cape May, 08204, (609) 884-8296, www.thelobsterhouse.com
You can't get fish much fresher than at this sprawling institution on the wharf in Cape May, where a view of the schooner *America* and a classic seafood menu sup-

plied by the restaurant's own fishing fleet have kept this old-timer happily afloat for 70-plus years. The cooking isn't always fabulous, but the deckside raw bar is great, and it still makes for a fun summer lunch.

Louisa's Cafe
104 Jackson St., Cape May, 08204, (609) 884-5882
This funky, hand-painted bungalow off Cape May's main drag is a favorite BYOB for seafood and vegetarian specials with a homemade, vaguely Provencale and tropical touch. It's a 20-seater, so prepare to wait. The owners can also be insufferably rude.

Lucky Bones Backwater Grille
1200 Rt. 109, Cape May, 08024, 609-884-2663
The owners of Cape May's Washington Inn have essentially recreated a more casual version of their now-closed Pelican Club in this spacious and friendly bar and grill, where fabulous brick-oven thin-crust pizzas are the highlight of a stylish, affordable menu that ranges from Cuban-spiced pork chops to steak with homemade frites.

Ma France Creperie
4901 Ventnor Ave., Ventnor, 08406, (609) 822-3067
Savor authentic Breton buckwheat crepes filled with ham and cheese followed by dessert crepes filled with chestnut creme, served up al fresco in a lovely garden. *Take-out.*

Mack's Pizza
3218 Boardwalk, Wildwood, 08260, (609) 522-6166
4200 Boardwalk, Wildwood, 08260, (609) 729-0244
Mack's rightly remains a touchstone of the Boardwalk summer, its happy pink and purple room uncompromised by the years, with a view of the carousel from its long formica counter. The pizza is also a classic, with an herby, orange sauce, addictively sharp cheese, and a thin crust that leaves a tricky dusting of flour on the finger tips.

Mac's Restaurant and Lounge
908 Shore Rd., Somers Point, 08244, (609) 927-2759, www.macsrestaurant.com
This classic Somers Point seafood house was in dire need of a fresh look, and it has gotten just that — a complete hipster renovation from the owners of Old City's Swanky Bubbles. The starters, desserts and cocktails are great, but the entrees — a mix of classic fish house, steaks, and more nouveau ideas — need some polish. *Take-out.*

Maui's Dog House
806 New Jersey Ave., North Wildwood, 08260, (609) 846-0444, www.mauisdoghouse.com
More than just a funky hotdog stand, the owner of this breezy Wildwood favorite is one of the last artisans left who actually makes his own dogs — both traditional and spicy white veal links — not to mention great, hand-cut fries. I find the buns a little too big, but there are so many toppings, you may need the extra room.

McGlade's on the Pier
Cape May Boardwalk, 722 Beach Ave., 08204, (609) 884-2614
Breakfast on the beach takes on extra weight at McGlade's, where chef Ginger Sulovsky has perfected the art of the giant omelette. Sit back on the canopied porch, listen to the morning surf, and behold her crepe-thin eggs stuffed, burritolike, with everything from garlicky shrimp to filet mignon and crab.

Mia
Caesars Atlantic City, 2100 Pacific Ave., 08401, (609) 441-2345, www.miaac.comwww.miaac.com
The high-profile French team behind Brasserie Perrier has cast its first chips onto the casino dining table at Caesars,

and the taste is something like the Brasserie with a more distinctly Italian flavor, from the homemade pastas to veal chops crowned with eggplant parmesan and excellent gelati. The cuisine, though, currently outclasses the space in the corner of Caesars' noisy lobby.

Mud City Crabhouse
1185 E. Bay Ave., Manahawkin, 08050, (609) 978-3660, www.mudcitycrabhouse.com
Don't be afraid to get your hands messy at this popular crab house across from Long Beach Island. The best crabs come topped with an addictive, finger-licking smear of garlicky breadcrumbs. *Take-out.*

Mustache Bill's Diner
8th and Broadway, Barnegat Light, 08006, (609) 494-0155
Summer on Long Beach Island wouldn't be complete without a visit to this beautiful deco diner where the seafood omelets and creamed chipped beef are first-rate. *Take-out.*

Nags Head Fine Foods
801 Asbury Ave., Ocean City, 08244, (609) 391-9080
Former Hatteras owners Bill and Ellen Rollins offer tasty regional American cooking in a no-frills dining room, scoring one of the Shore's best flavor values. *Take-out.*

Old Homestead Steak House
Borgata Hotel & Casino, 1 Borgata Way, Atlantic City, 08401, (866) 692-6742 (MY BORGATA) or 609-317-1000, www.thebor-gata.com
Home of the high-roller hamburger, this branch of the Manhattan red-meat institution has the casino's most stunning dining room, a super-modern steak house in the round with exotic woods and cool, West Coast colors. If only the meat tasted as good as the place looks.

Ombra
Borgata Hotel & Casino, 1 Borgata Way, Atlantic City, 08401, (866) 692-6742 (MY BORGATA) or 609-317-1000, www.thebor-gata.com
This subterranean grotto with vaulted ceilings evokes a Venetian hideaway ringed by a wine cellar behind walls of glass. The menu is an appealing take on Italian country cooking.

Opa Bar & Grille
1743 Boardwalk, Atlantic City, 08401, (609) 344-0094, www.opa1.com
One of the classier, non-casino-owned spots on a resurgent Boardwalk, this breezy, double-floored space near the Claridge Casino feels like an updated Greek taverna with a California touch, with giant mounds of salad and ouzo-flamed saganaki cheese, and blue martinis to wash down the bountiful pikilia platters of Mediterranean dips. Crab cakes and lamb chops also are superb. *Take-out.*

Plantation
7908 Long Beach Blvd., Harvey Cedars, 08008, (609) 494-8191, www.plantation-restaurant.com
The team behind Philly's Moshulu has transformed the old Owl Tree into one of the best upscale destinations on L.B.I. The custard-colored Victorian is fitted with a sexy South Seas look and plenty of great rum drinks, but it's the contemporary fusion cooking, from tortilla soup to pineapple-braised shortribs, that sets the sophisticated tone. *Take-out.*

Red Square
The Quarter at the Tropicana, 2801 Pacific Ave., Atlantic City, 08401, (609) 344-9100
Chill off in the vodka locker and drink a shot to capitalism at this fun, Vegas-style nightspot where Glasnost chic comes in the form of a beheadable Lenin statue, dry chicken Kiev, caviar-dabbed clams Kruschev, and enough high-end vodkas

(130 at last count; try the Polish Bison Grass) to cheer a czar.

Roma Pizza

656 Boardwalk (near Wonderland), Ocean City, 08226, (609) 399-6597
It looks like an ordinary Boardwalk pizza place (and the standard slices are pretty good), but in-the-know regulars call ahead to order the amazingly fresh, off-the-menu salad pie: a warm crust baked with olive oil and garlic that owner Dino Tredente mounds with spring mix and tomatoes dressed with extra-virgin olive oil.

Sails

998 Bay Ave., Somers Point, 08244, (609) 926-9611, www.njsails.com
Sip your cocktail with the chic martini masses by the bay at this sprawling, high-end marina nightspot in Somers Point. The former Waterfront space, stylishly retro-fitted by the group from (now closed) Mojo, also serves an impressive New American seafood menu. It's pricey but better than you'd expect from such a scene.

Sea Salt

8307 3rd Ave., Stone Harbor, 08247, (609) 368-3302, www.seasaltstoneharbor.com
Inventive New American cuisine meets South American inspiration at this charmingly personal BYOB from Argentine-born chef Lucas Manteca and wife Deanna. The old ice cream shop space has a simple elegance, but it's the creative cooking — from crab salad over savory gingerbread topped with rhubarb sorbet to Argentine chimichurra-laced barbecue — that is the draw.

Seablue

Borgata Hotel & Casino, 1 Borgata Way, Atlantic City, 08401, (866) 692-6742 (MY BORGATA) or (609) 317-1000, www.theborgata.com
West Coast fish wiz Michael Mina brings his caviar touch to Atlantic City with many of the contemporary seafood specialties he made famous at Aqua, ranging from Tunisian soft-shell crabs to Moroccan seafood tagines, wood-grilled fish, and the chef's signature lobster pot pie. Too new for a verdict.

The Sound of Philadelphia (TSOP)

The Quarter at the Tropicana, 2801 Pacific Ave., Atlantic City, 08401, (609) 887-2200, www.tsoplive.com
The crew behind Center City's Zanzibar Blue has collaborated with Philly soul legends Kenny Gamble and Leon Huff to funk it up in the Quarter with their posh music club and restaurant that presents live bands and a surprisingly tasty "soul fusion" menu ranging from honey-slicked skillet corn breads to cheesesteak spring rolls, seared tuna over black-eyed peas, shrimp scampi with grits, and decent gumbo.

Specchio

Borgata Hotel & Casino, 1 Borgata Way, Atlantic City, 08401, (866) 692-6742 (MY BORGATA) or 609-317-1000; www.theborgata.com
Chef Luke Palladino makes a dashing debut in this garish, upscale Italian dining room, where innovative flavors (beet ravioli) pair with sheer opulence (osso buco for two) to create an exciting restaurant for Atlantic City.

Steve and Cookie's by the Bay

9700 Amherst Ave., Margate, 08402, (609) 823-1163
This longtime, marina-side standout has the feel of a sleek yacht club with excellent service and wines, and one of the more sure-handed contemporary menus down the Shore. Past highlights have included scallops with gingered peach chutney, awesome bouillabaisse, chipotle-glazed pork, and peanut-butter mousse pie.

Suilan

Borgata Hotel & Casino, 1 Borgata Way, Atlantic City, 08401, (866) 692-6742 (MY BORGATA) or 609-317-1000; www.theborgata.com
Susanna Foo's second restaurant is a soaring ivory room with gliding glass doors, a wall of teapots, and a surprisingly noisy, open kitchen. The menu is similar to that at her French-Chinese jewel on Walnut Street, but more expensive, with bigger portions and slightly less vivid flavors.

Sweet Vidalia

122 N. Bay Ave., Beach Haven, 08008, (609) 207-1200
Chef/owner Michael O'Meara has one of the more ambitious eateries on Long Beach Island, with a New American menu that pays homage to good ingredients, especially the sweet onion that is its namesake. *Take-out.*

Sylvester's Fishmarket and Restaurant

21st and 5th Ave., Avalon, 08202, (609) 967-7553, www.sylvesters-avalon.com
This casual seafood market and restaurant has long been a favorite for a no-frills seashore fish fry, with great crab cakes and other basics for take-out or eating in the tented picnic pavillion. Word is that quality has stayed consistent since the ownership change.

Tucker's Steak and Seafood House

800 Bay Ave., Somer's Point, 08244, (609) 927-3100, www.tuckerssomerspointnj.com
Chef Joseph Tucker happily reemerged down the Shore a few years ago in this elegant Victorian manse by the bay with the kind of gutsy, upscale, South Philly Italian fare that made his name at Joseph's Seafood Italiano and Pompeii. Steaks are a worthy focus here, but also try the rich clams Pavarotti and blackened tuna Sambucca.

Voltaco's Italian Foods

957 West Ave., Ocean City, 08226, (609) 399-0753
The hoagies at Voltaco's, with their fresh meats and crisp-yet-light Jersey Shore rolls, might very well rank among the finest in the land. But it's the homespun Italian meals at this Ocean City take-out landmark that I find truly special. Eating the hearty lasagne is like traveling in a red-gravy time capsule back to 1954.

Washington Inn

801 Washington St., Cape May, 08204, (609) 884-5697, www.washingtoninn.com
The Craig family's gracious 1842 home is Cape May's grande dame of polished elegance, with an excellent French- and Italian-inspired menu from chef Mimi Wood and one of the Shore's most notable wine cellars.

White House Sub Shop

Mississippi and Arctic Aves., Atlantic City, 08401, (609) 345-8599
The light and crusty roll makes the steak and subs at this casino-city institution, but it's the sprinkling of sweet-hot pepper relish and the people-watching that give its sandwiches real panache. *Take-out.*

Wolfgang Puck American Grille

Borgata Hotel & Casino, 1 Borgata Way, Atlantic City, 08401, (866) 692-6742 (MY BORGATA) or (609) 317-1000, www.theborgata.com.
The first serious East Coast restaurant from the legendary innovator of California cuisine, Wolfgang Puck, offers a casual patio and a formal dining room for the chef's updated American cooking, ranging from wood-fired pizzas with smoked salmon, to grilled flat-iron steak with blue cheese to sole picatta. Too new for a verdict.

Yama

5305 Atlantic Ave., Ventnor, 08406, (609) 822-8007

Index by Category

Style

AFGHAN/PAKISTANI
Ariana (Afghan)
Kabobeesh (Pakistani)
Sansom Street Kabob House
    (Afghan)

AFRICAN
Abyssinia (Ethiopian)
Buka-Teria (Nigerian)
Dahlak (Ethiopian)
La Calebasse (West African)
Queen of Sheba Pub II
    (Ethiopian pub)

AMERICAN COMFORT
Curley's Fries
Honey's Sit 'n' Eat
Jones
Morning Glory Diner
Roller's

ASIAN FUSION
Bliss
Bubble House
BUDDAKAN
Coconut Bay
Cork
FuziOn
Ly Michael's
Mantra
NECTAR
Pod
RITZ SEAFOOD
Roy's
SUSANNA FOO
Teikoku
Twenty Manning

ASIAN, SOUTHEAST
Banana Leaf (Malaysian)
Indonesia
PENANG (Malaysian)

Rangoon (Burmese)
Vientiane Cafe (Laotian-Thai)

BBQ
Abner's Authentic Barbecue
Famous Dave's Barbeque
Fat Jack's BBQ
Red Hot & Blue
Rib Stand
The Smoked Joint
SWEET LUCY'S SMOKEHOUSE
Tommy Gunns
Zeke's Mainline Bar B Que

BEACH GRILL
Brown's Restaurant (donuts)
The Hula Grill (Hawaiian)

BELGIAN PUB
The Abbaye
The Black Door
Eulogy
MONK'S CAFE

CAJUN/CREOLE
CARMINE'S CREOLE CAFE
Crescent City
High Street Caffe
Melange Cafe

CARIBBEAN
Brown Sugar Bakery & Cafe
Denise's Soul Food
Jamaican Jerk Hut

CHEESESTEAKS
Abner's
Chick's Deli of Cherry Hill
Chink's Steaks
Cosmi's Market
Dalessandro's
Donkey's Place
Frusco's Steak Shop
Geno's Steaks
Grilladelphia
H&J McNally's Tavern

Jim's Steaks
JOHN'S ROAST PORK
Pagano's Market
Pat's King of Steaks
Pudge's
Rick's Philly Steaks
Sonny's Famous Steaks
Steve's Prince of Steaks
Tony Luke's
Tony Luke's Beef and Beer
    Sports Bar

CHINESE
Charles Plaza (vegetarian)
CHERRY STREET CHINESE
    KOSHER VEGETARIAN
    RESTAURANT (vegetarian)
Chung King (Szechuan)
Harmony Vegetarian
    Restaurant (vegetarian)
H.K. Golden Phoenix (dim
    sum)
Hunan
Imperial Inn
Joy Tsin Lau
LAKESIDE CHINESE DELI (dim
    sum)
Lee How Fook
MARGARET KUO'S
Margaret Kuo's Peking
    (Chinese/Japanese)
Mustard Green
Ocean City (dim sum)
Ray's Cafe & Tea House
Saigon Maxim Restaurant
Shiao Lan Kung
Singapore (vegetarian)
SZECHUAN TASTY HOUSE
    (Szechuan)
Yue Kee

CHINESE DUCK AND NOODLE HOUSE
Nan Zhou Hand-Drawn
    Noodle House
Ong's (noodles)
Pagoda Noodle Cafe
Sang Kee

SANG KEE ASIAN BISTRO
Sang Kee Peking Duck
Ting Wong

CHINESE/FRENCH

Chez Elena Wu
CinCin
Ly Michael's
Suilan
SUSANNA FOO
Yangming

CONCERT HALL

Chris' Jazz Cafe
World Cafe Live
Zanzibar Blue

CONTINENTAL

The Blue Bell Inn
DILWORTHTOWN INN
General Sutter Inn
Hotel DuPont
Meritage Philadelphia

CRAB HOUSE

Chickie's & Pete's
DiNardo's Famous Crabs
Howard House Tavern
Mud City Crabhouse

DELI, JEWISH

FAMOUS 4TH STREET
    DELICATESSEN
Kibbitz Down the Shore
Kibbitz Room
Koch's Deli
Murray's Deli
Pastrami and Things
Pikkles Plus

DESSERT/ICE CREAM

Apamate (churros)
Bassett's Ice Cream
Brulee
Cafe Sud
Miel
Roselena's Coffee Bar

DINER

Cafe Beach Club
Capogiro

Country Club Restaurant
Hank's Place
Mayfair Diner
Melrose Diner
Mustache Bill's Diner
Ponzio's
Silk City Diner (Lancaster)

EAST EUROPEAN

Balkan Express Restaurant
    (Balkan)
Blue Danube Restaurant
    (Hungarian)
Syrenka (Polish)
Warsaw Cafe

FISH HOUSE

Allen's Clam Bar
Busch's Seafood Restaurant
Dock's Oyster House
Lobster House
Mac's Restaurant and Lounge
Old Original Bookbinders
Pearl's Oyster Bar
SANSOM STREET OYSTER
    HOUSE
Snockey's Oyster and Crab
    House

FRENCH BISTRO/ FRENCH CAFE

Beau Monde (crepes)
Bistro Cassis (Pond)
Bistro St. Tropez
BRASSERIE PERRIER (lounge)
Cadence
Cafe Lutecia
Caribou Cafe
Claude's
Inn at Phillip's Mill
La Boheme
La Terrasse
Le Bar Lyonnais
Loie Brasserie
Ma France Creperie
Miel Patisserie
Overtures
PIF
ROUGE
Slate Bleu
Spring Mill Cafe
Taste
Vintage

FRENCH, CLASSIC UPSCALE

Deux Cheminees
Green Hills Inn
LE BEC-FIN

FRENCH, CONTEMPORARY

Alisa Cafe (Thai-French)
BIRCHRUNVILLE STORE CAFE
BRASSERIE PERRIER
Brasserie Perrier at Boyd's
Georges'
GILMORE'S
LE BEC-FIN
Nan (Thai-French)
Paloma (French-Mexican)
Pond (Bistro Cassis)
Posh (Thai-French)
Rat's
The Restaurant at Doneckers
Restaurant Taquet
SAVONA
Washington Inn

FUNKY BRUNCH

Azure
Carman's Country Kitchen
Honey's Sit 'n' Eat
Morning Glory Diner
SABRINA'S CAFE

GASTRO-PUB

Alfa
Bridgewater's Pub
Deuce Restaurant and Bar
Good Dog
Grace Tavern
Johnny Brenda's
The Latest Dish
McMenamin's Tavern
N. 3RD
New Wave Cafe
Race Street Cafe
REMBRANDT'S
Royal Tavern
Sidecar Bar and Grille
Society Hill Hotel
South Philadelphia Tap Room
STANDARD TAP

GERMAN

Ludwig's Garten
Old Guard House Inn
Otto's Brauhaus

GREEK

Athenian Garden
DMITRI'S
Effie's
Estia
Lourdes Greek Taverna
Olympic Gyro
Opa Bar & Grille
South Street Souvlaki
Zorba's Taverna

HOAGIES. *See* Italian
Sandwiches/Hoagies

HOT DOGS

Jimmy John's Pipin' Hot
Maui's Dog House
Wally's Wiener World

INDIAN

An Indian Affair
Cafe Spice
Coriander Indian Bistro
Desi Village Restaurant
DEVI (South)
Greater India Fine Dining
KARMA
Khajuraho
Nanee's Kitchen
Sitar India
Uduppi Dosa House (South)

IRISH PUB

The Bards
The Black Sheep
Fado Irish Pub
Plough and the Stars
Tir Na Nog

ITALIAN, CLASSIC UPSCALE

Giumarello's (upscale martini
bar)
La Collina
La Famiglia

La Veranda
Marco Polo
Monte Carlo Living Room
Ristorante La Buca
The Saloon
Tucker's Steak and Seafood
House

ITALIAN, CONTEMPORARY

August
Ava
Bacio
Caffe Aldo Lamberti
Davio's
Illuminare
KRISTIAN'S RISTORANTE
Le Castagne
Maya Bella
Mercato
Mia
Nonna's
Paradigm
PARADISO
Penne
POSITANO COAST BY ALDO
LAMBERTI
REMBRANDT'S
SOVANA BISTRO
(Italian/French Bistro)
Specchio
VETRI
Washington Inn

ITALIAN GELATI/ PANINI CAFE

Cafe Lift
Capogiro
Di Bruno Bros.
Paninoteca
Roselena's Coffee Bar (pas-
tries)
Teca (wine bar)
Tria (wine/beer bar)

ITALIAN RED GRAVY

Anastasi Seafood
Buca di Beppo (chain)
Casselli's
Criniti
Dante & Luigi's
Maggiano's Little Italy (chain)
Marra's

Pompeii
Ralph's
Tre Famiglia Ristorante
VILLA DI ROMA
Voltaco's Italian Foods (take-
out)

ITALIAN SANDWICHES/ HOAGIES

Boccella's (luncheonette)
Carmen's Famous Italian
Hoagies (H)
Chickie's Italian Deli (H)
Cosmi's Market (H)
DiNic's (pork)
Frusco's Steak Shop (pork)
JOHN'S ROAST PORK
Lombardi's Specialty Hoagies
(H)
Nick's Roast Beef
Pagano's Market (pork)
Porky's Point (pork)
Salumeria (H)
Shank's and Evelyn's Roast
Beef
Tony Luke's (pork)
Tony Luke's Beef and Beer
Sports Bar (pork)
Voltaco's Italian Foods
(take-out)
White House Sub Shop (H)

ITALIAN TRATTORIA

Basilicos
Bistro di Marino
Branzino
Brennan's by the Bay
Caffe Casta Diva
Cucina Forte
Domani Star
Ernesto's 1521 Cafe
Fish Tank on Main
Fitzwater Cafe
Gioia Mia
Hostaria Da Elio
Il Cantuccio
Il Tartufo
Joe Pesce (seafood)
Karina's (Italian/South
American)
KRISTIAN'S
La Fourno Trattoria

La Locanda del Ghiottone
La Viola
Laceno Italian Grill
L'ANGOLO
MELOGRANO
Mezza Luna
Nunzio's Ristorante Rustico
Ombra
Porcini
Prima Donna
RADICCHIO
Ristorante Panorama (wine
    bar)
Ristorante Pesto
Ristorante Valentino
Roberto Cafe
Sapori
Teresa's Cafe Italiano
Trattoria Lucca
Tre Scalini
Valentino on the Square

JAPANESE

Bluefin
Genji
Goji Tokyo Cuisine
Hikaru
Kami Sushi Express
Kisso Sushi Bar
MARGARET KUO'S
Margaret Kuo's Peking
    (Chinese/Japanese)
Megu Sushi
Mikado
Mikimotos
Miraku
MORIMOTO
Moshi Moshi
Oh Yoko!
Ooka Japanese Sushi and
    Hibachi Steak House
Osaka
Raw Sushi and Sake Lounge
Sagami
Sushikazu
Teikoku (Thai-Japanese)
Yama

JAPANESE/KOREAN

August Moon
Koja (truck)
Makiman
Tampopo

KOREAN

Anjou
Jong Ka Jib Soft Tofu
    Restaurant (tofu
    casseroles)
Kim's (BBQ)
Miran
Seo Ra Bol (BBQ)
Tampopo

LATINO

Alma de Cuba (nuevo)
Cafe Habana (Cuban)
Casona (Cuban)
Cuba Libre (nuevo)
El Bohio (Puerto Rican)
El Sol de Peru (Peruvian)
Isla Verde (nuevo)
Mixto
¡PASION! (nuevo)
Picanha Brazilian Grill
    (Brazilian)
Porky's Point (Puerto Rican)
Pura Vida
    (Mexican/Guatemalan)
Sabor Latino
Sea Salt (Argentine-Italian)
Shining Star (Puerto Rican)
TIERRA COLOMBIANA
Valanni (nuevo)

MEDITERRANEAN/ MEDITERRANEAN CONTEMPORARY

Audrey Claire
Aya's Cafe
Cafe Fresko
Citron
Figs
LaVa Cafe (coffee house)
MARIGOLD KITCHEN
Mezze (prepared foods)
TANGERINE
Valanni
Water Works Restaurant &
    Lounge

MEXICAN, CLASSIC

Las Cazuelas
LOS CATRINES RESTAURANT
    & TEQUILA'S BAR

MEXICAN, CONTEMPORARY

Cantina Los Caballitos
Coyote Crossing
El Sarape
EL VEZ
La Cava
LOLITA
Paloma
12th Street Cantina
Zocalo

MEXICAN TAQUERIA

El Fuego (Tex-Mex)
Jose's Tacos
La Esperanza
LA LUPE
Los Taquitos de Puebla
Lou's Restaurante (Tex-Mex)
Mexico Lindo
Restaurant Acapulco
Spice Mexican Food (cart)
Taco Riendo
Taqueria La Michoacana
Taqueria La Veracruzana

MIDDLE EASTERN/ PERSIAN

Aladdin (truck)
Aromatic House of Kebob
    (Persian)
Aya's Cafe (Egyptian)
Bitar's (falafel)
Christis's Unnamed Lunch Cart
Divan Turkish Kitchen
King of Falafel (lunch cart)
Konak (Turkish)
Maccabeam (kosher)
Mama's Vegetarian (falafel)
Marrakesh (Moroccan)
Maoz (falafel)
Mediterranean Grill (Persian)
Shouk (Israeli)
Shundeez (Persian)
Sila Turkish Restaurant

NEW AMERICAN

A Little Cafe
ALISON AT BLUE BELL
ANSILL
Astral Plane
Augusto's

Azure
Black Bass Hotel
The Black Duck on Sunset
Bleu
Bliss
Carambola
Catherine's
The Chef's Table at the David Finney Inn
Chloe
Coleman Restaurant
The Continental
Continental Mid-Town
Daddy O
Deep Blue
Derek's
DILWORTHTOWN INN
DJANGO
Domaine Hudson
Drafting Room
Eclipse Bistro
821
Elements Cafe
The Farmhouse
Farmicia
Fayette Street Grille
FORK (and FORK: ETC.)
FOUNTAIN RESTAURANT
Four Dogs Tavern
410 Bank Street
4th Street Cafe
Frenchtown Inn
FRIDAY SATURDAY SUNDAY
Funky Lil' Kitchen
Gables at Chadds Ford
GAYLE
Georges'
The Happy Rooster
The Harvest Moon Inn
Inn at St. Peter's Village
Island Grill
JAKE'S
Jonathan's on West End
Karen & Rei's
Krazy Kats
Lacroix at the Rittenhouse
Little Fish
LoBianco Coastal Cuisine
London Grill
Louisa's Cafe
Lucky Bones Backwater Grille
M/O Cafe
Mainland Inn
MAJOLICA
Mandoline

Marathon Grill
Marathon on the Square
MARIGOLD KITCHEN
MATYSON
Maya Bella
MORO
Mosaic Cafe
MOSHULU
Museum Restaurant
Next
The Orchard
Plantation
PUMPKIN
Red Sky
RESTAURANT ALBA
Rose Tattoo Cafe
Roux 3
Rx
Sails
Salt & Pepper Cafe
Sea Salt
Serrano
Simon Pearce on the Brandywine
SOUTHWARK
Steve and Cookie's by the Bay
Strawberry Hill
STRIPED BASS
Swann Lounge
Sweet Vidalia
333 Belrose
Trax Cafe
Twenty21
Umbria
Washington Square
White Dog Cafe
The Wild Onion
Winnie's Le Bus Manayunk
Word of Mouth
World Cafe Live
XIX NINETEEN

NEW AMERICAN HAUTE-HOTEL

FOUNTAIN RESTAURANT
Lacroix at the Rittenhouse
The Grill
SoleFood

PENNSYLVANIA DUTCH

Dutch Eating Place
Good 'n' Plenty

PIZZA

Couch Tomato Cafe
By George
Georges'
Illuminare
Joe's Pizza
La Fourno Trattoria
Lazaro's Pizza House
Lorenzo's Pizza
Mack's Pizza
Mama Palma's
Marra's
People's Pizza
Pietro's Coal Oven Pizzeria
REMBRANDT'S
Roma Pizza
Rustica
SOVANA BISTRO
Tacconelli's Pizzeria
Tacconelli's Pizzeria (New Jersey)
Teresa's Cafe Italiano

PREPARED FOODS

Bacchus
Brass Monkey
Carlino's
Di Bruno Bros.
FORK: ETC.
By George
Mezze
Taste Buds
12th Street Cantina

PUB

Bridgid's
Chaucer's Tabard Inn
Chris' Jazz Cafe
Copabanana; Copa Too
The Dark Horse (English)
Grey Lodge Pub
H&J McNally's Tavern
Iron Hill Restaurant & Brewery
Jolly's
Nodding Head Brewery & Restaurant
PJ Whelihan's Pub and Restaurant
Sly Fox Breweries
Tangier Restaurant
Ten Stone

RUSSIAN

Golden Gates
Paradise Restaurant
Red Square (nouveau)
Tashkent (Uzbekistan)

SEAFOOD

Classic Fish House
Allen's Clam Bar
Busch's Seafood Restaurant
Dock's Oyster House
Harvey Cedars Shellfish Co.
Lobster House
Mac's Restaurant and Lounge
Old Original Bookbinders
Pearl's Oyster Bar
SANSOM STREET OYSTER
   HOUSE
Seafood Unlimited
Snockey's Oyster and Crab
   House
Sylvester's Fishmarket and
   Restaurant

Contemporary Seafood

Alma de Cuba
Beach Creek Oyster Bar and
   Grille
Emerald Fish
Deep Blue
Little Fish
¡PASION!
POSITANO COAST BY ALDO
   LAMBERTI
RITZ SEAFOOD
Rock Lobster
SAVONA
STRIPED BASS
XIX NINETEEN

Crab House

Chickie's & Pete's
DiNardo's Famous Crabs
Mud City Crabhouse
Howard House Tavern
Lobster House

Greek Seafood

DMITRI'S
Estia

Italian Seafood

Anastasi Seafood
Branzino
Gioia Mia
Joe Pesce
La Collina
La Veranda
Laceno Grill
Marco Polo
RADICCHIO
Ristorante La Buca
Roberto Cafe

Japanese. *See* Food Features, Sushi

Seafood Chain

Bonefish Grill
Devon Seafood Grill
McCormick & Schmick's

SOUL FOOD

Corinne's Place
DeBreaux's
Delilah's Southern Cafe
Ms. Tootsie's Soul Food Cafe
The Sound of Philadelphia
   (TSOP)
Zanzibar Blue

SOUTHERN

CARMINE'S CREOLE CAFE
   (Cajun/Creole)
Crescent City (Cajun/Creole)
Down Home Diner
High Street Caffe
   (Cajun/Creole)
Jack's Firehouse
MARSHA BROWN
Melange Cafe (Cajun/Creole)
Nags Head Fine Foods

SPANISH (AND PORTUGUESE)

AMADA
Apamate
Bar Ferdinand
Taste of Portugal (Portuguese)

SPORTS BAR

Chickie's & Pete's

PJ Whelihan's Pub and
   Restaurant
Tony Luke's Beef and Beer
   Sports Bar
The Wild Onion

STEAK HOUSE

BARCLAY PRIME
Bridget's Steakhouse
THE CAPITAL GRILLE
The Chophouse
Davio's
Dock's Oyster House
Gallagher's Steakhouse
Knife & Fork Inn
Mac's Restaurant and Lounge
MARSHA BROWN
Old Homestead Steak House
The Palm
The Prime Rib
The Saloon
Tucker's Steak and Seafood
   House
Smith & Wollensky
Ted's Montana Grill
The Wooden Iron

TEX-MEX

El Fuego
Lou's Restaurante

THAI

Cafe de Laos
Chabaa Thai Bistro
Little Thai Singha Market
SIAM LOTUS
Teikoku (Thai-Japanese)

THAI/FRENCH

Alisa Cafe
NAN
Posh
Siri's Thai French Cuisine
Trio

TRUCK

Aladdin
Christis's Unnamed Lunch
   Cart
Denise's Soul Food
King of Falafel
Spice Mexican Food

The Creperie
Wally's Wiener World
Yue Kee

TURKISH
Divan Turkish Kitchen
Konak
Sila Turkish Restaurant

VEGETARIAN/VEGAN
Blue Sage
Charles Plaza (Chinese)
CHERRY STREET CHINESE
    KOSHER VEGETARIAN
    RESTAURANT (Chinese)
Citrus
Harmony Vegetarian
    Restaurant (Chinese)
HORIZONS (Vegan)
Mama's Vegetarian (Kosher)
Maoz (Kosher)
Singapore (Chinese)

VIETNAMESE
Ba Le Bakery
NAM PHUONG
O Sandwiches (hoagies)
Ong's (noodle house)
Pho 75
Pho Cali
Pho Ha
Saigon Maxim Restaurant
VIETNAM
Vietnam Palace

WILD GAME
Bridgewater's Pub
Sergeantsville Inn

Neighbor-hood

PHILADELPHIA

Chestnut Hill
CinCin
Citrus
H&J McNally's Tavern

Osaka
Roller's
Shundeez

Greater Center City
Avenue of the Arts District
Bliss
Buco di Beppo
Cadence
THE CAPITAL GRILLE
Capogiro
Chris' Jazz Cafe
Copa Too
EL VEZ
Ernesto's 1521 Cafe
Estia
Fado Irish Pub
Good Dog
The Grill
Jamaican Jerk Hut
Kami Sushi Express
La Viola
LOLITA
Ludwig's Garten
Marathon Grill
McCormick & Schmick's
Mercato
Miraku
Ms. Tootsie's Soul Food Cafe
Nodding Head Brewery &
    Restaurant
The Palm
Prima Donna
Raw Sushi and Sake Lounge
Ristorante Valentino
Sansom Street Kabob House
SANSOM STREET OYSTER
    HOUSE
The Smoked Joint
Ted's Montana Grill
12th Street Cantina
VETRI
Vintage
Warsaw Cafe
XIX NINETEEN
Zanzibar Blue

Chinatown
Banana Leaf
Charles Plaza
CHERRY STREET CHINESE
    KOSHER VEGETARIAN
    RESTAURANT

Chung King
Harmony Vegetarian
    Restaurant
H.K. Golden Phoenix
Imperial Inn
Indonesia
Joy Tsin Lau
LAKESIDE CHINESE DELI
Lee How Fook
Ly Michael's
Nan Zhou Hand-Drawn
    Noodle House
Ocean City
Ong's
PENANG
Pho Cali
Rangoon
Ray's Cafe & Tea House
Sang Kee
Shiao Lan Kung
Singapore
SZECHUAN TASTY HOUSE
Ting Wong
VIETNAM
Vietnam Palace
Zen Tea House

Fairmount/Art Museum
Bridgid's
Figs
Goji Tokyo Cuisine
Illuminare
Jack's Firehouse
London Grill
Museum Restaurant
REMBRANDT'S
Rose Tattoo Cafe
Trio
Water Works Restaurant &
    Lounge
Zorba's Taverna

Fishtown/Kensington
Johnny Brenda's
Taco Riendo
Taste

Fitler Square
Ants Pants Cafe
Bacchus
Balkan Express Restaurant
Cafe Lutecia
DIMITRI'S
Grace Tavern

Mama Palma's
MELOGRANO
Taste Buds

Graduate Hospital (and South Street West)

Ants Pants Cafe
Apamate
Astral Plane
Balkan Express Restaurant
Chaucer's Tabard Inn
Divan Turkish Kitchen
Grace Tavern
Jamaican Jerk Hut
LaVa Cafe
Lazaro's Pizza House
Meritage Philadelphia
PUMPKIN
Roberto Cafe
Sidecar Bar and Grille
Tangier Restaurant
Ten Stone

Loft District

Cafe Lift
Jose's Tacos
Siam Lotus
Spice Mexican Food (Broad Street)

Logan Square

Aya's Cafe
FOUNTAIN RESTAURANT
Swann Lounge
Tir Na Nog

Market Street

Bistro St. Tropez (west)
Christis's Unnamed Lunch Cart (west)
Maggiano's Little Italy (east)
Mama's Vegetarian (west)
Pagano's Market (east)
Pikkles Plus (west)
Reading Terminal Market (east)
SoleFood (east)
Twenty21 (west)

Northern Liberties

The Abbaye
Azure
Bar Ferdinand
Deuce Restaurant and Bar

Honey's Sit 'n' Eat
Il Cantuccio
Las Cazuelas
N. 3RD
Pura Vida
Rustica
SIAM LOTUS
SOUTHWARK
STANDARD TAP
Taste

Old City

AMADA
Anjou
Ariana
Aromatic House of Kebob
BUDDAKAN
Cafe Spice
Chloe
City Tavern
The Continental
Cuba Libre
DiNardo's Famous Crabs
Eulogy
Farmicia
FORK (and FORK: ETC.)
KARMA
Kisso Sushi Bar
Konak
La Famiglia
La Locanda del Ghiottone
Mandoline
Old Original Bookbinders
Pagoda Noodle Cafe
Paradigm
Plough and the Stars
POSITANO COAST BY ALDO LAMBERTI
Race Street Cafe
RADICCHIO
Red Sky
Ristorante Panorama
Serrano
Society Hill Hotel
Sonny's Famous Steaks
TANGERINE

Penn's Landing

La Veranda
MOSHULU
Rock Lobster

Reading Terminal Market

Bassetts Ice Cream
Carmen's Famous Italian

Hoagies
DiNic's
Down Home Diner
Dutch Eating Place
Four Seasons Juice Bar
By George
Little Thai Singha Market
Mezze
Nanee's Kitchen
Olympic Gyro
Pearl's Oyster Bar
Rib Stand
Rick's Philly Steaks
Salumeria
Sang Kee Peking Duck
12th Street Cantina

Rittenhouse Square and Restaurant Row (Walnut Street)

Alfa
Alma de Cuba
Audrey Claire
BARCLAY PRIME
The Bards
The Black Sheep
Bleu
Branzino
BRASSERIE PERRIER
Brasserie Perrier at Boyd's
Cafe Habana
Caffe Casta Diva
Capogiro
Cassatt Lounge and Tea Room
Continental Mid-Town
Davio's
Devon Seafood Grill
FRIDAY SATURDAY SUNDAY
Genji
Gioia Mia
Great Tea International
Joe's Pizza
Jolly's
The Happy Rooster
Lacroix at the Rittenhouse
Le Bar Lyonnais
LE BEC-FIN
Le Castagne
Loie Brasserie
LOS CATRINES RESTAURANT & TEQUILA'S BAR
Mahogany on Walnut
Mantra
Marathon Grill

Marathon on the Square
MATYSON
Miel Patisserie
Miran
MONK'S CAFE
Moshi Moshi
Paninoteca
¡PASION!
Pastrami and Things
Pietro's Coal Oven Pizzeria
Porcini
The Prime Rib
ROUGE
Roy's
Seafood Unlimited
Smith & Wollensky
STRIPED BASS
SUSANNA FOO
Tampopo
Tria
Twenty Manning
Valentino on the Square

Society Hill (and South Street East)

Ava
The Dark Horse
Copabanana
Crescent City
DJANGO
Jim's Steaks
La Fourno Trattoria
The Latest Dish
Maoz
Marrakesh
Monte Carlo Living Room
Ms. Tootsie's Soul Food Cafe
Next
Overtures
Pietro's Coal Oven Pizzeria
South Street Souvlaki
Tommy Gunns

Washington Square East/West

Caribou Cafe
Deux Cheminees
Effie's
El Fuego
Jones
La Boheme
Maccabeam
Mixto
MORIMOTO

Pompeii
Ristorante La Buca
Tampopo
Washington Square

Manayunk

An Indian Affair
Chabaa Thai Bistro
Couch Tomato Cafe
Derek's
Fish Tank on Main
Il Tartufo
JAKE'S
Tommy Gunns
Winnie's Le Bus Manayunk

Mt. Airy

Bitar's
McMenamin's Tavern
Umbria

North Philadelphia

The Creperie
El Bohio
Isla Verde
Jong Ka Jib Soft Tofu
    Restaurant
Kim's
Porky's Point
Seo Ra Bol
Shining Star
Taco Riendo
TIERRA COLOMBIANA

Northeast Philadelphia

Chickie's & Pete's
Chink's Steaks
Country Club Restaurant
Frusco's Steak Shop
Golden Gates
Grey Lodge Pub
Makiman
Mayfair Diner
Paloma
Paradise Restaurant
Picanha Brazilian Grill
Steve's Prince of Steaks
SWEET LUCY'S SMOKEHOUSE
Tashkent
Taste of Portugal
Zorba's Taverna

Port Richmond

Grilladelphia
Syrenka
Tacconelli's Pizzeria

Roxborough

Casselli's
Dalessandro's

South Philadelphia

Bella Vista

Beau Monde
Cafe Sud
Cucina Forte
Fitzwater Cafe
HORIZONS
Mezza Luna
Morning Glory Diner
SABRINA'S CAFE
The Saloon
Salt & Pepper Cafe
Shouk

Deep South Philadelphia: South of Washington Avenue, including East Passyunk

August
Cantina Los Caballitos (EP)
Carman's Country Kitchen
Chickie's & Pete's
Chickie's Italian Deli
Cosmi's Market
Criniti
Famous Dave's Barbeque
JOHN'S ROAST PORK
Karina's (EP)
KRISTIAN'S RISTORANTE
L'ANGOLO
Lombardi's Specialty Hoagies
Marra's (EP)
Melrose Diner
Nick's Roast Beef
PARADISO (EP)
Ristorante Pesto
Roselena's Coffee Bar (EP)
Royal Tavern
South Philadelphia Tap Room
Tony Luke's
Tony Luke's Beef and Beer
    Sports Bar
Trattoria Lucca (EP)
Tre Scalini (EP)

Italian Market

Anastasi Seafood
Bitar's
Cucina Forte
Dante & Luigi's
Geno's Steaks
LA LUPE
Lorenzo's Pizza
Los Taquitos de Puebla
Mezza Luna
O Sandwiches
Pat's King of Steaks
PIF
Ralph's
Restaurant Acapulco
SABRINA'S CAFE
Shank's and Evelyn's Roast
    Beef
Taqueria La Veracruzana
VILLA DI ROMA

Queen Village

ANSILL
The Black Door
DIMITRI'S
FAMOUS 4TH STREET
    DELICATESSEN
GAYLE
Hikaru
Hostaria Da Elio
Little Fish
Mustard Green
New Wave Cafe
Overtures
SOUTHWARK

Washington Avenue

Ba Le Bakery
Cafe de Laos
NAM PHUONG
Pho 75
Pho Ha
Snockey's Oyster and Crab
    House
Taqueria La Veracruzana

West Philadelphia
University City

Abner's
Aladdin
Bridgewater's Pub

Bubble House
Denise's Soul Food
Koja
La Terrasse
Lou's Restaurante
Marathon Grill
NAN
Penne
Pod
Sitar India
White Dog Cafe
World Cafe Live
Yue Kee
Zocalo

West of 40th Street

Abyssinia
Brown Sugar Bakery & Cafe
Buka-Teria
Dahlak
DeBreaux's
Delilah's Southern Cafe
Jim's Steaks
Kabobeesh
Koch's Deli
La Calebasse
MARIGOLD KITCHEN
Queen of Sheba Pub II
Rx
Vientiane Cafe
Zeke's Mainline Bar B Que

BEYOND PHILADELPHIA
Northern Suburbs

Abner's Authentic Barbecue
August Moon
Augusto's
Blue Sage
Bluefin
Boccella's
Brasserie 73
Bridget's Steakhouse
Carambola
Fayette Street Grille
Funky Lil' Kitchen
FuziOn
Greater India Fine Dining
La Cava
Mainland Inn
Marco Polo
Maya Bella

Mosaic Cafe
Otto's Brauhaus
Sly Fox Breweries
Spring Mill Cafe
Taqueria La Michoacana
Trax Cafe
Uduppi Dosa House

Blue Bell

ALISON AT BLUE BELL
The Blue Bell Inn
Bonefish Grill
Coleman Restaurant
El Sarape
Pudge's
Sushikazu

Doylestown

Domani Star
The Farmhouse (Lehigh
    Valley)
Ooka Japanese Sushi and
    Hibachi Steak House
Slate Bleu

Western Suburbs
Delaware County

The Countryside Market &
    Delicatessen
El Sol de Peru
Margaret Kuo's Peking
Sabor Latino

Main Line

Cafe Fresko
CARMINE'S CREOLE CAFE
Citron
Desi Village Restaurant (King
    of Prussia)
Georges'
Hunan
Khajuraho
La Collina
Lourdes Greek Taverna
MARGARET KUO'S
Mediterranean Grill
Murray's Deli
NECTAR
Old Guard House Inn
Pond/Bistro Cassis
Restaurant Taquet
SANG KEE ASIAN BISTRO
SAVONA

Teresa's Cafe Italiano
333 Belrose
The Wooden Iron
Yangming

West Chester (and Chester County)

BIRCHRUNVILLE STORE CAFE
Catherine's
Coyote Crossing
DEVI
DILWORTHTOWN INN
Drafting Room
Four Dogs Tavern
Gables at Chadds Ford
GILMORE'S
Hank's Place
High Street Caffe
Inn at St. Peter's Village
Iron Hill Restaurant & Brewery
Jimmy John's Pipin' Hot
MAJOLICA
The Orchard
RESTAURANT ALBA
Roux 3
Simon Pearce on the Brandywine
Sly Fox Breweries
SOVANA BISTRO
Teca
Teikoku
Wally's Wiener World

South Jersey

Camden and Camden County

Corinne's Place
Donkey's Place
Fat Jack's BBQ
La Esperanza
Mexico Lindo

Cherry Hill/ Marlton/Moorestown

Alisa Cafe
Caffe Aldo Lamberti
Chick's Deli of Cherry Hill
Emerald Fish
Famous Dave's Barbeque
Kibbitz Room
Megu Sushi
Melange Cafe
Miel Patisserie

Mikado
Nonna's
Oh Yoko!
People's Pizza
Pietro's Coal Oven Pizzeria
Ponzio's
Posh
Red Hot & Blue
Siri's Thai French Cuisine
Tacconelli's Pizzeria

Collingswood/Haddon-field/Haddon Heights

Bistro di Marino
Casona
Cork
Elements Cafe
Giumarello's
Nunzio's Ristorante Rustico
PJ Whelihan's Pub and Restaurant
Sagami
Sapori
Tre Famiglia Ristorante
Word of Mouth

Route 130

Bacio
Chickie's and Pete's
Sagami
Sila Turkish Restaurant

Voorhees

Chez Elena Wu
The Chophouse (Gibbsboro)
Coconut Bay
Coriander Indian Bistro
Laceno Italian Grill
A Little Cafe
M/O Cafe
RITZ SEAFOOD

Jersey Shore

Allen's Clam Bar (north of Atlantic City)
Athenian Garden (north of Atlantic City)
Basilico's (Sea Isle City)
The Black Duck on Sunset (Cape May)
Bobby Flay Steak (Atlantic City)
Brass Monkey (Brigantine)
Brennan's by the Bay (Sea Isle City)

Brown's Restaurant (Ocean City)
Brulee (Atlantic City)
Busch's Seafood Restaurant (Sea Isle City)
Cafe Beach Club (Ocean City)
Claude's (North Wildwood)
Curley's Fries (Wildwood Boardwalk)
Daddy O (Long Beach Island)
Dock's Oyster House (Atlantic City)
410 Bank Street (Cape May)
4th Street Cafe (Ocean City)
Gallagher's Steakhouse (Atlantic City)
Harvey Cedars Shellfish Co. (Long Beach Island)
The Hula Grill (Ocean City)
Island Grill (Cape May)
Joe Pesce (Ventnor)
Jonathan's on West End (Atlantic City)
Karen & Rei's (Mainland)
Kibbitz Down the Shore (Ocean City)
Knife & Fork Inn (Atlantic City)
LoBianco Coastal Cuisine (Margate)
Lobster House (Cape May)
Louisa's Cafe (Cape May)
Lucky Bones Backwater Grille (Cape May)
Ma France Creperie (Ventnor)
Mack's Pizza (Wildwood Boardwalk)
Mac's Restaurant and Lounge (Somers Point)
Maui's Dog House (North Wildwood)
McGlade's on the Pier (Cape May)
Mia (Atlantic City)
Mud City Crabhouse (Manahawkin/LBI)
Mustache Bill's Diner (LBI)
Nags Head Fine Foods (Ocean City)
Old Homestead Steak House (Atlantic City)
Ombra (Atlantic City)
Opa Bar & Grille (Atlantic City)
The Palm (Atlantic City)

Plantation (LBI)
Red Square (Atlantic City)
Roma Pizza (Ocean City)
Sails (Somers Point)
Sea Salt (Stone Harbor)
Seablue (Atlantic City)
The Sound of Philadelphia
    (TSOP) (Atlantic City)
Specchio (Atlantic City)
Steve and Cookie's by the Bay
    (Margate)
Suilan (Atlantic City)
Sweet Vidalia (LBI)
Sylvester's Fishmarket and
    Restaurant (Avalon)
Tucker's Steak and Seafood
    House (Somers Point)
Voltaco's Italian Foods (Ocean
    City)
Washington Inn (Cape May)
White House Sub Shop
    (Atlantic City)
Wolfgang Puck American
    Grille (Atlantic City)
Yama (Ventnor

New Hope/
Lambertville

Black Bass Hotel
Blue Danube Restaurant
    (Trenton)
Frenchtown Inn
The Harvest Moon Inn
    (Ringoes)
Inn at Phillip's Mill
MARSHA BROWN
Rat's (Hamilton)
Sergeantsville Inn

Delaware

The Chef's Table at the David
    Finney Inn
Deep Blue
Domaine Hudson
Eclipse Bistro
821
Hotel DuPont
The Howard House Tavern
    (Elkton, Md.)
Krazy Kats
Mikimotos
MORO

Lancaster/Berks
Counties

General Sutter Inn
Good 'n' Plenty
Green Hills Inn
The Restaurant at Doneckers
Silk City Diner
Strawberry Hill

Ambience/
Special
Features

BUSINESS DINING

BARCLAY PRIME
BIRCHRUNVILLE STORE CAFE
BRASSERIE PERRIER
BUDDAKAN
Caffe Aldo Lamberti
THE CAPITAL GRILLE
Coleman Restaurant
Davio's
Deep Blue
Deux Cheminees
DILWORTHTOWN INN
EL VEZ
Estia
FORK (FORK:ETC.)
FOUNTAIN RESTAURANT
GILMORE'S
The Grill
Hotel DuPont
JAKE'S
Krazy Kats
KRISTIAN'S RISTORANTE
La Famiglia
La Terrasse
LE BEC-FIN
Le Castagne
LOS CATRINES RESTAURANT
    & TEQUILA'S BAR
MARSHA BROWN
MORIMOTO
MORO
MOSHULU
NECTAR
The Palm
¡PASION!

PIF
Pod
Pompeii
Pond/Bistro Cassis
The Prime Rib
Rat's
The Restaurant at Doneckers
Restaurant Taquet
Ristorante Panorama
ROUGE
Roux 3
Roy's
Sagami
The Saloon
SAVONA
Simon Pearce on the
    Brandywine
Slate Bleu
Smith & Wollensky
SoleFood
STRIPED BASS
SUSANNA FOO
TANGERINE
Teikoku
Twenty21
VETRI
Washington Square
XIX NINETEEN
Yangming

CLASSICS

Philadelphia Classics

Astral Plane
Bassetts Ice Cream
The Blue Bell Inn
Chink's Steaks
Dalessandro's
Dante & Luigi's
Deux Cheminees
DILWORTHTOWN INN
DiNic's
DMITRI'S
FAMOUS 4TH STREET
    DELICATESSEN
FOUNTAIN RESTAURANT
FRIDAY SATURDAY SUNDAY
Geno's Steaks
H&J McNally's Tavern
Hotel DuPont (Wilmington)
Imperial Inn
JAKE'S
Jimmy John's Pipin' Hot
Jim's Steaks

JOHN'S ROAST PORK
Koch's Deli
La Famiglia
LE BEC-FIN
Lee How Fook
London Grill
LOS CATRINES RESTAURANT & TEQUILA'S BAR
Margaret Kuo's Peking
Marra's
Mayfair Diner
Melrose Diner
Monte Carlo Living Room
MOSHULU
Murray's Deli
Nick's Roast Beef
Old Guard House Inn
Old Original Bookbinders
Pat's King of Steaks
Ponzio's
Ralph's
Ristorante La Buca
Rock Lobster
Roller's
Rose Tattoo Cafe
Sagami
The Saloon
Sang Kee
SANSOM STREET OYSTER HOUSE
Shank's and Evelyn's Roast Beef
Shiao Lan Kung
Snockey's Oyster and Crab House
South Street Souvlaki
SUSANNA FOO
Tacconelli's Pizzeria
Tony Luke's
VIETNAM
VILLA DI ROMA
White Dog Cafe
XIX NINETEEN

Jersey Shore Classics

Allen's Clam Bar
Brown's Restaurant
Busch's Seafood Restaurant
Curley's Fries
Dock's Oyster House
410 Bank Street
Knife & Fork Inn
Lobster House
Louisa's Cafe
Mack's Pizza

Mustache Bill's Diner
Steve and Cookie's by the Bay
Voltaco's Italian Foods
Washington Inn
White House Sub Shop

DANCING

Golden Gates
Isla Verde
MOSHULU
Paradise Restaurant
TIERRA COLOMBIANA

DATE RESTAURANT/ FRIENDS NIGHT OUT/ ROMANTIC

ALISON AT BLUE BELL (F)
Alma de Cuba (F)
AMADA
ANSILL (D, F)
Ariana (D, F)
Audrey Claire (D, F)
August (D, F)
Ava (D, R)
Banana Leaf (D, F)
BARCLAY PRIME (D, R)
Beau Monde
BIRCHRUNVILLE STORE CAFE (D, R)
Bistro St. Tropez (D)
Blue Sage (F)
Branzino (D, R)
BRASSERIE PERRIER (D, R)
Buca di Beppo (F)
BUDDAKAN (D, R)
Cafe Sud (D)
Caffe Aldo Lamberti (D)
Caffe Casta Diva (D)
Capogiro (D)
Carambola (F)
CARMINE'S CREOLE CAFE (D, F)
Catherine's (D, R)
The Chef's Table at the David Finney Inn (F)
Chez Elena Wu (D, R)
Chloe (D, R)
Chung King (F)
CinCin (D)
Citron (D, R)
City Tavern (F)
The Continental (D, R)

Continental Mid-Town (D, R)
Coriander Indian Bistro (D)
Coyote Crossing
Cuba Libre (D, F)
Cucina Forte (D, R)
Davio's (F)
Deuce Restaurant and Bar (F)
Deux Cheminees (R)
DILWORTHTOWN INN (D, R)
DJANGO (D, R)
DMITRI'S (F)
Effie's (D)
EL VEZ (D, R)
Estia (D, R)
Eulogy (F)
FORK (FORK:ETC.) (D, R)
FOUNTAIN RESTAURANT (R)
Four Dogs Tavern (F)
FRIDAY SATURDAY SUNDAY (D, R)
Funky Lil' Kitchen (F)
Gables at Chadds Ford (F)
GAYLE (F, R)
Georges'
GILMORE'S (R)
Gioia Mia (F)
Golden Gates (F)
Grey Lodge Pub (F)
The Harvest Moon Inn
Hikaru (F)
HORIZONS (D, R)
Hotel DuPont (R)
Illuminare (F)
Inn at Phillip's Mill
Iron Hill Restaurant & Brewery (F)
Isla Verde (D, F)
JAKE'S (D, R)
Jamaican Jerk Hut (D, F)
Jones (D, F)
Karina's (D, F)
KARMA (F)
Khajuraho (D)
Konak (F)
Krazy Kats (D, R)
KRISTIAN'S RISTORANTE (R)
La Boheme (D, R)
La Collina (D, R)
La Famiglia (D, R)
LA LUPE (F)
La Terrasse (D)
L'ANGOLO (D, R)
Las Cazuelas (D, F)
LE BEC-FIN (F, R)
LOLITA (D, R)

London Grill (D)
LOS CATRINES RESTAURANT
& TEQUILA'S BAR
Mainland Inn (D)
MAJOLICA
Mandoline (F)
MARGARET KUO'S (F, R)
Margaret Kuo's Peking (F)
MARIGOLD KITCHEN (D)
Marrakesh (D)
Marra's (F)
MARSHA BROWN
MATYSON
Maya Bella
Melange Cafe (F)
MELOGRANO (D, R)
Mezza Luna (D, F)
MONK'S CAFE (F)
Monte Carlo Living Room (D, R)
MORIMOTO (D)
MORO (F, R)
Moshi Moshi (D)
MOSHULU
Ms. Tootsie's Soul Food Cafe (F)
Mustard Green (D, F)
N. 3RD (D, F)
NAM PHUONG (F)
NECTAR
Next (D, F)
Nonna's
Nunzio's Ristorante Rustico
Oh Yoko! (D, F)
Old Guard House Inn (D)
Old Original Bookbinders (F)
Ooka Japanese Sushi and
Hibachi Steak House (F)
The Orchard (D, R)
Overtures (D, R)
Paloma
Paradise Restaurant (F)
PARADISO
¡PASION!
PENANG (D, F)
Picanha Brazilian Grill (F)
PIF
Pod (D, R)
Pond/Bistro Cassis (D, R)
Porcini (D)
POSITANO COAST BY ALDO
LAMBERTI (D, F)
Prima Donna (D)
The Prime Rib
PUMPKIN

RADICCHIO (D, F)
Rat's
Ray's Cafe & Tea House (D)
REMBRANDT'S (F)
RESTAURANT ALBA
The Restaurant at Doneckers (D)
Restaurant Taquet (D, R)
Ristorante Panorama
Ristorante Pesto (D, F)
Ristorante Valentino (D)
RITZ SEAFOOD (D, F)
Rose Tattoo Cafe (D)
Roselena's Coffee Bar (D, R)
ROUGE (D, F)
Roux 3 (D, F)
Roy's
Rx (D, F)
SABRINA'S CAFE (D, F)
The Saloon
SANG KEE ASIAN BISTRO (D, F)
Sang Kee (D, F)
SAVONA
Seo Ra Bol (F)
Sergeantsville Inn (D, R)
Serrano (D, R)
Shouk (D, F)
SIAM LOTUS (D, R)
Simon Pearce on the Brandywine (D, F)
The Smoked Joint (F)
Society Hill Hotel (F)
SOUTHWARK
SOVALO
SOVANA BISTRO (D, F)
Spring Mill Cafe
STANDARD TAP (F)
STRIPED BASS
SUSANNA FOO
SWEET LUCY'S SMOKEHOUSE (F)
TANGERINE
Tangier Restaurant (F)
Taste of Portugal (F)
Teca (F)
Teikoku (D, F)
Teresa's Cafe Italiano (F)
333 Belrose (D, F)
TIERRA COLOMBIANA (F)
Tony Luke's (F)
Trattoria Lucca (D, F)
Tre Scalini (D, R)
Tria
Twenty Manning (F)

Umbria
Valanni (D, R)
VETRI
VIETNAM
Vietnam Palace (D)
VILLA DI ROMA (F)
Vintage (F)
Warsaw Cafe (D, R)
Washington Square (D, F)
White Dog Cafe (F)
Word of Mouth (D, F)
XIX NINETEEN (D, R)
Yangming (D, F)

HIDDEN GEMS AND WORTHY STOPS FAR AFIELD

ALISON AT BLUE BELL
August (H)
August Moon (H)
Augusto's (H)
Aya's Cafe (H)
BIRCHRUNVILLE STORE CAFE
Bluefin (H)
Brasserie Perrier at Boyds (H)
Cafe Lift (H)
Carambola (H)
CARMINE'S CREOLE CAFE (H)
The Chef's Table at the David Finney Inn
CHERRY STREET CHINESE KOSHER VEGETARIAN RESTAURANT (H)
Chickie's Italian Deli (H)
Chick's Deli of Cherry Hill (H)
Chink's Steaks (H)
Chris' Jazz Cafe (H)
Corinne's Place (H)
Cosmi's Market (H)
DeBreaux's (H)
Desi Village Restaurant (H)
DEVI
DILWORTHTOWN INN
Domani Star (F)
Eclipse Bistro (F)
821 (F)
Elements Cafe (H)
The Farmhouse (F)
Frenchtown Inn (F)
Frusco's Steak Shop (H)
Funky Lil' Kitchen
General Sutter Inn (F)
GILMORE'S (F)
Good 'n' Plenty (F)

Greater India Fine Dining (H)
Grey Lodge Pub (H)
Grilladelphia (H)
The Happy Rooster (H)
The Harvest Moon Inn
Hotel DuPont (F)
Isla Verde (H)
JOHN'S ROAST PORK
Jong Ka Jib Soft Tofu
    Restaurant (H)
Jose's Tacos (H)
Kami Sushi Express (H)
KARMA (Jersey location)
Kim's (H)
Krazy Kats (F)
La Esperanza (H)
LAKESIDE CHINESE DELI (H)
L'ANGOLO (H)
Le Bar Lyonnais (H)
MAJOLICA
Makiman (H)
Mandoline (H)

MARIGOLD KITCHEN (H)
Maya Bella (H)
Megu Sushi (H)
Melange Cafe (H)
Mexico Lindo (H)
Miraku (H)
MORO (F)
Moshi Moshi (H)
New Wave Cafe (H)
Oh Yoko! (H)
Ooka Japanese Sushi and
    Hibachi Steak House (H)
The Orchard
Pagano's Market (H)
Pagoda Noodle Cafe (H)
Paloma (H)
Picanha Brazilian Grill (H)
PIF (H)
Porky's Point (H)
Pura Vida (H)
RADICCHIO (H)
Rat's

RESTAURANT ALBA (F)
The Restaurant at Doneckers
    (F)
Ristorante La Buca (H)
Sansom Street Kabob House
    (H)
SAVONA (F)
Sergeantsville Inn (F)
SIAM LOTUS (H)
Sila Turkish Restaurant
Silk City Diner (F)
Slate Bleu (F)
South Philadelphia Tap Room
    (H)
SOVANA BISTRO
Spring Mill Cafe (H)
Strawberry Hill
Sushikazu (H)
SWEET LUCY'S SMOKEHOUSE
Taco Riendo (H)
Taste (H)
TIERRA COLOMBIANA (H)

Kid Friendly

Among the hundreds of restaurants we surveyed for this edition, all but a handful said they considered themselves to be "kid friendly." But what does this mean? Many (if not most) had high chairs and basic children's menus, but that wasn't the ultimate factor. In my experience, it is the restaurant's attitude, more than a handy box of crayons or a ready supply of chicken fingers, that makes a place truly accommodating to kids — a willingness to cook simple versions of menu items (or just plain pasta with butter) and a genuine openness to allowing them in the dining room.

We always call ahead to gauge a restaurant's feeling about younger diners. Some surprisingly upscale places have welcomed us with our two kids — the **Moshulu**, the **Fountain**, **Lacroix at the Rittenhouse**, **Nectar**, and **Georges'**, to name just a few. For a slightly less formal setting, but still a sure bet for genuinely cooked good food, ethnic restaurants are always a golden option, whether it's Chinatown (any restaurant), a South Philly red-gravy palace like **Villa di Roma**, or an Indian eatery, like **Desi Village** in King of Prussia.

Ultimately, though, I find it's up to the parents to decide where they're comfortable taking their kids. Like everything with raising kids, it might take some practice. But Philadelphia has no shortage of options to get the little ones out and started.

Trax Cafe (H)
Vientiane Cafe (H)

LIVE MUSIC

AMADA
The Bards
Bistro di Marino
Chris' Jazz Cafe
Golden Gates
Isla Verde
Jamaican Jerk Hut
Jolly's
MOSHULU
PARADISO
The Prime Rib
Serrano
The Smoked Joint (karaoke)
World Cafe Live
Zanzibar Blue

MOST COVETED TABLE

AMADA
BIRCHRUNVILLE STORE CAFE
BUDDAKAN
THE CAPITAL GRILLE
CARMINE'S CREOLE CAFE
Chloe
The Chophouse
DILWORTHTOWN INN
DJANGO
DMITRI'S
EL VEZ
FOUNTAIN RESTAURANT
GILMORE'S
L'ANGOLO
LOLITA
LOS CATRINES RESTAURANT
    & TEQUILA'S BAR
MAJOLICA
MARIGOLD KITCHEN
MATYSON
MELOGRANO
Mercato
MONK'S CAFE
MORIMOTO
Morning Glory Diner
NECTAR
PIF
Porcini
RADICCHIO
RESTAURANT ALBA
RITZ SEAFOOD
ROUGE

SABRINA'S CAFE
SANG KEE ASIAN BISTRO
SAVONA
SOUTHWARK
SOVALO
SOVANA BISTRO
STANDARD TAP
STRIPED BASS
SUSANNA FOO
TANGERINE
VETRI
VIETNAM

OUTDOOR DINING

ALISON AT BLUE BELL (patio)
Alma de Cuba (sidewalk)
An Indian Affair (sidewalk)
Anjou (sidewalk)
Apamate (sidewalk, patio)
Astral Plane (sidewalk)
Audrey Claire (sidewalk)
August Moon (sidewalk)
August (sidewalk)
Aya's Cafe (sidewalk)
Azure (patio, sidewalk)
Beau Monde (patio)
The Black Door (sidewalk)
Bleu (sidewalk)
Bliss (sidewalk)
The Blue Bell Inn (patio)
Boccella's (sidewalk)
Branzino (sidewalk)
Brasserie 73 (patio)
BRASSERIE PERRIER (sidewalk)
Buca di Beppo (sidewalk)
Cadence (terrace)
Cafe Beach Club (patio)
Cafe Lutecia (sidewalk)
Cafe Spice (sidewalk)
Caffe Aldo Lamberti (patio)
Caffe Casta Diva (sidewalk)
Capogiro (sidewalk)
Caribou Cafe (sidewalk)
Carman's Country Kitchen (sidewalk)
Casona (porch)
Cassatt Lounge and Tea Room (patio)
Catherine's (patio)
Chabaa Thai Bistro (sidewalk)
Chaucer's Tabard Inn (sidewalk)
The Chef's Table at the David

Finney Inn (patio)
City Tavern (garden, porch, veranda)
Claude's (patio)
Coleman Restaurant (patio)
Continental Mid-Town (rooftop patio)
The Continental (sidewalk)
Corinne's Place (backyard)
Cork (sidewalk)
Cosmi's Market (sidewalk)
Couch Tomato Cafe (sidewalk)
The Countryside Market & Delicatessen (patio)
Coyote Crossing (rooftop patio)
Crescent City (sidewalk)
Cuba Libre (patio)
Dahlak (patio)
Derek's (sidewalk)
Deuce Restaurant and Bar (sidewalk)
Devon Seafood Grill (patio)
DILWORTHTOWN INN (patio)
DiNardo's Famous Crabs (sidewalk)
DMITRI'S (sidewalk, Fitler Square)
Domani Star (sidewalk)
Drafting Room (patio)
Effie's (patio)
El Fuego (sidewalk)
Elements Cafe (sidewalk)
Ernesto's 1521 Cafe (sidewalk, patio)
Estia (sidewalk)
Fado Irish Pub (sidewalk)
The Farmhouse (patio)
Farmicia (sidewalk)
Fayette Street Grille (sidewalk)
Figs (sidewalk)
Fish Tank on Main (sidewalk)
Fitzwater Cafe (patio)
FORK (sidewalk)
Four Dogs Tavern (patio)
Frenchtown Inn (porch)
FRIDAY SATURDAY SUNDAY (sidewalk)
Funky Lil' Kitchen (sidewalk, courtyard)
FuziOn (patio)
Gables at Chadds Ford (patio)
GAYLE (patio)

Geno's Steaks (outdoor only)
Georges' (patio)
Gioia Mia (sidewalk)
Giumarello's (garden, patio)
Greater India Fine Dining (sidewalk)
Honey's Sit 'n' Eat (sidewalk)
Hostaria da Elio (patio)
The Hula Grill (patio)
Il Cantuccio (sidewalk)
Il Tartufo (sidewalk)
Illuminare (garden, patio)
Inn at Phillip's Mill (patio)
Iron Hill Restaurant & Brewery (patio)
Isla Verde (sidewalk)
Jack's Firehouse (sidewalk, patio)
JAKE'S (sidewalk)
Jamaican Jerk Hut (patio)
JOHN'S ROAST PORK (patio)
Jones (sidewalk)
Kabobeesh (sidewalk)
Karina's (sidewalk)
KARMA (sidewalk)
Konak (sidewalk)
KRISTIAN'S (sidewalk)
La Boheme (sidewalk)
La Cava (patio)
LA LUPE (sidewalk)
La Terrasse (terrace)
La Veranda (patio)
La Viola (sidewalk)
Las Cazuelas (sidewalk)
Little Fish (sidewalk)
LoBianco Coastal Cuisine (sidewalk)
LOLITA (sidewalk)
London Grill (sidewalk)
Lorenzo's Pizza (sidewalk)
LOS CATRINES RESTAURANT & TEQUILA'S BAR (sidewalk)
Lou's Restaurante (sidewalk)
Ma France Creperie (sidewalk)
Maggiano's Little Italy (sidewalk)
Mama's Vegetarian (sidewalk)
Mandoline (sidewalk)
Marathon Grill (sidewalk, patio)
Maya Bella (sidewalk)
McMenamin's Tavern (patio)
Megu Sushi (sidewalk)
Melange Cafe (sidewalk)
MELOGRANO (sidewalk)

Mercato (sidewalk)
Meritage Philadelphia (sidewalk)
Mikimotos (patio)
Mixto (sidewalk)
Morning Glory Diner (garden patio)
MOSHULU (deck)
N. 3RD (sidewalk)
Nags Head Fine Foods (patio)
NECTAR (patio)
New Wave Cafe (sidewalk)
O Sandwiches (sidewalk)
Old Original Bookbinders (sidewalk)
Opa Bar & Grille (boardwalk)
Otto's Brauhaus (beer garden, patio)
Pagoda Noodle Cafe (sidewalk)
Paradigm (sidewalk)
PARADISO (sidewalk)
Pat's King of Steaks (outdoor only)
Picanha Brazilian Grill (sidewalk)
Pietro's Coal Oven Pizzeria (patio, South St; sidewalk, Walnut St)
PJ Whelihan's Pub and Restaurant (sidewalk)
Plough and the Stars (sidewalk)
Pompeii (sidewalk)
Posh (sidewalk)
POSITANO COAST BY ALDO LAMBERTI (patio)
Prima Donna (patio)
Pura Vida (sidewalk, patio)
Race Street Cafe (sidewalk)
RADICCHIO (sidewalk)
Rat's (patio)
Red Hot & Blue (patio)
Red Sky (sidewalk)
REMBRANDT'S (sidewalk)
Restaurant Acapulco (sidewalk)
Restaurant Taquet (porch)
Ristorante Valentino (sidewalk)
Rock Lobster (deck)
Roselena's Coffee Bar (sidewalk, patio)
ROUGE (sidewalk)
Roux 3 (patio)

Rustica (sidewalk)
Rx (sidewalk)
SABRINA'S CAFE (sidewalk)
SANG KEE ASIAN BISTRO (sidewalk)
SANSOM STREET OYSTER HOUSE (sidewalk)
Sapori (sidewalk)
SAVONA (patio)
Seafood Unlimited (sidewalk)
Sergeantsville Inn (patio)
Shouk (sidewalk)
Shundeez (sidewalk)
Sidecar Bar and Grille (sidewalk)
Slate Bleu (terrace)
Sly Fox Breweries (Royersford, sidewalk; Phoenixville, patio)
Smith & Wollensky (patio)
Society Hill Hotel (sidewalk)
Sonny's Famous Steaks (sidewalk)
SOUTHWARK (patio)
SOVALO (sidewalk)
SOVANA BISTRO (patio)
Spring Mill Cafe (deck, porch)
STANDARD TAP (deck)
SWEET LUCY'S SMOKEHOUSE (sidewalk)
Tangier Restaurant (sidewalk)
Teca (sidewalk)
Ted's Montana Grill (sidewalk)
Teikoku (deck)
333 Belrose (patio)
Tir Na Nog (sidewalk)
Tommy Gunns (patio)
Tony Luke's (sidewalk)
Trattoria Lucca (sidewalk)
Trax Cafe (patio)
Tre Famiglia Ristorante (sidewalk)
Tria (sidewalk)
Trio (deck)
Tucker's Steak and Seafood House (patio)
Twenty Manning (sidewalk)
Twenty21 (patio)
Valanni (sidewalk)
Valentino on the Square (sidewalk)
Vintage (sidewalk)
Washington Square (patio, sidewalk)
White Dog Cafe (sidewalk)

Winnie's Le Bus Manayunk
(sidewalk)
Word of Mouth (patio)
XIX NINETEEN (patio)
Zeke's Mainline Bar B Que
(patio)
Zen Tea House
Zocalo (patio)

PEOPLE WATCHING

Alma de Cuba
BIRCHRUNVILLE STORE CAFE
BRASSERIE PERRIER
BUDDAKAN
THE CAPITAL GRILLE
The Continental
Continental Mid-Town
EL VEZ
FOUNTAIN RESTAURANT
Golden Gates
Isla Verde
Le Bec-Fin
MORIMOTO
NECTAR
Old Original Bookbinders
The Palm
ROUGE
STRIPED BASS
Tony Luke's
Washington Square

PRE-THEATER (-MOVIE) DINING

Bistro St. Tropez
Bliss
Buca Di Beppo
Cadence
Caffe Casta Diva
Caribou Cafe
Chez Elena Wu
Coriander Indian Bistro
Deux Cheminees
Ernesto's 1521 Cafe
Estia
Farmicia
La Viola
Miraku
M/O Cafe
Pagoda Noodle Cafe
Pompeii
POSITANO COAST BY ALDO
LAMBERTI
Prima Donna

The Prime Rib
Ristorante Valentino
RITZ SEAFOOD
Ted's Montana Grill
Valanni
Warsaw Cafe

TOURISTY

City Tavern
Geno's
Jim's Steaks
Maggiano's
Moshulu
Old Original Bookbinders
Pat's King of Steaks
Ralph's
Reading Terminal Market

VIEW

Beach Creek Oyster Bar &
Grille
Bistro St. Tropez
Black Bass Hotel
Bleu
Cadence
Devon Seafood Grill
Inn at St. Peter's Village
La Veranda
Lacroix at the Rittenhouse
Lobster House
MOSHULU
POSITANO COAST BY ALDO
LAMBERTI
REMBRANDT'S (upstairs banquet room)
Rock Lobster
ROUGE
Simon Pearce on the
Brandywine
Smith & Wollensky
Water Works Restaurant &
Lounge
XIX NINETEEN

WATCH THE GAME

The Black Sheep
Bridgewater's Pub
Chickie's & Pete's
The Dark Horse
Devon Seafood Grill
Fado Irish Pub
Iron Hill Restaurant &
Brewery

Isla Verde
Jolly's (19th St.)
New Wave Cafe
Nick's Roast Beef
PJ Whelihan's Pub and
Restaurant
Red Hot & Blue
REMBRANDT'S
The Smoked Joint
Taste of Portugal
Tony Luke's Beef and Beer
Sports Bar
The Wild Onion

Drink Features

BEER DESTINATION

ANSILL
The Bards
The Black Door
The Black Sheep
Bridgid's
Drafting Room
Eulogy
Fado Irish Pub
The Farmhouse
The Foodery Northern
Liberties
Grace Tavern
Grey Lodge Pub
Iron Hill Restaurant &
Brewery
Johnny Brenda's
Ludwig's Garten
McMenamin's Tavern
MONK'S CAFE
N. 3rd
Nodding Head Brewery &
Restaurant
Otto's Brauhaus
Plough and the Stars
Race Street Cafe
Sly Fox Breweries
South Philadelphia Tap Room
STANDARD TAP
Ten Stone
Tir Na Nog
Tria

BYOB

Abner's Authentic Barbecue (Jenkintown only)
Alisa Cafe
ALISON AT BLUE BELL
Allen's Clam Bar
An Indian Affair (soon to have liquor license)
Apamate
Ariana
Aromatic House of Kebob
Athenian Garden
Audrey Claire
August
Ava
Aya's Cafe
Bacio
Basilico's
BIRCHRUNVILLE STORE CAFE
Bistro di Marino
Bistro St. Tropez (with corkage fee)
The Black Duck on Sunset
Blue Sage
Bluefin
Boccella's
Branzino
Brasserie Perrier at Boyds
Brennan's by the Bay
Cafe de Laos
Cafe Fresko
Cafe Lift
Cafe Lutecia
Caffe Casta Diva
Carambola
CARMINE'S
Casona
Catherine's
Chabaa Thai Bistro
Charles Plaza
CHERRY STREET CHINESE KOSHER VEGETARIAN RESTAURANT
Chez Elena Wu
Chloe
Citron
Citrus
Claude's
Coconut Bay
Coriander Indian Bistro
Corinne's Place
Couch Tomato Cafe
Country Club Restaurant
The Countryside Market & Deli

Cucina Forte
DeBreaux's
Divan Turkish Kitchen
DJANGO
DMITRI'S (Fitler Square)
Domani Star
Effie's
Elements Cafe
Emerald Fish
Ernesto's 1521 Cafe (corkage fee)
Farmicia (no corkage fee)
Fayette Street Grille
Figs
Fish Tank on Main
Fitzwater Cafe
410 Bank Street
Funky Lil' Kitchen
FuziON
Gables at Chadds Ford (no corkage fee)
Georges' (Sunday)
GILMORE'S
Golden Gates
Greater India Fine Dining
Hank's Place
Harmony Vegetarian Restaurant
Harvey Cedars Shellfish Co.
High Street Caffe (corkage fee)
Hostaria da Elio
Il Cantuccio
Indonesia
Inn at Phillip's Mill
Island Grill
Jamaican Jerk Hut
Joe Pesce
Kabobeesh
Kami Sushi Express
Karen & Rei's
Karina's
Khajuraho
Kisso Sushi Bar
La Boheme
La Cava
La Locanda del Ghiottone
LA LUPE
La Viola
Laceno Italian Grill
LAKESIDE CHINESE DELI
L'ANGOLO
Las Cazuelas
Lee How Fook
A Little Cafe

Little Fish
LoBianco Coastal Cuisine
LOLITA
Lourdes Greek Taverna
Lou's Restaurante
Ma France Creperie
MAJOLICA
Makiman
Mama Palma's (wine only)
Mama's Vegetarian (kosher liquor only)
Mandoline
MARIGOLD KITCHEN
MATYSON
Mediterranean Grill
Megu Sushi
Melange Cafe
MELOGRANO
Mercato
Mezza Luna (and wine list)
Minar Palace
Miran
M/O Cafe
Mosaic Cafe
Mud City Crabhouse
Mustache Bill's Diner
NAN
Next
Nonna's
Ong's
Ooka Japanese Sushi and Hibachi Steak House
The Orchard
Picanha Brazilian Grill
PIF
Porcini
Prima Donna (with liquor license)
PUMPKIN
RADICCHIO
Ray's Cafe & Tea House
Restaurant Acapulco
RESTAURANT ALBA
Ristorante Pesto
Ristorante Valentino
RITZ SEAFOOD
Roberto Cafe
Roselena's Coffee Bar
Rustica
Rx
SABRINA'S CAFE
Sagami
SANG KEE ASIAN BISTRO
Sansom Street Kabob House
Sapori

Sea Salt
Seafood Unlimited (with
	wine list)
Shiao Lan Kung
Shundeez
Sila Turkish Restaurant
Singapore
Siri's Thai French Cuisine
Sitar India
SOVANA BISTRO
Spring Mill Cafe
Sushikazu
SWEET LUCY'S SMOKEHOUSE
Sweet Vidalia
SZECHUAN TASTY HOUSE
Taco Riendo
Taste
Teresa's Cafe Italiano
Tommy Gunns
Trattoria Lucca
Trax Cafe
Tre Famiglia Ristorante
Tre Scalini
Trio
Umbria
Vientiane Cafe
Word of Mouth
Zorba's Taverna (Fairmount)

GREAT BAR

Alma de Cuba (rum)
AMADA (Spanish wine bar)
ANSILL (beer, wine)
Astral Plane (Bloody Mary)
BARCLAY PRIME (great space)
The Bards (Guinness)
Beau Monde (L'Etage
	upstairs)
The Black Sheep (Irish
	whiskey, Guinness)
BRASSERIE PERRIER (cocktail
	scene)
Bridgid's (Belgian beer)
Cafe Habana (mojito)
THE CAPITAL GRILLE (Stoli-
	Doli)
Caribou Cafe (beer)
Chaucer's Tabard Inn (beer)
The Chophouse (martini)
The Continental (martini)
Copabanana; Copa Too (mar-
	garita)
Cuba Libre (rum)
The Dark Horse (scotch, beer)

Derek's (vodka)
Drafting Room (scotch)
EL VEZ (tequila)
Estia (ouzo, Greek wines)
The Farmhouse (scotch)
FRIDAY SATURDAY SUNDAY
	(Tank Bar upstairs)
Georges' (great space)
Giumarello's (martini)
Grace Tavern (beer)
The Grill (The Vault)
The Happy Rooster (cocktail
	scene)
HORIZONS (rum, tequila)
Jack's Firehouse (bourbon)
JAKE'S (classic spirits)
Le Castagne (grappa)
LOS CATRINES RESTAURANT
	& TEQUILA'S BAR (tequila)
Mahogany on Walnut
	(scotch)
McMenamin's Tavern
	(whiskey)
Old Original Bookbinders
	(historic)
¡PASION! (Latin cocktail)
Plough and the Stars
	(Guinness)
Posh (martini)
The Prime Rib (scotch)
Royal Tavern (scotch)
SoleFood (martini)
SOUTHWARK (classic cock-
	tails)
STANDARD TAP (beer)
333 Belrose (martini)
Twenty21 (spirits)
VETRI (grappa)
VIETNAM (tiki drinks)
Washington Square (al fres-
	co)
The Wooden Iron (martini)
XIX NINETEEN (wine bar,
	cocktail)

SAKE BAR

Anjou
BUDDAKAN
Genji
Haru
Mantra
MARGARET KUO'S
Margaret Kuo's Peking
MORIMOTO

NECTAR
Pod
Raw Sushi and Sake Lounge

TEA LIST

Bubble House
Cassatt Lounge and Tea
	Room
Great Tea International
Margaret Kuo's Peking
Museum Restaurant
Premium Steap
Remedy Tea
RITZ SEAFOOD
Ritz-Carlton. See The Grill
Zen Tea House

TEQUILA LIST

Cantina Los Caballitos
El Sarape
EL VEZ
HORIZONS
LOS CATRINES RESTAURANT
	& TEQUILA'S BAR
Zocalo

WINE DESTINATION

AMADA
ANSILL
Bar Ferdinand
THE CAPITAL GRILLE
DILWORTHTOWN INN
Domaine Hudson
FRIDAY SATURDAY SUNDAY
La Famiglia
Le Castagne
MORO
PARADISO
Penne
POSITANO COAST BY ALDO
	LAMBERTI
The Prime Rib
Rat's
Ristorante Panorama
SAVONA
Smith & Wollensky
Strawberry Hill
STRIPED BASS
Tria
Twenty21
VETRI
Vintage
XIX NINETEEN

Food Features

ADVENTURE DINING

Abyssinia
Alma de Cuba
AMADA
ANSILL
Balkan Express Restaurant
Banana Leaf
Bridgewater's Pub
Brown Sugar Bakery & Cafe
Buka-Teria
Carman's Country Kitchen
Charles Plaza
CHERRY STREET CHINESE
    KOSHER VEGETARIAN
    RESTAURANT
Chung King
City Tavern
Dahlak
DEVI
El Sol de Peru
FORK (FORK:ETC.)
GAYLE
HORIZONS
Indonesia
Isla Verde
Jack's Firehouse
Jong Ka Jib Soft Tofu
    Restaurant
Kabobeesh
Kim's
La Calebasse
LA LUPE
LAKESIDE CHINESE DELI
LE BEC-FIN
Los Taquitos de Puebla
MARGARET KUO'S
Margaret Kuo's Peking
MARIGOLD KITCHEN
Mexico Lindo
MORIMOTO
NAM PHUONG
Nan Zhou Hand-Drawn
    Noodle House
Paradise Restaurant
¡PASION!
PENANG
Pho 75
PIF

Porky's Point
Queen of Sheba Pub II
Rangoon
Seo Ra Bol
Sergeantsville Inn
Shining Star
SZECHUAN TASTY HOUSE
Taqueria La Michoacana
Tashkent
Taste of Portugal
TIERRA COLOMBIANA
Uduppi Dosa House
VETRI
VIETNAM

AUTHENTIC

Abyssinia
AMADA
Ariana
Aromatic House of Kebob
Ba Le Bakery
Balkan Express Restaurant
Banana Leaf
The Bards
Beau Monde
Blue Danube Restaurant
BRASSERIE PERRIER
Brown Sugar Bakery & Cafe
Buka-Teria
Cafe de Laos
Cafe Lutecia
Chung King
Dahlak
DEVI
El Bohio
El Sarape
El Sol de Peru
FAMOUS 4TH STREET DELI-
    CATESSEN
Golden Gates
JOHN'S ROAST PORK
Jong Ka Jib Soft Tofu
    Restaurant
Kabobeesh
KARMA
Kibbitz Room
Kim's
Konak
La Calebasse
La Esperanza
LA LUPE
LAKESIDE CHINESE DELI
L'ANGOLO
Las Cazuelas

Le Bar Lyonnais
Le Castagne
LOS CATRINES RESTAURANT
    & TEQUILA'S BAR
Los Taquitos de Puebla
Lourdes Greek Taverna
Mama's Vegetarian
MARGARET KUO'S
Margaret Kuo's Peking
MELOGRANO
Mexico Lindo
Mezza Luna
Miran
MONK'S CAFE
NAM PHUONG
Nan Zhou Hand-Drawn
    Noodle House
Ong's
Paradise Restaurant
PENANG
Pho 75
Pho Cali
Pho Ha
Picanha Brazilian Grill
Porky's Point
Pura Vida
RADICCHIO
Rangoon
Restaurant Acapulco
Sabor Latino
Sang Kee
SANG KEE ASIAN BISTRO
Sansom Street Kabob House
Seo Ra Bol
Shining Star
SIAM LOTUS
Sila Turkish Restaurant
Slate Bleu
South Street Souvlaki
SWEET LUCY'S SMOKEHOUSE
SZECHUAN TASTY HOUSE
Taco Riendo
Taqueria La Michoacana
Taqueria La Veracruzana
Tashkent
Taste of Portugal
TIERRA COLOMBIANA
Tre Scalini
Uduppi Dosa House
VETRI
Vientiane Cafe
VIETNAM
Vietnam Palace
Yue Kee

BAR DINING

Alma de Cuba
AMADA
ANSILL
BARCLAY PRIME
The Bards
Beau Monde
BIRCHRUNVILLE STORE CAFE
Bliss
BRASSERIE PERRIER
Bridgewater's Pub
Bridgid's
BUDDAKAN
Cafe Spice
THE CAPITAL GRILLE
Chaucer's Tabard Inn
Chickie's & Pete's
Cork
Cuba Libre
The Dark Horse
Derek's
Deuce Restaurant and Bar
Devon Seafood Grill
DMITRI'S (Fitler Square)
EL VEZ
Eulogy
FORK (FORK:ETC.)
FOUNTAIN RESTAURANT
FRIDAY SATURDAY SUNDAY
Gables at Chadds Ford
Georges'
Giumarello's
Good Dog
The Happy Rooster
HORIZONS
Iron Hill Restaurant &
    Brewery
Jack's Firehouse
Johnny Brenda's
Jolly's
Le Bar Lyonnais (LE BEC-FIN)
Le Castagne
London Grill
MARSHA BROWN
McCormick & Schmick's
McMenamin's Tavern
MONK'S CAFE
MORIMOTO
MOSHULU
NECTAR
New Wave Cafe
Nick's Roast Beef
Old Guard House Inn
Old Original Bookbinders
The Palm

Paradigm
Plough and the Stars
Race Street Cafe
Raw Sushi and Sake Lounge
Red Sky
REMBRANDT'S
Restaurant Taquet
Ristorante Panorama
Rose Tattoo Cafe
ROUGE
Royal Tavern
SANSOM STREET OYSTER
    HOUSE
Sergeantsville Inn
SIAM LOTUS
Slate Bleu
Society Hill Hotel
SoleFood
South Philadelphia Tap Room
SOUTHWARK
SOVALO
STANDARD TAP
STRIPED BASS
TANGERINE
Teikoku
TIERRA COLOMBIANA
Tir Na Nog
Twenty Manning
Valentino on the Square
Zanzibar Blue

CHEESES

ANSILL
DJANGO
FOUNTAIN RESTAURANT
Le Bar Lyonnais
LE BEC-FIN
MAJOLICA
MARIGOLD KITCHEN
PARADISO
Rat's
RESTAURANT ALBA
SAVONA
SOUTHWARK
SOVANA BISTRO
STRIPED BASS
Tria
VETRI

CHEF'S TASTING MENU

AMADA
BIRCHRUNVILLE STORE CAFE
CARMINE'S CREOLE CAFE

DILWORTHTOWN INN
FORK (FORK:ETC.)
FOUNTAIN RESTAURANT
GAYLE
Lacroix at the Rittenhouse
LE BEC-FIN
MARIGOLD KITCHEN
MATYSON
Meritage Philadelphia
MORIMOTO
MORO
¡PASION!
PIF
SAVONA
STRIPED BASS
SUSANNA FOO
Twenty21
VETRI

CUTTING-EDGE

Alma de Cuba
ANSILL
GAYLE
HORIZONS
Lacroix at the Rittenhouse
LE BEC-FIN
MARIGOLD KITCHEN
¡PASION!
STRIPED BASS
VETRI

DIM SUM

H.K. Golden Phoenix
Imperial Inn
Joy Tsin Lau
LAKESIDE CHINESE DELI
Ocean City
Saigon Maxim Restaurant

GREAT DESSERTS

ALISON AT BLUE BELL
Alma de Cuba
AMADA
ANSILL
Apamate
BARCLAY PRIME
BUDDAKAN
Capogiro
EL VEZ
FAMOUS 4TH STREET DELI-
    CATESSEN
FOUNTAIN RESTAURANT
FRIDAY SATURDAY SUNDAY

GAYLE
Georges'
GILMORE'S
JAKE'S
L'ANGOLO
Lacroix at the Rittenhouse
LE BEC-FIN
LOLITA
MARIGOLD KITCHEN
MATYSON
Miel Patisserie
¡PASION!
PUMPKIN
SOUTHWARK
SOVALO
STRIPED BASS
VETRI

GREAT PIZZA

Couch Tomato Cafe
Derek's
Di Bruno Bros.
By George
Georges'
Illuminare
La Fourno Trattoria
Lazaro's Pizza House
Lucky Bones Backwater Grille
Mama Palma's
Marra's
People's Pizza
REMBRANDT'S
Ristorante Pesto
SOVANA BISTRO
Teresa's Cafe Italiano

RAW BAR

Alma de Cuba (ceviche)
Beach Creek Oyster Bar and
    Grille
BRASSERIE PERRIER
Cadence
Deep Blue
El Sol de Peru (ceviche)
Lobster House
MARSHA BROWN
¡PASION! (ceviche)
POSITANO COAST BY ALDO
    LAMBERTI (crudo)
ROUGE
SANSOM STREET OYSTER
    HOUSE
Snockey's Oyster and Crab
    House

STRIPED BASS
XIX NINETEEN

SMALL PLATES/ TAPAS

AMADA
ANSILL
Bar Ferdinand
The Continental
Continental Mid-Town
Domaine Hudson
Elements Cafe
HORIZONS
Isla Verde
Mantra
POSITANO COAST BY ALDO
    LAMBERTI
Shouk
TANGERINE
Tria

SUSHI

Anjou
Bluefin
Genji
Goji Tokyo Cuisine
Hikaru
Kami Sushi Express
Kisso Sushi Bar
Makiman
MARGARET KUO'S
Margaret Kuo's Peking
Megu Sushi
Mikado
Mikimoto's
Miraku
MORIMOTO
Moshi Moshi
NECTAR
Oh Yoko!
Ooka Japanese Sushi and
    Hibachi Steak House
Osaka
Pod
Raw Sushi and Sake Lounge
Sagami
Seo Ra Bol
Sushikazu
Teikoku

VEGETARIAN FRIENDLY

ALISON AT BLUE BELL

AMADA
ANSILL
Audrey Claire
Azure
BRASSERIE PERRIER
Cafe Spice
Charles Plaza
CHERRY STREET CHINESE
    KOSHER VEGETARIAN
    RESTAURANT
DEVI
DJANGO
Farmicia
FOUNTAIN RESTAURANT
Harmony Vegetarian
    Restaurant
HORIZONS
JAKE'S
The Latest Dish
LE BEC-FIN
Mama's Vegetarian
Maoz
MORO
Next
Paninoteca
¡PASION!
RESTAURANT ALBA
Singapore
SOUTHWARK
STANDARD TAP
STRIPED BASS
Uduppi Dosa House

WHOLE FISH

Branzino
Divan Turkish Kitchen
DMITRI'S
Effie's
Estia
Gioia Mia
Joe Pesce
La Veranda
Laceno Italian Grill
Little Fish
LOS CATRINES RESTAURANT
    & TEQUILA'S BAR
Marco Polo
Margaret Kuo's Peking
MELOGRANO
Mercato
Mezza Luna
Monte Carlo Living Room
NAM PHUONG
PENANG

RADICCHIO
RESTAURANT ALBA
Ristorante La Buca
Ristorante Pesto
Ristorante Valentino
RITZ SEAFOOD
Roberto Cafe
SANG KEE ASIAN BISTRO
SAVONA
SIAM LOTUS
SOVANA BISTRO
SUSANNA FOO
VETRI
VIETNAM

Hours

BREAKFAST SCENE

Balkan Express Restaurant
Cafe Lutecia
Cafe Sud
Carman's Country Kitchen
Down Home Diner
FAMOUS 4TH STREET DELI-
    CATESSEN
Fitzwater Cafe
FOUNTAIN RESTAURANT
Hank's Place
Honey's Sit 'n' Eat
LA LUPE
Mayfair Diner
McGlade's on the Pier
Melrose Diner
Morning Glory Diner
SABRINA'S CAFE
Shank's and Evelyn's Roast
    Beef

BRUNCH

ANSILL
Apamate
Art Museum
Astral Plane
Ava
Azure
Balkan Express Restaurant
The Bards
Beau Monde
BIRCHRUNVILLE STORE CAFE
Bistro di Marino
Black Bass Hotel

The Black Sheep
Boccella's
Cafe Habana
Cafe Lutecia
Cafe Spice
Cafe Sud
Carman's Country Kitchen
Cantina Los Caballitos
The Chef's Table at the David
    Finney Inn
Coleman Restaurant
Continental Mid-Town
Corinne's Place
The Countryside Market &
    Deli
Coyote Crossing
Cuba Libre
The Dark Horse
Derek's
Devon Seafood Grill
DiNardo's Famous Crabs
Drafting Room
Ernesto's 1521 Cafe
Farmicia
Figs
Fish Tank on Main
FORK (FORK:ETC.)
FOUNTAIN RESTAURANT
Four Dogs Tavern
Frenchtown Inn
Georges'
The Happy Rooster
H.K. Golden Phoenix
Honey's Sit 'n' Eat
Hotel DuPont
Il Tartufo
Illuminare
Iron Hill Restaurant &
    Brewery
Jack's Firehouse
JAKE'S
Jim's Steaks
Johnny Brenda's
Jones
Khajuraho
Konak
Lacroix at the Rittenhouse
Las Cazuelas
London Grill
Mainland Inn
Mixto
M/O Cafe
MONK'S CAFE
MOSHULU
N. 3RD

New Wave Cafe
Old Original Bookbinders
PARADISO
Plough and the Stars
Pura Vida
Race Street Cafe
Rat's
REMBRANDT'S
Roller's
Roselena's Coffee Bar
ROUGE
Royal Tavern
Rx
Salt & Pepper Cafe
SAVONA
Sea Salt
Slate Bleu
Society Hill Hotel
SoleFood
SOUTHWARK
Spring Mill Cafe
STANDARD TAP
Swann Lounge
Twenty Manning
Valanni
White Dog Cafe
Winnie's Le Bus Manayunk
XIX NINETEEN
Zanzibar Blue

LUNCH SCENE

AMADA
Brasserie Perrier at Boyd's
Bubble House
BRASSERIE PERRIER
BUDDAKAN
Cafe Lift
Cafe Lutecia
THE CAPITAL GRILLE
The Countryside Market &
    Deli
Delilah's Southern Cafe
Di Bruno Bros.
DiNic's
El Fuego
Ernesto's 1521 Cafe
FAMOUS 4TH STREET
    DELICATESSEN
Fitzwater Cafe
FOUNTAIN RESTAURANT
The Grill
Hank's Place
Honey's Sit 'n' Eat
JOHN'S ROAST PORK

Jose's Tacos
Lacroix at the Rittenhouse
LAKESIDE CHINESE DELI
LE BEC-FIN
Little Thai Singha Market
MATYSON
Mezze
MORIMOTO
Morning Glory Diner
Olympic Gyro
Ong's
Pagano's Market
The Palm
Paninoteca
Pastrami and Things
Pikkles Plus
Ralph's
ROUGE
SABRINA'S CAFE
Salumeria
Sang Kee Peking Duck
SANSOM STREET OYSTER
  HOUSE
Shank's and Evelyn's Roast
  Beef
Siri's Thai French Cuisine
Tampopo
TIERRA COLOMBIANA
VIETNAM

LATE-NIGHT DINING

Alma de Cuba (limited,
  to 1 a.m.)
ANSILL (weekends to mid-
  night)
Aromatic House of Kebob
  (to 1 a.m.)
Banana Leaf (to 2 a.m.)
BARCLAY PRIME (to 10 p.m.)
The Black Door
  (to 12:30 a.m.)
Bleu (weekends to 11 p.m.)
BRASSERIE PERRIER (week-
  ends to 10:30 p.m.)
BUDDAKAN (F and Sa to
  midnight)
Cafe Spice (F and Sa to 1:30
  a.m.)
Capogiro (F and Sa to 1 a.m.,
  April-Oct)
Chickie's & Pete's (F and Sa to
  1 a.m.)
Chris' Jazz Cafe (to 1 a.m.)

Copabanana; Copa Too (to 1
  a.m.)
Cuba Libre (Th-Sa to 1 a.m.)
Dalessandro's (F to 1 a.m.)
Deep Blue (F and Sa, bar
  menu to 1 a.m.)
Deuce Restaurant and Bar (to
  1 a.m.)
Drafting Room (F and Sa to
  12:30)
El Fuego (to 1 a.m.)
Eulogy (F and Sa to 1 a.m.)
FORK (FORK:ETC.) (F and Sa
  to 1 a.m.)
FRIDAY SATURDAY SUNDAY
  (to 10:30 p.m.)
Frusco's Steak Shop (F and Sa
  to 3 a.m.)
GAYLE (Th-Sa to midnight)
Geno's Steaks (24 hrs.)
Giumarello's (F and Sa to
  midnight)
Golden Gates (to 2 a.m.)
Good Dog (to 1 a.m.)
Grace Tavern (to 2 a.m.)
Grey Lodge Pub (F and Sa to
  1 a.m.)
Grilladelphia (F to 4 a.m.; Sa
  to 2 a.m.)
HORIZONS (tapas menu)
Imperial Inn (to midnight)
Isla Verde (tapas every day to
  1 a.m.)
Jack's Firehouse (bar menu F
  and Sa to 1 a.m.)
JAKE'S (F and Sa to 10:30
  p.m.)
Johnny Brenda's (to 1 a.m.)
Jolly's (to 2 a.m.)
Joy Tsin Lau (to 12:30)
KARMA (F and Sa to 11 p.m.)
The Latest Dish (F and Sa to 1
  a.m.)
LaVa Cafe (Sa to 11 p.m.)
LOLITA (F and Sa to 11 p.m.)
London Grill (F and Sa to 1
  a.m.)
LOS CATRINES RESTAURANT
  & TEQUILA'S BAR (F and
  Sa to 11 p.m.)
Ludwig's Garten (to 1 a.m.)
MARGARET KUO'S (F and Sa
  to 11 p.m.)
Mayfair Diner (24 hrs.)
Melrose Diner (24 hrs.)

Mia (F & Sa to 1 a.m.)
MONK'S CAFE (to 1 a.m.)
MORIMOTO (F and Sa to mid-
  night; weekdays to 11
  p.m.)
MORO (to 11 p.m.)
N. 3RD (W-Sa to 1 a.m.)
NECTAR (F and Sa, sushi to
  midnight)
New Wave Cafe (to 1 a.m.)
Nick's Roast Beef (to 1 a.m.)
Ocean City (to 2 a.m.)
Opa Bar & Grille (Sa to 1 a.m.)
Pat's King of Steaks (24 hrs.)
PENANG (to 1 a.m.)
Plough and the Stars (to 1
  a.m.)
Ponzio's (to 1 a.m.)
POSITANO COAST BY ALDO
  LAMBERTI (F and Sa to 1
  a.m.)
Race Street Cafe (Tu-Sa to 1
  a.m.)
Red Sky (Tu-Su to 2 a.m.)
REMBRANDT'S (F and Sa to 1 a.m.)
ROUGE (Sa to 12)
Royal Tavern (to 1 a.m.)
Shiao Lan Kung (F and Sa to
  2 a.m.)
SIAM LOTUS (F and Sa to 11
  p.m.)
Sidecar Bar and Grille (F and
  Sa to 1 a.m.)
The Smoked Joint (to 2 a.m.)
Society Hill Hotel (to 1 a.m.)
SoleFood (to 2 a.m.)
Sonny's Famous Steaks (F
  and Sa to 3 a.m.)
The Sound of Philadelphia
  (TSOP) (F and Sa to 1 a.m.)
SOUTHWARK (F and Sa to
  11:30 p.m.)
STANDARD TAP (to 1 a.m.)
Steve's Prince of Steaks (F
  and Sa to 3 a.m.)
STRIPED BASS (F and Sa to 11
  p.m.)
SUSANNA FOO (F and Sa to
  11 p.m.)
Swann Lounge (lite fare to 1
  a.m.)
SZECHUAN TASTY HOUSE (to
  midnight)
TANGERINE (F and Sa to mid-
  night)

Teca (M-Sa to 2 a.m.)
TIERRA COLOMBIANA (F and Sa to 12:30 a.m.)
Tir Na Nog (bar menu to 1 a.m.)
Tony Luke's (F and Sa to 2 a.m.)
Tria (to 1 a.m.)
Twenty Manning (F and Sa bar menu to 1 a.m.)
Valanni (to 1 a.m.)
White Dog Cafe (F and Sa to 1 a.m.)

OPEN THANKSGIVING AND CHRISTMAS

Abner's (TG only)
An Indian Affair
Ariana (CH only)
Astral Plane (TG only)
August Moon (CH only)
Aya's Cafe
Bacio (TG only)
Banana Leaf
Black Bass Hotel (TG only)
The Black Door
Bleu (TG only)
Blue Danube Restaurant (TG only)
Brulee
Cafe Spice (TG only)
Carman's Country Kitchen (TG only)
CARMINE'S (TG only)
Charles Plaza
Chaucer's Tabard Inn
CHERRY STREET CHINESE KOSHER VEGETARIAN RESTAURANT
CinCin
Citron
City Tavern
Coconut Bay (CH only)
Coleman Restaurant
Coriander Indian Bistro
Country Club Restaurant (TG only)
Crescent City (TG only)
The Dark Horse (TG only)
Davio's (TG only)
Derek's (CH only)
Devon Seafood Grill (CH only)

Dilworthtown Inn (TG only)
Dock's Oyster House (TG only)
Eulogy
Fado Irish Pub (TG only)
FAMOUS 4TH STREET DELICATESSEN (TG only)
Farmicia (TG only)
FOUNTAIN RESTAURANT
Four Dogs Tavern (TG only)
FuziOn (CH only)
Gables at Chadds Ford
Golden Gates
Great Tea International (TG only)
Greater India Fine Dining
Grey Lodge Pub
The Grill
Harmony Vegetarian Restaurant
The Harvest Moon Inn (TG only)
Il Tartufo
Indonesia
Inn at Phillip's Mill (TG only)
Iron Hill Restaurant & Brewery (TG only)
Joy Tsin Lau
Kabobeesh
Karen & Rei's (CH only)
Karina's (TG only)
Khajuraho
Kibbitz Room
Knife & Fork Inn (TG only)
Konak
Krazy Kats
La Viola (TG only)
Laceno Italian Grill (TG only)
LAKESIDE CHINESE DELI (CH only)
L'ANGOLO (TG only)
Lee How Fook (CH only)
Little Fish
London Grill (TG only)
Ly Michael's (CH only)
Mainland Inn (TG only)
MARGARET KUO'S
Margaret Kuo's Peking
MARSHA BROWN (TG only)
Mayfair Diner (TG only)
McCormick & Schmick's
Megu Sushi (TG only)
Melrose Diner (TG only)
Meritage Philadelphia
Mia
Moshi Moshi

MOSHULU (TG only)
Mustard Green
NAM PHUONG
Next (TG only)
Nonna's
O Sandwiches
Ocean City
Ong's
Otto's Brauhaus (TG only)
Pagoda Noodle Cafe (CH only)
Paradigm (CH only)
PENANG
Penne
Plough and the Stars
Pompeii (TG only)
Pond/Bistro Cassis (TG only)
Ponzio's (TG only)
Porky's Point (TG only)
POSITANO COAST BY ALDO LAMBERTI (CH only)
The Prime Rib (TG only)
Queen of Sheba Pub II
Race Street Cafe (TG only)
Rangoon (CH only)
Red Square
Restaurant Taquet (TG only)
Ristorante Pesto (TG only)
RITZ SEAFOOD
Roux 3 (CH only)
Royal Tavern (CH only)
Saigon Maxim Restaurant
Sang Kee
SANG KEE ASIAN BISTRO (CH only)
SAVONA
Sergeantsville Inn (TG only)
Shiao Lan Kung
Shundeez
Sila Turkish Restaurant
Singapore
Siri's Thai French Cuisine
Sitar India
Smith & Wollensky
SoleFood
SUSANNA FOO
Sushikazu
Swann Lounge
SZECHUAN TASTY HOUSE
Taco Riendo
Tangier Restaurant (TG only)
Taste
Taste of Portugal (TG only)
Ted's Montana Grill (TG only)
Tir Na Nog (TG only)

Tucker's Steak and Seafood
House (TG only)
Vientiane Cafe
VIETNAM (CH only)
Vietnam Palace (CH only)
Warsaw Cafe (TG only)
Yangming (CH only)
Zen Tea House

Pricing

INEXPENSIVE (ENTREES $15 OR LESS)

Abner's
Abyssinia
Ariana
Aromatic House of Kebob
Ba Le Bakery
Beau Monde
Bitar's
Brown's Restaurant
Cafe Lift
Cafe Lutecia
CHERRY STREET CHINESE
KOSHER VEGETARIAN
RESTAURANT
Chink's Steaks
Coriander Indian Bistro
Corinne's Place
The Countryside Market &
Deli
Dalessandro's
The Dark Horse
DEVI
DiNic's
Donkey's Place
Down Home Diner
Dutch Eating Place
Effie's
El Bohio
El Fuego
El Sol de Peru
Fado Irish Pub
FAMOUS 4TH STREET DELI-
CATESSEN
Frusco's Steak Shop
Good Dog
Grace Tavern
Harmony Vegetarian
Restaurant
H&J McNally's Tavern

Honey's Sit 'n' Eat
JOHN'S ROAST PORK
Kabobeesh
Kibbitz Room
Koch's Deli
Koja
La Esperanza
La Fourno Trattoria
LAKESIDE CHINESE DELI
Lee How Fook
Lorenzo's Pizza
Los Taquitos de Puebla
Lou's Restaurante
Mama Palma's
McMenamin's Tavern
Melrose Diner
Mexico Lindo
Minar Palace
Morning Glory Diner
Ms. Tootsie's Soul Food Cafe
Mustard Green
NAM PHUONG
Nanee's Kitchen
O Sandwiches
Olympic Gyro
Ong's
Pagano's Market
Paninoteca
Pastrami and Things
Pat's King of Steaks
Pearl's Oyster Bar
Pho 75
Pho Cali
Pho Ha
Picanha Brazilian Grill
Pikkles Plus
Porky's Point
Pudge's
Pura Vida
Queen of Sheba Pub II
Rangoon
Ray's Cafe & Tea House
Restaurant Acapulco
Rib Stand
Rustica
Salumeria
SANG KEE ASIAN BISTRO
Sang Kee Peking Duck House
Sansom Street Kabob House
Shank's and Evelyn's Roast
Beef
Shiao Lan Kung
Shining Star
Sidecar Bar and Grille
Sila Turkish Restaurant

Silk City Diner
Singapore
Sitar India
Sonny's Famous Steaks
South Street Souvlaki
SZECHUAN TASTY HOUSE
Taco Riendo
Tampopo
Tangier Restaurant
Tony Luke's
Tony Luke's Beef and Beer
Sports Bar
12th Street Cantina
Uduppi Dosa House
Vientiane Cafe
VIETNAM
Vietnam Palace
Voltaco's Italian Foods
Yue Kee
Zeke's Mainline Bar B Que

GOOD VALUE

BRASSERIE PERRIER (lounge)
DMITRI'S
Kami Sushi Express
Le Bar Lyonnais
LE BEC-FIN (lunch)
Makiman
Miran
Moshi Moshi
N. 3RD
NAN
New Wave Cafe
PENANG
PUMPKIN
RADICCHIO
RITZ SEAFOOD
SOUTHWARK
SOVALO
Swann Lounge
VIETNAM
VILLA DI ROMA

ULTRA-EXPENSIVE (ENTREES $35 AND OVER)

BARCLAY PRIME
BRASSERIE PERRIER
Deux Cheminees
FOUNTAIN RESTAURANT
Gallagher's Steakhouse
La Famiglia
Lacroix at the Rittenhouse

Honey's Sit 'n' Eat (buyout only)
HORIZONS (buyout only)
Hostaria da Elio
Hotel DuPont
Il Tartufo
Illuminare
Indonesia
Iron Hill Restaurant & Brewery
Isla Verde
Island Grill
Jack's Firehouse
JAKE'S
Jamaican Jerk Hut
Johnny Brenda's
Jones
Joy Tsin Lau
Kabobeesh
Kami Sushi Express
Karen & Rei's
Karina's
KARMA
Khajuraho
Kisso Sushi Bar
Knife & Fork Inn
Konak
Krazy Kats
KRISTIAN'S
La Boheme
La Cava
La Collina
La Esperanza
La Famiglia
La Fourno Trattoria
LA LUPE
La Terrasse
La Veranda
La Viola
Lacroix at the Rittenhouse
L'ANGOLO
Las Cazuelas
LE BEC-FIN
Le Castagne
Lee How Fook
A Little Cafe
Little Fish
LoBianco Coastal Cuisine
London Grill
LOS CATRINES RESTAURANT & TEQUILA'S BAR
Lou's Restaurante
Ludwig's Garten
Ly Michael's
Ma France Creperie
Mac's Restaurant and Lounge

Maggiano's Little Italy
Mainland Inn
Mandoline
Marco Polo
MARGARET KUO'S
Margaret Kuo's Peking
MARIGOLD KITCHEN
Marra's
MARSHA BROWN
Maya Bella
McCormick & Schmick's
Mediterranean Grill
Megu Sushi
Melange Cafe
MELOGRANO
Mercato
Meritage Philadelphia
Mezza Luna
Mia
Mixto
M/O Cafe
Monte Carlo Living Room
MORIMOTO
MORO
Mosaic Cafe
Moshi Moshi
MOSHULU
Ms. Tootsie's Soul Food Cafe
Mud City Crabhouse
Murray's Deli
Mustard Green
N. 3RD
NAM PHUONG
NECTAR
New Wave Cafe
Next
Nonna's
Nunzio's Ristorante Rustico
Ocean City
Old Guard House Inn
Old Homestead Steak House
Old Original Bookbinders
Ombra
Ong's
Opa Bar & Grille
The Orchard
Otto's Brauhaus
Overtures
Pagoda Noodle Cafe
The Palm
Paloma
Paradigm
PARADISO
¡PASION!
Penne

Pietro's Coal Oven Pizzeria (South St.)
PJ Whelihan's Pub and Restaurant
Plantation
Plough and the Stars
Pod
Pompeii
Pond/Bistro Cassis
Ponzio's
Porcini
Posh
POSITANO COAST BY ALDO LAMBERTI
Prima Donna
The Prime Rib
PUMPKIN
Pura Vida
Queen of Sheba Pub II
Race Street Cafe
Ralph's
Rangoon
Rat's
Raw Sushi and Sake Lounge
Red Hot & Blue
Red Sky
Red Square
REMBRANDT'S
RESTAURANT ALBA
The Restaurant at Doneckers
Restaurant Taquet
Ristorante La Buca
Ristorante Panorama
Ristorante Pesto
Ristorante Valentino
RITZ SEAFOOD
Rock Lobster
Roller's
Rose Tattoo Cafe
Roselena's Coffee Bar
Roux 3
Roy's
Rx
SABRINA'S CAFE
The Saloon
Salt & Pepper Cafe
Sansom Street Kabob House
SANSOM STREET OYSTER HOUSE
Sapori
SAVONA
Sea Salt
Seo Ra Bol
Sergeantsville Inn
Serrano

Shouk
Shundeez
SIAM LOTUS
Sidecar Bar and Grille
Sila Turkish Restaurant
Suilan
Silk City Diner
Simon Pearce on the
  Brandywine
Singapore
Siri's Thai French Cuisine
Slate Bleu
Sly Fox Breweries
Smith & Wollensky
The Smoked Joint
Snockey's Oyster and Crab
  House
SoleFood
The Sound of Philadelphia
  (TSOP)
South Street Souvlaki
SOVANA BISTRO
Spring Mill Cafe
Strawberry Hill
Suilan

SUSANNA FOO
Swann Lounge
SWEET LUCY'S SMOKEHOUSE
Sweet Vidalia
SZECHUAN TASTY HOUSE
TANGERINE
Taste
Taste of Portugal
Ted's Montana Grill
Teikoku
333 Belrose
TIERRA COLOMBIANA
Tir Na Nog
Tommy Gunns
Trattoria Lucca
Trax Cafe
Tre Famiglia Ristorante
Tre Scalini
Trio
Tucker's Steak and Seafood
  House
Twenty21
Twenty Manning
Umbria
Valanni

Valentino on the Square
VETRI (buyout only)
Vientiane Cafe
VIETNAM
Vietnam Palace
VILLA DI ROMA
Vintage
Warsaw Cafe
Washington Inn
Washington Square
White Dog Cafe
The Wild Onion
Word of Mouth
World Cafe Live
XIX NINETEEN
Yangming
Zanzibar Blue
Zeke's Mainline Bar B Que
Zocalo
Zorba's Taverna

Acknowledgments

It's a good thing I love to eat, because reviewing restaurants for a living will put even the most enthusiastic appetite to the test. But undertaking a restaurant guide of this magnitude — on top of a weekly column — brings the challenges to an entirely new level, and far beyond matters of mere digestive prowess.

This project was a huge undertaking in time, effort, expense, and the tireless pursuit of details, and I'm indebted to so many people for making it happen. Thanks first and foremost to my wife, Elizabeth, and kids, Alice and Arthur, for allowing me the slack to squeeze 60 extra restaurant visits into an already busy eating schedule over the course of 10 months. I especially loved the occasions when we revisited those favorites as a family, and missed you when you stayed home. Thanks for giving me so many weekend afternoons and random spare hours to write when we could have been doing something fun instead.

Thanks especially to Kim Volcy, who was an indispensable assistant on this book, who fact-checked the hundreds of phone numbers and lists of index details, re-checked details I forgot, organized a flood of information, and made it all look easy. Without her color-codes, and amazingly efficient phone work, I'd still be stuck somewhere in the Fs.

There are a number of other colleagues at *The Inquirer* to whom I'm also grateful. Thanks to the fabulously smart assignment editors — Maureen Fitzgerald, Linda Harris, Avery Rome, Barbara Sadek, and Chris Gray — who whipped my raw copy into coherent columns over the past few years. Thanks to folks in the higher ranks — Tom McNamara, Sandy Clark, Nancy Cooney, Anne Gordon, and Amanda Bennett — for believing strong restaurant coverage is essential to *The Inquirer's* mission, and giving me the support to do it right. Thanks to Karen Knoll for paying all the bills.

Thanks to all my photographer friends — especially Eric Mencher, Michael Wirtz, Michael Bryant, photo editor Margaret Grace, and Michael Perez — who gave artful pictures to my words and withstood interrogations from nervous restaurateurs during photo assignments without giving up a bell. Thanks to Michael Klein for the latest line in restaurant gossip — and helping to keep this book up to date until press. And thanks to Rick Nichols, my good buddy, wise counselor and encyclopedia of Philadelphia culinary history, for giving me at least one hysterical laugh each day, a good "book stomp" every month, and a restaurant exclusive every so often.

Thanks to Susan Dilanni, *The Inquirer* ambassador who is really responsible for making this second edition of my restaurant guide a possibility. Thanks to Edward Jutkowitz at Camino Books for believing this book was worthwhile and helping to make it a success. Thanks to Barbara Gibbons for her careful editing and unflappable patience as I submitted a steady stream of tweaks to the manuscript, both small and large, until the final hours. Thanks to the uber-talented Matt Ericsson, whose amazing efforts in designing my first guide, *Savoring Philadelphia*, made this edition that much easier. Thanks to Robin Gillespie for making me pedal hard in a vain attempt to keep all the calories at bay.

I couldn't have done all this eating without the help of a first-rate posse, and there are dozens of people with whom I've shared memorable meals. But I must thank some of the regulars for their insight and reliable company: Kaitlin Gurney and Patrick Kerkstra, Dave and Nika Haase, Jen Moroz, Jennifer Weiner and Adam Bonin, Alfred Lubrano, Tom Avril, and Hansjakob Werlen (Mr. Slow Food). Thanks to Paul Jablow, Rob Watson, and others already mentioned here for sharing their hot lists of date restaurants. Thanks to my brother, Terry, and sister-in-law, Patty Rich. Thanks to the A Street Gang, the greatest neighbors in America. Thanks to Mom and Dad, Joyce and Myron LaBan. Thanks to Barbara Trostler, the classiest mother-in-law a guy could ever live three blocks away from. And a special thanks to Angie Benson, baby-sitter extraordinaire and unofficial family, who always makes my work nights out seem like a special treat for the kids.

Of course, this job (and this book) would be no fun at all if it weren't for the hundreds of talented chefs and servers that make our restaurant scene so special. I learned more than ever from this second go-round how much they strive for excellence, and for that I'm forever grateful. Not to mention almost always well fed.

About the Author

Craig LaBan is the restaurant critic for *The Philadelphia Inquirer*. Before coming to *The Inquirer* as a staff writer in 1998, he worked as the restaurant critic for the *Times-Picayune* in New Orleans, as a general assignment reporter for *The Inquirer's* South Jersey bureau, and was a freelance food writer for *Boston* magazine, *Saveur, Eating Well, Food Arts,* and many other publications. He has a bachelor's degree in French from the University of Michigan, a master's degree in journalism from Columbia University Graduate School of Journalism, and a culinary degree from Ecole de Cuisine la Varenne in France.

LaBan has won the James Beard Foundation Award for his restaurant reviews, and has been named three times by the Association of Food Journalists as one of the top three newspaper restaurant critics in the country.

He is married and lives in Philadelphia with his wife, Elizabeth, and their two children, Alice and Arthur.